DATE DUE

#47-0108 Peel Off Pressure Sensitive

Other Books by Robert I. Rotberg

The Rise of Nationalism in Central Africa:
The Making of Malawi and Zambia, 1873–1964

A Political History of Tropical Africa

Christian Missionaries and the Creation of
Northern Rhodesia, 1880–1924

Joseph Thomson and the Exploration of Africa

Editor

Protest and Power in Black Africa

Africa and its Explorers

Strike a Blow and Die

HAITI

The Politics of Squalor

by

Robert I. Rotberg

with Christopher K. Clague

A Twentieth Century Fund Study

HOUGHTON MIFFLIN COMPANY
19·BOSTON·71

FIRST PRINTING W

For Toussaint, Christophe,
and other freedom-loving Haitians

Foreword

THE TWENTIETH CENTURY FUND has a long tradition of sponsoring scholarly studies of countries and regions — studies designed to provide thorough and objective analyses in order to achieve a better understanding of their peoples and their problems. This study of Haiti by Robert I. Rotberg not only conforms to the Fund's tradition; in its comprehensiveness, its intellectual rigor, and its scholarliness, it may well become the standard work on one of the world's poorest and most troubled states.

A considerable volume of material is available concerning Haiti — on Toussaint and Christophe, on corruption and *vodun*. In other respects, too, research on Haiti might appear to present few difficulties. The country is not large (it was the first independent micro-state), does not possess a very advanced or complex economy, and does not pursue an active or complicated role in international affairs. Yet Haiti is among the most enigmatic and perplexing nations to study because of the skimpiness of accurate data, the murkiness of its history, and the mysterious and quixotic nature of its ruler, who has concocted a bloody, grim, and perverted parody of the concept known as "Black Power."

It was largely because Haiti presents such a confusing, tragic, and potentially volatile element in the far from tranquil Caribbean area that the Fund's Trustees decided to sponsor a research project that would provide a detailed analysis of its development. Mr. Rotberg proved a most fortuitous choice as research director for the project because of the very special qualities he brought to it. As a student of Africa, he had peculiar insight into Haiti's social structure and the background of her long-suffering people. And, as a painstaking scholar, he was able to assemble a wealth of information — historical, economic, psychological — that is essential for an objective analysis of Haiti's many dimensions. He is also a courageous man, for he recognized that drawing an authentic and vivid portrait of Haiti depended on seeing both President Duvalier and his opponents; he has modestly refrained from describing his adventures with the demi-monde of intriguers and informers who are so integral a factor in any serious attempt to know and understand Haiti.

Despite the lushness of its landscape and the colorfulness and friendliness of its people, Mr. Rotberg's view of Haiti is bleak and sobering. The Haitians have suffered grievously before and since independence, and they seem destined to suffer still more. The plight of the country and its people demands attention and concern, although Mr. Rotberg makes clear that Haiti's future depends primarily on the Haitians themselves. The most that the outside world can do is to provide material help and technical assistance when it is evident that such assistance and help can be fruitfully employed.

The Fund and its staff are grateful to Mr. Rotberg and Christopher K. Clague for carrying out their assignments with such studiousness, energy, and commitment. And the Fund shares with Mr. Rotberg the hope that Haiti's future will be more constructive and more peaceful than its past or present.

M. J. Rossant, Director,
The Twentieth Century Fund

New York

Preface

EARLY IN 1968 the Twentieth Century Fund asked me to undertake a study of the problems of contemporary Haiti. The Fund sought to determine whether conditions in our neighbor to the south were in fact as dreadful as they had been described. If so, we wanted to dissect the character of Haiti under Duvalier, laying bare its strengths and weaknesses in as objective a manner as possible. We would naturally also want to isolate the reasons why Haiti — once the most glorious colony in the world — had fallen upon such hard times. Finally, any examination of the Haitian dilemma needed to be directed to the future: How could Haiti extricate itself, or be assisted to extricate itself, from its present morass? This book is a product of such a multifaceted, multidisciplined, and necessarily swift inquiry.

Research on these problems in Haiti was possible only with the personally granted authorization of Dr. François Duvalier, President à Vie. I remain grateful to him for permission to carry out our investigation, and for the consequent willingness of his cabinet ministers and civil servants to cooperate and be of assistance. Several dozen Haitians of all classes, and a number of foreigners resident in Haiti, also contributed significantly to our project, but to mention their names and thus associate them with us and this book could well result in unfortunate consequences for them and their families. If silently expressed, our debt to them individually and collectively is large and deeply felt.

In both obvious and subtle ways this book is a product of many minds and hands. Christopher K. Clague was responsible for the materials in Chapters VIII and IX, and for extending the analysis of economic matters throughout. Henry W. Vaillant contributed to the discussion of problems of population and health, which so bedevil Haiti. Stephanie D. Jones, for whose unstinting and devoted efforts no praise can be too lavish, skillfully organized and coordinated the supportive research, supervised the transformation of the authors' original into fair copy, and helped to give the prose its final polish. Our eventual product was enriched by the research assistance of Caroline Lincoln, Claire Kramsch, Dale Foreman, Virginia Rowland, and Emily Barclay, and the translations of Gabriel Grasberg and Joep van der Linden. Edna Oakeshott, John Adams, John Demos, Roy Feldman, Ted Robert Gurr, Colonel Robert Debs Heinl, Jr., Albert O. Hirschman, Stanley N. Katz, F. Xavier Pi-Sunyer, Kent Ravenscroft, Jr., Gunter Schramm, Vito Tanzi, and James Thomson generously read portions of the book in draft and made numerous constructive suggestions. David Raynolds of the United States Embassy in Port-au-Prince was a source of invaluable data and dialogue. I am also grateful for the encouragement, lengthy discussions, stimulating suggestions, the loan of unpublished manuscripts, and/or the kind of moral backing without which a book like the present could not have been written or deadlines met, to Captain Edward L. Beach, Adolf A. Berle, Paul H. Douglas, Emerson Douyon, Ralph Dungan, Elizabeth Frawley, William B. Gates, Jr., James N. Goodsell, Senator Ernest Gruening, Mary Henderson, Francis Huxley, Hélio Jaguaribe, Kendall W. King, Abraham Lowenthal, Jason McManus, the late Max F. Millikan, Sidney Mintz, Harry Montgomery, Melville Osborne, Elizabeth Peer, John N. Plank, Vera Rubin, Richard P. Schaedel, Arthur M. Schlesinger, Jr., and Bishop C. Alfred Voegeli. I am also grateful to the Harvard University Center for International Affairs for valuable bibliographical assistance and a general responsiveness which cannot be quantified, and to the director and staff of the Twentieth Century Fund for doing everything to make this book possible. Roger Dennis Hansen and Joseph S. Nye, Jr., friends and colleagues who should have known better, deserve a special note of appreciation for bringing Haiti and the author together. Most of all, this book could not have been written, and certainly not within the allotted span of time, without my wife's extensive and unremitting support, her resourcefulness, and her attention to the details of form and style, and the forbearance and understanding of Rebecca, Nicola, and Fiona.

R.I.R.

Chocorua
SEPTEMBER 1, 1969

Contents

List of Tables

HAITI
The Politics of Squalor

I

The Matrix of Haitian Politics

HAITI is many things. To the visitor a picture of the country consists of a collection of overlapping, highly diverse, often contradictory, and sometimes startling sensory images. Haiti is a panorama of tropical vegetation where the rain comes suddenly, in angry torrents. It is quaint, gaily painted, almost ramshackle nineteenth-century houses with balconies that jut out over the narrow streets of Port-au-Prince, the capital, and Cap Haitien, in the north. Urban Haiti is mad driving, nimble pedestrians, constant horn-blowing, red-flagged taxis which lurch to sudden stops, colorfully converted pickup trucks crammed full of humanity, mangoes, goats, and the varied products of a peasant economy. Rural Haiti conveys a sense of movement and teeming population: every spring or waterhole is surrounded by women and children washing, pounding clothes, and swimming. Haiti is rutted roads of crushed rock and oozy, axle-deep mud — blocked, as often as not, by tethered cattle — sugar cane waving in the wind, tiny groves of coffee, gaunt horses, snorting long-nosed pigs, and *mapou* or baobab trees revered as the haunts of *vodun* spirits and therefore worshipped in regularly arranged eclectic ceremonies where candles are burned to deities. And Haiti is hunger: "At any hour of the day or night, wherever you go, people are stripping sugar cane, peeling bananas, crunching bits of fried pork, buying food, selling it at every corner, eating and being still hungry. Even the skinny, spitting lizards work their mouths constantly." [1]

1 Herbert Gold, "Haunted Haiti," *Holiday*, XXXVII (March 1965), 68. The folly, grandeur, and dizziness of modern Haiti are nowhere more successfully and descriptively captured than in the opening chapters of Francis Huxley, *The Invisibles* (London, 1966).

But Haiti is more. When bombs drop from slow-flying Constellations, Haitian automobiles whirl wildly in circles, then suddenly plunge madly across darkened streets, careening into parked cars as they go. Haiti is the paralytic fear of a capricious dictatorial regime of unusual malevolence; none but the most secure Haitians are immune from the stabbing anxiety which afflicts all days and nights. Open criticism of the regime has long ago been eschewed; the most confident talk guardedly of their antagonism to the dictatorship of François Duvalier, President à Vie, only to trusted friends, and in moving vehicles or other places where eavesdropping is impossible. Even then, they look continually over their shoulders and, if they are men of substance, always attempt to maintain their contacts with someone close to the president or a high-ranking, pistol-carrying *tonton macoute*. The dominant feature of the dictatorship is its arbitrariness: the blue-serge-suited Al Capone-like figures who live in the white rococo presidential palace have never thought twice about drawing a revolver from their shoulder holsters and mutilating someone suspected of antagonism, disobedience, or mere idiosyncratic behavior. If they themselves are sufficiently powerful, they act without the authorization of Duvalier; otherwise, virtually nothing in Haiti of any moment happens without his specific approval.

This is not to say that the dictatorship is efficient: Haiti is a lackadaisical state, and the trains, none of which now carries passengers, have never run on time. Customs officials rarely inspect the luggage of incoming visitors, and checks at roadblocks are simultaneously suspicious and cursory. Often roadblocks exist in pairs, one manned by the army and the other, in order to keep an eye on the army, by the *tonton macoutes*. But, at both, the gendarme manning the barrier simply peers into the interior of a vehicle, asks names and destinations, and, if he can write, indicates the answer on the back of a scruffy envelope or some other piece of loose paper.

It would be a mistake, however, to conclude that this quintessential Haitian combination of dictatorship, cavalier planning, and splendid incompleteness is particularly new. In an earlier time of instability, for example, a visitor from overseas was impressed — as a modern tourist might be — with the careful way in which "everything is arranged . . . by a paternal government." But for him, too, the illusion faded. The electric light plant was there, "but it did not act. It was the same with the cannon. There are cannon, but they won't go off. It was the same with their railways. They were being 'hurried forward,' but they never progressed. It was the same with everything." He went, for example, to the prisons. "I had read a notable code of rules referring to them, drawn up with a view to their proper maintenance. Had the rules been carried out the result would have been more than satisfactory. On reading it one pictured a model house of detention, ruled wisely by grave officials with one eye on the regulations and the other on the welfare of their prisoners. [Then] I went to the prison. The grave officials of fancy were replaced by a dozen truculent vagabonds with cocomacaque clubs. The place was the haunt of disease, blow-flies, and vermin, a pestiferous swamp, surrounded by ramshackle walls, inhabited by starving and naked prisoners. . . . The code of regulations was for show, the prison for use." [2]

Haiti is brutal and rapacious tyranny. It is a country without due process, or any understanding of the meaning of the term, where all trials are show, arrests and imprisonments are whimsical — but brutal — and no ordinary man wants more than to be left alone. It is a country where rumor is the usual and preferred form of communication, where any incident will, within hours, give rise to thirty different, hectically elaborated interpretations passed from house to house by word of mouth. The sound of shooting near the palace, even if it is the result of an accidental triggering of a rusty antiaircraft gun, within minutes is known in the purlieus of the city and the suburb of Pétionville, three miles uphill into the mountains; there the rumor mill churns frantically. *"Chut. Ne passez pas en ville,"* a hotel proprietor told one of his guests when the guns began firing wildly. *"Le coup est commencé, comprenez?"* The army and the *tonton macoutes* were fighting for control — or so he hoped. But the dark is a time of danger anyway, and few Haitians care under normal circumstances to venture out of their houses at night; even if they can avoid the *tonton macoutes,*

2 H. Hesketh Prichard, *Where Black Rules White: A Journey Across and About Hayti* (2nd ed., London, 1910; 1st ed., 1900), 345–346.

spirits may lurk in the shadows. And danger of all kinds is to be avoided. Instead, there are states of mania and depression and paranoia, the magnification of imagined slights, and a kind of sullenness that seems to be as much a product of healthy apathy as of fear. Tension, too, rises, ebbs erratically and slowly, and always lingers in some form or another. Sudden movements, unaccustomed behavior, coincidental timing, and prescience are all signs of possible evil.

Haiti is much else. It is an army colonel who is a sociologist *manqué* and a competitive buyer of antiquarian books, a judge in a civil case who extorts the necessary emoluments from the defendant in open court, swimming pools that take three days to fill, an exporter who regularly sends overweight and extralength parcels by bribing the postal clerk, peasants who are extraordinarily friendly and civil servants who can be incredibly bureaucratic, soldiers sleeping on duty, rurally based *tonton macoutes* running through the streets with old Springfield rifles and bandoliers of cartridges, well-made-up, high-cheekboned girls dressed in the latest fashions jostling pipe-smoking wrinkled crones astride decrepit donkeys, men pushing iron-wheeled carts throughout the capital selling concoctions of colored water to passersby, artistry of the canvas and gimcrack tourist crafts, soldiers who poke guns at tourists who so much as glance at the presidential palace, a military band which marches to "The Halls of Montezuma" and, certainly not least, an elite which treats the common man, all dark-skinned foreigners, and almost everything that is neither culturally French nor efficiently American with unconcealed contempt.[3] The extent of vitriol, invective, bitterness, and discourtesy toward one's compatriots, relatives, or mistresses surpasses imagination. There is gaiety on the surface and antagonism beneath. It is a society that

---

[3] One example of the contempt of the elite for the masses appeared in scientific guise: The character of the primitive, concluded Louis Mars (later a cabinet minister) three decades ago, is due not so much to a lack as to a lethargy in his logical powers. He seems to have little ability for discovering the laws of nature. He suffers from a laziness of mind: he prefers to accept the old explanations for things rather than to make the effort to find new ones. "In short, the primitive mentality is a mentality gangrened by ignorance and magic, closed to progress and light, plunged in the deepest darkness." "La Mentalité Haitienne et la Psychiatrie," *Revue de la Société d'Histoire et de Géographie d'Haiti*, VIII (March 1937), 26.

has been molded by its physical surroundings, shaped by its tortured history, and conditioned by a national character which reflects the heritage of slavery as much as the politics of the twentieth century. They are a people, and it is a republic, caught firmly in the grip of a viselike social structure.

Seen from the air Haiti is a jumble of wild cliffs and mountains, rent by plunging, tortuously twisted streams and narrow, steep-walled canyons. The sweep of the great northern plain, the broad central plain following the valley of the Artibonite River, the coastal plain of Arcahaie between Port-au-Prince and St. Marc, the plain of the Cul-de-sac between the brackish lake Etang Saumâtre and Port-au-Prince, and the other pockets of extensive cultivation in the south are all visible; the mottled and attractive green of the growing sugar cane, coffee, rice, and sisal contrasts vividly with the visually pleasing earthy reds and browns which, however, reveal the extent of Haiti's well-advanced soil erosion. The peaks and sides of all but her highest mountains have been denuded of trees for fuel and, with the help of violent tropical storms, the richer topsoils. Her rivers consequently run brown, clogged with the humus and detritus of severe ecological neglect. There is little terracing and even less contour plowing in a land of obsessively individualistic peasant farmers whose holdings have been fragmented for generations.

Haiti, the western third of the Antillean island of Hispaniola, is about 600 miles from the United States and occupies an area of about 10,700 square miles, roughly the size of Maryland. But to be small is not necessarily to be compact. The Gulf of Gonave cuts into the heart of the country, making Haiti resemble a crocodile that is about to swallow the desiccated satellite island of La Gonave and, in time, attack the neighboring nations of Cuba and Jamaica. Port-au-Prince, a mere thirty miles from the rugged, often-closed land frontier with the Dominican Republic, guards the apex of the bay. But the narrow belt of land widens on each side of the capital; Haiti's longest and widest dimensions are 183 and 114 miles. Because the coastline is irregular and the northern and southern peninsulas are so elongated (stretching as they do the equivalent of the distance between Harrisburg in the south and Scranton in the north to New York City), different sections and peoples of the country have remained unusually isolated, internal communications have always been excessively difficult, life in the rural fastness has proved markedly resistant to change, and the port towns have developed apart from the surrounding hinterlands. (Yet communications with the outside have been facilitated by the long coastline; no point in Haiti is far from the sea, which explains why nineteenth-century Haiti could export coffee without roads.) These tendencies have been accentuated by the thoroughly crumpled terrain; the mountain ranges rise abruptly to about 3000 feet — some peaks reach 9000 — and bisect the country from west to east in three major and innumerable minor places. The southwestern peninsula is virtually one range with no level ground beyond Léogane except for the plain of Cayes. Of the entire land surface 21 per cent lies below 700 feet and 35 per cent over 1600 feet.

These physical divisions have obviously had an inhibiting effect upon the extension of the services and facilities generally associated with national governments and, equally, with the ability of a poorly funded central administration to govern at all. They have also hindered the fabrication of durable economic ties between the countryside and the capital and villages and port towns. The character of the terrain has also made the construction and maintenance of normal infrastructural requirements — roads, telephones, electric power, and telegraphs — unusually complicated and expensive. In 1969, outside the capital and its suburbs and the main towns, there were less than fifty miles of properly surfaced, fully repaired highway, another 200 miles of once-paved, badly surfaced main roadway (tiny Barbados in 1964 had a total of 1287 miles of paved roads), and another 2000 miles of the most execrable roads in the world; no passenger railways; a mere 2000 functioning telephone lines and 4400 telephones (about 1 per 1000, the lowest percentage in the Western Hemisphere; in 1966 the comparable figures for Barbados were 63.0 per 1000, Jamaica, 27.2, Cuba, 20, and the Dominican Republic, 8.5), nearly all of which are in the capital, and only a few of which worked consistently in 1969; the fewest radio receivers in the Western Hemisphere, about 13 per 1000; a minimal daily newspaper circulation of 6 per 1000; and 73 million total KWH capacity or 17.4 KWH per capita (compared with per capita figures for Cuba of 537 KWH, Jamaica, 540, Barbados, 320, and the Dominican Republic, 164) largely supplied by petroleum-fired plants in the main towns and small diesel engine generators in the smaller market centers (where the proprietors still charge per outlet, or burning lightbulb, per month). Only 2.6 per cent of all dwellings in Haiti have piped water; in Guatemala 12.1 per cent do, in Paraguay 16, and in the United States, in 1963, 79.8. There are almost no houses with piped water outside of Port-au-Prince and Cap Haitien, yet 60 per cent of the houses of the capital lack piped water, and only 21 per cent of houses in all urban areas boast a piped water supply. The comparable hemispheric figures are Paraguay 20.7 per cent, Guatemala 43 per cent, and the United States 99.9 per cent. Whereas even Paraguay is credited with a figure of 22.8 (U.S. = 81 per cent) for urban dwellings with inside water-borne sanitation, the figure for Haiti is so negligible that it must be listed as .01 per cent.[4]

Haiti, like eighteenth-century Sicily, has always been a place apart. Historically both have shared the acute sense of isolation which is common to many island cultures. In Haiti, as in Sicily, the mountains impede cross-country communication, and in both a third of the land is about 1500 feet above sea level. Until recently both, lacking decent roads, depended almost exclusively upon water-borne means for long-distance communication, their urban centers being seaports and their interiors remaining comparatively isolated and backward. Both have squandered their natural resources, improvidently cut down their trees for firewood, laid bare the peaks of mountains, and, in Sicily in the early nineteenth century and in Haiti by the end of that century, processes of erosion commenced which have proved virtually irreversible. As a result, in twentieth-century Haiti as in nineteenth-century Sicily, agricultural productivity per cultivated acre has declined drastically.

Sicily and Haiti have both moved through history with a pen-

4 The above data are derived primarily from C. Paul Roberts (ed.), *Statistical Abstract of Latin America, 1967* (Los Angeles, 1968), 122, 161, 174–175, 177–178. Bruce M. Russett *et al., World Handbook of Political and Social Indicators* (New Haven, 1964), credits Haiti with 7 radio receivers per 1000 in 1961 (placing Haiti 104 of 118 countries world-wide) and with a daily newspaper circulation of 11 per 1000 in 1960 (ranking Haiti 91 of 125 world-wide), 109–111, 120–122.

chant for the bizarre and the grotesque — for idiosyncratic twists
of fate which have usually accentuated the monstrousness of life.
In both the traditions of the Enlightenment were, and are, weak.
Illiteracy has always been high (58 per cent in Sicily and 92 per
cent in Haiti in about 1900) and passive obedience the norm. The
index of corruption has never deviated from its apogee, and violence — Sicily's "only prosperous industry" — and brutality have
been the natural means of handling independence and non-
conformity. Fear and arbitrary proceedings were the methods used
by successive governments of both island states to impose their
will. And neither experienced benevolent authority more than
briefly. Sicily, to cite one example of a ruler whose methods were
analogous with those who presided over Haiti, knew Queen Maria
Carolina during the Napoleonic Wars. She organized a private espionage system, took deposits from charities and the Palermo bank,
and tried to engross the local road-building fund. Three decades
later, wrote a contemporary, there was "scarcely a single official
. . . who does not intend to profit from his post."

In both countries notions of public service and social conscience
atrophied early. A late nineteenth-century commentator observed
that "the great majority of Sicilians have no idea of any such thing
as a social advantage distinct from individual interests and superior
to them." Admiration was reserved for those who knew how to
defend and enrich themselves by their own strength and influence.
Even killing innocent people was a justifiable means of inculcating fear and obtaining respect. The noble and disinterested were
rare and the vicious and rapacious common. Both have also long
been closed societies in which becoming a man of respect and
achieving status have traditionally seemed aspirations more important than mutual activity directed at the furtherance of the commonweal. Indeed, neither society has probably ever articulated a
notion of benevolence which was shared by more than a minute
fraction of its citizenry. In the nineteenth century, Sicilians, like
Haitians in more modern times, disregarded official channels and
depended upon their relations with a local boss, a "big man."
In dealing with the threatening world of non-kin, Haitians and
Sicilians have relied upon the intercession of friends or friends of

friends — upon patronage and contacts. In Sicily this was a revived feudalism, in Haiti simply a perpetuation of the kind of personalization of power which had proved efficacious during and
since the days of slavery. Suspicion predominates in such societies,
and association with others is anathema. Nor does benevolent rule
provide an antidote. After 1886 the people in Sicily still "had no
vote, since they were illiterates; hence no one courted their favour,
and hence the schools were not built which would have equipped
them to vote. Some villages continued to lack either school or doctor: apart from the priest, there was only the local witch or magi-
cian to take their place. The rich, on the other hand, even when
illiterate, were always a power and could extract plenty of concessions from Rome; yet they were not interested in improving the
conditions of the poor; if anything, they understood their interest
to lie in depressing it." [5] Both Sicily and Haiti are states where
the capacity for cooperative action eroded very early — in Sicily
because of the helotry of the peasant estate, in Haiti because
of slavery — "so that collective action to resist injustice or hardship has usually been impossible except under the temporary stimulus of blind fury." [6]

Poverty and neglect, the extent of which is merely hinted at by
the absence of a functioning modern infrastructure, are ineradicably Haitian. Together they condition the direction of contemporary and future political development. The national average
per capita gross national product is the equivalent of about $67,[7]
the median is even lower and, according to any of the accepted
indices of national wealth, Haiti ranks at the bottom of the Latin
American and near the bottom of most global scales. Her people
are poorer than those of Bolivia, at $164, the second lowest in the
Western Hemisphere; the Dominican Republic, $230; Barbados,
$370; Martinique, $440; Jamaica, $460; Zambia, $200; and even
India, $90. Haitians ranked on this same scale of relative poverty
with Tanzania, $73, and Chad, $72, and per capita in advance only
of such countries as Botswana, $55, Malawi, $52, and Ethiopia, $52

5 Denis Mack Smith, *Modern Sicily* (London, 1968), 337, 369, 465, 467, 469.
6 Lead review in *The Times Literary Supplement*, February 13, 1969. For a discussion of "amoral familism," see below, 366.
7 See also W. Brand, *Impressions of Haiti* (The Hague, 1965), 67–68.

— and these are all figures for 1965 and 1966, since which time
Haiti's relative position probably has worsened.[8]

Standard numerical equivalents cannot begin to describe the extent and impact of Haitian poverty. It is equally apparent in the
fetid and extensive slums of the capital — they rival the *barrios* of
Caracas, the *favellas* of Rio de Janeiro, and the *pondokis* of Cape
Town and Johannesburg in squalor and misery — and one or two
other ports, and in cramped rural villages and pole and dried-earth
hutments reminiscent of tropical Africa. The swollen bellies of
children and the tattered raiments of their elders, the kind and
quantity of consumer goods in most shops and markets (rural ones
never sell hammers or screwdrivers), the long distances women
travel in order to obtain water or to sell a handful of mangoes, the
absence of shoes, and the omnipresence of maimed and mutilated
beggars all testify to the corrosive continuation of depressed conditions.[9]

Neglect, which naturally accompanies poverty and, at times,
feeds upon it, is omnipresent: Haiti is official signs everywhere that
have not been repainted for generations, airports where vital damage takes years to restore, miles and miles of spectacular potholes,
smartly uniformed soldiers shod in loafers, antiaircraft guns which
misfire in moments of crisis, impressive steel bridges rusting in the
sun for want of minor repairs, splendid edifices begun and never
completed, precious public records dumped willy-nilly in a massive
heap in the attic of the national archives, where they can be attacked by mildew and nibbled by mice, the government printer's
perpetual inability to locate copies of government publications,
and sections of the capital which disappear under water whenever
it rains.

Poverty, nutritional failures, and the spread of endemic diseases
all go together in a cycle of underdevelopment that limits the
effectiveness of modernizing initiatives. Haiti is fortunate to be
free of schistosomiasis and fly-borne human encephalitis, but tuberculosis and tetanus are endemic, malaria has not as yet been

---

8 *World Bank Atlas* (Washington, 1967); U.N., *Statistical Yearbook, 1967* (New York,
1968), 582 ff.; Roberts (ed.), *Statistical Abstract*, 181.
9 For a further discussion of peasant life, see below, 17–19, 63, 73, 149–151, 277–282.

fully eradicated, intestinal disorders (bacterial and parasitic) are prevalent, and kwashiorkor, a protein deficiency of children, is widespread. Between 7 and 15 per cent of all Haitian children die during the first eight weeks of life from umbilical tetanus; about 50 per cent of all children die before they are five years old. Haiti had less than 1 physician per 15,000 inhabitants in 1969, being approached with respect to this overall figure in the Western Hemisphere only by Guatemala with 1 per 6700 persons; Paraguay had 1 per 2000 inhabitants and the United States 1 per 788. (There are 300 M.D.'s in Haiti, 200 of whom are in the capital, and 84 per cent of all Haitian nurses are located in Port-au-Prince.) Haiti also had 0.6 general hospital beds per 1000 (of the 25 hospitals, 12 are in Port-au-Prince) compared with 1.9 in the Dominican Republic and 2.0 in Jamaica.[10]

Life expectancy averages about thirty-three years. And, even if Haitians survive, life on the brink of existence is anything but full. A survey in the late 1950's established that the nutritional status of the people of Haiti was probably the worst in the Western Hemisphere. In particular, preschool children were in a precarious position bordering on malnutrition. Other investigators have confirmed the findings of this survey and, as a result of further longitudinal studies, have demonstrated that, although children of the Haitian elite grow at North American rates, children of the mass of Haiti's population, particularly those who reside in the rural areas, show marked retardation. Teen-age boys in one rural sample averaged six inches shorter and fifty pounds lighter than their urban counterparts. These discrepancies are strictly environmental, becoming noticeable at about six months and marked after ten. They result from inadequate lactation, inappropriate supplementation, and low levels of sanitation leading to intestinal infections. In two rural villages only 9 per cent of all three-year-olds

[10] Russett, *World Handbook*, 204–206; Brand, *Impressions*, 70; Roberts (ed.), *Statistical Abstract*, 109. A Dutch sociologist reported at the beginning of the Duvalierist period that in the most important Haitian towns he saw only badly equipped hospitals; in the rural areas he found "annexes managed by political favorites without medical training." Harmannus Hoetink, "Over de Sociaal-Raciale Struuctur van Haiti," *Tijdschrift van het Koninklijk Nederlandsch Aardrijksundig Genootschap,* LXXVIII (1961), 150.

were of or above normal weight. In one community 11 per cent of the children showed indications of protein deficiency and about 20 per cent showed at least one overt sign of malnutrition. Infestation by intestinal parasites — 100 per cent in at least one community — obviously was a contributing factor in addition to inadequate diet.

Haitian adults also suffer from nutritional insufficiencies. "Caloric deficit in a manual labor society is particularly damaging because it erodes the economic value of the output of an hour's work." Surveys in a major town and four villages indicated that the male laboring age group was receiving about 27 per cent fewer calories than the minimum daily requirement. Some rural men claimed to subsist in the "dead" summer season by eating mangoes and unharvested sugar cane. The shortage of calories clearly makes a major contribution to the impression of laziness and lethargy that is often given by Haitian laborers, and has been overcome in some instances only by factory lunch programs.[11] It is not inappropriate to conclude that the prevalence of disease and nutritional deficiencies has seriously hindered Haitian economic and, it can be argued, political development.

In addition to high levels of morbidity and mortality, Haiti is saddled with the most densely packed rural population in the Western Hemisphere and, next to Java and the Egyptian delta, in the world. Although her estimated 4.6 million (with a natural increase of about 2.3 per cent)[12] average out to about 430 per square mile, far less than Mauritius (961), Martinique (769), the United Kingdom (583), Puerto Rico (777), and Barbados (1365) — but more than the neighboring Dominican Republic (199) and El Salvador (316) — over half of Haiti's population lives on the 23 per cent of the land mass which is arable, and there is no easy escape, as there was in the Anglophone West Indies, for her surplus

11 Kendall W. King, "Nutrition Research in Haiti," in Richard P. Schaedel (ed.), *Research and Resources of Haiti* (New York, 1969), 347–370; W. H. Sebrell, Jr., *et al.*, "Appraisal of Nutrition in Haiti," *American Journal of Clinical Nutrition*, VII (1959), 1–48; Derrick B. and E. F. Patricia Jelliffe, "The Nutritional Status of Haitian Children," *Acta Tropica*, XVIII (1961), 1–45. For a more detailed elaboration of these problems, see Chapter VII, below.
12 For a fuller discussion of Haiti's demographic base and epidemiological horizons, see Chapter VII, below.

population. Fewer than 500,000 persons, by the most generous estimate, inhabit Port-au-Prince and environs — a smaller proportion than any of the other capital cities of the Caribbean islands (23 per cent of Jamaica lives in Kingston, 22 per cent of Martinique in Fort-de-France, and only 13 per cent of the Dominican Republic in Santo Domingo). Aside from the capital there has been little growth of urban centers since the revolution of the early nineteenth century. Few new towns of more than 5000 people have come into existence since colonial times. And, to take a not atypical example, the rich Artibonite Valley, which had a population in 1960 of about 300,000, boasted no village larger than about 3000.[13] The older urban centers have, it is true, lost population to Port-au-Prince. Overall, the rural share of the population has remained at about 89 per cent — the highest in the Western Hemisphere. In terms of rural persons per square mile of arable land, Haiti's dire position is even more marked: the figure for Haiti is 1600, only slightly less than the most crowded parts of central Java and the Egyptian delta; in Peru, 515; the Dominican Republic, 516; El Salvador, 617; Barbados, 839; and Jamaica, 945.[14] Or, to make this point somewhat differently, Haiti has less than half an acre of arable land per person. (There is no direct correlation between land per head and income per head, but considering the predominantly rural character of Haiti's population and the absence of manufacturing and extractive industries, the paucity of cultivatable land per capita is significant.) Given the poor and obviously declining capacity of the land, this is a spectacular burden to be borne by any underdeveloped country, much less one of the least efficient.

Haiti's soil is no longer so fertile as it was during the eighteenth century, and only the well-watered northern plain can still be exploited without the extensive irrigation which, since the revolution of 1791, has been lacking in the Artibonite Valley, the plain

[13] U.N., *Demographic Yearbook, 1967* (New York, 1968), 14; Roberts (ed.), *Statistical Abstract*, 64; Richard P. Schaedel, "The Human Resources of Haiti," unpub. typescript (1962), 14.
[14] Main source: Roberts (ed.), *Statistical Abstract*, 68–69, 78. For Java, see Clifford Geertz, *Agricultural Involution: The Processes of Ecological Change in Indonesia* (Berkeley, 1963), 12. However, Adiwerna, an alluvial region in north-central Java, carries about 3200 persons per square mile.

of the Cul-de-sac, and elsewhere.[15] Because of Haiti's peculiar pattern of *minifundia*, her customs of inheritance, and excessive fragmentation, few peasants are in a position to grow both cash and
subsistence crops. As a result of these factors, disease, economic
and political disincentives, and a number of interrelated influences
which will be elaborated subsequently,[16] agricultural production
in Haiti has declined both in per capita terms and absolutely.
During the late 1950's and early 1960's, Haiti was the only country in the Caribbean which showed a decrease in total agricultural
production. Along with Cuba, Haiti's decline in agricultural productivity per capita exceeded that of all of the other nations of the
Caribbean; Haiti's rate of growth per head was roughly *minus* 25
per cent. Furthermore, the decrease was proportionally greater in
the important export-earning sphere of non-food agricultural production. Haiti ranks lowest among all of the Caribbean and Central American countries in average food availability per capita. In
terms of livestock production per capita, it was ousted from the
bottom rung of the scale only by Honduras.[17] Haiti, in sum, has
failed to match population growth with agricultural productivity.
Its inhabitants were dramatically less well equipped during the
1960's than they were both a decade and a century earlier to feed
themselves and provide export-earning surpluses.[18]

The lack of a firm agricultural base would be less damaging if
Haiti were more richly endowed with natural resources. Comparatively small deposits of bauxite and low-grade copper have been
mined since the late 1950's, but the reserves of both are limited
and, in 1969, neither operation was proving excessively profitable.

15 See below, 49–50, 70.
16 See below, 277–294.
17 Arthur W. Peterson, "Man-Land Relations in the Caribbean Region," in A. Curtis
Wilgus (ed.), *The Caribbean: Its Health Problems* (Gainesville, 1965), 44–50.
18 The Haitian experience in several important respects parallels that sketched by
Geertz (*Agricultural Involution*), and it may prove fruitful to view the "shared
poverty" of Haiti as a case of what he has called "involution" (after Alexander
Goldenweiser). There is the "flaccid indeterminateness [which is so] highly functional
to a society which is allowed to evade, adjust, absorb, and adapt but not really
allowed to change . . . the diversity, variability, fragility, fluidity, shallowness, and
unreliability of interpersonal ties" (103). Haiti, like Indonesia, can be called an
"anthology of missed opportunities, a conservatory of squandered possibilities" (130).
But until studies have been made of the ecological basis of Haitian society (her
ecosystem), Geertz's work must remain, for Haiti, more suggestive than conclusive.

Otherwise, drilling for oil had proved nugatory, and no base minerals — not even the gold that attracted Christopher Columbus to Haiti in 1492 — had been discovered in concentrations which were even marginally attractive to investors. Without its exports of coffee, sugar, and sisal, tourism, remittances from Haitians abroad, and disguised foreign aid, Haiti's already parlous and impoverished economy would have been declared irredeemably bankrupt.[19] Instead, by deliberate and astute legerdemain and desperate contortions, Haiti managed throughout the 1960's to pay its debts and somehow stagger from budget to budget without being compelled to declare the extent of its insolvency. In the process, the living standard of the majority of its people has fallen (in 1957–59 dollars, the gross domestic product — GDP — per capita was around $82 in the middle 1950's, as compared with less than $70 in the late 1960's), but persons with severely depressed levels of consumption and expectation seem to be able to take batterings of this kind with less distress than can the inhabitants of more developed societies. Furthermore, although the differences between grinding poverty (the minimum daily wage is 70 cents [U.S.], but this statutory requirement is still honored more in the breach than in fact, and many workers are employed only on a seasonal basis) and excessively grinding poverty can probably be measured per capita, once a man is inured to living on the most precarious of margins, increasing the thinness of the margin tends to produce no newly accentuated emotional response.

Politics in Haiti reflects and is constrained and conditioned by these many physical and socioeconomic hardships. The continued domination of an urban elite, and the style of dictatorship to which Haitians have become accustomed, has also been assisted by the maintenance of a restricted and inappropriate system of education and the perpetuation of antimodern modes of thought and patterns of behavior. Schooling, in theory accessible to all Haitians, has in practice been limited since the early nineteenth century to members of the urban elite and the families of relatively advanced rural peasants. Some presidents have appropriated large sums of money for rural schools, and in 1969 CARE (Cooperative for

19 For a lengthy discussion of these points, see Chapter IX, below.

American Relief Everywhere) distributed American surplus foodstuffs to a network of village-level schools in the north and northwest; but no matter how often Haitian governments speak of their
concern for the expansion of educational facilities (including basic
alphabetization) in the countryside, there has been only slight improvement in either the availability or the quality of Haitian education.

Teachers, like the newly trained doctors who are obliged to
spend their first two years in a village hospital or clinic, disdain
their rustic surroundings, are poorly motivated, have little equipment, and probably find it stultifying to try to convey the
elements of a French classical education to their charges. The lessons are meant to be taught in French, which few rural pupils can
read or speak. In recent years there has been serious talk of curriculum reform and, almost simultaneously, of a vast campaign to
teach illiterate adults to read and write in Creole, an extended version of seventeenth-century Norman French influenced by Bantu
grammatical constructions and vocabulary and still the sole language of about 90 per cent of the population. But despite the attention which has been paid to these problems by Haitians, a
plethora of missionary organizations, and the United Nations
Educational, Scientific, and Cultural Organization, Haiti still
possesses the lowest level of functional literacy in the Western
Hemisphere — between 7 and 10 per cent. An African country
like Zambia, with a comparable population, has a much higher
level of literacy (40 per cent), and in the Caribbean and Central
America 93 per cent of the inhabitants of Barbados, 85 per cent of
Costa Rica, 82 per cent of Jamaica, 77 per cent of Cuba, 60 per
cent of the Dominican Republic, and 49 per cent of El Salvador
are literate. The Yemen (97.5 per cent), Ethiopia (97.5 per cent)
and Moçambique (99 per cent) are among the few countries
which exceed Haiti's rate of illiteracy.[20]

Together with low levels of educational attainment in a rural
setting go the parochialism and resistance to change which have so
often been attributed to peasants largely cut off from mass media

20 Russett, World Handbook, 222; U.N., Compendium of Social Statistics, 1967 (New
York, 1968), 313 ff.

or easy access to urbanity. The pace and pursuits of the mass of rural Haitians seem to have changed little since the early nineteenth century; according to a variety of indices, the countryside has experienced "surprisingly little social evolution since the first years of independence." [21] For the Haitian farmer, there has been every incentive to turn his back on developments in the capital, or even in the small towns along the coast. Neither the heritage of slavery, the cataclysm of revolution, nor the widened gulf between *rus* and *urb* which was such a feature of the nineteenth century (factors which are discussed in succeeding chapters) encouraged peasants to seek their security elsewhere than in their isolated mountain and valley retreats. Freedom and independence were more important to ex-slaves than higher levels of prosperity. Cut off as they were — and the bulk of Haiti's population still is — from the communications inputs which might have inculcated a sense of relative deprivation, and uninfluenced by missionaries (of which there were few in the rural areas until the mid-twentieth century) or immigrants from other cultures (of which there were none) or the towns (a universally rare phenomenon), self-preservation has dictated an overwhelmingly apathetic response to the course of Haitian politics. On an experiential basis, disengagement has proved a policy of prudence. Peasants still have no reason to suppose that anything but harm comes from involving themselves in national politics; at the local level the question hardly arises since there has never been any effective politics in the sense in which the term is usually employed. Colonial-style military rule is the pattern in the rural sections and districts. It must also be said that citizens of a predatory state,[22] many of whom lease their land from the state, quickly learn, as a function of existence, to conserve their resources and avoid the kinds of economic or political behavior which would subject them to functionaries or rivals with licenses to plunder.

Nearly all Haitians share the attitudes of rivalry, suspicion, and intrigue that are so particularly apparent in rural life.[23] Except to

[21] Schaedel, "Resources," 3.
[22] For discussion of the nomenclature, see below, 342.
[23] Rémy Bastien, "Haitian Rural Family Organization," *Social and Economic Studies,* X (1961), 483–484; Huxley, *Invisibles,* 26.

the extent that sophistication and education have altered their perspectives, urban-dwelling Haitians also share a cast of mind which
is noticeably their own, has influenced their political and economic
responses, and appears to be derived from the necessary mental ac-
commodation with slavery: The first Haitians were rootless, lacking any bonds common to them all except revolution. They were
originally of many tribes and languages of Africa, and naturally
lacked the cement of a shared culture, religion, language, or, as
time went on, even — as peasants and freed men — the group socialization which might have been conveyed by a modern colonial
experience. Instead, separated as they had been from kith and kin
and denied the normal rights of assembly and standard acquaintance with the possibilities of cooperation, they retained the combination of submission to authority and the ability — deviously if
necessary — to cope under stress, which was a by-product of the
slave estate. Even within the nucleated family there was competition and calumny.

Mistrust was and is the habitual response of Haitians of all
classes to all other Haitians. To persuade rural and urban Haitians to cooperate, or to concert their efforts to a mutually desirable end, is difficult and usually unrewarding. The central element in one of Haiti's most powerful novels of rural life is the
struggle to bring together feuding village families in order to irrigate their fields mutually. The hero, a peasant who had spent
many years in Cuba, looks forward to the time when peasants will
"no longer act like mad dogs to other peasants. Each man will
recognize his equal, his likeness, and his neighbor." [24] He is murdered, however, by a peasant from the other faction, and — as in
real Haitian life — bitterness remains a constant.

Until recently, to call a peasant a Haitian was to insult him
grossly; a man had very specific ties to a locale, and no supralocal or
national links to which he gave real credence. Xenophobia of the
most virulent kind complemented parochial pride and a robust
mental self-sufficiency. After all, the world was cruel and dangerous, and only fools relied upon the assistance and promises of

24 Jacques Roumain (trans. Langston Hughes and Mercer Cook), *Masters of the Dew*
(New York, 1947), 109.

others. Even residents of the urban areas have long known insecurity and fear; from an early age they have recognized that survival could best be insured by a combination of wary distrust, caution, and deception and, toward superiors, flattery. A disgusted Haitian summed up this last aspect of the character of his fellow citizens as long ago as 1901: "Everyone has two faces — one for those above him and one for those below. Flattery is preferred to frankness. A friend is abandoned as soon as he is no longer useful. Those in power also appear to have lost any ability to discriminate, for they are taken in by all manner of lies, they give favors to those who deceive them, and they are angry with those who are too proud to sink to the indignities of flattery. In a land of hunchbacks the straight man is unwelcome." [25] And these are defensive postures which are well wedded to the underlying ethic of submission.

From the psychological point of view, there is a further element in the mental configuration of non-elite Haitians that, it can tentatively be argued, makes dictatorship and brutality possible. It is probably wise to digress here in order to introduce the kinds of psychological insights and background information which may contribute to a greater appreciation of the historical and political problems which are discussed at some length in the remainder of the book. It is suggested that this psychological dimension may contribute significantly to an understanding of Haiti's history and modern development and, finally, of Duvalier's personality and techniques of government.

Child-rearing patterns may provide one of the keys to Haitian political problems and personality difficulties at the group and national level. According to what little, largely unpublished, data are available, most Haitians seem to rear their children in a manner that is traumatic and conducive to later conflict. Throughout what we can call the oral stage, and perhaps through and beyond the normal stage of autonomy, Haitian children are highly indulged. They receive and learn to expect immediate and intense physical gratification, but lack the concurrent satisfaction of equally fundamental ego-sustaining and ego-developing nurturance. For reasons that are related to the quality — not the quan-

25 Dantès Bellegarde, *Dessalines à Parlé* (Port-au-Prince, 1948), 303–304.

tity or the level of indulgence — of the maternal relationship, Haitian children become deficient in what Erikson has called basic
trust. During their first two or three years Haitians seem unable to
learn or are prevented from discovering that "one may trust oneself
and the capacity of one's own organs to cope with urges; and that
one is able to consider oneself trustworthy enough so that the pro-
viders will not need to be on guard lest they be nipped." Mothers
elsewhere "create a sense of trust in their children" by inculcating
"a firm sense of personal trustworthiness within the trusted framework of their culture's life-style. This forms the basis in the child
for a sense of identity which will later combine a sense of being 'all
right,' of being oneself, and of becoming what other people trust
one will become." The earliest (oral) stages of life seem to introduce "a sense of inner division and universal nostalgia for a para-
dise forfeited." And, says Erikson in words aptly descriptive of
Haiti, "it is against this powerful combination of a sense of having
been deprived, of having been divided, and of having been abandoned — that basic trust must maintain itself throughout life." [26]

The handling of the next stages of Haitian child rearing, we may
continue to speculate, deepens the developmental crisis and increases the likelihood that Haitians, particularly Haitian males,
will, as adults, find it difficult, if not impossible, to cope with responsibility and aggression. In Haiti the transition between total
dependency on the mother and what would in other circumstances
be a normal development of an independent sex identity, is usually
abrupt and traumatic. After the child has been weaned but before
he has attained a meaningful autonomy, understood the critical
distinctions between initiative and guilt, and managed to resolve
the oedipal problems of identity, the parameters of his existence
shift radically. Virtually overnight the Haitian child is compelled
— perhaps for historical reasons connected with plantation slavery
and the rearing patterns which were then imposed — to assume a
behavioral role which is much more appropriate to late adolescence. In the process, stages of development which we have come
to accept as normal are omitted (foreclosed) or compromised.

The Haitian child may therefore be prevented from experienc-

26 Erik H. Erikson, *Childhood and Society* (New York, 1963), 248–250.

ing the bearable levels of tension which are fundamental to healthy growth. Among the Sioux, for example, a boy was emancipated from his mother, and regressive fixations upon her prevented, "by an extreme emphasis on his right to autonomy and on his duty of initiative." He learned gradually, within an atmosphere of boundless trust, to treat his mother with reticence and respect, to direct frustration and rage into the chase after game, and to take up his rightful role as a male.[27] But the institution of slavery, it is suggested, inhibited such culturally sanctioned maturation, as does the overall pattern of child behavior in contemporary Haiti. Training in autonomy — in any event difficult without "a firmly developed and convincingly continued state of early trust" — is either much delayed, totally absent, or suddenly (and tardily) thrust upon the child. The natural desire to choose is repressed and, clinically, he is overcome by shame and doubt.[28] As a result, the turning of the child toward adulthood from an exclusive, pregenital attachment to his mother is made difficult and his development and understanding of the essence of initiative emasculated. (In adulthood this residual conflict over initiative seems to become hysterical denial, inhibition, impotence, and overcompensatory exhibitionism — the Haitian syndrome.) The Haitian boy is unready for justice, stunted in his appreciation of the meaning of moral responsibility and, during what Freud called the latency period, he despairs of his own potency as an autonomous individual. Because of the harsh ways in which he is forced to grovel before authority, he begins to think of himself as inferior and inadequate, rejects the impulses toward cooperation and mastery which are normal and, if never expressed or always suppressed, may atrophy and cause subsequent anxiety.

In light of the slim evidence available it seems that the Haitian male child fails to develop the critical role identification that is a product of a healthy latency period. Hitherto totally dependent, he is suddenly encouraged to become completely independent — to react to his mother and other kin in a manner which is harshly differentiated from the old. He, speaking archetypally, also assumes

[27] *Ibid.,* 143–144.
[28] *Ibid.,* 84–85.

a lowly status and is expected to obey the authority of elders without question. When he disobeys or tries to disobey anyone, especially his mother, the oedipal-aged child is faced with maternal (anxiety-based) tantrums and severe corporal punishment. He rapidly learns to submit totally, to repress his aggressive, masterly responses, and never to express independent autonomous resistance to authority and the discipline of authority. Furthermore, when normal seeking of attention and assistance, and cries of distress, elicit little immediate attention or attract rage, the child fails to appreciate that he can have an effect upon the world. Instead, he learns helplessness and despair. The balance of sheer physical power is decisive. As at least one result, it is possible to suppose that Haitian children develop a syndrome of severe anxiety which is associated with the ongoing conflict between dominance and submission and, it has been suggested, mastery impulses which are repressed are then lost "to conscious awareness and to the personality. . . . The mastery impulses will remain buried below consciousness and thus unintegrated with his active personality." [29] Once unleashed — typically during young adulthood when the first major conflicts occur — these impulses may give rise to renewed anxiety and, instrumentally, to inaction.

During adolescence, a Haitian child typically learns to fear and unquestionably to obey his father. Even young men submit to their fathers, and are whipped by them for infractions of household rules as well as social deviance. "It is papa who has most authority. Fathers of families insist upon their rights, and will beat disobedient children even when these children are forty years old: rights reinforced by the ever-increasing shortage of land, and the need for a man to inherit from his father." [30] In several senses we may say that Haitian young adults remain hostages of the guilt of the unresolved oedipal phase. Later, of course, serious conflict develops between felt inadequacy and the need for an assertion of mastery. It is during this crisis that a Haitian male may regress to the period of the rejection of autonomy and unconsciously use the

29 Kent Ravenscroft, Jr., "Spirit Possession in Haiti: A Tentative Theoretical Analysis," unpub. scholar of the house B.A. (hons.) thesis (Yale, 1962), 40. The above paragraph draws upon the data in Ravenscroft's suggestive dissertation and discussions with him during 1970.
30 Francis Huxley, "Haiti Chérie," *Geographical Magazine*, XXXVI (June 1963), 77.

histrionic techniques employed against him then by his mother, thus identifying with the aggressor, a normal defensive mechanism used by the ego in its conflicts with authority and its attempts to cope with objects of anxiety.[31] Erikson has noted that "one of the deepest conflicts in life is the hate for a parent who served as the model and the executor of the superego [here the 'Papa'] but who (in some form) was found trying to get away with the very transgressions which the child can no longer tolerate in himself."[32] This kind of identification also represents an intermediate stage in the development of paranoia.[33] Casual observers have also noted the unusual extent to which paranoia — well-systematized delusions of persecution and/or grandeur, the elaborations of which are logically constructed on false premises — seems to afflict elite and peasants equally.[34]

The need to be simultaneously submissive and independent gives rise, it seems, to complicated tensions. Traditionally Haitians have tried to alleviate these tensions by aligning themselves with a patron, a "big man." This rural pattern is not unique to Haiti, but in Haiti it also seems to have been carried over in a very basic way into politics. A Haitian, writing recently from exile, explained that the political and social structure of his people had been molded by absolute power used absolutely. Autocrats have traditionally used terror to keep the lower classes and the elite submissive. "Our souls," he wrote, "are like dead leaves. We live in indifference, are silently malcontent [and] the most flagrant violation of our rights and the most outrageous abuse of authority provokes among us merely submission. We retreat, in the manner of an *escargot*."[35] Presidents are often called "Papa" — a trivial but not completely irrelevant indication of basic identifications — and

31 Anna Freud (trans. Cecil Baines), *The Ego and the Mechanisms of Defense* (New York, 1966; orig. ed., 1936), 120.
32 Erikson, *Childhood and Society*, 257.
33 Ari Kiev, "Research and Resources in Psychiatry in Haiti," in Schaedel (ed.), *Research*, 428–440. Emerson Douyon, a Haitian psychiatrist, also argues that the possession states of *vodun* are channels for otherwise unexpressible aggressiveness and symptoms of repressed conflicts and serve "as a last resort against deeper mental illness." "Research Model on Trance and Possession States in the Haitian Voodoo," *ibid.*, 415–427.
34 For example, see Herbert Gold, *The Age of Happy Problems* (New York, 1962), 174–175. See also Huxley, *Invisibles*, 42.
35 Placide David, *L'Héritage Colonial en Haiti* (Madrid, 1959), 210–211.

have been overthrown, it may be conjectured, when they vitiated
their responsibilities as parental surrogates. If so, the problems of
oedipal adjustment would also tend to be projected onto and resolved by identification with a "big man" or a head of state.
(Everyone wants to be a "boss.")[36] In later life, this transference
provides an unexpectedly firm and docile body of support for any
strong leader. If this analysis is at all valid, the severity and violence of authority figures re-enact the basic childhood conflict, and
harsh behavior is accepted as a necessary concomitant of leadership. Haitians therefore can be said to need and expect strong dictatorship; accordingly, democratic politics revives the kinds of tensions which Haitians would prefer to avoid and the decisions which
they find difficult to make.

The contemporary problems of Haiti can be fully understood
only by reference to the national psychology and its elaboration
over time. The man who is limned in the cities and villages as
"Papa Doc à Vie," and the engine of total repression which he has
cannily and masterfully crafted since 1957, is no aberration. Duvalier and Duvalierism, the violence, the corruption, the poverty,
the hopelessness, and even the absurdity of a recurrent budget of
between $33 and $40 million (depending upon how it is calculated) which is devoted almost entirely to salaries and wages —
40,000 of the 100,000 nominally employed in Haiti work for the
government — fit securely in the framework of Haiti's past and
rest upon the psychological bases of the nation. The Duvalierist
dictatorship is harsh and by no stretch of the imagination benevolent. But it differs from its predecessors only in degree, and in the
measures it uses to maintain its effective grip on power. Modern
Haiti is a prisoner of its past, and the next four chapters are intended to place the politics of squalor as fully as possible in historical context.

[36] Huxley, *Invisibles*, 39, 100, 102.

II

The First Revolution
and Its Effects

ON THE EVE of the French Revolution Haiti, then called Saint-Domingue, was the veritable Pearl of the Antilles. It was France's most prosperous colony, it outranked any of the British possessions in their contributions to the wealth of the mother country, and, in contemporary as well as historic lights, Haiti was the wealthiest European outpost in the New World.

This prosperity was all the more prized for having been achieved late and enjoyed to its fullest extent only during the fading years of the *ancien régime*. Columbus made landfalls on the northern shore of Haiti in 1492. He and his successors established Spanish settlements, the aboriginal population largely disappeared due to disease and cruelty and, after 1513, African slaves began to replace Carib Indians in the plantation and pearl-fishing economy of Hispaniola, the name by which the entire island was known to the Spaniards.[1] But the Spanish developed the western or Haitian portions of their première possession less extensively than they did the part subsequently called Santo Domingo. In the forests of what was to become Haiti wild cattle roamed; there was little gold, and, largely because of the extremely rugged nature of the terrain and the concomitant absence of navigable waterways, there was a paucity of Spanish administrators and settlers.

---

[1] For a discussion of the aboriginal population, see Jean Price-Mars, "L'archéologie, l'ethnologie et la linguistique: état actuel de ces sciences appliquées à l'aire géographique du Golfe du Mexique et du bassin des Caraibes, études comparatives et possibilités de coordination scientifique," *Revue de la Société d'Histoire et de Géographie d'Haiti*, XII, 41 (April 1941), 1–12; Herbert M. Kreiger, *The Aborigines of the Ancient Island of Hispaniola* (Washington, 1929); Louis E. Elie, *Histoire d'Haïti* (Port-au-Prince, 1944), I, 71–112, 239–256.

By 1629 the presence of such resources and the absence of *de facto* administration had attracted adventurers of many European nationalities, would-be pirates, fugitives from justice, shipwrecked sailors, and a multitude of men of kindred spirit to Tortuga Island off the northwestern coast of Hispaniola. Thirty years later Norman and Breton buccaneers forcibly established their ascendancy over this riff-raff. Systematically they raided Spanish settlements on Hispaniola and British outposts on nearby Jamaica. With the direct encouragement of Louis XIV, who sanctioned the importation of slaves, they began to grow indigo, cotton, and cacao in the fertile plains of northern Haiti. Despite numerous concerted British and Spanish expeditions against this burgeoning outpost of France, the buccaneers never ceased to maintain their position in Haiti and to harass the established colonies. By 1694, after receiving important naval assistance from a French fleet, the hold of the buccaneers on Cap Français (later Cap Haitien) finally seemed secure.[2]

The War of the League of Augsburg and the Treaty of Ryswick by which it was concluded, in 1697, confirmed French possession of the western third of Hispaniola. Its inhabitants included about 6000 adult white and mulatto males and about 50,000 black slaves. Until the end of the Seven Years' War in 1763, the plantations of Saint-Domingue were expanded gradually, especially in the north and south, and sugar and coffee joined the export crops of the seventeenth century. The slave population (it was an estimated 250,000 in 1775) also increased as a result of forced immigration, a new class of aristocratic settlers (there were about 15,000 resident adult whites in 1775) added a veneer to the social complexion of the colony, and some fortunes were made from Saint-Domingue by the importers and exporters of Nantes, Bordeaux, and Le Havre. Although Martinique preceded Saint-Domingue in the develop-

[2] Interesting discussions of this period will be found in George-Ary Chevalier, "Étude sur la colonisation française en Haïti: Origines et développement des propriétés Collette," *Revue de la Société d'Histoire et de Géographie d'Haïti*, IX, 31 (October 1938), 13–37; Ricardo Pattee, *Haiti: Pueblo Afroantillano* (Madrid, 1956), 21–36; Pierre de Vaissière, *Saint-Domingue: La Société et la Vie Créoles sous l'Ancien Régime (1629–1789)* (Paris, 1909), 2–24, 45, 52–55. The fullest contemporary account is Pierre-François Xavier de Charlevoix, *Histoire de l'Isle Espagnole ou de S. Domingue* (Amsterdam, 1733), III and IV, *passim*.

ment of both sugar and coffee, Saint-Domingue had passed Martinique in sugar production by 1742[3] and in coffee production by 1776, despite the almost continuous political discord there between the *colons* and the French Intendant. There also were conflicts over the treatment of slaves, the extent of French taxation, and the restrictive mercantile policies of the Empire.[4]

France's loss of Canada and the American Revolution contributed to the accelerated growth of the economy of Saint-Domingue. French merchants concentrated their efforts on the island and new markets became available. During the decade and a half of peace following the Seven Years' War, the planters of Saint-Domingue approximately doubled their exports: in 1767 about 72 million pounds of raw sugar, 51 million pounds of white sugar, 1 million pounds of indigo, 2 million pounds of cotton, and large amounts of coffee, tobacco, cocoa, rum, molasses, and hides were shipped to France, the United States, and Jamaica, the coffee and cocoa being particularly prized in Paris because of their quality.[5] From this time, too, and especially after a hurricane in 1766 and a plague of ants in 1775 had slowed the development of Martinique and Sainte-Lucie, Saint-Domingue became the brightest jewel in France's Caribbean crown.

The economic development of Saint-Domingue in the three decades prior to the revolution is indicated in Table 1. This table includes only the legal exports to France. The contraband exports consisted of molasses and sugar to the northern colonies of the United States, and indigo, cotton, and sugar to Jamaica. After the trade liberalization by the French government in 1784, Saint-Domingue's legal exports to the United States rose in 1788 to 3.7 million francs (approximately equal to livres tournois), while the

[3] David MacPherson, *Annals of Commerce* (London, 1805), under the year 1748. Reprinted in *East India Sugar, Papers Respecting the Culture and Manufacture of Sugar in British India* (London, 1822), 94–104.

[4] There is a fascinating analysis of the complex commercial mechanisms of this period in Richard Pares, *War and Trade in the West Indies, 1739–1763* (London, 1936), 326–343. Cf. Gaston Martin, *Nantes au XVIII⁰ Siècle; l'Ere des Négriers (1714–1744)* (Paris, 1931), 200–265, 368–382.

[5] There is some confusion with regard to the precise figures, but see R. Lepelletier de Saint-Remy, *Saint-Domingue: Étude et Solution Nouvelle de la Question Haitienne* (Paris, 1846), I, 18–24. See also Placide-Justin, *Histoire Politique et Statistique de l'Ile d'Hayti, Saint Domingue* (Paris, 1826), 113–124.

Table 1

Exports of Saint-Domingue, in Current and Constant Prices,
Selected Years, 1767 to 1787–89
(All figures in millions of colonial livres, worth one-third less
than livres tournois)

I.   Constant (1787–89) prices

	Sugar	Coffee	Cotton	Indigo	Tafia & Molasses	Others	Total
1787–89	75.0	71.5	12.31	9.16	3.1	1.2	172.3
1783–84	76.2	48.8	8.91	15.41	2.8	1.2	153.3
1774–76	61.0	43.7	4.62	15.82	2.6	1.2	128.9
1767	65.2	12.2	5.49	15.92	2.6	1.2	98.8

II.   Current prices

	Sugar	Coffee	All Others[a]	Total
1787–89	75.0	71.5	25.8	172.3
1783–84	70.2	36.6	28.3	134.9
1774–76	58.6	26.2	24.2	109.0
1767	65.2	14.6	25.2	105.0

[a] These figures are the sum of cotton, indigo, tafia-molasses, and others. The constant-price figures were used for these products, in the absence of reliable price series.

legal imports were 7 million francs, but the contraband trade was undoubtedly much larger.[6] The planters depended on slaves smuggled from Jamaica, and on stock fish, an important item in the slave diet, from the United States.[7] Ten to 15 per cent should be added to official exports to France to allow for legal and illegal exports to other countries.[8]

[6] Alain Turnier, Les Etats-Unis et le Marché Haïtien (Washington, 1955), 31; Prosper Boissonade, Saint-Domingue à la Veille de la Révolution (Paris, 1906), 24.
[7] Dubucq and Dubuisson estimate the contraband trade (imports plus exports) in 1784 at 15 to 20 million livres (presumably livres tournois). Ragatz cites a figure of 28 million pounds of French sugar smuggled into the British market in 1785. If two-thirds are from Saint-Domingue, and we estimate the price at 0.4 colonial livres per pound, the total comes to 7.5 million livres. J. B. Dubucq and P. U. Dubuisson, Lettres Critiques et Politiques sur les Colonies et le Commerce des Villes Maritimes de France, adressées à G. T. Raynal (Geneva, 1785), 115; Lowell Joseph Ragatz, The Fall of the Planter Class in the British Caribbean, 1763–1833: A Study in Social and Economic History (New York, 1928), 103.
[8] Venault de Charmilly, whose interests would incline him to inflate the figure, says

Table 1 also reveals the shifting composition of exports. Sugar production increased only moderately during the thirty years prior to the revolution (although 1767 seems to have been a fairly good year for sugar exports). Coffee exports grew greatly during the period. D'Auberteuil estimates that the coffee plantations absorbed 60 per cent of the new slave imports in the 1767–1774 period, and that they must have taken a similar percentage in 1783–1789. On the eve of the French Revolution, Saint-Domingue grew about 60 per cent of the world's coffee.[9]

The French islands had wrested the continental sugar market from the British during the 1720–1740 period, and they never relinquished it, aside from periods of war, until after the revolution.[10] The relative cheapness of French sugar is also attested by the continued smuggling of it into the British islands for sale in the protected British market. Had there been free trade in sugar, Saint-Domingue's share of the combined French and British islands' sugar would probably have exceeded its actual share of about 40 per cent.[11] Another indication of the superior competitive ability of Saint-Domingue was its willingness to pay more than the British islands for slaves.[12]

---

that contraband exports came to at least one-fourth the value of official exports. Venault de Charmilly, *Lettre à Bryan Edwards* (London, 1797), 77; Guillaume T. Raynal, *Histoire Philosophique et Politique des Etablissements et du Commerce des Européens dans les Deux Indes* (Geneva, 1782), VII, 145–146, indicates that contraband trade was very important in the period about 1775.

[9] Hilliard d'Auberteuil, *Considérations sur l'Etat Présent de la Colonie Française de St. Domingue* (Paris, 1776), I, 68; Jean Barré de St. Venant, *Des Colonies Modernes sous la Zone Torride, et Particulièrement de celle de Saint-Domingue* (Paris, 1802), 255–256.

[10] Richard Pares, "The London Sugar Market, 1740–1769," *Economic History Review*, IX (1965), 254–270. Bryan Edwards, *An Historical Survey of the French Colony in the Island of St. Domingo* (London, 1797), II, 599, gives British sugar exports on the eve of the revolution.

[11] This figure was calculated in the following way:

All British islands, 1787–1790 (Edwards, *St. Domingo*, II, 597)	195.0 million French pounds
Saint-Domingue, 1787–1789 (See Table 1)	187.5 million French pounds (Muscovado equivalent)
Other French islands (one-third of Saint-Domingue's exports)	63.0 million French pounds
Total	445.5

With these figures, Saint-Domingue's share was 42 per cent.

[12] Dubucq and Dubuisson, *Lettres Critiques*, supplement, 10; Venault de Charmilly, *Lettre*, 78.

Whether the competitive edge of Saint-Domingue over the British islands was due to the superior fertility of its soil or to the skill and industry of the French is a matter on which the British and French disagreed. Edwards estimated the sugar yields per acre to be two-thirds greater in Saint-Domingue than in Jamaica, but he attributes this result entirely to the better irrigational possibilities and superior soils in Saint-Domingue. Venault de Charmilly asserts that the French planters were more innovative and industrious, in part because absenteeism was less prevalent than in Jamaica.[13]

Ragatz, who is very critical of the entrepreneurial failings of the British planters, indicates that the French might have been more enterprising. He attributes inertia in large measure to absenteeism.[14] Perhaps one reason for the industry and enterprise of the Saint-Domingue planters was the migration there in the seventeenth century of French Protestants.[15]

Saint-Domingue also had the benefit of a somewhat more en-

[13] Edwards, *St. Domingo*, III, 145–146 and 241–242. But Edwards' own figures indicate that, even on non-irrigated land, Saint-Domingue's yields were about a third higher than those of Jamaica. On this point see also Noel Deerr, *The History of Sugar* (London, 1950), II, 425.

[14] Ragatz, *Planter Class*, 61, 79. But, regarding absenteeism, Ragatz says: "The fundamental cause is to be found in the fact that the French holdings, save only St. Domingo, were developed by small resident owners while, with the single exception of Antigua, all of the long-held British colonies were cultivated under the direction of large absentee proprietors' representatives, which made operating expenses markedly lower in the former." (*Ibid.*, 126–127.)

[15] Maurice de Young, *Man and Land in the Haitian Economy* (Gainesville, 1958), 12–13. For further discussion of the reasons for the French competitive advantage see William E. Gordon, "Imperial Policy Decisions in the Economic History of Jamaica, 1664–1934," *Social and Economic Studies*, VI (1957), 3–4.

The British and French planters were frequently criticized for failure to adopt the plow (e.g., Young, *Man and Land*, 16). It is wise to be skeptical of this sort of criticism, however, for it implies that the writer, frequently not a planter, knew more about the business than the man on the spot. The plow was, in fact, introduced to most of the British and French islands, but found to be less efficient, at the going price of labor, than the use of the hoe. (Deerr, *Sugar*, II, 353–354.)

Cane-hoeing was a backbreaking task, and part of the propaganda in favor of the plow was motivated by humanitarian considerations. As the price of labor increased, and especially after the abolition of slavery, the plow came into more general use, though cane-hoeing was continued in some places into the twentieth century. Barré de St. Venant (*Colonies Modernes*, 340–341) provides an interesting insight into one of the problems attending the use of the plow. It was supposedly difficult for the planter to hire white plowmen to come to the West Indies and ply their trade because the slaves "made fun" of any white man who worked with his hands.

lightened colonial policy than that applied to the British islands. British development of clayed sugar was prevented by discriminatory duties. Coffee-growing in the British islands was retarded prior to 1783 by duties equal to four or more times the price of the product. After the American War of Independence, the British government declared trade with the United States to be illegal, and interfered more with that trade than did the French government.[16]

Still, that Saint-Domingue was more prosperous was not solely a function of differences in colonial policy vis-à-vis the British-held islands. Saint-Domingue's soils were fertile and extensive, and her French owners had put their talents and their savings to work to create an impressive and efficient economic machine. By 1783 it was producing two thirds of French-grown tropical produce, nearly as much sugar — more than 100 million pounds — as all of the British possessions in the Caribbean, 42 million pounds of coffee, 5 million pounds of cotton, and 1.7 million pounds of indigo.[17] New towns and roads were constructed (but not without the waste and graft which have always accompanied such operations in Haiti), the ports were improved, a measure of self-government was granted to newly created communal councils of settlers (very few whites lived in the interior), and more than 13,000 white and mulatto males were enrolled in the local militia. To be sure, slaves provided the energy of the society, and much of the great wealth of the colony accrued to merchants of Bordeaux and Nantes, but by about 1783 Cap Français and Port-au-Prince were places of more than parochial importance. Culturally, if not physically, they rivaled Charleston and Savannah, and conveyed more of a French provincial than a Caribbean air.

Books were published in Saint-Domingue as early as 1725, the first weekly newspaper appeared in 1764 (at one time fifty substantial newspapers or reviews were regularly published in the colony), from 1784 there was a literary and arts and sciences society which published a number of scholarly papers, and there were

16 Deerr, *Sugar*, I, 232; Edwards, *St. Domingo*, II, 339, 349; Paul Leroy-Beaulieu, *De la Colonisation chez les Peuples Modernes* (4th ed., Paris, 1891), 126, 169.
17 Ragatz, *Planter Class*, 125–126.

flourishing repertory theaters in Port-au-Prince,[18] Cap Français, Les Cayes, Léogane, St. Marc, and Jérémie. Of the approximately 3000 theatrical productions between 1764 and 1791, a large number were naturally by the dramatists then popular in France: Molière, Rousseau, Voltaire, Racine, and Beaumarchais. But there were productions by local authors as well, readings of poetry composed by inhabitants of the colony, concerts by local performers, and a flourishing *salon* life.

Between the end of the American War of Independence in 1783 and the French Revolution, Saint-Domingue greatly increased its production of primary crops (in the case of coffee and cotton by more than 50 per cent) as a result of rising demand in the United States and Europe. Of the 4100 ships registered as entering and leaving the ports of Saint-Domingue in 1789, more than 2500 were from the United States. There then were 792 sugar estates (of 200 or more hectares each), 2810 smaller coffee plantations, 705 producers of cotton, and more than 3000 smaller cultivators of indigo, their licit exports surpassing those of all of the British possessions in tropical America. Of even greater significance, in 1789 Saint-Domingue was responsible for more than 40 per cent by value of the foreign trade of France; no other colony contributed so much to the economy of its mother country. Furthermore, only about one third of the goods imported into France were consumed there, the remainder being re-exported after the addition of further units of value. It has been estimated that of the 27 million Frenchmen about 5 million depended directly upon the trade with Saint-Domingue. The prosperity of Nantes, Bordeaux, and Marseilles, and, to a lesser extent, Orléans, Dieppe, and Bercy-Paris, was based upon the refining of raw sugar from Saint-Domingue; the cotton spinners of Normandy drew their supplies from the same source; and the exporters of a dozen prominent French cities and regions relied upon the sale of flour, salted meat, wines, cheese, wax candles, soap, tallow, oil, beer, vegetables and preserved fruit, fish, butter, dry goods, and much else to the inhabitants of Saint-Domingue.[19]

18 See Dantès Bellegarde, *Histoire du Peuple Haitien (1492–1952)* (Port-au-Prince, 1953), 48–54; Elie, *Histoire,* II, 227–235; and Vaissière, *Saint-Domingue,* 333–334. But see *ibid.,* 255–275.

19 Léon Deschamps, *Les Colonies Pendant la Révolution* (Paris, 1898), 5–6; Edwards,

The population of Saint-Domingue on the eve of the revolution consisted of about 30,000 whites, 27,500 free mulattoes and blacks, and 465,000 slaves.[20] Many of the mulattoes had been educated in France, owned prosperous estates, and contributed to the defense of the colony. Most mulattoes were free but, although equal before the law in France as a result of measures introduced during and after the Seven Years' War, at the behest of the *colons* they were subject to severe discrimination in Saint-Domingue. The *colons* feared their increasing prominence, saw the mark of color as the only obvious distinction between themselves and the vastly more numerous slave population, and dreaded being overwhelmed by an inexorable tidal wave of color; like so many of their kind who had savored the fruits of prejudice, the whites sought both to humiliate and to harass the mulattoes by the use of every and any means which ingenuity and malice could devise. Mulattoes were forbidden to meet together on any pretext, to remain in France, to play European games, to take the titles of monsieur and madame, to wear European dress, to purchase ammunition or wear swords, to take advanced degrees, to be priests, lawyers, physicians, goldsmiths, apothecaries, or schoolmasters, to accept military commissions, and to eat with whites. "I must further observe to you," Baron Wimpffen wrote in 1788, that "the male and female mulattos, in spite of the acquisition of liberty, remain in a state of abjectness, which not only disqualifies them from any public employ, but forbids them to contract with the whites a sufficient degree of intimacy, I will not say to sleep with them, but even to eat. If I visit a rich mulatto, he will call me *sir,* and not *master,* like the rest. I call him *friend, dear friend,* &c. and he will ask me to dinner; but if he

St. Domingo, 206; Ragatz, *Planter Class,* 204–205; Candelon Rigaud, "Influence des Colonies Françaises sur le Commerce de la Métropole," *Revue de la Société d'Histoire et de Géographie d'Haiti,* II (December 1926), 18–26; Henock Trouillot, "Economie et Finances de Saint-Domingue," *Revue de la Société Haitienne d'Histoire, de Géographie, et de Géologie,* XXXIII, 110 (January–April 1965), 123–132; Herbert Ingram Priestley, *France Overseas Through the Old Régime: A Study of European Expansion* (New York, 1939), 266; Tadeusz Lepkowski, *Haiti: Początki Państwa i Narodu* (Warsaw, 1964), 58. See also François Alexandre Stanislaus de Wimpffen (trans. J. Wright), *A Voyage to Saint Domingo in the Years 1788, 1789, and 1790* (London, 1817), 85–89.
20 Cf. Vaissière, *Saint-Domingue,* 153–154; Deschamps, *Colonies,* 290; Priestley, *Overseas,* 267.

be correct, he will not presume to sit at table with me." [21] The sum of these various regulations, in spirit as well as in law, constituted an atmosphere akin to *apartheid*. As James has remarked, "the only privilege the whites allowed them was the privilege of lending white men money." [22]

The slaves, most of whom were black, constituted an even more intractable problem. The majority were very recent arrivals, and a surprisingly small proportion of the adults had been born or, presumably, socialized in Saint-Domingue. During the 1720's Saint-Domingue regularly imported only about 4000 slaves yearly. In 1753, 5000 slaves were introduced. By 1771, the numbers had increased: 10,000 slaves were landed in Saint-Domingue. But in 1786, 27,000 slaves reached Saint-Domingue and, during each of the succeeding three years, about 40,000 slaves arrived. Although it has been widely assumed that most of these slaves were shipped to Saint-Domingue from Dahomey and the Guinea coast, the sources upon which everyone relies provide little hard evidence of the provenance of the mass of slaves. Nor do we know the composition of individual shiploads at specific times. That slaves during the 1780's and earlier were imported from what is now Senegal, Mali, Guinée, Liberia, Ghana, Dahomey, the Congo, Angola, etc., is clear, but, despite the reputed ritual similarities between old Dahomey and Haiti, nothing indicates that the slave markets of Saint-Domingue were ever supplied overwhelmingly from that quarter. A careful examination of the eighteenth-century accounts reveals that the slaves stemmed from at least thirty-eight different regions, and from three or four times as many tribes.[23] They lacked com-

21 Wimpffen, *Voyage*, 62.
22 Cyril L. R. James, *The Black Jacobins: Toussaint l'Ouverture and the San Domingo Revolution* (2nd ed., New York, 1963), 5. For a detailed exposition of color discrimination in eighteenth-century Saint-Domingue, see Auguste Lebeau, *De la Condition des Gens de Couleur Libres sous l'Ancien Régime* (Poitiers, 1903), 67, 93, 147, and *passim;* Harry H. Johnston, *The Negro in the New World* (New York, 1910), 141. For the United States, see Winthrop D. Jordan, *White Over Black: American Attitudes Toward the Negro, 1550–1812* (Chapel Hill, 1968), 167–178. For a discussion of the position of *affranchis* (free blacks), see Hoetink, "Sociaal-Raciale Struuctur," 148.
23 The most comprehensive collation of the origins of Haitian slaves is James G. Leyburn, "The Making of a Black Nation," in George Peter Murdock (ed.), *Studies in the Science of Society* (New Haven, 1937), 381–386. For contemporary numbers and discussions of provenance, see Vaissière, *Saint-Domingue*, 164; Edwards, *St.*

mon languages, religions, social principles, and technologies, being assembled in Haiti only because they were black and readily salable, and were brought together on a particular plantation strictly by chance. It is possible to say, however, that the newest and least Westernized slaves were wanted and used during the 1780's for the opening up of the hitherto largely virgin interior of Saint-Domingue. The heightened demand for the agricultural products of Saint-Domingue obviously encouraged the exploitation of the central and northern uplands. We can conclude that the great increase in the absolute number of newly landed slaves filled the colony, and particularly its rural areas, with a mass of inexperienced, intractable, very densely settled, probably resentful, and not yet broken Africans who remembered their lost freedom. These slaves had little to lose by rebellion. If discontent is generated by discomfort, tribulation, and oppression, they formed a sizable pool of persons antagonistic to the established order.

The onerous conditions of field slavery in Saint-Domingue are well documented. Work in the sugar fields was hard, and equally inhumane — by the standards of a later day — in Saint-Domingue, the southern United States, and the sugar isles of the Caribbean.[24] The slaves were ill-housed, ill-fed, ill-cared for, and continually abused; a catalogue of their mistreatment and the detailing of specific cases are unnecessary here, but in addition to brutal whippings and the pouring of salt and pepper into their wounds, slaves were mutilated for trivial offenses or in order to prevent the enjoyment of pleasure; they were shackled, and some overseers affixed

---

Domingo, 212 (slightly lower figures). The assumptions regarding provenance are weighed judiciously in Bellegarde, *Peuple Haitien,* 25; Melville J. Herskovits, *Life in a Haitian Valley* (New York, 1937), 17–25. Herskovits relies heavily on Charlevoix, *Histoire de l'Isle Espagnole,* IV, 362–363; Médéric-Louis-Élie Moreau de Saint-Méry, *Description Topographique, Physique, Civile, Politique et Historique de la Partie Française de l'Isle Saint-Domingue* (Philadelphia, 1797; Paris, 1958); and cognate studies. See also "Le Vodou, La Religion des Masses Haitiennes," *Bulletin du Bureau d'Ethnologie de la République d'Haiti* (February 1948), reprinted in François Duvalier, *Oeuvres Essentielles* (Port-au-Prince, 1968; 2nd ed.), I, 277–285, esp. 278–279. 24 There is a good description of life on a sugar plantation in Justin Girod-Chantrans, *Voyage d'un Suisse dans Différentes Colonies d'Amerique* (Neuchatel, 1785), 136–138. Two other case studies are found in Gabriel Debien, *Plantations et Esclaves à Saint-Domingue* (Dakar, 1962). For the United States, see Jordan, *Over Black,* 128–135.

tin-plate masks in order to prevent the slaves from eating sugar cane. There are recorded instances of owners pouring burning wax or boiling cane sugar onto slaves for punishment or sport, of slave roasts, and of torture of every known perverse devising. It was reported that a planter at La Grande-Rivière had nailed a slave to a wall by his ears, sliced them off, grilled them, and fed them to the earless slave. The case of the infamous coffee planter Le Jeune, of Plaisance, was brought to the attention of the French Assembly in 1788. Suspecting poisoning and witchcraft, he killed four slaves and sought to extort confessions by torture from two women. After some of the other slaves complained to magistrates in Plaisance, a commission visited the plantation and found the two women chained, with elbows and legs decomposing. Yet a judicial hearing acquitted Le Jeune.[25] It is true that many domestic slaves were treated more humanely, and that both Henri Christophe (born in St. Kitts) and Toussaint Bréda (later L'Ouverture), who were of the house and the kitchen rather than the fields, served considerate masters, gained an education, and could, in time, probably have obtained their freedom by non-martial means, but the lot of most slaves was vile, and almost beyond modern appreciation.

The whites of Saint-Domingue meanwhile enjoyed an almost caricatured colonial life. The sophisticated urbanities of Cap Français or Port-au-Prince were equalled, in their way, by the rustic luxury of the great houses of the plantations. Only for Brazil has this kind of life been described in lavish detail, yet upper-class whites in Saint-Domingue could, before 1791, have cultivated an elegant, graciously affected life of comparative ease. In Cap Français which, in 1789, counted a population of 20,000, half of whom were slaves, they could expect to live in stone houses (the materials for which were often carried from France) constructed around tree-lined public squares near imposing churches. The town boasted several of the country's newspapers, a printing works, a small theater with a permanent company of actors, a bookstore, public baths, and shops where the latest Parisian fashions could be

25 For details of this case, and of other horrors, see Vaissière, *Saint-Domingue*, 186–188. Other stories, and eyewitness accounts, are retailed by Wimpffen, *Voyage*, 216–218.

purchased. The governor and his assistants were based there, in preference to earthquake-prone Port-au-Prince, and it had a military barracks, hospitals, and a prison. The town, moreover, did not lack its pleasures: there were gambling dens, dance halls, and a series of celebrated brothels, all of which testified to the booming nature of the economy as well as to the typicality of the colonial culture.[26]

Port-au-Prince approached le Cap in depravity if not in culture and size, but the remainder of the urban centers were no more than villages. Léogane had 300 houses, St. Marc 150, and Jacmel, an important town of the south, only 40. These were all coastal centers, emphasizing the extent to which Haiti, always looking outward, consistently failed to develop inner resources or any self-sustaining sense of national identity. On the eve of the revolution it is clear that the fabric of Saint-Domingue, like so many scattered, sparsely populated European outposts dependent upon the export of raw materials to a distant mother country, rested on illusory foundations. There was no indigenous mechanism of unified administration and government. A distant, absolute monarchy, influenced by absentee landlords and entrepreneurs in France, depended for the administration of justice, the economic exploitation, and the maintenance of law and order in Saint-Domingue upon the machinations of an uninspired exiled bureaucracy and the sullen acquiescence of squabbling *colons* and silent blacks. Furthermore, society was highly stratified. Nobody shared power with or participated in the administration except officials sent from France. The governor only rarely took advice from the communal councils. The bureaucrats tolerated the *seigneurs* — the *grands*

---

[26] There is a detailed description and history of Cap Français in Moreau de Saint-Méry, *Description Topographique*, 296–482. Baron Wimpffen, however, did not share the usual view of Port-au-Prince: "When a person has been acquainted in France with colonists, and above all with Creole colonists, he cannot approach Port-au-Prince . . . the capital of the richest country on the face of the globe! the most fertile in delights! the throne of luxury! the center of voluptuousness! without experiencing that secret shivering, that pleasing and vague anxiety which precedes admiration, and prepares the soul for enthusiasm — To be brief, I entered between two rows of huts, jolting along a dusty track called a street, and searching in vain for Persepolis, amongst a chaotic mass of wooden barracks! . . . The comparison which most forcibly strikes one, at the first sight of this famous city, is, that of a Tartar camp. . . ." *Voyage*, 206, 208.

blancs — and despised the *petits blancs,* the mulattoes, and the slaves. The *grands blancs* feared the *petits blancs* and the rest; the *petits blancs* disliked classes above and below; the mulattoes wreaked vengeance on the blacks; and the slaves for the most part maintained a complex attitude of fatalism and submission. There is no gainsaying that the ingredients of a violent protest were at hand, but what is of even greater importance for us is that the political and economic machinery of the colony was exclusively French. No blacks or mulattoes, and only a very few white *colons,* participated in the governance or commerce of the colony. After the revolution there existed no fund of indigenous administrative experience, and no pool of governmental or technical skills. The revolution, when it came, had both a purging and a scourging effect.

The economic contrast between pre-revolutionary Saint-Domingue and independent Haiti is striking. To keep this contrast in perspective, however, it is essential to stress certain economic frailties which might have manifested themselves in Saint-Domingue even in the absence of any revolution. Among the primary weaknesses of Saint-Domingue must be mentioned the loss of soil fertility through intensive use. In the history of the sugar industry, production repeatedly shifted away from the first settled islands, the soils of which became exhausted, toward the fresh soils of new producers. Barbados lost out to Jamaica, Jamaica to Saint-Domingue and then, after a brief revival following the revolution, to Cuba and elsewhere. As the price of sugar fell during the first half of the nineteenth century, Saint-Domingue undoubtedly would have suffered along with Jamaica, although perhaps not to the same degree. This is not to say that the French planters could not have made the adjustment to the use of fertilizers; but costs would have risen and development would have been slowed down. A similar situation existed in the coffee industry; the intensive French methods of cultivation, so profitable in their time, were very destructive to soil-carrying capacity.[27]

The second weakness was the reliance of the economy on the

27 D'Auberteuil, *Considérations,* I, 239. Paul Moral, "La Culture du Café en Haiti: Des Plantations Colonials aux 'Jardins' Actuels," *Cahiers d'Outre-Mer,* VIII (1955),

continued importation of slaves. There was a considerable excess of deaths over births in the slave population, a fact that speaks volumes about the brutality of the system.[28] In this connection it is interesting to examine the role of slave imports in the balance of payments of Saint-Domingue.

	Exports	*Imports*	*Exports minus Imports*	*Slave Imports*
1762–1776	74.4	49.5	24.9	17.7
1784–1789	128.8	62.1	66.7	48.5

These figures are in millions of livres tournois, and, although the method of calculation is not very exact, the broad picture is fairly clear.[29] If the supply of slaves had been cut off, Saint-Domingue would have had to make a serious economic adjustment, namely

---

233–256. Haitian methods, in particular the shading of the trees, were less productive but also took less out of the soil.

28 Placide-Justin (*Histoire Politique,* 147) notes that during the eighteenth century 900,000 slaves had been brought to Saint-Domingue; yet in 1789 only about 465,000 remained. Many probably died during the famines accompanying wars, but even in normal times the death rate of the adult population was high. Raynal (*Histoire Philosophique,* VII, 123) says the annual loss of slaves from natural causes was one-twentieth, and accidents raised this to one-fifteenth. The high infant mortality rates are less an indication of undernourishment and overwork than of infectious disease (mainly tetanus), and were probably little affected by independence. The evidence on slave mortality is discussed in T. Lothrop Stoddard, *The French Revolution in San Domingo* (Boston, 1914), 51–53.

29 Priestley, *Overseas,* 267, gives the following figures (in millions of livres tournois) for trade between the Antilles and France:

	Antilles Exports to France	*Antilles Imports from France*
1762–1776	111.6	74.2
1777–1783	108.7	50.6
1784–1789	193.25	93.1

Assuming Saint-Domingue accounted for two thirds of both imports and exports, we obtain the figures given in the text. Slave imports were 26,000 in 1786 and about 40,000 per year in 1787–1789. If we take an average of 35,000 for 1784–1789, and multiply these by an average price of 1387 livres (Edwards, *St. Domingo,* III, 220), we obtain the 48.5 million livres cited in the text. Slave imports in the 1767–1774 period were 17,000 per year (D'Auberteuil, *Considérations,* 67–69); the price of 1040 for 1770 (Vaissière, *Saint-Domingue,* 164) gives a value of 17.7 million, as shown in the text.

In fact, the price of slaves was rising rather sharply. Vaissière (*ibid.*) gives the following figures (in livres tournois): 773 in 1750; 1040, 1770; 1267, 1778; 1467, 1785.

Young (*Man and Land,* 26–27) proposes a peculiar economic model to account for

the conversion to productive techniques that maintained and increased the labor force. Again, such a conversion would not have
been impossible, but it would have raised costs.

On the eve of the revolution, the ruling classes of Haiti were
committed economically, socially, and politically to the perpetuation of a highly privileged and very rewarding system of exploitation. There were obvious inequities, but Haiti had proved such a
successful colony that the possibility of radical change naturally
seemed as unthinkable to those who were profiting from the system
as it made psychological sense to the oppressed. The myriad details
of the development of the revolution need not detain us unduly,[30]
but if we are to appreciate the impact of the revolutionary experience on the Haitian political, social, and economic heritage, and
the profound way in which the inner dynamic of the revolution
molded Haiti — perhaps for all time — then it is necessary to discover by what process Saint-Domingue was transformed into Latin
America's first independent nation.

The summoning by Louis XVI of the Etats-Généraux sent an

---

the rising price of slaves. He feels that the phenomenon is paradoxical in the light
of the falling price of sugar and constant technology. He concludes that the price
of slaves must have exceeded their marginal revenue product, and he explains this
by arguing that the value of the slave to the planter was not just the value of the
output he produced, but also the value of the land which he enabled the planter
to acquire.

This explanation, however, is hard to accept and unnecessary. A much more
orthodox model can explain Young's data. Our model relies on the difference between total costs and variable costs, or between the cost of producing sugar by clearing new land and the (lower) cost of continuing to produce on existing plantations.
(This latter cost is lower for some years, until the soil becomes exhausted.) Probably
until the late 1770's there was considerable clearing of new land for sugar production. After that date, the price of slaves continued to rise as a result of the demands of the coffee and cotton industries, and the slave price was too high to
justify land clearing for sugar, but sugar production continued at the same level
because the variable costs of sugar production were still below the price of sugar.
This set of circumstances would account for a falling sugar-slave price ratio, even
with constant technology. In this model the price of the slave is always equal to his
marginal revenue product.

Furthermore, Young's statistics can be questioned. According to our figures for
the London and Nantes sugar markets, there was no decline in the price of sugar
from the mid-1770's to 1789. And there may well have been some improvements in
techniques of sugar production; perhaps not in the fields, but in the manufacturing
part of the process some technical advance was made.

[30] It is, nevertheless, a fascinating period, and for those who wish to be detained
the most accessible studies are James, *Jacobins;* and Bellegarde, *Peuple Haitien,*
55–83.

initial shock wave across the Atlantic, the fall of the Bastille increased its amplitude, and the debates in the Assembly in early 1790 between the abolitionists and their opponents, the bourgeois supporters of the colonial interests, intensified the existing animosity between the different classes of whites, and whites and mulattoes. Louis XVI's submission had immediately led to a clamor for rights, and to the formation of constituent assemblies in St. Marc and other towns of the colony. The *petits blancs,* who excluded the mulattoes, were in the vanguard of the democratic attack on the commercial and political domination of the colonies by the metropole (the privileges of the nobility and the church were not at issue in Saint-Domingue since they did not exist) and, at first, they were joined by the settler aristocracy and opposed by the French bureaucracy and, because of their exclusion, by the mulattoes. Subsequently the leading *colons* joined hands with the mulattoes (and free blacks) against the *petits blancs,* warfare between the two sides becoming endemic. The slaves remained on the sidelines. The French Assembly then discussed the colonial problem and, in its instructions, albeit equivocally, in March 1790 decreed universal franchise for all persons who paid taxes and could meet certain residential qualifications.

The *petits blancs* could not admit (as they did in Brazil) that mulattoes were persons, for if they were, then so were slaves. Yet in Haiti this was only one of the many issues; when the instructions of March finally reached Haiti and inflamed the local white deputies, the royalists had already mounted a counterrevolutionary offensive against the local assemblies which proved successful. It demonstrated, to any who remained skeptical, that the verdicts of justice were still made by force of arms.

Had the mulattoes, already humiliated by the *petits blancs,* been permitted to share the royalist triumph, then Saint-Domingue might have been spared the cataclysm by which it was ultimately engulfed. A number of influential young mulattoes had observed the events of Paris and experienced their own final rejection by whites of both camps at home. Vincent Ogé went from Paris to London, received encouragement from Thomas Clarkson and other English antislavers, sailed to the United States, purchased weapons in Charleston, and soon landed east of Cap Français. To-

gether with Jean-Baptiste Chavannes, a mulatto who had fought
for the United States in the War of Independence, he demanded
the promulgation of the instructions of the French Assembly, refused to contemplate arousing the slaves, and instead attempted to
march on Cap Français with a mere 400 mulattoes. A first engagement went to the mulattoes, but a larger force of indigenous whites
— both revolutionary and counterrevolutionary — and black vol-
unteers soon overwhelmed the mulatto force. Ogé and Chavannes,
and a number of their co-conspirators, were tortured, broken alive
on the wheel, and beheaded, their bodies left to rot.[31] The imprint
of their trial and execution for long remained on the hearts of mulattoes. In death, if not in life, Ogé made mulattoes reconsider
their loyalties.

In Saint-Domingue, as in France, the masses were slow to make
the revolution their own. In Saint-Domingue the blacks observed
the struggle between white and mulatto, felt the hitherto secure
colonial structure crumble, compared their own deprived lot with
the hesitant liberal promises of the National Assembly, pondered
(possibly misreading) the lesson of the mulattoes, gradually
understood the strength of numbers, and harbored the sparks of
insurrection. In August 1791, after several tentative essays of revolt had failed to arouse the slaves, Boukman, the headman of a
plantation in the northern plain, used the informal network of
vodun (voodoo) priests, and the mystery of *vodun* ritual, to acquire and retain the support of 40,000 slaves throughout northern
Saint-Domingue.[32] They sought revenge as well as freedom and,
once the revolution had been unleashed, raped, tortured, and
killed whites, and pillaged and destroyed white-owned property.

[31] For Ogé's final statement and contemporary documents see Edwards, *St. Domingo*,
39–50, 223–231. Clarkson explicitly denied abetting Ogé's plans. See Clarkson's
letters of 1828 in Charles Mackenzie, *Notes on Haiti Made During a Residence in
that Republic* (London, 1830), II, 246–258, 304–306.
[32] Partaking of the ritual was thought to provide invulnerability to adherents; the
superior fire power of the French *colons* would thereby be negated by the superior
efficacy of the black man's religion. And oaths sworn religiously could not in theory
be disregarded in the heat of battle. For some African comparisons see Terence O.
Ranger, *Revolt in Rhodesia* (London, 1967), 127–162; Robert I. Rotberg, "Resistance
and Rebellion in British Nyasaland and German East Africa, 1888–1915: A Tentative
Comparison," in Prosser Gifford and William Roger Louis (eds.), *Britain and Germany in Africa: Imperial Rivalry and Colonial Rule* (New Haven, 1967), 667–690.

Before too long all of the rural areas of Saint-Domingue were dominated by the only loosely coordinated slave bands, and much of the northern plain was in flames. "We arrived in the harbour of Cape François," Edwards wrote of a visit in September, ". . . and the first object which arrested our attention . . . was a dreadful scene of devastation by fire. The noble plain adjoining the Cape was covered with ashes and the surrounding hills, as far as the eye could reach, every where presented to us ruins still smoking, and houses and plantations at that moment in flames. It was a sight more terrible than the mind of any man . . . can easily conceive."[33]

In the west the mulattoes, led by André Rigaud, an educated goldsmith who had fought in the American war, rose a few days after Boukman had exhorted the blacks. Their initial victories were followed by a white-inspired counterrevolution, the total destruction of Port-au-Prince, and the mobilization by mulattoes of the slaves. In the south, where the mulattoes had also risen, the blacks at first joined the whites in their antagonism to the counterrevolution. Confusion, chaos, and destruction penetrated everywhere; the strength of the prosperous colony ebbed as rebellion replaced cultivation as the central preoccupation of the inhabitants of Saint-Domingue.

The blacks — Boukman soon being captured and decapitated — lacked the leadership and decision necessary to transform their revolutionary fervor into a victorious movement of independence. The whites thus managed to retain control of Cap Français and most of the other principal towns of the colony, and to maintain their hegemony in the south. And there were periods of intermittent negotiation during which the colonists, with the exercise of some restraint, could have curtailed hostilities. For the most part, however, conditions of civil war and anarchic violence prevailed, neither whites nor blacks being capable of realizing a *détente* by force of arms, throughout 1792 and most of 1793. In the latter year, too, as a result of a quarrel between the commissioners repre-

[33] Edwards, *St. Domingo*, V, 77–78. See also *ibid.*, 216–222; [James Barskett], *History of the Island of St. Domingo from its First Discovery by Columbus to the Present Period* (London, 1818), 142–156; Antoine Métral, *Histoire de l'Insurrection des Esclaves dans le Nord de Saint-Domingue* (Paris, 1818), 21–27.

senting the Republic and the local *colons,* 3000 slaves ransacked
and fired Cap Français. Two thirds of the city was destroyed and
10,000 whites fled — compounding Saint-Domingue's misery and
losses — to the United States.

The end of the monarchy, and the culmination of the revolution
in France, had already begun to alter the course of the civil war in
Haiti. The commissioners, led by a forceful Jacobin and assisted
by 6000 French soldiers, had begun to suppress the rebellion in
Saint-Domingue when Spain and Britain extended their war
against the Republic in Europe to the islands of the Caribbean.
The blacks of Saint-Domingue promptly joined forces with the
Spaniards of Santo Domingo against the representatives of the Republic, and the smoldering war once again burned with a violent
intensity. The slaves, a contingent of whom were led by Toussaint Bréda, now fought for the counterrevolution and the lapsed
monarchy against the liberal, even radical, agents of republicanism.
In an effort to stem the rebellion, the leading commissioner even
declared the end of all slavery in Saint-Domingue, but his proclamation was received distrustfully and Toussaint, who called himself "General of the Armies of the King, for the Public Good," issued the first of his proclamations: "I have undertaken vengeance.
I want Liberty and Equality to reign in San Domingo. I work to
bring them into existence. Unite yourselves to us, brothers, and
fight with us for the same cause, etc." [34]

The jackboots of war continued relentlessly to trample the di-
sheveled body of Saint-Domingue. In the south the blacks sun-
dered their alliance with the whites and fought both white and
mulatto soldiers. In the west the mulattoes temporarily gained
control, and in the north and east Toussaint and the other ex-slave
generals campaigned successfully against the French. In December
1793, Toussaint marched into Gonaïves, captured Plaisance, and
accepted the surrender of the garrisons of St. Marc, Verrettes, and
Arcahaie. By the beginning of 1794 the Spaniards and Toussaint
had established a clear hold over most of northern Saint-Domingue

---

[34] Quoted in James, *Jacobins,* 125. There is a brief but tantalizing essay on the
slaves of the Bréda plantation before the rising in the north in Gabriel Debien,
Études Antillaises (XVIIIe Siècle) (Paris, 1956), 161–173.

and, to complicate the story, British troops had conquered much of the south, the west except for Port-au-Prince (which fell in June), and the Môle St. Nicolas. But it was at this time, when Saint-Domingue needed peace if it were to recover economically from the steady deterioration of its resources, that the Convention abolished slavery. When news of this decree reached Saint-Domingue, perhaps together with the information that a mulatto-led Republican force had ousted the British from Guadeloupe, Toussaint — opportunistically or idealistically, his many biographers differ — agreed to desert the Spaniards and many of his ex-slave colleagues, and take his followers into the service of Étienne Laveaux, the French general whose movements had been restricted to the little town of Port-de-Paix, west of Cap Français.[35]

Toussaint, now a French general, quickly demonstrated a capacity for carefully conceived campaigns against his erstwhile allies. His troops drove the Spaniards out of the Artibonite plain, pushed the British southward, and assisted Laveaux in the campaign to recapture the north. During these last months of 1794, too, a number of blacks who were subsequently to lead Haiti distinguished themselves in Toussaint's army. Henri Christophe, Jean-Jacques Dessalines, and Moyse Toussaint (the nephew of Toussaint L'Ouverture) all became prominent. Despite their efforts, however, Toussaint proved unable to bring the reconquest to a rapid conclusion. He quarreled with mulatto leaders and, to an extent, chafed under Laveaux's inconsistent generalship. Then, because of events in Europe, Spain surrendered its portion of Hispaniola to France and left the battlefield in the autumn of 1795. The British, however, still hoped to master the island and to succeed where France had failed. Until 1798 they retained a grip on the far southwest and the Môle, Toussaint opposing them in a desultory fashion north of the Artibonite River and Rigaud strengthening his independent, mulatto-dominated position in Les Cayes, Jacmel, and Saltrou. But in the autumn of that year, after attacks of fever (7300 of 18,000 men perished from malaria) and logistical

---

[35] For Toussaint's letters of this period to Laveaux, see Gérard M. Laurent (ed.), *Toussaint Louverture: A Travers sa Correspondance (1794–1798)* (Madrid, 1953), 112–120.

problems had finally weakened the British determination, Toussaint won a series of victories on the battlefield, which encouraged the British to end their occupation of the south, albeit hesitantly, and liberate the Môle.[36] Toussaint's mastery was unquestioned: In 1796 he had gently but firmly compelled Laveaux's return to France. In 1797 he had become commander in chief of the French armies in Saint-Domingue and strengthened an alliance with Rigaud. After overcoming the British he took advantage of the perfidy of his nominal superior, the local representative of the Republican regime, ousted him, and thereafter alone ruled what was still the colony of Saint-Domingue. "Remember that there is only one Toussaint L'Ouverture in San Domingo," he said, "and that at his name everybody must tremble." [37]

Only the existence of a mulatto-dominated state in the south challenged Toussaint's pre-eminence. Rigaud was not spoiling for a fight, and probably would have clung to his earlier alliance if Toussaint had but contrived a way of recognizing the autonomous nature of Rigaud's enclave. There a wealthy plantation-owning class had managed both to prosper, despite continuing warfare, and to maintain harmonious relations with their black laborers. But their way of life may have seemed a threat to Toussaint, as his certainly worried them. Most of all, however, Toussaint feared that an autonomous south would ally itself with France when and if the Republic attempted to reimpose its will by force of arms. He sought to leave no flank unprotected.

Rigaud disavowed racial antagonism: "I have consecrated my life to the defence of the blacks. From the beginning of the revolution I have braved all for the cause of liberty. I have not betrayed my principles and I shall never do so. Besides, I am too much a believer in the Rights of Man to think that there is one colour in nature superior to another. I know a man only as a man." [38] Many of his mulatto followers, however, distrusted the blacks. They fought as valiantly against Toussaint as they had against the Brit-

36 For the wars with the British, and a reflection of favorable contemporary British accounts of Toussaint's methods and character, see Barskett, Island of St. Domingo, 163–203.
37 Quoted in James, Jacobins, 220.
38 Quoted in ibid., 229–230.

ish, and sustained their independence until, after a siege that lasted five months, Alexandre Pétion and the defenders of Jacmel succumbed. By the end of 1799, Toussaint's forces controlled all of the south.

Toussaint was sufficiently statesmanlike to realize that Saint-Domingue must now, after so many years of warfare, be allowed a respite. He had a nation to construct out of a motley collection of slaves, antagonistic mulattoes, and whites both scheming and loyal. There were plantations to be restored and trade relations to be restructured. But Santo Domingo, although still garrisoned by the Spaniards, was nominally French. Toussaint wanted to be secure in his island. Thus he sought, sensibly so, to safeguard his revolution and to deprive the French of an employable base on the island. In late 1799 his troops marched across the mountains to the capital city of Santo Domingo, and fought a series of brief battles with the Spanish garrison, gaining unquestioned control early in 1800. An island almost as large as Ireland had thus been cleansed of white aggressors. In all but name, Toussaint's enlarged Saint-Domingue was independent. The revolution had reached its apogee. Only Napoleon Bonaparte, who had meanwhile come to power in France, posed a clear and present danger to the embryo nation.

Toussaint's genius, hitherto exercised primarily in pursuit of martial goals, accepted the challenge of peace. After a decade of warfare, the air of Saint-Domingue was redolent of destruction and decay more than of prosperity.[39] War and neglect had ruined the elaborate irrigation works constructed by the French and made their repair unlikely. It is not known how many hectares of cane, coffee, cotton, and indigo had been spared the ravages of war, how many sugar mills still functioned, or the exact state of the country's infrastructure in 1800, but there is no doubt that constant fighting across the body of Saint-Domingue had severely dislocated its export economy and permanently altered the pattern of production

[39] For the devastation of Cap Français, see the contemporary description in Marcus Rainsford, *An Historical Account of the Black Empire of Hayti: Comprehending a View of the Principal Transactions in the Revolution of Santo Domingo: With Its Ancient and Modern State* (London, 1805), 217–218. See also Placide-Justin, *L'Ile d' Hayti,* 328–331; Lepkowski, *Początki Państwa,* 99.

and trade. Of presumably even greater significance (despite the absence of precise quantification) had been the flight of trained persons and the resulting loss of administrative and technical skills. Perhaps 20,000 of the 30,000 whites resident in Saint-Domingue before the revolution had been killed or compelled to emigrate. Ten thousand of the 40,000 mulattoes and freed blacks had disappeared, and more than a third of the slave population of 500,000 were no longer alive. If we assume that men in the prime of life were most apt to have lost their lives on the battlefields of Saint-Domingue, then the demographic data disclose an even more tragic decline in Saint-Domingue's human resources.[40] Furthermore, of the ex-slaves who had survived, many of the more spirited had drifted away to the mountains, where they remained. There they could subsist with a minimum of effort and gather "wild" coffee to sell. Despite the valiant efforts of Toussaint, Dessalines, and Christophe, it proved impossible to re-establish the intensive agriculture on which the prosperity of Saint-Domingue had been based. Coffee displaced sugar as the country's major cash crop, and the methods and approach of the peasant smallholders became the economic norm. Continuous warfare had also given the people of Saint-Domingue, and their leaders particularly, a taste for blood. They had learned that might made right, that ends justified the use of virtually any means, and that grievances were susceptible to instant redress by violence. James makes this point with characteristic pungency: "For nearly ten years the population, corrupt enough before, had been trained in bloodshed and soaked in violence." [41]

Toussaint bravely attempted to restore order and a measure of prosperity. Conditions in the countryside were desperate, a French attack was expected at any time, the British were generally hostile, and relations between the previously free and ex-slave, and the new self-appointed mulatto aristocracy and the masses who had won their freedom and feared a reimposition of slavery, were tense. Indeed, the behavior of Dessalines, to whom Toussaint had devolved authority in the south, only exacerbated these tensions.

40 For some figures, see Barskett, *Island of St. Domingo*, 203.
41 James, *Jacobins*, 242.

Unlike Toussaint and Christophe, before the revolution Dessalines had been a field hand of the least highly regarded kind; his employer was himself a black, and Dessalines physically had suffered much. As a result, and because he had so dramatically risen from a particularly low social and economic estate, he wreaked his vengeance on the whites, mulattoes, and ex-freed blacks of Jacmel, Les Cayes, Jérémie, and the other towns of the south. Toussaint tried to restrain him, and refused by his own actions to worsen relations between classes and castes divided by color. If anything, blacks resented Toussaint's seeming partiality to whites and his reliance upon white and mulatto advisers. Color, despite or, let it be said, probably because of the revolution, continued to count in the calculations of Saint-Domingue.

Thoroughgoing social revolutions — and Haiti's was particularly extreme — often lead to despotism. Although Toussaint intuitively recognized the importance of nation-building, he seems to have lacked what in modern terms can be called an appreciation of the extent to which long-term national development depended upon the mobilization of popular support. The long term also was of less consequence to him than the present; viability had to be restored before the French sought to reassert metropolitan control over their colony. Discipline was an obvious prerequisite. Without it he could hardly hope to weld a mass of ex-slaves, many of whom were roaming the countryside like the buccaneers of old, into a cohesive army of free laborers motivated by macro- as well as micro-economic considerations. Development was uppermost in his mind and, he was able to see, irrelevant to theirs. They wanted to enjoy their freedom to the fullest, subsisting on the easily obtained bounty of Saint-Domingue's fertile soil. But subsistence negated rapid resuscitation and development. Toussaint therefore adopted a system of *fermage* which had already been introduced in the north by Christophe and a white adviser. The new government took over the abandoned plantations and refused to break up the remaining estates. The former and many of the latter were leased to members of the victorious elite; each was responsible for maximizing the production of his plantation and caring for the workers, but the government provided a compliant labor force by ordering the ex-slaves and persons without urban trades or other gainful employment back to the fields. Movement between plantations, or plantations and the towns, was forbidden and heavily penalized. Everyone worked under military supervision, too, and, although the laborers were paid in kind — virtually as sharecroppers — and their hours regulated by law, the ex-slaves were in fact impressed, and compelled to cultivate, in a manner reminiscent of the slave days. Certainly there were punishments which recalled the arbitrary usages of the past: Idlers were forced to run a gauntlet of soldiers; persistent offenders were shot; and Dessalines, always brutal, buried incompetent overseers and troublesome workers alive.

These methods restored a degree of prosperity, and Leyburn may be correct in saying that the "return to prosperity between 1799 and 1802 was amazing" if he means that any production above a subsistence level was remarkable considering the tribulations that the colony had endured. In 1802 only two thirds of the pre-revolutionary acreage was under cultivation and the production of sugar, coffee, cotton, and indigo was derisory compared with the figures for 1791. Sugar, by far the most important export commodity, was down between two-thirds and three-quarters, the production of coffee had fallen to one half of its previous level and that of cotton to two thirds, and the cultivation of indigo had almost disappeared.[42]

The weakness of Saint-Domingue's governmental apparatus also needs to be appreciated. Statistics are unavailable, but it seems that in 1800 Saint-Domingue could boast virtually no experienced administrative cadre. The middle-level technocrats and bureaucrats had long since fled with their superiors; many mulattoes had commercial and agricultural experience, and there was no shortage of persons to buy and sell, but men of governing abil-

---

[42] James G. Leyburn, *The Haitian People* (New Haven, 1941 and 1966), 27. For the figures, which are the best available approximations, see *ibid.*, 320; Paul Moral, *Le Paysan Haitien; Etude sur la Vie Rurale en Haiti* (Paris, 1961), 20; Auguste Nemours, *Histoire Militaire de la Guerre d'Indépendance de Saint-Domingue* (Paris, 1925), I, 17–18; François Joseph Pamphile Lacroix, *Memoires pour Servir à l'Histoire de Saint-Domingue* (Paris, 1819), II, 35. But see Lepelletier de Saint-Remy, *Saint-Domingue*, II, 170.

ity were scarce. Toussaint accordingly ran the country in as direct and centralized a fashion as possible. He delegated tasks and supervision, but little real power, and his advisers seem to have counseled rather than guided. Toussaint thus governed by inspiration. He established administrative divisions, created courts of law, stabilized the currency, established uniform tariffs, levied a property tax, tried to discourage smuggling, built roads, sponsored schools, rebuilt Cap Français, revived the theater and, hoping to fix the future in the present, in 1801 granted Saint-Domingue (still a colony) its first constitution.

The individual provisions of the constitution, and their provenance, are less interesting for us than the import of the whole for the future and its immediate impact on France. The document enshrined Toussaint's belief in the efficacy of autocratic benevolence. Power was concentrated in his hands: He alone could propose and promulgate legislation; the military, the church, and every branch of the administration were subordinate to him. The members of the assembly were elected, but by administrators appointed by the governor. And the constitution named Toussaint governor for life, with the power to name his successor.[43] There were numerous other provisions, two of which simultaneously outlawed slavery on the island and, albeit in a veiled manner, encouraged the landing of workers, presumably slaves from Africa, but it was the centralizing and authoritarian aspects of the document which provided a model for so many subsequent Haitian constitutions and, in certain respects, molded the governmental expectations of the Haitian ruling class. If Haiti had somehow emerged from the crucible of revolution believing in the values and virtues of democracy as well as liberty and equality, and with the urge and the informal attitudes and ability to make representative government work, then Haitian history might conceivably have followed a radically different path. But Toussaint was otherwise disposed, and the mass of ex-slaves and their new superiors were unprepared to produce and run other than an autocratic state.

43 Nemours, *Histoire Militaire*, I, 98–112, includes a complete text, as does Louis-Joseph Janvier, *Les Constitutions d'Haiti (1801–1855)* (Paris, 1886), 7–23.

From Napoleon's point of view, the implications of the constitution were anathema. "The Constitution that you have made," wrote Napoleon to Toussaint, "in reaffirming many good things, contains in it things contrary to the dignity and the sovereignty of the French people, of which Saint-Domingue forms but one portion." [44] Yet, by its promulgation Saint-Domingue had declared its absolute local independence, admittedly within the orbit of France and without breaking legally or overtly from France, and made it clear that France was welcome to assist and advise, but never to govern. It was an adroit attempt to satisfy both the Francophile and Francophobe elements within Toussaint's government (Dessalines, for one, demanded real independence), and to retain the French assistance which Saint-Domingue needed while preventing any diminution of indigenous control. (Unhappily, however, Napoleon refused to play the role that Charles de Gaulle later, with reference to Africa, assumed with ease.)

The ensuing war of independence destroyed much that had been so carefully restored since the revolution. Napoleon soon sent an army to reclaim his colony, and violent war convulsed the island. Christophe, retreating before the French troops in 1802, fired le Cap: "By eleven o'clock the city resembled a vast funeral pyre, flames shooting through the roofs of houses and linking in great fiery arcs across the streets, the buildings themselves cracking and crumbling and rocking the earth with the shock of their collapse. At midnight the main powder magazine exploded with a terrifying roar that filled the sky with fire and smoke and burning debris. By dawn only one house in every ten remained unburned. Property worth one hundred million francs had been reduced to smouldering embers. The only living persons in the town were the looters, exhausted and drunk." [45] Dessalines destroyed St. Marc, the plains were set alight, and everywhere in western and northern Haiti (the south did not resist) conditions resembled those of the early years of the revolution. Ten thousand French troops drove the black soldiers into the hills, and for several months ambush and counter-ambush occupied the two

44 Napoleon to Toussaint, quoted in Janvier, *Les Constitutions*, 23–24.
45 Hubert Cole, *Christophe: King of Haiti* (London, 1967), 88.

fighting forces. Finally, however, Christophe, and then Toussaint and Dessalines, submitted to the French, and Toussaint, after being beguiled and tricked, was captured and sent to France, where he subsequently died on April 27, 1803, in a dank cell in Fort de Joux in the Jura Mountains. Christophe and Dessalines loyally served the French; other blacks and mulattoes formed guerrilla bands in the mountains—like the later *cacos*—and harassed the French and fought armies commanded by Christophe and Dessalines. But during the latter half of 1802 Napoleon indicated that he intended to reimpose slavery in Saint-Domingue. The guerrilla fighters then escalated the level of their attacks on the French, Dessalines began covertly to treat with the guerrillas and prepare a new insurrection and, in the autumn, Pétion (now a colonel in a French regiment) led a successful mutiny, Christophe and Dessalines went over to the guerrillas, and the war entered an entirely new phase. It was clear, by then, that the French army was seriously weakened by fever and the absence of reinforcements from Europe. The French, however, devised new and unusually loathsome ways to fight the war and deal with prisoners; throughout 1803 both sides sought to outdo the other's atrocities.[46]

Once more the body of the colony was clawed and marked, its agricultural potential deformed, and its towns gutted. Neither side could hope to win, and hostilities might have continued indefinitely if the peace in Europe (from late 1801 until the spring of 1803) had not come to an end. Napoleon could spare no more thought or men for Saint-Domingue. With British assistance Dessalines, Christophe, Pétion, and the leaders of the many guerrilla bands finally obtained the submission of the remaining French troops in November 1803 and, on New Year's Day 1804, the colony of Saint-Domingue became the independent state of Haiti.[47]

The formal declaration of independence marked neither the

---

[46] Rainsford's description of the war and its atrocities is contemporary: *Black Empire*, 324–328.

[47] Haiti, meaning the land of the mountains, was the Carib name for the island. For the changing British attitudes toward the black struggle against the French, see H. B. L. Hughes, "British Policy Towards Haiti, 1801–1805," *Canadian Historical Review*, XXV (1944), 397–408. A translation of the independence proclamation can be found in Rainsford, *Black Empire*, 439–441.

end of one era nor the well-defined beginning of another. Not until the new nation had lost its fear of renewed hostilities with France could it be said that the revolution had been brought to a conclusion or a new way of national life begun. In any event, the accession of Dessalines provided no real break with the past. With respect to the problem of restoring productivity and order to a land again chaotic, he simply followed Toussaint, with added cruelty, and reintroduced the *fermage*. Again Haitians were commanded either to cultivate or to serve in the army, the cultivators being tied, as before, to specific plantations (and employers). Dessalines also embarked upon a program of building impregnable fortresses in the hills, compulsory labor naturally being utilized. The overweening role of the army was continued, with fairly obvious consequences for the future: "A military mentality was nourished, the people early learning the lesson (apparently unchallenged by any liberal) that the army should rule and the people obey." [48] Additionally, the supply of able-bodied manpower was monopolized by the army when it might have been more useful on the plantations.

Like Toussaint, Dessalines was an autocrat, but he failed lamentably to temper his despotism with benevolence; *liberté* he regarded highly while despising *egalité* and *fraternité*. Nor, despite Toussaint's careful lessons, did he seek to revive the spirit of his people or the mechanisms of government. He was more rapacious and avaricious than necessary and, like so many men who come to power by the sword, he enjoyed the authority and the trappings more than the responsibilities of power. (Not wanting to be outdone by Napoleon, he proclaimed himself emperor in 1805.) Where Toussaint had schemed for his people as much as for himself, Dessalines simply schemed. The circumstances of his accession, and his consuming fear of French reprisals, also blinded him (unlike Toussaint, and Christophe later) to the immediate needs of a a country lacking trained manpower and administrative and commercial expertise. He himself was illiterate, as were many of his leading followers. Instead of conserving the few pools of learning

[48] Leyburn, *People*, 37. See also James Franklin, *The Present State of Hayti* (London, 1828), 188–192, 324–325.

and technical ability available within Haiti, Dessalines confiscated land owned or managed by whites and mulattoes, decreed that no white could ever again own land in Haiti (a decree obeyed until the American occupation) and, in innumerable petty ways, widened the gulf between light- and dark-skinned Haitians. Of immediate practical importance because it impoverished the country economically and spiritually, and contributed directly to the deadening isolation of nineteenth-century Haitian life, he systematically extirpated whites. Whether he did so to prove himself, because of paranoia, as an expression of sadistic tendencies, or to remove a potential pro-French fifth column is less important than the fact that extirpation represented an irreversible step backward—a reduction of the new state to ground zero.

Contemporary horror stories are many; to a people accustomed to cruelty and bloodshed they may simply have represented a more extreme exercise of arbitrary rule. Being merely extensions of the norm, they also provided comfortable parameters within which the actions of future leaders could be judged. In 1804, at le Cap, Dessalines agreed with Christophe that only Frenchmen should be killed. An American observer recalled the "night of horrors": "At short intervals [we] heard the pick-axe thundering at the door of some devoted neighbour, and soon forcing it. Piercing shrieks almost immediately ensued, and these were followed by an expressive silence. . . . A proclamation was published . . . stating, that . . . all who had escaped the massacre [should] appear on the parade, and receive tickets of protection [but] . . . most of whom now came forth from their hiding places . . . were instantly led away to the place of execution and shot. The rivulet which runs through the town of Cape François was literally red with their blood." [49] In Port-au-Prince a British naval officer reported that Dessalines had ordered all white men in the town to be put to death in any fashion his black soldiers chose: "Some they shot having tied them from 15 to 20 together. Some they pricked to death with their bayonets, and others they tortured in such a manner too horrid to be described. In the span of 8 days no less

[49] Paraphrased in Barskett, *Island of St. Domingo*, 305. See also Placide-Justin, *L'Ile d'Hayti*, 412–426.

than 800 were actually murdered by these assassins and their
bodies thrown into the bogs and marshes to rot away." In Jérémie
more than 400 whites were similarly killed after Dessalines had
confiscated their property. The same observer assured his admiral that it was "horrid to view the streets in different places
stained with the Blood of these unfortunate people, whose
bodies are now left exposed to view by the river and sea side. In
hauling the seine the evening we came to our anchor several
bodies got entangled in it. . . ." [50]

Haiti thus commenced its independent existence amid an atmosphere of squalor. Dessalines defeated the French, but otherwise offered to his people only continued destruction, militarism,
and autocracy, and the reimposition of servitude.[51] As events
proved, these were hardly adequate as bases of political development, but Dessalines (like his Haitian contemporaries) lacked any
political or administrative training and followed the only patterns
of rule with which he was familiar — those of the colony of Saint-
Domingue and the rebel army. Haiti was, and for long remained,
"nothing more than an isolated encampment in a perpetual state
of emergency." [52] Dessalines' policies, too, unmarked as they were
by any productive vision of the future, intensified internal tensions and widened the divisions between black and mulatto, north
and south, and the ex-colony and the mother country. His behavior worried foreign governments (several of the most important
refused to recognize or trade with his regime)[53] and accentuated
the self-imposed isolation which was for long to prove Haiti's bane.
He provided nothing durable upon which his successors could
build. By this time, sugar, indigo, and cotton — all of which required large capital investments — had disappeared from the list
of Haiti's exports and coffee had dropped 25 per cent (the United
States had recently banned trade to Haiti) in relation to what its

50 Perkins to Sir John Thomas Duckworth, quoted in Cole, *Christophe*, 141–142.
51 But see François Mathon, "Dessalines, Législateur: Deux Aspects du Statut Familial Haitien sous le Premier Empire (1805)," *Revue de la Société d'Histoire et de
Géographie d'Haiti*, XI, 35 (October 1939), 1–14; Duraciné Vaval, "Le Gouvernement
de Dessalines," *Revue de la Société Haitienne d'Histoire, de Géographie, et de
Géologie*, XXVIII, 99 (October 1955), 63–74.
52 Alfred Métraux (trans. Peter Lengyel), *Haiti: Black Peasants and Voodoo* (New
York, 1960), 22.
53 For U.S. attitudes, see Jordan, *Over Black*, 378–391.

level had been in 1802. Nor did he even begin to offset the ravages of war. For all of these reasons, because of the arousal of personal jealousies and antagonisms, and also because the Haitian elite was tired of turmoil and disgusted with displays of naked power, in late 1806 Pétion and other officers carefully ambushed their dictator and used his torso for bayonet practice.

Haitians had accustomed themselves to solving complicated problems directly and simply. This approach was integral to the revolutionary ardor which still animated the former colony, and which continued to find martial as well as less sanguinary expression in national life. This is not to say that Haitians of all classes and regions favored identical policies of national development. As before, and by way of an omen for the future, the death of Dessalines encouraged the north and the south, and mulatto and white, to follow separate social, political, and economic paths; indeed, until the end of the revolutionary era in 1820, tiny Haiti and the relatively few Haitians (the total population in 1807 was only about 400,000) were effectively bifurcated and subjected to radically different administrations.

After the assassination of Dessalines, Christophe regarded himself, and was generally presumed to be, the rightful heir. But there was no mechanism for eliciting an indication of the popular will and, in any event, Pétion and his largely well-educated and light-skinned followers were reluctant to permit Christophe and his black soldiers and white advisers to benefit from the mulatto-inspired coup. For all of the obvious reasons, they no longer wanted to be subjected to rule by largely illiterate ex-slaves. They probably also disliked the *fermage,* or at least those aspects of it which denied economic freedom of choice. Accordingly, Pétion and his followers managed to dominate the constituent assembly of late 1806 by packing it with mulatto supporters. Their blueprint for the new Haiti provided for a virtually powerless president and a strong chief of the national assembly.[54] Christophe, who, by pridefully staying away from the assembly, probably for-

[54] For the constitution see François Dalencour, *La Fondation de la République d'Haïti par Alexandre Pétion* (Port-au-Prince, 1944), 134–162, 281–295; Janvier, *Constitutions,* 49–73. For another view of Pétion and the constitution, see Duraciné Vaval, "Alexandre Pétion: L'Homme et sa Vie," *Revue de la Société d'Histoire et de Géographie d'Haïti,* III, 7 (July 1932), 1–34.

feited his chance to rule the entire country, was elected president,
and Pétion became head of the assembly. But if the mulattoes
had ever really expected to deal so deftly with Christophe, they
were soon disappointed. He led the army of the north on St. Marc
and Arcahaie, and, by early 1807, Haiti was again rent by strife.
With the line of the Artibonite River as their mutual border,
each side raided the other and, together, sustained a level of
strife sufficiently high to threaten any return to antebellum neutrality. Christophe and Pétion each proclaimed the other an out-
law, and each — Pétion styling himself President of the Assembly
of the Republic of Haiti, and Christophe at first using the title
Commander in Chief of the Army of the Empire and then being
elected President of the State of Haiti by a new assembly of
northern representatives — began to govern his half of the former colony.

Their methods and their approaches to the problems of nation
building were radically different. Christophe combined the best
qualities of Toussaint and Dessalines with an enhanced appreciation of the nature and pressures of the international system. Dynamic, energetic, imaginative, and vain, Christophe consciously
planned the economic development of his half of Haiti. To do so,
he maintained the autocratic machinery developed by Toussaint
and Dessalines, but did so with an application of paternal benevolence rather than naked tyranny. However, the structure of the
fermage continued virtually unchanged: the estates belonging to
the government were leased to entrepreneurs and worked by
blacks bound in perpetuity to their places of occupation; the lives
of the cultivators were strictly regulated and the degree of their
exertion strictly enforced; one fourth of the total crop on any
plantation supposedly went to the workers. Christophe's reign
also contributed to the growing rigidity of the country's class
structure, especially after he had himself crowned king of Haiti
in 1811. The lessees of landed estates already constituted a favored class and, by the creation of a titled nobility after the coro-
nation, Christophe sanctioned class (or caste, as some writers
have loosely phrased the term) distinctions. In the towns especially, he widened the economic and social gulf between worker

and overseer, and between those who worked with their hands and those who pushed paper and guided the destinies of the state.

His policies were not, however, simply a perpetuation of the past. Although he was as hostile as Dessalines was to mulattoes, Christophe was particularly friendly to foreign-born whites. Like Theodorus of Ethiopia he was not loath to use their services for the economic betterment of the state. Indeed, with the help of such persons, many of whom were British, Christophe rationalized the administration of his state, strengthened the currency and the overall financial structure, improved marketing arrangements overseas, and established a rudimentary educational system. He even tried, but failed, to mechanize prevailing methods of agriculture by introducing the plow. He codified the laws of the state in 1812 and introduced a number of benevolently paternal measures which might, in time, have redounded to the benefit of the peasant cultivators of the north. Like his mid-nineteenth and mid-twentieth century successors, he also understood the need to surround himself with an armed force loyal primarily to his person rather than to the state: he obtained 4000 recruits from Africa, armed them and called them the Royal Dahomets. They constituted an effective personal bodyguard and incorruptible agents of his rule in the hinterland.[55] In sum, Christophe was a modernizer who subordinated the masses for the good of the state and, because of their exertions and despite remittent hostilities with the armies of the south and occasional disputes with Britain, restored a level of prosperity to the north. Sugar, indigo, and coffee once more flowed profitably from the plantations to the markets of the United States and Europe, Cap Henri (as Cap Français had become) flourished as a commercial center, and the cultural embellishments of Toussaint's day again (and until the early end of the regime in 1820) thrived under Christophe's patronage.

A contemporary English visitor concluded his detailed description of Christophe's capital with careful praise: "In few places of

[55] Jonathan Brown, *The History and Present Condition of St. Domingo* (Philadelphia, 1837), II, 189–199, 203–205, 207, 210–211, 212; Franklin, *Present State,* 198–199, 210. See also Duraciné Vaval "Le Roi d'Haiti Henri Christophe; L'Homme et son Oeuvre de Gouvernement," *Revue de la Société d'Histoire et de Géographie d'Haiti,* II, 3 (June 1931), 7–20; Lepkowski, *Początki Państwa,* 161.

commerce could there be seen greater regularity in the despatch
of business, greater diligence displayed by those engaged in it, or
more evident marks of a prosperous state of things. Every man
had some calling to occupy his attention; instances of idleness or
intemperance were of rare occurrence; the most perfect subordination prevailed; and all appeared contented and happy. They
were satisfied with their government, because they found it
adapted to their state; and though somewhat less attached to their
sovereign than at the commencement of his reign . . . they were
still proud of having a monarch of their own race so ably qualified
to govern. So striking, in short, was their improvement, that a
foreigner would have found it difficult to persuade himself, on his
first entering the place, that the people whom he now beheld so
submissive, industrious, and contented, were the same who, a few
years before, had escaped from the shackles of slavery." [56]

Under Pétion, by contrast, the south experienced an era of decay and disinvestment. Prior to his reign Haiti had known only
large estates. Its main exports were based on a plantation economy and, although Toussaint, Dessalines, and Christophe had all
appropriated land on behalf of the state, it had been worked
in the manner of plantations. Even during the first years of the
demi-republic, Pétion assisted the proprietors of the plantations
— the landed gentry. He altered the tax base in a manner favorable to them, and subsidized their operations during years of
drought or oversupply. He supported floor prices for the usual
tropical products. But with each improvement in the lot of the
smallholders, the plantations of the south tended to be cultivated
more haphazardly. Then, in 1809, for reasons which were unspe-
cified but which probably reflected the republic's shortage of cash
and its attempt to meet financial obligations by the distribution of
assets, Pétion began to parcel out the arable property of the state.
Some went to soldiers in five carreaux (15 acre) lots; officers took
some, and everyone ultimately had the opportunity to purchase
government-owned plots for modest fees. Squatters also obtained

[56] William Woodis Harvey, *Sketches of Hayti; From the Expulsion of the French
to the Death of Christophe* (London, 1827), 263–264. For Christophe's military, educational, and agricultural policies, see *ibid.*, 169–232, 249–251.

arable land without difficulty. (Later, invalids and non-active military, non-commissioned officers, and soldiers all received 5 carreaux; lieutenants and captains, 10; officers in active service — under-lieutenants, 20; lieutenants, 25; captains, 30; and chiefs of battalions or squadrons, 35.) He may also have wanted to pacify his potentially unruly subjects by transforming them from tenants and serfs into peasants, or he may consciously (like the physiocrats and Thomas Jefferson) have wanted to make conditions in the south appealing to the hard-pressed masses in the north. Whatever the explanation, Pétion certainly could not have intended to break the power of his own class, and to have elevated the ex-slaves to positions of some independence.

The entire agricultural base of the society was greatly altered by Pétion's largess. The majority of the inhabitants of the south were no longer willing to cultivate sugar, coffee, and indigo. Instead they grew garden crops for home consumption, the economy of the south rapidly becoming more subsistence- than cash-oriented. Since the owners of the remaining estates also had difficulty obtaining labor, tenant-farming arrangements were soon developed which further limited the number of carreaux which continued to be devoted to export crops. To be sure, coffee was still harvested, but only where it grew wild. The quality as well as the quantity of the Haitian crops suffered and, as Leyburn has so aptly stated, "Petion's careful planning resulted consequently in an entirely unplanned, accidental, and automatic adjustment to new conditions of life." [57] The GNP undoubtedly declined steadily in the south. And as it declined, so Pétion, whose motives were surprisingly humane, unerringly found a supposed way of bringing about additional "improvements" which, in fact, only accelerated decay. The common man may not have cared, however, and was probably more content under Pétion than ever before. By the end of Pétion's reign he was, typically, secure on a small plot of fertile land. An ex-slave who had experienced conditions similar to serfdom under Toussaint and Dessalines, he had become a peasant, and enjoyed the new landed status. Unlike the remainder of Latin America, in southern Haiti (as later also in the north)

[57] Leyburn, *People,* 59. See also Franklin, *Present State,* 219–226, 326–327.

there was no *latifundia*. The ex-slave could probably grow sufficient to feed his immediate family and to provide a little extra for
sale. He also welcomed Pétion's gentle, *laissez-faire* methods of administration. Even when Rigaud gained control of the southwest
and, for a year, waged war on Pétion's republic, or, during the
various periods of war against the north, Pétion, the respected
soldier, refused to impose his will upon his people. Discipline disappeared, but the masses were happy and the elite, too, was reasonably content. For if its prosperity had waned, its pretension had
been recognized and largely confirmed. Inertia reigned everywhere, neglect captured the countryside, and the mulattoes ran the
state. A subsequent visitor compared the two administrations of
Haiti: "While Christophe was wielding an iron despotism which
pressed his subjects to the earth, it was the policy of Pétion to hold
the reins of government lightly, and to give the negroes under his
rule their hearts' content of indolence, raggedness, and disorder.
A cautious, wily system of promotions and appointments among
the military and civil authorities, filled the ranks of power with
mulattoes, and prepared the political system of the republic for a
mulatto dynasty to continue in perpetuity." [58] Pétion, who was reelected president in 1811 and 1815 and, ominously enshrining the
principle of "the indispensable man," had himself elected president for life in 1816, ruled serenely and, in Haitian terms, reasonably benignly until his death in 1818.

With the merging of the north and south in 1820, after Christophe's tragic suicide, the period of revolutionary adjustment was
concluded. Jean-Pierre Boyer, Pétion's mulatto successor, ended
internal war, obviated the threat of fresh hostilities with France by
agreeing to a crippling annual indemnity, and began to build a
new nation from the separate sections bequeathed to him by his
predecessors. However, in some ways, as shall be seen, their legacy was unassailable. Building upon Pétion's foundations, Haiti

[58] Brown, *St. Domingo*, 201. The fullest study of the problem is Henock Trouillot,
"La République de Pétion et le Peuple Haïtien," *Revue de la Société Haitienne
d'Histoire, de Géographie, et de Géologie*, XXXI, 107 (April 1960), 36–57, 131–149.
See also Lepkowski, *Początki Państwa*, 169–183, 338–389. It should be said, however,
that in 1819 Christophe finally began to distribute land to his officers. Colonels received 20 carreaux each, soldiers 1.

became a land of smallholding, black, Creole-speaking peasants more interested in subsistence than in producing for the cash economy, divorced from the mulatto-dominated towns, and isolated from the main currents of change elsewhere. The wars of the revolution had produced such destruction and personal misery that the majority of the ex-slaves were content to remove themselves from any future sources of strain. Although they were poor, they were free, secure in the *status quo,* and resigned — once Christophe's death had ended compulsory labor and agricultural misery — to their state of stagnation. And the elite was for the most part anxious that this situation should continue, provided that their own ascendance should prevail. They, and town dwellers generally, also inherited a complete lack of familiarity with governmental processes, a tendency toward solving political problems violently, a tolerance of military interference in the affairs of state, a confusion of color and status, and a personalization of politics which provided the context within which Haiti lurched from instability to internal chaos to the American occupation.

By 1820, class consciousness, sectionalism, and individualism were all ready to be carried to political and social extremes. Under Boyer and his successors these and the other natural tendencies of an untutored population intent on survival at all costs and subject to the direction of lettered but intensely self-serving townsmen were encouraged and perpetuated. A pattern of government was soon impressed upon the republic which was institutionally deficient and very highly personalized. Loyalty was accorded — given Haitian psychology — to a man, never to an impersonal abstraction like a state, facilities for communication were conspicuous by their absence, and funds were lacking with which to realize the potentials of republican parliamentary government or make its apparatus meaningful. Only the army maintained a semblance of institutional coherence and continued to play a vital and influential national role. Above all, neither the army nor the politicians ever internalized the notion of a public interest. Nor did either accept a conceptualization of the state which would have encouraged the growth of consensus or made possible national integration. Instead, the presidency was equated with license to plunder and all energies, military and civil, were consciously devoted to the acquisition or retention of that license. The turmoil and trauma of the revolution, the incessant internecine conflicts of Dessalines, Pétion, and Christophe, the externally generated tensions of the period of transition, Pétion's distribution of lands and consequent fostering of a self-sufficient peasantry, the decline in Haiti's export earnings, and the lack, perhaps, of any influential men of vision were factors that, when accentuated by the events and experience of isolation of the nineteenth century, presupposed continued internal conflict and national instability during the twentieth.

III

The Impact of Isolation:

The Lost and Chaotic Years

IT WAS DURING the long reign of Jean-Pierre Boyer that Haiti cast off its revolutionary mantle and resolutely sought to regularize its role in world commerce and affairs. Yet the very effort to achieve normalcy, the fevered negotiations with France, the reintroduction of compulsory labor, the careful avoidance of situations which might lead to color conflict, and modernization in general — indeed all of the well-intended postures of the Boyer regime — resulted in a steady deterioration of the fortunes of Haiti. Even the tranquillity of Boyer's twenty-five years in office was in some senses counterproductive.

Haiti slipped into the pattern of stagnation which conditioned politics until the rise of Duvalier. Under Boyer Haiti lost the thrust and ardor of the revolutionary era and the dynamism identified with Christophe. Instead, Haiti lowered its sights, accepting less ambitious goals and declining productivity. When Boyer, who had served many years as Pétion's secretary, came to power, he had an implicit sense of the need to build a nation of the disparate, variously ruled peoples of Hispaniola. An overriding consideration for him, too, was the need finally to eradicate the threat of renewed foreign claims to the territory and intervention in the affairs of Haiti. The Spaniards, who had reassumed their administration of the eastern portion of the island in 1809, posed an obvious danger to Haitian security. The royalist Spaniards were not present in strength, however, and, in November 1821, a Creole group overcame desultory resistance and created the independent state of Spanish Haiti within Simon Bolivar's Federation of Columbia. This was a weak nation, and two months later it succumbed

to the dictates of Haitian strategy and ambition. Boyer's army easily overwhelmed its neighbor and Haiti began two decades of
what proved a culturally and economically stultifying rule over
the Dominican part of the island.[1]

The French, who refused to recognize the independence of
Haiti (none of the other great powers accorded Haiti recognition
until 1826) and who had on several occasions evinced a desire to
restore its colonial status, worried Boyer beyond measure. Without an agreement with France, Boyer reasoned, Haiti could never
be secure. Like Dessalines and Christophe before him, Boyer was
obsessed by the danger of another invasion. But whereas Dessalines and Christophe prepared their military defenses and otherwise sought to reimpose internal discipline, Boyer concentrated
primarily upon negotiation as the best means of avoiding conflict.
The attendant diplomatic maneuvers, intricate and interesting
though they were, need not be reviewed in detail: at first France
threatened to impose a protectorate by force, and tried to legitimate such an action by prior agreement. But neither this tactic,
nor Haiti's counter-attempt to obtain recognition without conced-
ing commercial advantages, proved efficacious. A parley in Brus-
sels in 1823 also proved sterile, and in 1824, after further French
entreaties, Haitian agents offered an indemnity to the former colonists in exchange for recognition of Haitian sovereignty. Charles X
still thought, however, that France should retain ultimate suzerainty while devolving local autonomy to Haitians. In 1825, he
peremptorily brought the tortuous negotiations to an end by
issuing an ordinance which, while patronizingly recognizing the
independence of Haiti, obtained preferential tariff arrangements
for goods bound to or from France, and compelled Haiti to pay 150
million francs in five annual installments.[2] Three squadrons (14
men-of-war) of the French fleet accompanied the presentation of

---

[1] For a Haitian point of view, see Jean Price-Mars, "L'Unité Politique de l'Ile
d'Haiti," *Revue de la Société d'Histoire et de Géographie d'Haiti*, VIII, 27 (1937),
16–27. Cf. Moral, *Paysan Haitien*, 38, who contends that the occupation of the
Dominican portion of the island was inspired in part by agricultural covetousness.
[2] For the text, and a detailed discussion of the negotiations, consult R. Lepelletier de Saint-Remy, *Saint-Domingue: Étude et Solution Nouvelle de la Question
Haitienne* (Paris, 1846), II, 11–65.

the ordinance to Boyer in Port-au-Prince; the use of gunboat diplomacy thus made it difficult for the Haitians to refuse to accept such a heavy indemnity. Boyer therefore acceded. But by so saddling the republic with debt (Haiti immediately floated a heavily discounted loan in Paris and drained the country of specie in order to pay the first installment) and by drastically curtailing revenue derived from imports and exports, Boyer severely mortgaged the potential for Haitian economic development.

These new burdens crippled Haiti in both the short and long term; although Haiti began to default on the installments of the indemnity (finally securing a reduction in the total to 60 million francs in 1838) and gradually managed to make French importers and exporters pay full rather than partial rates, the remittance of portions of the indemnity and the loss of some customs revenues severely limited Haiti's ability to function financially.[3] The issue of paper currency with insufficient backing also hindered the republic's development. But in terms of the economic growth of the republic, the most debilitating result of the negotiations with France was the outbreak of security. Without the threat of a French invasion to motivate Boyer's supporters and countrymen, they relaxed. Vigilance seemed unnecessary, discipline an imposition, and the expenditure of unusual energy wasteful. Freedom, having been recognized as well as achieved, could at last be enjoyed. Psychologically, the republic accepted its hard-won ease and, despite all of Boyer's efforts to the contrary, rapidly shed the posture of industry which had brought such prosperity to the French colony and Christophe's kingdom.

Boyer's initial inclination had been to pursue the *laissez-faire* policies of Pétion. The surplus bequeathed by Christophe, and the comparatively high prices realized between 1820 and 1822 by Haitian coffee and sugar, at first provided funds sufficient to maintain the state. But by 1823 Christophe's surplus had been exhausted, the price of coffee had been halved (on the French market) and, in general, the refusal of the state to intervene in the agricultural life of the country had enhanced the effect of Pétion's

[3] Further discussion of the economic effects of the indemnity will be found below, 77–78, 86, 93, 101–102 and in Appendix B. In 1838 60 million francs equaled $11.6 million.

encouragement of economic and agricultural individualism.
Sugar, the crop that demanded the most concerted effort, was no
longer being cultivated in a serious manner; coffee tended more
and more to be collected in the mountains rather than harvested;
and cultivation of cotton and cacao were everywhere neglected.
As peasants more concerned to consume than to sell hard-won
crops on a declining market, Haitians — beholden to no one — began to grow maize, millet, and beans where they had once been
compelled to tend sugar or other plantation crops. On the plantations that remained, too, there was a serious shortage of labor.
Voluntary inducements proved insufficient to attract labor, even
as sharecroppers; there was no shortage of land; most Haitians had
the usufruct of a plot of their own, and, as Leyburn has put it, "the
average Haitian preferred to be his own master, working only
when he wished, and particularly working only for himself and
his family." [4]

The recognition of Haiti's independence by France only exacerbated this unwillingness to labor for others or to resume the
burdens and conditions of plantation life. As a result, Boyer was
persuaded to abandon his reliance upon exhortation and encouragement (on his own plantations, though, foreign observers saw
laborers "working under the terror of the bayonet and the sabre
. . . ");[5] no longer could he afford to assume that the increased
prosperity of the state could best be secured by individuals pur-
suing their own preferred economic goals. Consequently the
Code Rural which he promulgated in 1826 represented a drastic,
thoroughgoing exercise in *étatisme*. Boyer sought to reintroduce
the compulsory methods which had served Toussaint, Dessalines,
and Christophe so effectively. To this end he and his collaborators
forged a very complicated, carefully and cleverly calibrated legal
instrument which was designed for each and every agricultural
and personal contingency. Once again a Haitian head of state re-
asserted the obligation of his people to work on the land. Workers,
reattached to specific estates in the manner of the Toussaint era,
were denied the right to leave the plantations, to send their chil-

4 Leyburn, *People*, 65.
5 Franklin, *Present State*, 334.

dren to town, to open a shop, to form cooperatives — in sum, to engage in pursuits which would not directly contribute to the production of cash crops. A rural constabulary was reintroduced to enforce these regulations, in particular to arrest vagrants — those rural dwellers who refused to work for a landed proprietor. They were also to direct the daily exertions (Boyer's code spelled them out in tedious detail) on the plantations and to discipline the laborers on behalf of the proprietors and the state.[6]

Discipline, in fact, proved the commodity in scarcest supply. A foreign observer who was among the staunchest supporters of the code predicted that compulsion was no longer feasible: "I am inclined to think that [the Haitians] have been too long indulged in those vices which seem inherent [in them] to be brought to obedience; and that too rigid an enforcement will bring on discontent, and finally a general resistance."[7] Haitians had enjoyed their liberty, and the promulgation of the code was greeted by inertia on the part of many potential workers, by flight away from the plains into the mountains, and by open antagonism. Of importance, too, was the extent to which vast numbers of Haitians had already become the proprietors of plots of land, and were thus exempted from the new regulations. There were, in fact, far fewer plantations in existence than there had been at the beginning of Christophe's reign. But, of greater significance, the code could have been administered only by a large corps of functionaries, and Haiti lacked such a reservoir. Nor, after the settlement with France, could the army be relied upon to supervise the exacting requirements of the code. As a result, Haitians became confirmed in their predominant methods of small-scale, unmechanized cultivation. They avoided the plains, the sugar plantations being abandoned — "the fields are dead," a visitor remarked[8] — and concentrated, where they cropped for cash at all, on the sale of coffee and dyewood, neither of which demanded much cultivation.

[6] For an English text, see *ibid.*, 337–342. There is a partial French text in Mackenzie, *Notes*, II, 294–297.
[7] Franklin, *Present State*, 342–343. See also Samuel Hazard, *Santo Domingo, Past and Present: With a Glance at Haiti* (New York, 1873), 164–165.
[8] Victor Schoelcher, *Colonies Étrangères et Haiti: Résultats de l'Émancipation Anglaise* (Paris, 1843), II, 261.

Furthermore, when the owners of the few large estates saw that they yielded little profit, they moved permanently into the towns, turning their hands to commerce and abandoning the plantations to squatters.

By the end of Boyer's first decade of rule it had become apparent that the Code Rural could not be implemented and that Haiti, for the balance of the nineteenth century, would be content to remain a republic of peasant proprietors producing largely for internal consumption and concerning themselves rarely with economic, political, and social trends elsewhere. Of the once flourishing plantations in the south and southwest, little remained: "In the neighbourhood of Aux Cases [Cayes] the soil . . . has gone into great neglect, and exhibits on the face of it that relaxation in culture which is so general throughout the republic. Indeed in the whole of this part . . . the cane plantations are but little attended to; they are allowed to go on years in succession without cleaning, without manure, or any other requisite to render them productive. . . . In the district of Jeremie . . . the finest plantations of the French are now totally obscured and overspread with the creeper. . . . In vain does the traveller look for those settlements which wore the gay appearance of culture, and for those plantations that enriched the proprietors. . . . Instead of such a scene, the whole country, as we approach towards the capital, exhibits nothing but neglect and waste, and their concomitants, poverty and wretchedness." [9] In the vicinity of Port-au-Prince, another contemporary observer reported, "The very little field labour effected is generally performed by elderly people, principally old Guinea negroes. No measures of the government can induce the young creoles to labour, or depart from their habitual licentiousness and vagrancy. The whole body of proprietors constantly lament the total incapacity of the government to enforce labour." [10] Jacmel, once a prosperous trading port in the south, like Gonaïves and Cap Haitien in the north, no longer ex-

[9] Franklin, *Present State*, 302–304. For comments on the deterioration of plantations and aqueducts in the north as well as the south, see Mackenzie, *Notes*, I, 82–83, 91, 102, 191–192, 322–323. See also S. W. Hanna, *Notes of a Visit to Some Parts of Haiti* (London, 1836), 24, 128–129.
[10] Mackenzie, *Notes*, I, 100.

uded an air of confident wealth. Even Port-au-Prince had fallen upon hard times: "The stranger on first landing at Port-au-Prince," wrote a sympathetic English visitor, ". . . feels greatly disappointed. Instead of a handsome city, such as it appears from the ship's deck at sea . . . you enter into streets of wooden buildings, with the pavement dislocated or broken up, the drains neglected, and filth and stable dung interrupting your steps in every direction. . . . Port-au-Prince, with all its advantages of situation, with every inherent capability of being made and kept delightfully clean, is perhaps the filthiest capital in the world." [11] The roads, which had once been so well-kept, had also fallen into disrepair; there was an absence of inns, and a paucity of bridges over swift-flowing rivers. The infrastructure (to use modern terminology), according to the travelers of the 1820's, was almost nonexistent. Indeed, their commentaries have a distinctly modern ring: "It is almost impossible to describe the state of the roads. . . . It is evident that, notwithstanding the heavy contributions levied for their repair, they have remained untouched since the revolution, and there seems a disposition on the part of the government to efface every vestige of the former roads, leaving the people who travel to beat out their own way in the most easy manner they can." [12]

It is evident that the economy of Boyer's Haiti experienced both an absolute and a relative decline. Once the premier sugar producer in the Caribbean, by 1842 Haiti produced virtually no sugar for export. (A proportion was made into *tafia*, a rough rum, and consumed locally.) Although the production of cotton had increased somewhat from the 1820's to the 1830's, the average production in the latter decade (about 1.3 million pounds) was

[11] John Candler, *Brief Notices of Hayti: With its Condition, Resources, and Prospects* (London, 1842), 69. This reaction to Port-au-Prince was echoed by successive foreign visitors, the most lurid descriptions being contributed by James Anthony Froude, *The English in the West Indies, or the Bow of Ulysses* (New York, 1900; 1st ed., 1888), 342–343, who visited Haiti during the mid-1880's and called Port-au-Prince the "Paris of the gutter"; and Prichard, *Black Rules White*, 46, 53–55, who spent several months in Haiti immediately before the turn of the century. Cf. Johnston, *Negro in the New World*, 174.
[12] Franklin, *Present State*, 306; Hanna, *Visit*, 22, 41; Lepelletier de Saint-Remy, *Saint-Domingue*, II, 97.

but half of Haiti's exports in 1804 and one quarter of the exports in 1791. The production of coffee increased about in proportion to the population over the 1820's and 1830's, but the average for the five years around 1840 (41.7 million pounds) was only about two thirds of the total produced in 1791.[13] Indigo had ceased to be grown although logwood was beginning to appear in the export lists. Tobacco was exported in substantial quantities, but this came from the eastern, or Spanish, portion of the island. Mainly as a result of the halving of the price of coffee from the early 1820's to the early 1840's, the dollar value of total Haitian exports declined from $6.0 million in 1821–25 to $4.5 million in 1838–42. Since this was a period of general price declines, there was probably some reduction in the average price of Haitian imports. (Lacking a better measure, we shall use a U.S. wholesale price index as an index of Haitian import prices.) The purchasing power of Haitian exports, then, in 1910–14 prices, fell from $5.87 million in 1821–25 to $4.6 million in 1838–42. As exports fell, so, with the necessary lag, Haitians were unable to import the manufactured articles and foodstuffs which customarily came from the United States, France, and Britain. The prices of urban and rural land also slumped dramatically. The finest waterfront plots sold for no more than $60 an acre, in the rich plains of the Artibonite small stands were worth no more than $40 an acre, and in the north the best watered, most luxuriant pasture lands — if they could be sold — fetched no more than $40. Even in Port-au-Prince the price of land had failed to increase and was even expected, by knowledgeable visitors, to decline in value.[14] It is clear that the increased taxes which were imposed in order to pay the French indemnity had an inhibiting effect on the making of commercial and agricultural decisions, as had the reduced world price for coffee.

These statistics need not imply that individual Haitians were more impoverished than they had been after the declaration of

13 There are statistics (which vary) in Leyburn, *People*, 320; Lepelletier de Saint-Remy, *Saint-Domingue*, I, 184–185; Placide-Justin, *L'Ile d'Hayti*, 499–506; Mackenzie, *Notes*, II, 158–170; Candler, *Hayti*, 105–111; Alain Turnier, *Les Etats-Unis et le Marché Haitien* (Washington, 1955), 120–121.
14 Franklin, *Present State*, 316.

independence. Rather, there were more of them — about 750,-
000 — and the majority of the population had chosen to follow a
rather different way of life than their forebears. Perhaps a third
of the population were peasants: they owned their land in fee
simple (the largest holdings consisting of about thirty acres); the
most fortunate kept a horse, a cow, goats, and pigs, raised yams
and bananas, and sold coffee, cotton, castor oil, or a little fruit at
the local market. Another third or so of the rural population
were sharecroppers who, although they worked for a fixed percentage of the yearly crop, often acted with an independence of
spirit that made them the equal of peasants.[15] By the close of
Boyer's reign many of the estates worked by sharecroppers had,
because of the myriad problems associated with supervising men
who preferred their own methods to those of an absentee land-
lord, for all practical purposes been broken up and distributed
among the tenants. It is even possible that the workers who
gained control of the estates voluntarily collectivized them in
order to facilitate improvements; for a time they may have
worked plots jointly and elected their own leaders.[16] This fragmentation and dispersal led to the disappearance of the moderate-
as well as the large-sized plantations, to the deterioration of the
fixed assets of many of these habitations, and to a rapid decline in
rural investment. (The peasants were responsive then, as now, to
declining returns.) Government-owned properties were overrun
by squatters who enjoyed their usufruct, every tenant and laborer
would have his own smallholding on which he could subsist with
some comfort — providing that he did not object to remoteness or
height — and the national transformation in land use begun by
Pétion was in effect continued under Boyer after the failure to
implement his code.[17] Plantations were abandoned and the elite,
now devoid of any direct economic stake in agriculture, lacked the
motivation to devote scarce government funds to roads, irrigation
facilities, and rural education. They crowded into the cities, es-

15 Candler, *Hayti*, 122–127.
16 Moral, *Paysan Haitien*, 36.
17 "Good land may be had of the government in every part of the island at a low
price; and any man not satisfied with his condition as a private labourer, may
easily buy it, and become a freeholder in his own right." Candler, *Hayti*, 38.

pecially Port-au-Prince, and turned their backs on the peasants and their ways.

Some authors also blame Boyer for fixing class distinctions irrevocably on a basis of color. For the first few years of his long reign he opened the ranks of the bureaucracy to blacks, in preference to persons of his own light color, but too few blacks were literate and he soon began to appoint more and more mulattoes to positions in the civil service. The army stressed literacy less, however, and blacks in number found places in its service. By the end of his presidency, blacks had achieved a dominant position in the military, and mulattoes dominated the civil arm of the state. This precarious balance was maintained, it seems, primarily by the force of Boyer's personality and a general acceptance of his good intentions.[18] Certainly there was no concerted attempt to improve the rudimentary educational system of the republic, or to extend the benefits of education to the overwhelmingly black lower classes. The absence of Roman Catholic missionaries (there was no concordat with the Vatican until 1862) further inhibited educational growth and intensified the country's isolation. The few Protestant missionaries at first concentrated their efforts in the towns. Missionaries elsewhere in the world established rural schools well in advance of the state; because of its international ostracism, Haiti lacked this attention, its development consequently being retarded.

During the 1830's about 1000 children attended school throughout all of Haiti, and fewer than 300 persons subscribed to periodicals. Despite the initial promotion of blacks in the bureaucracy, the black ascendancy in the army, and Boyer's personal lack of manifest discrimination, most educated and wealthy Haitians were light-skinned. They constituted an obvious ruling elite which perpetuated itself because of its monopoly of educational opportunity, its control of capital, and the maintenance of an informal network of family relationships. An American visitor noted the virulence of prejudice in Haiti: blacks hated mulattoes, and mulattoes despised blacks with equal vehemence. "The pre-

18 Cf. Jonathan Brown, *The History and Present Condition of St. Domingo* (Philadelphia, 1837), II, 259.

judice of color existing among the mulattoes in relation to their fellow citizens," he observed, ". . . is almost as great as that once entertained by the whites of the colony against the class of mulattoes. Intermarriages between the two castes are extremely rare, and such unions are regarded by many of the mulattoes with absolute disgust. The habitual hauteur and assumed pretensions of the mulattoes are a perpetual source of irritation to the vanity of the blacks, and thus the breach between them is every where widened and made permanent." [19]

If we are to understand Duvalier's Haiti and the heritage on which it draws, it is also important that we appreciate the manner in which Boyer's Haiti was — if the word is appropriate — governed. In the first place, by 1835 the financial state of the country had become parlous as a result of its agricultural failings and what a contemporary called the "utmost inefficiency" of the civil service. The receipts of the government regularly fell short of expenditures by $1 million or so, the deficiency being made good by the emission of paper currency, which in turn periodically depreciated in value and was widely unacceptable in the interior. "Amidst this abject poverty of the treasury, and the total non-existence of any public credit, the hirelings and petty subalterns of the government swarm among the population of every commune, like so many vampyres exhausting the life blood of the country; as with responsibility to the chief of the government, which is merely nominal, these public agents make little pretensions to the vulgar qualities of honesty and conscientiousness, and immense sums are annually lost to the treasury by means which are perfectly inexplicable to the treasurer general." [20]

Dishonesty, according to contemporary observers otherwise partial to Haiti, was less injurious to the welfare of Haiti than the sheer ignorance of the functionaries of government. Important official details were either awkwardly performed or neglected altogether through the want of a sense of public responsibility. Provincial administrators, furthermore, depended upon instructions from

[19] *Ibid.*, II, 283; Pattee, *Pueblo Afroantillano*, 154–160. With regard to education, see Candler, *Hayti*, 75–76; David, *L'Héritage Colonial*, 169–170.
[20] Brown, *History*, II, 263.

Port-au-Prince for the interpretation of even the most innocuous
ordinances. The president often altered the legislative intentions
of his chambers — either by fiat, by neglecting to execute, or by
obliging the government printing house to revise meanings —
and was the final interpreter of the actions of the judiciary. Boyer's government was a "military despotism in the hands of a single
man; mild and merciful it must be confessed, and desiring the
welfare of his country; but mistaken in some of his views, and
therefore acting on some occasions in a manner utterly opposed to
the public good." [21] Boyer's government was sustained by the bayonet, but also by the reverence accorded to the president because
of his character and revolutionary associations. (The parliamentary election of 1826, like so many subsequent ballots, was clearly
rigged. Ballot boxes were stuffed and opponents of the regime
prevented from canvassing.)[22] As a basis for future governments
of Haiti, Boyer's regime lacked the stability that would endure,
and that could only have been derived from the solid backing of a
bourgeoisie which was absent in Haiti. Instead, Boyer's support
rested upon the acquiescence of the elite, the only temporary
dampening of latent class-color and sectional antagonisms, the
apathy of the great mass of the apolitical peasants and, as he and
his successors were pained to discover, the non-interference of the
black-officered army.

The Haitian army, despite the contempt with which it has been
described, has, since Boyer's time, represented an important component of the population — the upwardly mobile, semiliterate
blacks who, frequently, assumed that they could govern or misgov-
ern Haiti with a facility equal to that of the elite of Port-au-Prince
or Cap Haitien. Yet in Boyer's day, if contemporary descriptions
can be credited, the troops were already "mere hireling cut-throats,
without character or habits of industry, and ever ready to employ
themselves in scenes of disorder and depredation." [23] They were
arbitrary, and preyed upon the citizenry; the civil service was
everywhere subservient to the military, and the president's au-

21 Candler, *Hayti*, 90. Cf. Mackenzie, *Notes*, II, 105–106; David, *L'Héritage*, 166.
22 Mackenzie, *Notes*, II, 111.
23 Brown, *Condition*, 267. See also Hanna, *Visit*, 56–57; Mackenzie, *Notes*, I, 114–
116; II, 202; Candler, *Hayti*, 91–94.

thority was upheld in large part merely because he was chief of the army. In turn, by maintaining a comparatively large standing army — about 30,000, plus a militia as numerous — agriculture was neglected, and money that could have been employed for public works and civil development was squandered on a host of officers. (On a per capita basis, Haiti in 1842 had a standing army more than twice as large as that of Britain and most other European countries. Including the militia, one in every fifteen inhabitants was under arms despite the absence of any foreign involvements.) In fact, because Haiti was freed from external conflict, rivalry within the army was more worrisome, and the intrainstitutional antagonisms which erupted could be resolved only by resort to *coup d'état.*

Boyer failed to place Haiti on any meaningful road toward national development. He was unable to build upon the foundations constructed by Christophe, probably largely because the threat of invasion was removed, and nearly all of the actions of his government tended to perpetuate the natural inclinations of an untutored population intent, naturally and rightfully, upon maximizing their individual economic and social well-being. The pattern of government that was impressed upon the country was institutionally deficient and very highly personalized. Face-to-face relationships were prized, communications were poor, and money was lacking to make the government relevant to the rural masses. Only the army maintained a heritage of institutional coherence, and thus continued to play an important national role. Above all, only a minute fraction of the population (much less than in comparable societies) was involved in the affairs of state and in sharing the spoils of government.

By the end of Boyer's reign, politics had become a monopoly of town dwellers, and more and more the peasants left the political arena to the educated elite who so enjoyed its complicated machinations. Haiti was at peace but had little to show for it. The republic was agriculturally backward, politically primitive, and socially fragile. In material terms, it was also onerously saddled with large external debts owed to France — $9.82 million on account of the indemnity and $5.26 million as a result of the loan of 1825, both of which could be paid only in specie. (Payments on these debts had been highly irregular under the Boyer regime. After initial payments totalling $1.2 million in 1825 and 1827, practically nothing was paid until the 1839–43 period, when payments averaged $0.8 million, or nearly 60 per cent of government tax receipts.) This, the legacy of Boyer, shaped the history of nineteenth-century Haiti. And isolation — for Haiti was a French-speaking independent micro-state in a sea of English- and Spanish-speaking colonies and was denied a regular open relationship with the slaveholding United States — only accentuated the parochial weaknesses of an inbred republic.

The ouster of Boyer by force of arms inaugurated a long era when the *coup d'état* became a prime fact of Haitian life and the instability of governments approached endemic proportions. In 1843 Major Charles Hérard-Rivière, a mulatto officer of some experience but little education, raised the banner of revolt on a plantation near Cayes, gained supporters in Jérémie (who had themselves already risen to protest high prices), and marched toward Port-au-Prince. Although Hérard-Rivière may himself have possessed no ideological grievances against the government of Boyer, the men of wealth and education of Cayes (notably the Salomons) who initially encouraged him to overthrow the regime, and those persons in the capital who welcomed his initiative, knew no other way to dislodge their president for life, whose actions had begun to appear more and more dictatorial.

Opponents of Boyer for several years had favored the democratization and modernization of the regime: they demanded a free press, a vastly expanded educational system, the return of effective power to the legislature, the dismantling of the government's network of spies, and the reintroduction of compulsory labor as a means of restoring the country's declining prosperity.[24] In addition, among the elite of the south there was widespread dissatisfaction with the overweening economic, social, and political importance of Port-au-Prince, and the increasing dominance of its

---

24 See Mark B. Bird, *The Black Man: or Haytian Independence, Deduced from Historical Notes and Dedicated to the Government and People of Hayti* (New York, 1869), 230. H. Paulèus-Sannon, *Essai Historique sur la Révolution de 1843* (Les Cayes, 1905), is also an important source, but it was unavailable to me.

inhabitants. Boyer's rule had also brought Haiti to the verge of bankruptcy; usurers backed the peasants in the absence of other sources of credit, and the paper money in peasant hands had fallen sharply in value. The rapid decline in the export volumes of Haitian commodities, notably coffee, also contributed to Boyer's loss of popularity. In 1841 coffee fetched the equivalent of nine cents a pound. By 1843 the price had slumped to 6.9 cents. Boyer's inability to relieve the suffering of the inhabitants of Cap Haitien, Port-de-Paix, Fort Liberté, and Môle St. Nicolas after the great earthquake of 1842 may also have hastened his loss of popularity. Finally, it is one of the axioms of Haitian politics that "devotion to the country in Hayti goes for nothing; it is the devotion to a leader or individual that is the act of virtue." [25] By 1843 Boyer, who had failed to build a nation, had forfeited his earlier widespread acceptance and, as the history of Haiti has almost continuously demonstrated, others — with their followings — had become rivals for the spoils of office.

Hérard-Rivière, who had collected 4000 troops, overwhelmed soldiers loyal to Boyer at Léogane while other revolutionaries, under their own officers, marched on the capital from the north. Boyer might have defended the city, and prolonged his rule for a number of months but, in accord with the unwritten rules of supplantive violence, especially as practiced in Haiti before 1957, he chose to minimize the kind of conflict which might destroy the capital and the property of the elite. He accepted the loss of his mandate, abdicated, and sailed — with his family and possessions — aboard a foreign warship to Jamaica and France, where he subsequently died.

Thus commenced a seventy-two-year cycle of twenty-two governments, only one of which completed its term without interruption. Fourteen were ended by revolts after, in most cases, but a fraction of their stated incumbency; the heads of three died in office, one resigned, one was blown up in the palace, another may have been poisoned, and yet another was pulled apart by an urban mob. This succession of unstable administrations was a product of the failure of Haitians to harness the energies of their revolu-

[25] Hazard, *Santo Domingo*, 425.

tion to the political and social development of the new republic. Boyer's reign marked the watershed, and his failure was accentuated by an era of economic decline and compounded by social and political miscalculations. His successors, devoid of any connections to the revolutionary epoch, seemed even less aware of the need to develop Haiti. Each was a representative of a faction; and each seemed to be more interested in being president and in the perquisites of power than in the future of the republic. At least none of the twenty-two regimes, nor the movements which put them into office, was actuated or sustained by more than evanescent ideologies. The character of the regimes, furthermore, was influenced more by the personality of the president than by other than pragmatic persuasions. Even color and the north-south split — important though they may have been in shaping Haitian society throughout the nineteenth century — may have counted for less in politics than usually has been supposed. Politics, after all, remained the concern and game of the numerically small ruling elite (fewer than 1000 persons) and the army only.[26] The changing alliances and factions within these groups struggled largely to get and keep the spoils of office; there were no other important rewards and, conversely, all rewards depended upon the ability to gain access to and to control the highest offices of state.

The four regimes which followed the downfall of Boyer were each a product of military intervention. All lasted less than a year and were inherently unstable; they epitomized the politics of recirculating cliques. Hérard-Rivière, who ruled Haiti as the head of the provisional government of 1843 and, after a *coup d'état,* as president during the first four months of 1844, proved an inept representative of his predominantly mulatto backers. They had provided him with the extremely liberal constitution of 1843: it broadened the hitherto narrowly restricted franchise by at last giving peasants the vote, abolished the presidency for life, returned legislative prerogatives to the Chamber of Deputies and the Senate, introduced trial by jury, and demanded that the

26 For the comparable situation in Central America, see Kalman H. Silvert, *The Conflict Society: Reaction and Revolution in Latin America* (New York, 1968), 14, 63.

military be subservient to the civil authorities.[27] But Hérard-Rivière, like most presidents of Haiti, chose to ignore the constitution; he once again ruled Haiti by the sword, thereby losing liberal favor. On behalf of the landed families of the south he also forfeited the support of the peasants who had been promised the vote by exiling Lysius Félicité Salomon, their leader in Cayes, and by too openly championing the predominantly mulatto elite.

Hérard-Rivière's downfall came, however, after his failure to contain the secession from Haiti of the Spanish-speaking two-thirds of the island (which in 1844 became the Dominican Republic) had established his vulnerability and ineffectuality. Subsequently, there were revolts in Cayes and Grande-Anse in the south and at Cap Haitien (which seceded), and in Port-au-Prince. These were largely revolts of blacks against mulatto rule, although color mattered less than the favoritism which Hérard-Rivière had openly shown to his backers. General Philippe Guerrier, an aged general who had been Christophe's Duke de Marmalade and who now commanded the garrison at Cap Haitien, marched on the capital, where he was accepted as the strongest of the rebel leaders and, in the absence of Hérard-Rivière and his army, was proclaimed president in May 1844. Hérard-Rivière sailed for Jamaica, where he died.

The three short-term successors to Hérard-Rivière were elderly black military officers from the north. The first two, Guerrier and Louis Pierrot, were octogenarians (eighty-seven and eighty-four respectively) who ruled autocratically, without the assistance of the legislature. But both were beholden to a council of state, some of the influential members of which were mulattoes. Both are also said to have been ignorant, and there is some evidence that both were mere front men manipulated by the traditional elite, the first in Port-au-Prince, the second in Cap Haitien (where Pierrot established his capital). Neither managed to accomplish very much during his eleven months in office; true, both on several occasions sent the Haitian army into battle against the Dominicans, but these skirmishes had no important issue. During their periods in office, encouragement was also given to the opening of new

[27] For the text, see Janvier, *Constitutions*, 154–186.

schools in Port-au-Prince, but rural education continued to remain essentially exiguous. Guerrier, who drank heavily, died in office and, as a result of the deliberations of the council of state, Pierrot was asked to assume the presidency. But by creating official positions for the peasant leaders of the south, and by waging war too assiduously and unsuccessfully against the Dominicans, he soon displeased the council of state, which forced his resignation in March 1845 and transferred the presidency to Jean-Baptiste Riché, a sixty-year-old.

Although Riché was also illiterate, may have been addicted to drugs, and was immediately faced with a peasant uprising in the south, he possessed a willingness to rule democratically. He commanded the preparation of yet another constitution — "in order that we may be in harmony with the leading ideas of the present age" — and, after his admittedly brutal suppression of the uprising near Cayes, proceeded to dismantle the dictatorial apparatus of his immediate predecessors.[28] Why he was so motivated is not very clear, but he chose to return to the constitution of 1816, with the addition of many modifications from the constitution of 1843. Presidency for life was once again enshrined, and the council of state became the Senate — without elections — but the remainder of the document was in intent essentially republican. Even so, before he could begin to rule according to these precepts, Riché died, in February 1847. At this point, with the nation comparatively tranquil, Haiti could conceivably have rejected the continued dominance of generals. Financially the country was still impoverished, however — the indemnity remaining outstanding and coffee prices low — and the army, to which the major portion of the budget was devoted, clung tenaciously to its recently won role of dominance. The Senate, which largely represented the elite, may also have felt inclined to elect another weak man who could be dominated. Therefore, when the senators deadlocked in the voting between two prominent generals, they turned to the illiterate sixty-two-year-old head of the presidential guard, one Faustin Soulouque, and elected him to the presidency.

It is said that Soulouque at first refused to take his election seriously. He was uninterested in politics and in no way had ex-

28 Quoted in Bird, *Black Man*, 280.

pected to be summoned to high office.[29] But his qualities, and conceivably his expectations, were more extensive than the standard accounts would have us believe. Despite his illiteracy, he had established an enviable reputation as a result of his military exploits against Christophe. Boyer had given him the command of Plaisance, and Riché, who presumably had a high regard for his ability and loyalty, had placed him in command of the palace guard. In that position he could not have been unaware of the labyrinthine intrigues of Haitian politics. If so, his nomination by the Senate may have astonished his knowledgeable contemporaries less than subsequent historians. Apparently, he was a vain man with no small regard for his abilities. He was also ambitious, and his career pattern reflected political as well as military talent. His *vodun* associations may also have been critical, as was his standing in the army. Yet it is also likely that his strength of character and innate shrewdness were underestimated by the "coterie which, having governed pretty much the country through his predecessors, expected to find in him the easy tool or lay figure with which to work." [30]

Soulouque, like Duvalier 110 years later, surprised his sponsors and confounded the optimistic calculations of those who so wholeheartedly had endorsed his candidacy. He read the lessons of his predecessors and quickly set about entrenching himself in power. Simultaneously he strove to make himself independent of the predominantly mulatto "coterie" to whom he owed his accession by purging the army and placing in positions of importance only those loyal to him. He replaced the members of the cabinet whom he had inherited from Riché with less qualified and darker-skinned men of his own choice. He also organized a secret police, charging it with the prevention of subversive activities. In addition an informal paramilitary group, called *zinglins,* operated in Port-au-Prince as an effective instrument of terror.[31]

For the first time since the revolution prominent Haitians, espe-

29 Dantès Bellegarde, *Histoire du Peuple Haitien (1492–1952)* (Port-au-Prince, 1953), 153.
30 Hazard, *Santo Domingo,* 427.
31 Pattee, *Pueblo Afroantillano,* 176, describes the *zinglins* as a species of Gestapo, but if we possessed more concrete evidence of their activities a comparison with the *tonton macoutes* of Duvalier might be more appropriate.

cially mulattoes, were made to fear the arbitrary, irrational actions of illiterate and irresponsible blacks. Soulouque was also
never loath to employ assassination as a political weapon; he eliminated his potential opponents and, even before his period of rule
was a year old, ordered the murder of prominent persons who
spoke out against the excesses of his regime. The capital thus lived
in perpetual disquiet. For all of those reasons he was easily able in
1848 to crush a mulatto-inspired rebellion in Port-au-Prince, and
to repress a peasant uprising in the south. The brutal massacres
of that year effectively destroyed any threat of elite-inspired revolt
for at least a decade.

By the middle of 1849, despite the first of many abortive attempts to reconquer the Dominican Republic, Soulouque had consolidated his position in Haiti. He was sufficiently strong, having
already arrogated dictatorial powers and abrogated the constitution of 1846, to emulate Dessalines. In August 1849, conceivably
as a means of mobilizing mass support, he proclaimed himself
(with the approval of the Senate) Emperor Faustin I, and proceeded to make the most of his vainglorious pretensions. For the
next nine years Port-au-Prince remained in a state of agitation,
while the emperor, assisted by the army and the *zinglins,* ruled
autocratically and impetuously through the proliferation of un-
relenting terror. "Justice and vengeance," as Soulouque's most
recent biographer has noted, "became tragically confused." [32] He
also used *vodun* and the *vodun* priesthood as instruments of social
control.

Unlike most authoritarian regimes, however, Soulouque's was
as inefficient and corrupt as several more recent Haitian governments. The customs house, upon which Haiti depended for a
large proportion of her recurrent costs, had become a sieve, and
administrative officials, when they did anything at all, prevari-
cated and peculated. The economy also suffered: the treasury
defaulted on the French loan, agricultural production declined
because so many able-bodied men had been recruited into the

---

[32] Murdo J. MacLeod, "The Soulouque Regime, 1847–1859: A Reevaluation," unpublished paper delivered at the first seminar of the Center for Haitian Studies, in
Cambridge, Mass. (April 1969), 11.

army,[33] the currency was debased anew, there were heavy commercial failures as a result of the world recession of 1857–58, and the empire had begun to live from hand to mouth. These conditions helped prepare the path for yet another *coup d'état,* but it was the disastrous campaign of 1855–56 against the Dominicans which finally encouraged a group within the army to bring about the emperor's demise.[34] General Fabre Nicolas Geffrard, a southerner who had commanded the outstanding battalion during the war of 1855, gathered support in the north and marched on the capital from Gonaïves. Early in 1859 Soulouque, his magic having deserted him and his policies having contributed to the accelerating political, social, and economic decline of Haiti, fled to Jamaica.

By the time of the accession of Geffrard, more than half a century after independence, Haiti had acquired a set of political, social, and economic responses which tended to determine the nature of national life until the American occupation and, in certain respects, until the present. Most of these responses have already been enumerated: Since the rural masses of Haiti were illiterate, and were exposed to no modernizing influences, and also because of the complete absence of a meaningful infrastructure, only inhabitants of the few Haitian towns, and a very small proportion of the periurban peasantry, played any role in national politics. At the same time, the availability of land — Geffrard renewed the sale of state-owned lands on easy terms and was lenient toward squatters — minimized the likelihood of rural discontent and, by accentuating the existing individualism of Haitian peasants, lessened the likelihood that the peasants — who lacked the vote — would ever become sufficiently unified to pose a serious political challenge to the largely self-perpetuating cliques who fought for power at the center. Obversely, too, politicians naturally sought to do nothing that would disturb the docility of the peasants; after Boyer, little — either positive or negative — was ever done (except by Salomon) to attempt to increase the production of

[33] For a contemporary description of the way in which the army recruited its soldiers, see Bird, *Black Man,* 296–297.

[34] For a list of their ostensible grievances, see Antoine Michel, *Avènement du Général Fabre Nicolas Geffrard à la Présidence d'Haiti* (Port-au-Prince, 1932). The whole of this book is an attack upon Geffrard and a lavish apologia for Soulouque.

Haitian primary crops. Exports did in fact increase, in large part because population increased. Haitian peasants could gather coffee, cacao, and logwood for export without benefit of any technical assistance and even without roads. The quantity of exports, measured in 1910–14 prices, increased from $3.6 million in 1821–25 to $4.8 million in 1838–42 to $5.7 million in 1859–61.[35] On a per capita basis, exports remained about constant ($6.06, $6.53, and $6.14 for the three periods specified above).

There were no conscious attempts to foster manufacturing industries through tariff protection,[36] and nothing — by way of import substitution — was manufactured in Haiti. Financially, of course, the governments of Haiti were continually in difficulty. The indemnity, until it was paid off in 1888, consumed the balance of customs revenues and any occasional surpluses; the loan of 1825 was also a burden; and, whenever Haiti could not do without capital installations, it borrowed again from foreigners and saddled the impoverished republic with yet another expensive and hard-to-service debt. Payments on the foreign debts, after being suspended from 1843 to 1848, averaged $0.84 million annually during the Soulouque period. During these years, the emission of paper money reached new heights: the rate of exchange between the gourde and the Spanish silver piaster was 1:1 in the early 1820's, between 2.5:1 and 3:1 in the last years of Boyer's regime, 5:1 in 1847, and 20:1 in 1859.[37]

There was never any money for development, and little for essential services in the capital, nearly all of the available resources

35 The quantity of exports, calculated by multiplying quantities of individual items by 1910–14 export prices, is not to be confused with the purchasing power of exports, which is calculated by dividing exports in current dollars by an import price index.

36 In view of the extremely small size of the Haitian market for manufactures and the lack of security, physical infrastructure, and industrial entrepreneurship, tariff protection would have had to have been extremely high to have induced the setting up of any factories. There was in fact considerable unconscious encouragement through tariffs of production for the domestic market, in the form of high import and export duties. (A duty on all exports of x per cent encourages import substitution to the same degree as a uniform import duty of x per cent.) But because of the obstacles mentioned above, this encouragement did not result in any manufacturing activity.

37 Robert Lacombe, Histoire Monétaire de Saint-Domingue et de la République d'Haiti (Paris, 1958), 64.

of the country being consumed, decade after decade, by the still enormous standing army, renewed wars against the Dominicans, and frequent *coups d'état*. Foreign observers were unanimous in their condemnation of the excessive militarization of Haiti in mid-century: "The energies of the country are entirely expended under an unhappy military system," wrote one experienced resident, "which, while it turns everything out of course, as to general produce and industry, at the same time corrupts, demoralizes and in fact ruins the entire youth of the nation." An American consul believed that "the greatest bar to the industry, and therefore to the general progress of Haiti, is her army. . . . The largest standing army in the world . . . supplies no national want. . . . All their military appointments, therefore, but serve to stimulate factions among themselves, arm one against the other, destroy property, and keep the people from their work."[38]

Throughout Haitian life there was never any sense of or regard for the commonweal. During the nineteenth century, it is clear, this concept was entirely wanting in Haitian national life. The men at the center of Haiti, whether wealthy mulattoes or *ancien libres*, parvenu blacks, or the emergent soldiers, concentrated on acquiring and consuming as much as possible of the very limited Haitian economic and political pie. Rewards outside of politics or the bureaucracy were limited and comparatively hard-won. In politics, however, the control of or access to the presidency permitted the sharing of enormous riches and the abundant spoils of office. Retaining public office, by declaring oneself president for life, or by military reinforcement, was an obvious temptation. Geffrard received an annual salary of $40,000, an enormous sum for the time, and increased his overt emoluments by another $10,000 despite a promise to reduce governmental expenditures. Not unexpectedly for Haitian heads of state, he also spent at least another $20,000 on a spy network, purchased land with national funds, and paid for his family's food and drink from the budget of the marching band and, on occasion, from that of a hospital. The

[38] Bird, *Black Man*, 406; [Benjamin S. Hunt], *Remarks on Hayti as a Place of Settlement for Afric-Americans; and on the Mulatto as a Race for the Tropics* (Philadelphia, 1860), 19.

British consul in Haiti, who reported the above excesses and, notwithstanding, was one of Geffrard's staunchest supporters, supplied
a general axiom of nineteenth-century Haitian politics: "Every
Haytian appears fully persuaded that his countrymen never seek
office except for the purpose of improving their private fortunes.
. . ."[39] By Geffrard's time the presidency had come quite openly
to be regarded as "the juiciest financial plum in Haiti," and one
which could justify any and all contingent expenses.[40]

Despite the emergence of political labels (there were Liberals,
who largely represented the mulattoes of Port-au-Prince, and Nationalists, who were black members of the elite or upwardly mobile provincials) from the time of Geffrard, between Soulouque
and the American occupiers, politics in Haiti was largely a game of
changing cliques. There were no issues or ideological discrepancies, and the differences between presidents — in terms of the ways
in which they chose to rule — are slight and largely stylistic. The
structure of Haitian society — and it is this structure which is so
important if we are to understand Duvalier's role — only reinforced the tendency to ignore the long-term importance of developing consensus and to evade the necessity to construct more permanent alliances in a society where trust reposed only in persons
— in face-to-face ties — and never in institutions. Leyburn was
certainly correct to conclude that the absence of universal education was a basic weakness, and that without it Haiti could never
rise above autocratic rule by shifting cabals.[41] By 1858, too, no
president had ever been removed by unquestionably fair electoral
procedures, the legislature had never been able to check the executive, and the judiciary had remained a creature of successive rulers.
Soulouque had shattered faith in indirect mechanisms, and, by the
end of his reign, political inbreeding, when coupled with a national isolation that was only very marginally relieved by American recognition in 1862, denied to Haitians any very easy escape
from the dreary round of factional competition or, indeed, an
awareness that the Haitian paradigm was not inevitable. In addi-

39 Spenser St. John, *Hayti, or the Black Republic,* (2nd ed.; New York, 1889), 183–
185.
40 Cf. Leyburn, *People,* 224.
41 *Ibid.,* 224–225.

tion, the presence of a large standing army, and the availability for employment of southern and northern guerrilla bands, exaggerated the oscillations of factionalism.

Although any discussion of the course of Haitian politics from Geffrard to the American occupation must of necessity take on the repetitive character of a catalogue, it is essential, in what follows, to stress the repetitiveness and, by particularizing it, to make more meaningful the generalizations that have already been drawn. Furthermore, Duvalier's regime is the heir to the misgovernment of these nineteenth-century years, and the institutionalized chaos which became standard after Soulouque reflected Haitian structural realities which persisted until Duvalier's accession to power and have, together with the underlying national psychology, contributed to his ability to rule.

Geffrard, the first of many similar presidents, governed Haiti for eight years, from 1859 to 1867. To his credit, he attempted to improve the cultivation of cotton in order to take advantage of the enormous rise in cotton prices induced by the northern blockade of the southern United States, reorganized the medical school and established a law school and additional urban secondary schools, regularized Haiti's relations with the Vatican and, after siding with the North in the American Civil War, at last entered upon diplomatic relations with the United States. As president, Geffrard behaved with the kind of license, and the accentuation of personal gain, that Haitians had come to accept in their leaders. He was less brutal than Soulouque and hewed closely to the local norms of personal rule but, like so many others, he welcomed the presidency for life and made it evident that he intended to retain power for as long as possible. He dissolved the legislature in 1862, replacing the deputies and senators with men of his own choice, maintained a secret police, and lost few opportunities to act arbitrarily. Geffrard survived both an attempted coup and an attempted assassination at the very beginning of his reign, the threat of a Spanish bombardment of Port-au-Prince (the Spaniards were again ruling the eastern two thirds of the island), abortive uprisings in Gonaïves, Cayes, and Cap Haitien in 1861, 1862, 1863, and 1864, a much more serious insurrection in 1865, led by Major Sylvain Sal-

nave, which was contained only after a British warship had shelled
the insurgents in Cap Haitien, and subsequent attempted revolts
(with accompanying incendiarism) in Port-au-Prince, St. Marc,
and Cap Haitien. There were crop failures in 1865 and 1866, the
arsenal in Port-au-Prince was destroyed in 1866, and there was a
mutiny of troops in Port-au-Prince in 1867. Geffrard took the hint
and fled to Jamaica while Salnave, his strongest opponent, re-
grouped his troops in Cap Haitien and began the long march
southward.

The presidency of Salnave, which lasted from June 1867 to December 1869, was the *reductio ad absurdum* of Haitian government. From his seizure of power from the provisional government
(initially as "Protector of the Republic") of Generals Nissage
Saget and Victorin Chevallier to his own execution, it was an inter-
minable demonstration of the Haitian predilection for the martial
settlement of political issues. In June 1867 the constituent assembly proclaimed a new constitution for the republic, which abolished the presidency for life and fixed the term at four years. Simultaneously, Salnave sent a mob to frighten the members of the
assembly; *l'épée à la gorge,* they elected Salnave, a dark north-
erner, president. Salnave was supposedly a Liberal, and it was assumed that he would try to govern Haiti in a markedly progressive
manner. By the autumn, however, it was clear that he had no administrative ideas, that he was a libertine, and that, like so many of
his predecessors, he could think only of plunder. After differences
of opinion between the executive and a body of legislators, Salnave
led his guards into the National Assembly and effectively ended
parliamentary government. There were riots in the capital, and
deputies from the provinces escaped to their constituencies in
order to raise troops against yet another dictator. Meanwhile, the
cacos, guerrillas of the north who had been attacked by Salnave
when he was master of Cap Haitien, began to march southward.
They joined the townsmen who had been rallied by their deputies. Nissage Saget, in command at St. Marc, led one large contingent, and General Michel Domingue started northward from
Cayes at the head of other troops. There were also dissidents in
Jérémie, Léogane, and l'Anse-à-Veau, in the south, and troops

under General Boisrond Canal near Port-au-Prince. The remainder of Salnave's term was one long civil war, but surprisingly, because they were divided, he was able to withstand his attackers for a considerable period and to win a number of victories. There were confrontations at sea as well as on land, a siege of Port-au-Prince which failed, contests for nearly every commune and, to the dismay of peasant farmers, much desultory skirmishing. Finally, however, the insurgents managed to attack Port-au-Prince from the sea; a newly acquired gunboat trained its fire on the palace, blew up the presidential powder magazine, and compelled Salnave to take to the hills with his followers. Eventually captured, he was summarily tried, tied to a pole set up on the smoking ruins of the executive mansion, and shot — thus ending what the resident British consul called the most trying year the consul had ever known.[42]

Until Duvalier, no president of Haiti after Salnave ventured to accept or to assume the presidency for life. Nissage Saget, who was elected to a four-year term by the National Assembly in March 1870, became the first president to fulfill his prescribed term of office and retire gracefully to private life. He refused all blandishments to extend his term in any way, suffered only one insurrection, and successfully remonetized Haiti's depreciated paper currency and silver and gold coinage.[43] His regime enjoyed favorable coffee prices and good crops (coffee exports alone exceeded $10 million in 1873 and 1874), and part of the proceeds were used to improve the quality of urban schooling, but he seems to have had little interest in doing more than to survive his term. His presidency, though it provided a welcome oasis of calm in the midst of conflict, hardly affected the republic's fundamental political malaise. His ministers were as corrupt as before and, according to a contemporary, the Saget regime was no less a military despotism than its predecessors. Passes were still required if rural dwellers

---

[42] St. John, *Hayti*, 118. For a view of the conflict in the south, see Nerva Lataillade, "Broussais Brice, Dit Brice Aîné, 1868–1870," *Revue de la Société d'Histoire et de Géographie d'Haiti*, III, 8 (1932), 26–34. It may be relevant that, from the fall of Geffrard to the fall of Salnave, the exchange rate rose from 20 gourdes to the Spanish piaster, to 4000. See Lacombe, *Histoire Monétaire*, 64–65.
[43] Michel Fièvre, "Nissage Saget, 1810–1880," *Revue de la Société d'Histoire et de Géographie d'Haiti*, IV, 11 (1933), 30–31.

wanted to visit the towns, the only police were soldiers, and the bloodiest outrages were committed with impunity against the peasants and the workers of the towns. There was no freedom of opinion of any kind, neither foreigner nor Haitian dared express views which were not in accord with those of the government. Nor did Saget attack the more basic problems of the republic. There was still no general means of communication, "except by roads ordinarily fit only for animals," which dated from colonial days, bridges were never repaired, there was a paucity of steam sugar mills and, despite a soil conducive to coffee growing, the government did too little to encourage its proper cultivation. "There cannot be said," Hazard wrote, "to be a dozen coffee estates in the island, and . . . even the coffee, which, left thus in its wild state, grows in such abundance that it cannot all be harvested, is in the marts of commerce valued as an inferior article, not from any demerits of its own, but from the fact that the people are too lazy to clean and prepare it for market." [44]

Saget's peaceful retirement occasioned renewed turmoil. Despite the popularity of the black Liberal candidate, General Pierre Monplaisir Pierre, the outgoing council of ministers managed, after Saget's retirement, to summon an unnecessary constituent assembly. Supporters of the government were elected under military

[44] Hazard, Santo Domingo, 434–435. The deterioration in the quality of Haitian coffee is indicated by the comparison of the unit values (according to U.S. import statistics) of Haitian and total coffee imports into the United States (unit values in U.S. cents per pound):

	Haitian Unit Values	Total Unit Values
1821–25	17.00	16.20
1843–47	5.67	6.16
1883–87	8.46	8.80
1910–14	9.05	11.29

Source: Foreign Commerce and Navigation of the United States. Though Haitian coffee was slightly more valuable than the average of all coffee in the 1821–25 period, its price fell more than the average of all coffee as the century progressed. (For 1913, quoted prices on the New York market are available. They are consistent with the relative unit values for that period: 10.42 cents for "Haitian unwashed" compared with 12.10 cents for an average of eight types of coffee, weighted by U.S. imports. See Lloyd Shaulis, "Prices of Tea, Coffee, and Cocoa," War Industries Board Price Bulletin, 18 [Washington, 1919], 12–13.)

pressure, and they in turn unanimously elected as president Michel Domingue, another illiterate, who was known to be the military front man of Septimus Rameau, a powerful mulatto politician from Cayes. Rameau ruled more overtly than earlier backers of soldier-presidents, and very early showed the kind of domineering tendencies which had for so long plagued Haiti. He was also avaricious and, despite the prosperity engendered by favorable coffee prices, he negotiated a ruinous $6.8 million (later reduced to $4.05) loan from French bankers which endeared the Domingue government to few of the leaders of Port-au-Prince, particularly since the proceeds were shared only among the inner circle of the ministers. The blatant assassination of Monplaisir Pierre and another Liberal general (a third, Boisrond Canal, escaped), and the subsequent banishment of the opponents of the regime, indicated that political violence was still endemic. It reminded the inhabitants of Port-au-Prince of the bad old days of Soulouque and Salnave. There ensued a degree of unrest in the capital until Rameau, a prudent man, decided to sail for Cayes with the contents of the vaults of the Bank of Haiti. This was the final humiliation; a mob killed Rameau in the streets of Port-au-Prince, Domingue fled to the French legation and eventually sailed to Jamaica, and, once again, in 1876 Haiti enjoyed a new government.

Boisrond Canal was a mulatto and a Liberal from the south who wrested the presidency from Jean-Pierre Boyer Bazelais, another mulatto and the leader of the Liberals in the legislature. A distinguished general, Canal brought a degree of disinterestedness to the executive branch of the government. Believing that Haiti's political difficulties resulted from the arbitrary character of her presidents, he sincerely sought to subordinate himself to the law — the restored constitution of 1867 — and in this regard he was thoroughly successful. But, because he deferred to the legislature, nothing very much was accomplished, and reforms proposed by the president and promised by the Liberal party were in fact never enacted. For the most part the deputies figuratively preened themselves in the chamber and in petty ways asserted their supremacy over the executive. Futility thus replaced venality, but even Boisrond Canal's administration could not escape strife. Compara-

tively honest parliamentary elections marked the end of Boisrond
Canal's four-year term in 1879 and gave the Nationalists a majority
and thus the presidency. Boyer Bazelais tried to upset the results
by force and arson (there were riots in Port-au-Prince and a separate revolt in the west), being prevented from doing so only by the
intervention of Boisrond Canal, who still had enough influence in
the Liberal party to suppress Boyer Bazelais' efforts. Then the
president resigned and sailed, like so many of his fellow chief executives, to Jamaica.

Most of the remaining twelve presidents of Haiti who ruled during the twenty-six years before the American occupation were
black generals of the same stamp as their immediate predecessors.
They continued the internecine wars to which Haiti had become
accustomed, did little to assist the republic's escape from the cycle
of near-bankruptcy and ruinous loans which defeated nearly all attempts at economic development, focused their political energies
on system maintenance rather than the building of a lasting base,
paid only lip service to the idea of reform and, except for the very
first, totally ignored the masses. Louis Lysius Félicité Salomon,
who remained in office for a seven-year term, and even began another (1879 to 1888), was among the most qualified of the presidents; he had served as Soulouque's minister of finance, was of a
revolutionary land-owning family of Cayes, was modern-minded
and socially conscious, and had lived in France for eighteen years.
Because Boisrond Canal had provided a comparatively free legislative election, and because Salomon possessed sufficient resources to
purchase the votes of the members of the chamber[45] and obtain the
acquiescence of the army, he became president on behalf of the
Nationalists. Despite this awareness of ideology, however, and although he brought several uneducated men of a lower-class background into his government, Salomon proved no more able than
his predecessors to effectuate significant change in Haiti. He did
provide for a national bank, and for telegraphic links overseas, arranged the admission of Haiti to the Universal Postal Union, and

45 Cf. Leslie F. Manigat, *Un Fait Historique: l'Avènement à la Présidence d'Haiti
du Général Salomon: Essai d'Application d'un Point de Théorie d'Histoire* (Port-au-
Prince, 1957), 26.

reorganized the law school. In 1883 he also permitted impecunious citizens to purchase plots of land from the state if they would agree to cultivate sugar, coffee, cotton, cacao, and tobacco over a period of two to five years. By this means Salomon may have hoped both to increase his popularity and, conceivably, to coerce peasants into growing cash rather than subsistence crops. But the Haitian peasant would not be regimented, and the law of 1883 changed the complexion of rural Haiti little. Peasants still squatted on government lands and grew whatever they liked; they gained effective freehold rights as usucapients.

Salomon, by his fundamental if ill-articulated partiality for the socialism of the day, and even more by his evident antagonism for and persecution of mulattoes, abraded Haiti's most painful sore. Tension between the classes — and class then and later was at least partially conditioned by color — was exacerbated lastingly by Salomon, especially after Boyer Bazelais returned from exile in Jamaica in 1883 and attempted unsuccessfully to overthrow Salomon by force. Port-au-Prince was fired and, with official American assistance, there were attacks on Miragoâne and other southern towns, but Boyer Bazelais lost his life, the Liberal party was permanently destroyed, and Salomon intensified his persecutions of mulattoes, especially in the capital.[46] His downfall, however, came not as a result of the kind of despotism which had come to be expected of Haiti's rulers. Rather, after the rebellion was repressed and Haiti had enjoyed an interlude of peace, Salomon's supporters urged him to accept a new term of office. The constitution was duly amended, and in 1886 Salomon was given a second term of seven years. But, no matter how innocently intended, this perpetuation of one man's and one clique's rule produced the standard reaction. General Séide Thélémaque, the commandant of Cap Haitien and a mulatto, declared his opposition and prepared to march south. There were riots in Port-au-Prince led by sympathizers of Thélémaque, notable among whom was former President Boisrond Canal, acting on behalf of François Denis Légitime, Sal-

[46] For quotations and details, see Bellegarde, *Peuple,* 192; St. John, *Black Republic,* xvi–xviii. For the events of 1883–84 see Jean Price-Mars, *Jean-Pierre Boyer Bazelais et le Drame de Miragoâne* (Port-au-Prince, 1948).

omon's minister of agriculture, and encouraged by the resident British and French ministers.[47] In August 1888 Salomon and his family retired to France.

Throughout the remainder of 1888 and the first nine months of 1889, two governments competed for national recognition. In the north, General Florville Hyppolite, a supporter of Salomon and Salnave's secretary of war, succeeded to the mantle of Thélémaque, who had been assassinated, probably by Légitimists, in Port-au-Prince. Légitime became the candidate of the south. Each side convened an assembly and named its man president of the republic. The Légitime faction retained control of Port-au-Prince, but for the balance of the year it proved too weak to assert its authority over the departments of the Artibonite, the north, the northwest, and the southern commune of Jacmel. "If they want a civil war," Légitime was said to have declared, "I will give them a civil war. I have more resources than they and I will see the country totally destroyed before I allow these ignorant people to put me down." [48] He controlled the capital, with its armaments and other resources of war, as well as the national treasury, and he had the ships with which to mount a blockade of the ports loyal to Hyppolite. Nevertheless, with the help of agents in New York, Hyppolite obtained sufficient arms via the Dominican Republic and, by May 1889, had advanced to within sight of Port-au-Prince.[49] By August the "ignorant people" had put Légitime down, and he sailed, like so many others, for foreign parts.

Despite the political chaos, the early 1890's represented a high point in the economic fortunes of nineteenth-century Haiti. Coffee prices were up, and the logwood boom was in full swing. The quantity of exports (in 1910–14 prices) had increased since 1859–61 at about the same rate as the population, to a total of $8.2

47 Ludwell Lee Montague, Haiti and the United States, 1714–1938 (Durham, 1940), 132–133.

48 John E. W. Thompson, Minister of the United States Legation in Port-au-Prince, to Secretary of State Thomas F. Bayard, October 18, 1888, quoted in ibid., 135–136.

49 The United States government maintained an official position of neutrality between the two factions, despite the contention to the contrary in Jacques Nicolas Léger, Haiti: Her History and her Detractors (New York, 1907), 244. See Rayford W. Logan, The Diplomatic Relations of the United States with Haiti, 1776–1891 (Chapel Hill, 1941), 399–400.

million in 1888–92, maintaining per capita exports at $6.06. But because of the rise in export prices and the presumed decline in import prices (the U.S. wholesale price index fell 11 per cent from 1859–61 to 1888–92), the purchasing power of exports per capita rose from $7.42 to $12.41.[50] Even during this period of export boom, however, the absence of fundamental structural change in the economy is striking. Haiti was a classical example of an economy lacking the "capacity to transform." [51] Almost the only change in the structure of exports over the whole of the 1821–1914 period is the rise and decline of logwood, a highly resource-intensive commodity that required no skill, no long-term investment, and no physical infrastructure to gather and ship abroad. The problem was not that Haitian peasants were unresponsive to price incentives (witness the rapid expansion of cotton production during the

---

[50] The statistics for the whole of the nineteenth century are gathered in the following tables:

Exports per Capita, 1821–1914,
in 1910–14 Prices

	Average Exports (million dollars)	Population (million)	Exports per Capita
1821–25	3.596	.593	$6.06
1838–42	4.775	.731	6.53
1859–61	5.739	.935	6.14
1888–92	8.208	1.355	6.06
1910–14	8.217	1.778	4.62

Sources: See Appendix B.

Purchasing Power of Exports
per Capita, 1821–1914

	Exports in Current Prices (million dollars)	Purchasing Power of Exports[a]	Purchasing Power of Exports per Capita
1821–25	5.989	5.872	$ 9.90
1838–42	4.516	4.603	6.30
1859–61	6.400	6.941	7.42
1888–92	13.683	16.809	12.41
1910–14	8.217	8.217	4.62

[a] Exports in current prices divided by U.S. wholesale price index (1910–14 = 100).

Sources: See Appendix B.

[51] Charles Kindleberger, *Foreign Trade and the National Economy* (New Haven, 1962), 99–115.

period of astronomic cotton prices occasioned by the American Civil War). The major reasons were the chronic political instability and governmental plundering of the private sector, which made investment in physical capital a highly risky venture, and the utter neglect of the transport network.

Jamaica provides a revealing contrast. The development of the road and railway network there laid the basis for a banana boom from the 1890's to the 1920's.[52] The physical and climatic conditions were equally favorable in Haiti, but the development of bananas there had to wait until the 1930's. Yet Jamaican development in the nineteenth century was not a resounding success: There was a difficult period of readjustment following the abolition of slavery in the 1830's, especially before the British government took over the reins of the colony in 1866.[53] The ex-slaves, detesting anything that smacked of the slave routine, took to the hills in large numbers and must have lived much as their Haitian counterparts did. The social cleavage between white (2 to 4 per cent of the population), mulatto (about 18 per cent), and black was no less severe than between mulatto and black in Haiti. But what Jamaica enjoyed — and Haiti lacked — was a government that provided a basic physical infrastructure (mainly a transport network) and political and administrative security for private undertakings.[54]

The next three black generals from the north ruled during relatively untroubled times. The inhabitants of Jacmel were in rebellion throughout the 1890's, and Port-au-Prince, Cap Haitien, and Petit Goâve witnessed battles between contending electors in 1902, but presidents Hyppolite (1889–1896), Tirésias Augustin Simon

---

52 William F. Maunder, "Notes on the Development of Internal Transport in Jamaica," *Social and Economic Studies*, III (1954), 161–185.

53 See Gisela Eisner, *Jamaica, 1820–1890* (Manchester, 1961), *passim*.

54 The results of this favorable environment are shown in the following table of exports and GDP per capita. The latter is the appropriate measure for overall economic growth: The figures show very slight growth from 1870 to 1890 and a gradually accelerating growth rate thereafter. (From 1910 to 1930, the rate of growth of GDP per capita was 0.7 per cent.) The export figures are given in the table for purposes of comparison with Haiti. In 1890, exports per capita were not too different in the two islands: $10.10 in Haiti versus $12.65 in Jamaica. This was an abnormally high period for Haiti, but a typical period for Jamaica. Haiti was merely benefiting from very favorable coffee prices, and could do nothing to keep

Sam (1896–1902), and Nord Alexis (1902–1908) otherwise were not faced (until the close of Alexis' term) with the tumultuous excesses which were the lot of their successors.[55] Hyppolite died in office; Simon Sam, whose subordinates had condoned brutality in the capital and had persecuted opponents of the regime, thought it prudent to withdraw; and Alexis, a doughty eighty-one-year-old warrior with autocratic ideas, whose election was accomplished by mob action and sustained by various assassinations and terrorism, sailed for Jamaica after General Antoine Simon had raised the banner of revolt in the south.

During their terms of office, Hyppolite, Sam, and Alexis were builders of public works — Hyppolite was responsible for the imposing iron markets of Port-au-Prince and Cap Haitien, numerous bridges, the digging of canals in towns, the stringing of telegraph lines between the towns, and the repair of the country's road network. Simon Sam constructed official buildings in Port-au-Prince and started to link Port-au-Prince and Lake Etang Saumâtre, on the Dominican border, and Cap Haitien and Grande Rivière by rail. During their presidencies, too, there was a considerable increase in educational activities; by 1895 some 9800 students were being taught in "national religious" schools which received some financial support from the state and were run by various sectarian

---

her exports up as coffee prices fell. Jamaica was developing a new export industry which kept her exports increasing as fast as population for the next forty years.

GDP per Capita in Jamaica, 1832–1930
(Figures in U.S. dollars)

	Exports in Current Prices per Capita	*Purchasing Power of Exports per Capita*[a]	*GDP per Capita, 1910 prices*
1832	28.69	30.20	75.5
1850	11.16	13.29	59.0
1870	10.95	n.a.	57.6
1890	12.65	15.43	60.0
1910	14.99	14.55	66.3
1930	18.83	14.94	76.0

[a] Exports in current prices per capita divided by the U.S. wholesale price index (1910–14 = 100).

Source: Eisner, *Jamaica*, 119, 289.

[55] For an amusing description of Alexis, see Stephen Bonsal, *The American Mediterranean* (New York, 1912), 77–79.

bodies. There were about 26,600 students in public primary schools — 13,050 in urban areas and 13,550 in rural areas. The statistics on rural schools are very misleading, however, since many existed on paper rather than in fact. In addition, 6500 students were enrolled in private primary and secondary schools (this category includes some religious schools receiving little or no support from the state), and 1670 were enrolled in post-primary schools: high elementary (970), lycées (600), and higher education (100). At this time, the primary enrollment ratio was around 7.5 per cent, excluding the rural pupils.[56]

The national religious schools were among the best in Haiti. The presence of foreign (largely French) teachers made these schools attractive to Haitian families, and the encroachment of the religious on the public secular schools was a matter of concern to Haitian governments.[57] The religious schools occupied an increasing share in Haitian education up to 1895; disregarding the rural pupils, the national religious schools accounted for one third of all primary and secondary school students (the private schools accounting for another 20 per cent). Judging by the experience of the 1950's, the desertion rates were substantially lower in the national religious than in the urban public schools, a fact which implies that, among secondary students, the national religious share was larger than one-third.[58]

[56] The total number of pupils in public urban primary, plus the national religious and private secondary and primary schools, was 29,300. From these must be subtracted an unknown number of secondary students in the national religious and private schools. Estimating secondary students at 20 per cent leaves 26,500 primary students, which implies the 7.5 per cent enrollment rate.

[57] Catts Pressoir, "Historique de l'Enseignement en Haiti," *Revue de la Société d'Histoire et de Géographie d'Haiti*, VI (1935), 33–57. *Exposé Général de la Situation de la République d'Haiti*, 1892, 90–91. *Exposé*, 1905, 81.

[58] The statistics (such as they are) on total enrollment in publicly supported schools are shown in the following table. Year-to-year changes should be treated with great caution, since the national religious schools were not always included. Very broadly, what the table shows is substantial educational activity from 1859 to 1865, a considerable increase from 1865 to 1895, a sharp cutback in 1904–05, and a recovery to roughly the 1895 level by 1912–13. (The data on school formation for 1859–65 are confirmed in *Exposé*, 1875, 40. The data on the number of pupils in 1904–05 are confirmed by budgetary statistics. Expenditure for salaries was $640,000 in 1895, but only about 600,000 gourdes in 1904–05, or the equivalent of $109,000 at the exchange rate of 5.5 gourdes to the dollar. See Logan, "Education," 433.) By and large, the changes in school enrollments parallel changes in economic activity as a whole (as measured by export earnings).

Aside from letting the public schools deteriorate, Nord Alexis decided to issue paper money in vast quantities, thus bringing about serious inflation at a time when, with the floating debt consolidated, it might have been possible to avoid being damagingly beholden to foreign creditors. The inflationary spiral naturally worried the townsmen more than the rural masses, but even the country markets felt the effects of Alexis' manipulation of the currency. Foreign merchants were equally concerned, and all three elements assisted the rebels in bringing about Alexis' departure in late 1908.

The swirling eddies of Haitian instability gathered a cumulative momentum. Between 1908 and 1915, they surged with rapidly increasing impetus. Financially, the republic was even more vulnerable than before. Although the burdensome indemnity had at last been refunded (Haiti had never defaulted, presumably because of her fear of foreign intervention), ruinous and heavily discounted French loans of 1875 and 1896 were still outstanding.[59] Average

Number of Pupils in Publicly Supported Schools		
	Total	*Total, excluding National Religious*
1820	1,100 (Christophe only)	
1842	at most 1,000	(no national religious
1860	10,000	in existence)
1865		15,697[a]
1875 or 1877		19,250
1881–82		23,745[a]
1889		29,164[a]
1891		33,391[a]
1895	38,039	
1904	probably under 27,000[b]	
1912–13	38,000 to 39,000	

[a] Not clear whether national religious are included or not.

[b] From Fleury Féquière, *L'Education Haitienne* (Port-au-Prince, 1906), 480–481. He gives 27,063 for what seems to be all schools, but he has no statistics for Cap Haitien. *Exposé*, 1905, gives 30,000 for the total number of pupils, including private schools.

Source: Logan, "Education," 422, except as indicated above.

[59] It is sometimes said that the burden of this indemnity was a major reason for Haiti's failure to progress in the nineteenth century. See Logan, *Haiti and Dominican*, 195. The indemnity had a negative influence, but it was certainly not decisive. Because of the political situation, in Haiti there was a negligible propensity to invest. Additional income did not lead to sufficient capital formation which could in future raise production significantly. (The weak correlation mentioned above between educational activity [a type of capital formation] and export earnings provides a slight — but only a slight — qualification to this statement.)

annual payments on these loans had run around $500,000 from
1876 to 1885 (14 per cent of customs receipts), declined somewhat
to 1895, and then rose to $800,000–$900,000 from 1896 to 1910
(20 to 25 per cent of customs receipts). In 1910 a new French loan
raised the total foreign debt from $11.7 million to $24.3 million;[60]
annual payments from 1912 to 1914 were $1.6 million, or 30 per
cent of customs receipts. These figures do not include a series of
short-term "internal" loans, subscribed to largely by foreigners. In
1913 and 1914, the annual payments on the internal debts were
$1.2 million and $1.0 million respectively.

Foreigners, especially the Germans (who controlled wholesale
and retail trade), the French, to whom Haiti sold nearly all of her
coffee and about half of her total exports, and the Americans, who
supplied the major portion of the republic's imports, dominated
what remained of the once flourishing economy. Customs revenues had been pawned to pay off the loans, and a number of dubious and costly concessions had been granted to unscrupulous foreign promoters. Funds were not lacking in selected private hands,
particularly to support movements of rebellion, but the
government itself lurched precariously from pay day to pay day,
and even the army was encouraged to forage for itself.

In nearly all other respects, Haiti clung tenaciously to its traditions. The educational system was still excessively classical, with
access to it, and hence also to the escalator of upward mobility,
limited largely to the elite (both black and mulatto). In 1908 a
visitor with considerable African experience described the continued inability of successive Haitian governments to ameliorate the
republic's schools: "Large sums of money are appropriated annually in the Haitian budget for the maintenance of schools in all the
communes of Haiti. This appropriation is one of the many cruel
tricks played on the Haitian people by its Government. In the
beautifully printed 'Budget Général' (which is published annually at Port-au-Prince), under the head of the Department of Public Instruction, there is a *cadre* providing for the education of
Haiti — primary, secondary, and advanced — with a detail and

[60] See slightly different figures in Montague, *Haiti*, 23; Arthur C. Millspaugh, *Haiti
under American Control, 1915–1930* (Boston, 1931), 18n.

completeness worthy of Switzerland or Germany. Yet much of this organisation exists only on paper, and the funds appropriated for this splendid purpose find their way into the pockets of Government officials, or possibly never leave the Treasury. There are fairly good schools in Port-au-Prince and in the eleven or twelve principal coast towns of Haiti. I doubt if there are any rural schools at all, in spite of the fact that 500 are provided for in the budget; or, if they exist, they do so as a means for providing a petty sustenance for some totally incompetent person. The plain fact remains that something like 2,500,000 out of the 3,000,000 of Haitians cannot read or write, and are as ignorant as unreclaimed natives of Africa." [61]

Despite the efforts of Geffrard, Hyppolite, and others, the infrastructure remained exiguous and, for the old cultural and geographical reasons, the republic continued to consist of six urban centers, a string of comparatively isolated coastal villages, and clusters of remote and largely uninvolved hamlets. The soldiery was as numerous, ill-paid, undisciplined, and ready to side with an insurgent movement as before. "Hayti is governed by Generals in all sizes," one admittedly flamboyant visitor noted. "The General is so ubiquitous that it leads you to doubt whether it may not be possible that while to be a General is no compliment, not to be one is in the nature of a slap in the face." [62] The practice of employing guerrilla or bandit groups to foment a revolution had become ingrained, particularly in the north where groups of *cacos* responded willingly to financial inducement and then marched southward from Cap Haitien to Gonaïves and on to the gates of Port-au-Prince. German merchants had begun to supply the wherewithal for these uprisings, apparently solely because of the profits which might accrue. An American diplomat described the enduring pattern: "Politicians who are at any time willing to inaugurate a revolution, are abundant, and with a comparatively small sum of money can obtain an army and take the field against the Government. In this emergency the man with the money appears — almost invariably a German merchant who looks upon the financing

61 Johnston, *Negro in the New World*, 187.
62 Prichard, *Black Rules White*, 60.

of a revolution as a straight business proposition. The revolutionary leader gives his paper for not less than double the amount borrowed, and when the revolution succeeds the merchant receives his money again with 100 per cent or more interest. As most revolutions succeed, there is little risk in such loans and they are easily obtained." [63]

By this time there was a widespread acceptance of disorder and instability. Only a handful of intellectuals, notably the followers of Joseph-Anténor Firmin, a journalist, author, lawyer, cabinet minister (under Hyppolite), and rebel (against Nord Alexis), consciously argued that the executive should be the servant, not the master, of the state, that class divisions should be eschewed, and that the rural masses should be integrated into the fabric of the state.[64] The majority of the membership of the civil and military oligarchy which ruled the republic preferred to maintain its own grip — despite internecine squabbles, sometimes openly racial or sectional — over the division of the spoils. Elections were no cleaner than in earlier decades: "I have seen in Port-au-Prince," a minister at the American legation wrote, "the soldiers come up in companies and remain all day voting and repeating at the command of their officers, while none of the better or middle or common classes were trying to vote, if indeed, it had been possible." [65] As before and since, the government was run exclusively for the benefit of the particular clique in power — upon the smallest flea fed a whole series of large fleas.[66] Had those who really held the

63 Madison Smith to William Jennings Bryan, February 21, 1914, quoted in Dana G. Munro, *Intervention and Dollar Diplomacy in the Caribbean, 1900–1921* (Princeton, 1964), 329–330. An equally cynical observer was Captain Edward Latimer Beach, who served with the American occupation forces: "A revolution was bought and paid for at an agreed upon price. . . . It would seem that in the years immediately preceding 1915, any Haitian could be president who could raise sufficient funds. In some cases the cost was as low as $30,000, in others as high as $50,000. Except for the politicians engaged, and the troops hired to depose and the other troops hired to defend, no other Haitians were concerned in the revolution." "Haiti and its People," unpub. typescript (1919), 27–27a, privately held. See also John H. Allen, "An Inside View of Revolutions in Haiti," *Current History*, XXXIII (May 1930), 329.
64 See Léonce Viaud, "La Personnalité de Joseph-Anténor Firmin," *Revue de la Société d'Histoire et de Géographie d' Haiti*, XIX, 68 (1948), 4–20.
65 Henry Watson Furniss to Philander C. Knox, August 29, 1907, quoted in Munro, *Intervention*, 329. Cf. Bonsal, *American Mediterranean*, 66–67.
66 With apologies to Prichard, *Black Rules White*, 74.

reins of power knowledge or experience sufficient to do otherwise?

In a society thrust before time into the Western idiom, wholly unintegrated, totally lacking in any kind of consensus, racked with poverty and deprived of the natural resources or knowledge with which to escape the dreary cycle that necessitated the renewed mortgaging of the national patrimony, and prey to the machinations of outsiders, it is no wonder that the inherent instability of the nineteenth century was amplified at the state level by the conditions of the early twentieth. Coffee prices declined sharply in the late 1890's and remained low until just before World War I. The logwood boom petered out, and its decline was only partly offset by expansion in cotton and cacao. From 1888–1892 to 1910–1914, total exports in 1910–14 prices remained constant, per capita exports declining from $6.06 to $4.62. But in current dollars total exports fell from $13.7 million to $8.2 million, and as a result of the presumed rise in import prices (measured again by the U.S. wholesale price index), the purchasing power of exports per capita fell from $12.41 to $4.62.

The weaknesses of Haiti were also apparent on an entirely different level. It was difficult then, as later, to transform plans into reality — to get anything very significant done. A commentary of 1900 is apposite: "Everything was arranged. Everything was drafted upon paper. It seemed as if, with a people so hedged in, nothing could go wrong, that they simply could not get off the paths of progress. And yet, and yet — they began everything — and dropped it." [67]

Between 1908 and 1915 there were seven presidents and about twenty uprisings and attempted insurrections. (There had been sixty-nine between 1806 and 1879). Simon, a nearly illiterate peasant who had risen through the ranks of the army, was president from 1908 to 1911. His government negotiated a loan from the Banque de l'Union Parisienne for 65 million francs ($12.5 million) at 5 per cent per year, 10 million of which were meant to be devoted to monetary reforms and the redemption of paper currency, and only 47 million of which were actually realized by Haiti. His government was also persuaded to let this same French

[67] Prichard, *Black Rules White*, 345.

bank assume the responsibilities and privileges of the national
bank, and to embroil itself in a number of similarly complicated
and disadvantageous ways with a host of other foreign concession-
aires — each of whom presumably offered suitable inducements.

The first uprising against Simon came from the south, but a second organized by Cincinnatus Leconte, a former cabinet minister
under Simon Sam, and the leaders of several bands of *cacos,* spread
southward along the Gonaïves–St. Marc axis to Port-au-Prince.
Simon fled. Although Leconte is highly praised by Haitian historians for trying to reform the army and improve the schools, his presidency lasted less than a year. In August 1912 the presidential palace was blown up; Leconte and more than 300 members of the
palace guard perished.[68] Tancrède Auguste, a mulatto former senator and cabinet minister under Hyppolite and Simon Sam, was
named president by the National Assembly. He pledged to follow
the policies of Leconte, even paying off the *cacos,* but he lasted
only eight months, dying either of pernicious anemia and complications, or, as was thought at the time, of poison.

There was an immediate scramble for the succession. Even
while the body of the ex-president was lying in state in the cathedral, firing began throughout the town and spread to the interior
of the cathedral as Edmond Defly, a locally based general, and his
followers attempted to guarantee his own selection by the assembly. They surrounded the assembly but were opposed by soldiers
and police loyal to Generals Justin Poitevien and Maurice Ducasse,
the latter of the palace guard. Poitevien's favorite, Senator Michel
Oreste, a prominent lawyer and orator, was named president. The
leading American diplomatic representatives in Haiti reported
that each senator and deputy had received a promissory note from
the successful candidate and that these were later honored by the
national treasury.[69]

Oreste is remembered for having established a paramilitary body
reminiscent of the *zinglins* in order to strengthen his intelligence
and security operations and, during the legislative elections of

---

[68] Although the events were suspicious, it is still not known whether or not Leconte
was the victim of circumstance or a plot.
[69] Munro, *Intervention,* 329.

early 1914, to intimidate his opponents and ensure the success of his own hand-picked candidates.[70] Simultaneously, he also tried to weaken the army by depriving it of appropriations. But these maneuvers were too obvious, and Oreste's power base was too restricted. Shortly after the elections, in January 1914, Senator Davilmar Théodore led an army of *cacos* toward Gonaïves from Cap Haitien, there being ousted by General Oreste Zamor, who enlarged the rebellious force, burned Gonaïves, and marched on Port-au-Prince. Michel Oreste fled to Jamaica after seven months as president.

Troops loyal to Théodore and Zamor fought throughout the early part of the presidency of the latter. It lasted eight months, during which the funds of the government were in large part devoted to paying off the *cacos* and preventing defections to Théodore and the interference of German merchants. Théodore, however, was equal to the test of mercenaries; at the head of a *caco* army he reached Port-au-Prince in October 1914, assumed the presidency, and immediately began to defend his office against yet another rising in the north while the *cacos*, who had remained in the capital, treated it like a conquered city. At the same time as General Vilbrun Guillaume Sam, Théodore's representative in the north, was slowly leading his own *cacos* southward along the tortuous road to Gonaïves, Théodore's government began raising money by issuing unsecured bank notes and continuing the recently introduced practice of floating loans domestically which were largely subscribed to by the foreign commercial community and secured by a slice of the customs revenues that had already been pledged on an external loan. These financial manipulations hardly endeared Théodore to the governments and investors of France, Germany, and the United States, all of which had begun — especially after the outbreak of World War I — to pay close attention to the affairs of the rapidly changing Haitian governments. In December 1914 American Marines had even entered the national bank and taken $500,000 in gold to New York for safekeeping. It is unclear how much foreign support was given to

---

[70] Interestingly, Oreste, like Duvalier later, chose to finance his security operations from the proceeds of a special tobacco levy.

Guillaume Sam, but American detachments accompanied him to the outskirts of Port-au-Prince, which his forces entered in late February 1915.[71] He became president in March, and the American envoy immediately attempted to negotiate a devolution of Haitian sovereignty to the United States. Although this transfer of authority to the United States was in no way conceded, conditions in Haiti made it almost impossible for Sam to govern. The state was virtually bankrupt, the *cacos* and the army were restless, and the foreign powers were constantly competing among themselves and intriguing with Haitians. Sam was not popular, and soon his own minister of the interior began yet another northern revolt in May 1915. Before this newly assembled army could sweep southward, however, conditions in Port-au-Prince deteriorated. Sam, whose attempts to cling to power were increasingly desperate, epitomized Haitian life and politics from 1790 to 1915 by massacring all of the persons whom he had recently imprisoned in Port-au-Prince for political reasons. The response of the citizens of the capital was to storm the palace and, after the president had scurried to the French legation, to rout him out of his sanctuary and pull him limb from limb. Considering the strategic and commercial anxieties of the United States, conditions in Haiti were ripe for intervention.

71 H. P. Davis, *Black Democracy: The Story of Haiti* (New York, 1936), 155–156.

IV

The American Occupation

THE UNITED STATES intervened in Haiti in July 1915 and ruled
there until 1934. It occupied, pacified, and administered, introduced new methods of solving old problems, suggested and provided an array of technological innovations, added significantly to
the fragile and fragmentary infrastructure, improved medical and
educational facilities, sought to develop the country in a general
way and, like colonial powers nearly everywhere, strove diligently
to make the pattern of life in its subject dominion conform as
closely as possible, and certainly in external aspects, to the cultural
expectations of the dominant society. Considered as an intervention, the occupation of Haiti was of a piece with the virtually simultaneous American takeovers of Nicaragua and the Dominican
Republic, but the impact of the policies of the occupiers depended
as much upon the character and responses of the receiving as the
sending culture. Haiti certainly absorbed and reacted to American
initiative in a particularly Haitian manner; it is also evident that
the nature of the occupation contributed in a number of ineradi-
cable ways to the tensions and the methods of manipulating Haitian society.

The decision to intervene was no sudden, capricious response to
Haitian political and financial destitution. There were precedents
and important strategic and commercial considerations; indeed, it
is more surprising that the Americans waited until 1915 than that
they intervened at all. Throughout the first half of the nineteenth
century southern Americans sought to isolate Haiti in order to
prevent the possible spread of "black power" to the United States,
while their cousins from New England pushed the sale of fish and

rum there as intensively as they could. However, during the last
thirty or forty years of the century — especially after the recognition of the republic by the United States in 1862 — the Americans
grew more aware of the potentialities of Haiti, and looked with a
covetous eye upon the Môle St. Nicolas, a well-protected harbor on
the northwestern coast of Haiti and a mere sixty miles across the
Windward Passage from Cuba. American policy essentially consisted of ignoring Haitian internal problems and of making absolutely certain that no foreign power gained control of the Môle.
At times American administrations sought to persuade Haitian
governments to cede the Môle, and there were some influential
Americans who were willing to use martial means in order to acquire it, but successive Haitian leaders resisted all blandishments
and promised firmly to oppose any and all encroachments upon
Haitian sovereignty. Nevertheless, the American navy successfully visited Haitian ports in order to protect American life and
property on eight occasions between 1857 and 1900. After the
turn of the century, when the construction of the Panama Canal
made the Môle strategically that much more important, and when
Haitian instability became even more apparent, ships of the U.S.
Navy interfered on behalf of Americans and American interests an
additional eleven times.[1]

Between 1870 and 1913, the United States increased its share of
the Haitian market from 30 to about 60 per cent. Haitian imports
from the United States, primarily in pork, lard, flour, soap, fish,
and cotton textiles, were worth about $6 million, but this figure
represented less than 2 per cent by value of total U.S. exports.
Nor were American investments of startling magnitude. Two
wasteful railway concessions (of 1876 and 1904) were originally
owned by Americans, but by 1910 both had been assumed by German firms. In that same year James P. McDonald, an American
entrepreneur, gained control of a comprehensive port improvement and rail network concession for which the government of
Haiti guaranteed to all investors, in exchange for evidence of progress, the payment of principal and interest on its construction

1 Details in Hans R. Schmidt, Jr., "The United States Occupation of Haiti, 1915–
1934," unpub. Ph.D. thesis (Rutgers, 1968), 23–24.

bonds. (McDonald had intended to grow bananas along the line of rail, with Haitians, typically, expecting to defray the bond guarantees by the payment of export taxes on the bananas.) A New York syndicate led by W. R. Grace & Co. and numbering among its stockholders several officers of the National City Bank of New York purchased half of McDonald's concession, the other half going to a British syndicate. It was intended that this consortium should build a national railway from Port-au-Prince to Cap Haitien, but by 1914, when Haiti grew dissatisfied with the line and refused to make further payments, the company could claim merely to have constructed three poorly maintained and badly separated sections of the railroad. There were lengthy gaps between St. Marc and Gonaïves and Ennery and Bahon; through traffic was impossible, three sets of rolling stock had to be maintained, what was completed seemed shoddy, and, as if to add insult to injury, the main station had been sited two miles out of Port-au-Prince, in the middle of a mire.[2]

American interest in the railway coincided with and contributed to an involvement in the only other significant American investment in Haiti before 1915. The republic's Banque Nationale had been controlled by French investors since its inception in 1881. It collected the principal revenues of the country, acted as a depository for official funds and the national paymaster and, in sum, exerted a control over the republic's finances which was intended primarily to serve the interests of foreign creditors. In 1905, after the discovery of blatant and outrageous frauds (several men who subsequently became presidents of Haiti were implicated along with the bank's French directors), the Banque Nationale lost its most lucrative quasi-governmental functions. In 1909–10, however, after the inauguration of a new Haitian government, French and German interests sought a contract for a reorganized Banque which would enable them to collect Haiti's customs revenues, obviously the republic's most accessible and most negotiable financial resource. By this time the Germans in Haiti numbered about 200.

2 Paul H. Douglas, "The National Railway of Haiti: A Study in Tropical Finance," *Nation*, CXXIV (January 19, 1927), 59; *idem.*, "The American Occupation of Haiti," *Political Science Quarterly*, XLII (1927), 233–235; Munro, *Dollar Diplomacy*, 255–256, 331–332.

They controlled nearly 80 per cent of all international commerce (imports of textiles and consumer goods and exports of coffee), owned the public utilities in Cap Haitien and Port-au-Prince, the main wharf in the capital, the Chemin de Fer de la Plaine du Cul-de-sac (the railway serving the sugar-producing area near Port-au-Prince), and the tramway in Port-au-Prince. In addition, the Hamburg-American was the principal steamship line serving Haiti. And we have already noted the willingness of German firms to sponsor internal disorder for short-run financial gain.[3]

The National City Bank, to a large extent because of the personal interest of two of its officers in the national railway, had become equally interested in obtaining access to Haitian revenues which could easily be earmarked.[4] At the same time, the State Department in Washington indicated its unwillingness — for strategic reasons already implied by the Roosevelt corollary to the Monroe Doctrine — to accept increased German and French economic influence in Haiti. They were less opposed to financial hegemony *per se* than to the possibility that such financial stakes would, in the event of future Haitian instability, provide an excuse for German or French intervention and occupation of an island commanding the Windward Passage. The American government forcibly made its opposition known to the Haitians as well as the German and French consortia. Yet, this antagonism to an agreement "so detrimental to American interests, so derogatory to the sovereignty of Haiti, and so inequitable to the people of Haiti," [5] failed to deter the Haitians, many of whom hoped to profit personally from signing away their national financial independence. But it gave the Franco-German consortia pause. The German banking interests decided to play a less dominant role; 40 per cent of the ownership of the Banque was divided among four American firms, including National City, and the remaining German financial house, having 10 per cent ownership, agreed to subordinate itself to American leadership. The French consortium retained a 50 per cent stake. Even so, the State Department was only with reluctance persuaded by National City personnel to withdraw its objec-

3 See above, 103–104.
4 See Frank A. Vanderlip, President of the National City Bank to Secretary of State Philander Knox, May 1, 1911, quoted in Schmidt, "Occupation," 36.
5 Quoted in Munro, *Dollar Diplomacy*, 251.

tions to the Banque contract. The department finally acceded to the very profitable arrangements whereby the new bank would collect a commission on all monies received and expended on the government's own account, with a further commission for payments in foreign currencies, would purchase a French loan at a mere 72.3 per cent of par (a recent Dominican bond issue had been bought at 98.5 per cent), and would replace the existing and depreciated paper currency with imperfectly secured notes of its own issue.[6] In addition, the Banque became responsible for the service of external debts (in which its managers obviously had a distinct personal interest) and, onerously, the supply — on a monthly basis — of the operating funds of the Haitian government. But the State Department balked at Haiti's own willingness to transfer control over customs revenues to the Banque, and this provision, which was to become an important source of friction, was eliminated from the concession as implemented from 1911.

It immediately became apparent that the directors of the National City Bank regarded Haiti with special concern. Roger L. Farnham, a vice-president of National City, became a central figure in the operations of the Banque Nationale and the national railway. Still, overall American investment (in the railway, the Banque, a cotton plantation, a small copper mine, and other miscellaneous operations) amounted in 1913 to no more than $4 million at a time when total American direct investments in Latin America amounted to $1.7 billion, including $800 million in Mexico and $220 million in Cuba.[7] Considered as an aspect of dollar diplomacy, therefore, Haiti was of only marginal concern to the United States before 1915. Yet it was geographically proximate and, Washington tended to argue, if it fell into the wrong hands, it could prove a source of acute embarrassment to the United States.[8]

---

[6] O. Ernest Moore, "Monetary-Fiscal Policy and Economic Development in Haiti," *Public Finance,* IX (1954), 231.

[7] Max Winkler, *Investments of United States Capital in Latin America* (Boston, 1928), 275.

[8] An influential statement of the importance of Haiti for the strategic posture of the United States was contained in a short book published on the eve of the intervention by a former governor of West Virginia—William A. MacCorkle, *The Monroe Doctrine in its Relation to the Republic of Haiti* (New York, 1915). The author was particularly alive to the German threat to the Panama Canal, noting that Haiti guarded one of the main routes thither. See especially 28–39, 91–96.

President Wilson and William Jennings Bryan, his first Secretary of State, were unusually fearful of strategic embarrassment in the Caribbean. They persuaded themselves that interference and intervention in the affairs of smaller countries represented a legitimate exercise of American power if the implicit and explicit aims of each intervention were demonstrably progressive. The Haitian policy of the Wilson administration, although falling within this rubric and its corollary — that the introduction of American capital into the Caribbean would, in accord with a new Gresham's law, drive out the lucre of Europe — was also directly influenced by the fact that Bryan depended primarily upon one man — Farnham of the Banque Nationale, the railway, and National City — for information about Haiti.[9] At the same time, Farnham and his colleagues contributed to the continued instability of Haiti (by restricting the income of the Haitian government and causing defaults on debts) in an attempt to compel the introduction of an American-run customs receivership and, ultimately, American intervention.[10] There was the Dominican precedent, and there is abundant evidence that Farnham continually pressed the short-lived Haitian governments of 1912–15 for a voluntary cession of their customs houses. As a result of his influence upon Bryan, Farnham was ideally placed to encourage a decision to intervene. He was able to magnify the threat of German and French interference, and, after the outbreak of World War I, to remind Bryan and Wilson of the (then improbable) prospect that Germany would find the Môle St. Nicolas an attractive coaling station for her warships and an ideal harbor for her U-boats. Simultaneously, Farnham and the Banque could tighten the screws internally and stress the dangers of Caribbean instability when advising Bryan and Wilson.

War in Europe intensified the pressures on Haiti. As a proportion of the funds of the Banque Nationale were tied up in France, credit became tighter, and the customary advances to exporters,

9 See Arthur S. Link, *Wilson, the Struggle for Neutrality: 1914–1915* (Princeton, 1960), 522–524; Munro, *Dollar Diplomacy*, 338; and the sources cited in Schmidt, "Occupation," 324–326.
10 Raymond Leslie Buell, "The American Occupation of Haiti," *Foreign Policy Information Service*, V (November 27–December 12, 1929), 336–338, 340; Douglas, "Occupation," 236–237.

and to the *speculateurs,* or middlemen, upon whose efforts the collection of the 1914–15 coffee crop depended, were largely denied. Combined with a shortage of shipping, this meant that the movement of coffee was severely curtailed. Subsequently, too, France ceased all purchases of the Haitian coffee on which the republic's economy largely depended. The Banque, which had always serviced debts before supplying the government with funds for its own purposes, became even more reluctant to provide monthly "allowances." The Banque finally promised funds, but only if the government would accept an American receivership. In turn the Haitian government, driven by financial necessity and alarmed at the quality of its three-piece railway, defaulted on national railroad bonds, threatened to seize the line, and raised punitive loans internally, the majority of which were subscribed to by the German business houses. Politically, too, Haiti had reached the brink of chaos.[11] *Cacos* held successive governments at their mercy and no single man, or group of men, seemed capable of overcoming the structural shortcomings of the country. Certainly, the officials of the Banque, and the equally grasping German and French representatives, actively undermined what was left of Haitian stability. By early 1915 the machinations of these various parties had even resulted in abortive negotiations for a voluntary occupation. Bryan and Wilson, pushed by Farnham and frightened that the Germans and French might — even in the middle of a distant war — choose to intervene, were disposed to act pre-emptively themselves.

Although the excesses of Vilbrun Guillaume Sam's government, the resultant disorders in Port-au-Prince, and the possibility of renewed clashes between the forces of President Sam and Dr. Rosalvo Bobo, his sometime minister of the interior, provided the immediate pretext for American interference in the affairs of Haiti, Wilson's government had long before decided upon the desirability of American occupation and had drafted the necessary plans. Landing operations were sanctioned as early as July 1914, notices of an occupation of Haiti, with spaces for the appropriate day and month, were prepared at about the same time, and there was a "Plan for Landing and Occupying the City of Port au Prince"

11 See above, 105–108.

which dated from November 1914. American warships cruised in Haitian waters throughout this period, and made their presence felt during the abortive negotiations of 1915. Only the departure of Bryan from office in June 1915, his replacement by Robert Lansing, who distrusted Farnham but was also a pronounced Germanophobe, and the outbreak of renewed disorders (any riots would do) were needed to make the contingency plans real. Wilson declared that the intervention in Haiti was a humanitarian response to the total collapse of indigenous abilities to maintain law and order, but a compassionate examination of the available evidence suggests a deeper concern for America's national interests than for her moral responsibilities in a troubled and disturbed world.[12] Furthermore, the decision to intervene was made before the Port-au-Prince mob had violated the French legation and dismembered President Sam. No Americans or American property had been threatened.

The manner by which the intervention was accomplished established a pattern for Haitian-American relations. On July 28, 1915, Admiral William B. Caperton, commanding the U.S.S. *Washington*, landed 330 sailors and Marines in Port-au-Prince. Meeting almost no organized resistance, Caperton very quickly gained command of the city. By the end of the first week, the American military command had made its presence felt in nearly all of Haiti's major towns. Within the first six weeks Marines (there soon were 2029) had taken over the country's customs houses and assumed control of its other administrative organs. By then, too, the Marines had disarmed and dispersed the 1500 *cacos* who had accompanied Bobo to the portals of the capital and had postponed the session of the Haitian legislature which would have elected Bobo president. Caperton, on orders from Wilson, had also started

---

[12] Schmidt, "Occupation," 73, 76–77, who has recently looked at the remaining documents, makes a good case for this conclusion. He disagrees with the sense of Munro, *Dollar Diplomacy*, 351–354, who seems inclined to accept the rhetoric of America's decision to intervene at face value. See also Dantès Bellegarde, *La Résistance Haitienne* (Montreal, 1937), 35; Link, *Wilson*, 527, 534, 549; Montague, *Haiti*, 211, which supports Schmidt. In examining the reasons why the United States was willing to intervene, it is relevant to remember that both Lansing and Daniels held blacks in low esteem. For interesting quotations and discussion, see Logan, *Haiti and Dominican*, 126–127.

searching for a suitable substitute. Both Wilson and Lansing knew that the American occupation rested upon no legally secure ground; instead of straightforward direct rule by the military, they sought to install a pliable Haitian government which could be counted upon to cooperate with the United States and, most importantly, to sign a treaty of abnegation. Philippe Sudre Dartiguenave, the mulatto president of the Senate, offered himself as president after three other distinguished Haitians declined to sully their patriotism and Bobo had been rejected as a candidate by Caperton's chief emissary. "For you," he told Bobo, "I have nothing but kindly feelings . . . but Admiral Caperton directs me to inform you that you are not a candidate for the Haitian presidency. And further, that instead of being a patriot, you are a menace and a curse to your country." [13]

The election of an acquiescent president was only the beginning of American involvement. Widely expressed disaffection in Port-au-Prince, and Dartiguenave's own anxieties, encouraged Caperton to declare martial law (censorship accompanied it) on September 3, 1915. And "martial law," as an American editor later wrote, "is martial law. It cannot be camouflaged into a tea-party or a benefit performance." [14] This state, which lasted until 1929, permitted political offenders to be dealt with according to American military codes (military justice in contemporary Haiti, which is widely used for political offenders, is still based on U.S. naval regulations).[15] Martial law, the threat of military pressure, and the withholding of budgetary support also facilitated the passage through the reluctant Haitian legislature on November 11, 1915 (the U.S. Senate ratified it in February 1916) of a treaty which,

[13] Edward Latimer Beach, "Admiral Caperton in Haiti," unpub. typescript (1919), 57, privately held. Captain Beach was the emissary. Despite this conversation, and Caperton's unmistakably coercive comments to the legislature before the election (*ibid.*, 70–71), Beach persisted in believing that "no Senator or Deputy was coerced, or ever had any intimation as to whom Admiral Caperton desired elected" (*ibid.*, 55). For an eyewitness account of the first stages of the occupation, see Beach, "From Annapolis to Scapa Flow," unpub. typescript (1919), 252–256, privately held. On the election see also A. A. Vandergrift (ed. Robert B. Asprey), *Once a Marine* (New York, 1964), 47.
[14] Ernest H. Gruening, "Haiti Under American Occupation," *Century Magazine*, CIII (1922), 845.
[15] See below, 358.

technically at least, legitimized the occupation.[16] It provided for unquestioned American control of Haiti's finances, the consequent appointment of American advisers and receivers, the establishment of an American-officered constabulary (the Gendarmerie d'Haiti), the creation of American-run public health and public works services, and daily supervision of nearly all other aspects of the government of the republic. No relations with other nations could be entered into without American consent. Article XIV even permitted renewed American intervention at any time (during the duration — extended from ten to twenty years in 1917 — of the treaty) for any reasons.[17]

By 1916 the Americans had — unwittingly — laid the groundwork for a fairly typical colonial enterprise, with its usual poorly thought out mixture of idealism, paternalism, and benevolent and not-so-benevolent brutality, reliance upon coercion, hypocrisy, and double standards of conduct and morality. As in so many African colonial ventures, in Haiti there was also confusion about whether to depend upon indirect or direct methods of rule and with regard to the precise aims of the occupation: Was it intended merely to bring order to a land racked by anarchy? Or were there more long-run goals? Did the Americans intend to nurture Haiti economically until it could reach the point of what can now be called developmental takeoff? Or was it more important to open up Haiti to American investors? Did the Americans hope to remake the political structure of Haiti? Were they making Haiti safe for democracy? Definitive answers to these and a number of other obvious questions always proved elusive, but the ways in which answers were suggested, and the very extent to which Americans attended to or neglected these questions, were relevant to the political modernization of Haiti.

---

[16] The following message was sent on September 8, 1915, from Caperton to Captain William Durrell of the U.S.S. *Connecticut*, then stationed at Cap Haitien: "After encountering many difficulties treaty situation . . . looks more favorable than usual. This has been effected by exercising military pressure at propitious moments in the negotiations. Yesterday two members of the cabinet who had blocked negotiations resigned. . . . At present am holding up offensive operations and allowing President time to complete cabinet and try again. Am therefore not yet ready to begin offensive at Cape Haitien but will hold them in abeyance as additional pressure." Documents in Ernest H. Gruening collection.
[17] For the complete treaty, see *The Nation*, CXI (1920), 254–255.

The notion of modernization does not necessarily imply an over-arching framework or a series of carefully wrought programs. The Americans had no grand design for Haiti. Instead, policy-makers in Washington responded to the perceived threat or particular prejudices of the moment, and directed their subordinates in Port-au-Prince accordingly. No one planned, not even — except at lower levels of operations — within the colonial administration in Haiti. Improvisation and random attention to the most immediate problems was the rule, as it has been in most colonial situations. But the Americans were inexperienced colonizers, and the Marine Corps, which provided the local leadership in many spheres of activity and the grand commissar from 1922 to 1930, were more amateur than most. Their horizons, like those of their superiors in Washington, were understandably narrow, and the maintenance of law and order in the district supervised by each rural adminis-trator (a corporal or sergeant in the Marine Corps became an officer in charge of a district in the Gendarmerie) was of primary importance. Funds were short, too, the U.S. Treasury Department objecting during the war years, and afterward as well, to giving aid to Haiti. For all of these reasons, and also because the area was culturally strange to Americans (few of the Marines spoke French), because even doing nothing well was difficult, and be-cause the Marines — unlike administrators in Africa or Asia — could look to no local career and therefore had no long-term stake in Haiti's success, the American occupation was static, planless, and disappointing to those who hoped for the inducement of substan-tial change in a society too long isolated from the main currents of world progress.

During the war and postwar years, the occupying forces treated Haiti as if it were a minor satellite capable of being manipulated at will. A few days after the intervention, Caperton proclaimed that the United States had no object in view "except to insure, establish and help to maintain Haitian independence, and the establishing of a stable and firm government by the Haitian people." [18] But the Americans were more concerned to maintain order, to provide an atmosphere conducive to American investment, and to construct basic public works. After the first year during which the Marine

[18] Quoted in Buell, "Occupation," 345.

Corps managed to buy peace with bribes and to mount successful assaults upon the less mercenary *caco* leaders, conflict in the rural areas of Haiti was kept to a minimum until 1918. During this initial period, however, Marine search-and-destroy operations, which included the spectacular capture of a series of *caco* strongholds, resulted in the loss of Haitian lives sufficient to alarm Washington, which curbed the more enthusiastic field commanders.[19] Thereafter (in common with Puerto Rico and Cuba previously), Haiti was pacified and largely administered by a hastily recruited Gendarmerie, the officers of which were drawn primarily from the Marine ranks and the soldiery from among the undernourished Haitian peasantry. In theory, the Gendarmerie (total strength 336) was responsible to President Dartiguenave, but Smedley D. Butler, the Marine major who became the Gendarmerie's first commandant and its major general after battling the Boxers in China and fighting in Honduras, Nicaragua, Panama, and Mexico, took orders from no Haitian. At least once he publicly manhandled Dartiguenave and, when traveling with the president, he always usurped the best or the only bed.[20]

By 1925 the Gendarmerie numbered 2700, of whom 160 were officers (53 were Haitian), but initially a handful of Marines assumed the military command of the eighteen districts of the republic. Within each they exercised normal police functions, supervised travel and traffic and weights and measures, prevented smuggling, collected vital statistics, enforced the sanitation code, supervised the prisons and, simply speaking, were fully "in charge"

---

[19] The Marines used a variety of tactics to persuade the *cacos* to desist. Bribery was among them. Fifty thousand gourdes was paid to each of 1000 *caco* soldiers in the north after they had proceeded to Gonaïves or Cap Haitien, surrendered their rifles and ammunition, and agreed in writing not to oppose the government of Haiti. Payment was personally made by American officers. For details, see Richard L. Schreadley, "The American Intervention in Haiti," unpub. M.A.D.L. thesis (Fletcher School, 1969), 104–105. For the campaigns, see James H. McCrocklin (ed.), *Garde d'Haiti; 1915–1934: Twenty Years of Organization and Training by the United States Marine Corps* (Annapolis, 1956), 30–37; Lowell Thomas, *Old Gimlet Eye: The Adventures of Smedley D. Butler* (New York, 1933), 181–208; Clyde H. Metcalf, *A History of the United States Marine Corps* (New York, 1939), 380–386; Robert Debs Heinl, Jr., *Soldiers of the Sea: The United States Marine Corps, 1775–1962* (Annapolis, 1962), 174–178.

[20] Frank Freidel, *Franklin D. Roosevelt: The Apprenticeship* (Boston, 1952), 279; Thomas, *Gimlet Eye*, 235.

of their rural fiefs. Like district administrators in colonial Africa, an officer in the Gendarmerie found himself with virtually unlimited power. "He is the judge of practically all civil and criminal cases," wrote a contemporary observer. "He is the paymaster for all funds expended by the national government, he is ex-officio director of the schools, inasmuch as he pays the teachers. He controls the mayor and city council, since they can spend no funds without his O.K. As collector of taxes he exercises a strong influence on all individuals in the community." [21] One Marine, Sergeant (local lieutenant) Faustin E. Wirkus, commanded the subdistrict of the Ile de la Gonave, where he was known as the "White King." [22] In these respects the officers of the Gendarmerie behaved as local Haitian warlords had always behaved. Power came out of the barrel of a gun, or at least from a fat wallet. To Haitians, these white commandants and *chefs de section* were no less arbitrary than their black predecessors. Their probity was probably more evident, but their adherence to wholly unfamiliar, and sometimes incomprehensible, standards often vitiated whatever advantages veracity might promise.

It was their effort to build roads on the cheap (the Haitian government could hardly afford to pay laborers) that embroiled the Marines and the Gendarmerie in fresh hostilities. Aside from a few *pistes* dating from prerevolutionary times, in 1915 Haiti lacked anything that could be called a road. Certainly there were none suitable for automobiles. Yet, by invoking nineteenth-century legislation, which permitted the exaction of three days of free work a year, Butler justified a *corvée* and, by impressing peasants into the service of the state for a few days, weeks, or months of each year, by 1917 had managed to construct a passable road from Port-au-Prince to Gonaïves and Cap Haitien, a distance (then) of 175 miles. However, Haitian peasants were no more receptive to their treatment by gendarmes overseeing recruitment for and work on the roads than were Congolese during the days of King Léopold II. Brutality was not unknown; laborers were roped together in a

[21] Samuel Guy Inman, *Through Santo Domingo and Haiti: A Cruise with the Marines* (New York, 1919), 68–69.
[22] See Faustin E. Wirkus and Taney Dudley, *The White King of La Gonave* (Garden City, 1931); W. B. Seabrook, *The Magic Island* (New York, 1929), 171–226.

manner reminiscent of the slave era, recruits were illegally transported beyond their own districts — particularly from the plains
into the mountains — and the duty of serving in a *corvée* team fell
unequally and too often on the least privileged within each local
community. As Butler reported, "It would not do to ask too many
questions as to how we accomplished this work, it is enough to say,
that the people are satisfied and pleased, everyone from the President down." [23]

Aware of the extent to which the *corvée* was increasing tension in
the rural areas of Haiti, particularly in Jacmel, the Marine commandant abolished it in late 1918. Yet in and around Hinche,
which had always been a troubled district, the major in charge secretly maintained the *corvée* and a concomitant reign of terror
which resulted in the loss of numerous Haitian lives. It was in this
region that the *cacos*, led in part by Charlemagne Peralte and
Benoit Batraville, revolted during the final months of 1918. They
commanded up to 40,000 followers, perhaps only 5000 of whom
were armed (with machetes, pikes, and old rifles). But nearly all,
because of their faith in the efficacy of *vodun* potions, exuded a
sense of invincibility. They proved far tougher than the Gendarmerie, even daring to attack Port-au-Prince. Marine reinforcements, with air support, were needed before Peralte and Batraville
could be shot and the rebellion ended. Slightly more than 2000
Haitians and a few whites were killed during the pacification.
Both sides were guilty of atrocities. One officer estimated that 400
prisoners had been shot.[24] Subsequent investigations indicated, on
the basis of a chain of admittedly circumstantial evidence, that
these were but particularly extreme manifestations of the inability
of the Marines to cope with the frustrations of warfare in Haiti.
Although they overcame the *cacos* in the end, the Marines probably caused more devastation and loss of life than had ten prior

[23] Quoted in Freidel, *Roosevelt*, 282. See also Carl Kelsey, "The American Intervention in Haiti and the Dominican Republic," *Annals of the American Academy
of Political and Social Science*, C (1922), 137; Schmidt, "Occupation," 125–127.
[24] Major T. C. Turner, quoted in the *New York Times*, October 27, 1921; Ernest H.
Gruening, "The Senators Visit Haiti and Santo Domingo," *Nation*, CXIV (January
4, 1922), 8; Buell, "Occupation," 376. For the campaign, see Heinl, *Soldiers*, 234–
245.

civil wars involving *cacos*.[25] Their methods were also seen to be squarely within the Haitian tradition; once again oppression had been coupled with the exercise of naked force. And, for the first time in a century, the agents and the ostensible benefactors had been whites.

On the civil front, the actions of the Americans further confirmed Haitian notions of public responsibility, the meaning and personalization of power, and the authoritarian, self-serving character of a ruling class. Despite the expectations of at least nominal independence — or of independence within a context of interdependence — with which President Dartiguenave might justifiably have commenced his tenure in office, he found his American advisers unwilling, for the most part, to share more than a minute portion of their power. Only lip service was paid to the concepts of trusteeship and tutelage which were the ultimate justifications for the occupation, and at no time during the first seven years of American responsibility for Haiti's destiny were the representatives of the ruling power willing to accept and honor indigenous political sensitivities. Even President Dartiguenave, a client wholly dependent upon the physical and financial backing of the United States, visibly chafed against the tight rein with which his government was held in check. Whenever he protested, or tried to ignore or modify American requests, he was reminded of the ease with which he could be replaced. Although there was continuity of institutional forms, with Haitians occupying executive positions, and the treaty of 1915 offered a legal excuse for the American presence, it was daily re-emphasized to Haitians that whites were once again in complete command. The local Marine Corps brigadier and the national financial adviser gave the orders which were obeyed by Haitian officials, and Haitians of all classes, and eventually executed by other American "advisers" in the towns and the rural districts. It is also true that from the point of view of the Haitian peasant, the initial impact of the occupation, aside from the *corvée*, was probably minimal. He had always been ruled arbitrarily, and the substitution of white for black overseers affected

25 But see the McCormick Senate Committee *Hearings,* quoted in Millspaugh, *Control,* 95–96, which whitewash these episodes.

him only after the Marines had managed to entrench themselves in the countryside and begun to interfere in heavy-handed ways with traditional agricultural, marketing, and religious modes of behavior. The townsman was more intimately involved with Americans, obviously experienced the impact of the occupation more intensely, and, especially if he were a member of the mulatto and emergent black elite, felt psychologically threatened by the intimidating presence of a superimposed regime. For many, it denied hard-won personal esteem, and contributed to a widespread feeling of failure and inferiority which discriminatory behavior served to reinforce.

In the political sphere, it was evident that the Americans expected and would, if necessary, compel the Haitian government to respond faithfully and promptly to the dictates of its advisers. The direction of the policy of the United States was made perfectly clear in a letter from the Department of the Navy to its representative in Haiti: The United States was prepared to "support Dartiguenave so long as he conducted his administration in accordance with correct principles and the agreements entered into between Haiti and the United States." Hostile actions on the part of legislators would be assumed to be "activities of a revolutionary and disorderly political character," and no *putsches* or *coups* could be countenanced.[26]

The occupying forces permitted the election of a new legislature in early 1917 (the former having been dissolved in 1916) and apparently felt no need to influence the result. But when the deputies and senators proved reluctant to declare war against Germany, or to accept without question a Haitian constitution drafted in Washington which, *inter alia,* for the first time since 1806 permitted foreigners to own land, a second dissolution seemed inevitable.[27] The constitution also created a council of state, the twenty-one members of which would be appointed and subject

[26] Quoted in Munro, *Dollar Diplomacy,* 368–369.
[27] Franklin D. Roosevelt, then Assistant Secretary of the Navy, claimed in 1920 personally to have written the constitution. But he exaggerated, for it was drafted by F. L. Mayer of the State Department after only desultory consultation with the Department of the Navy. See Freidel, *Roosevelt,* 284; Schreadley, "Intervention," 122–123. For the prohibition against foreign ownership, see above, 55.

to removal by the president, to perform legislative functions; permitted judges to be removed for cause during the six months following the promulgation of the constitution; stipulated that treaties were superior to laws of the assembly; and, by a special article, validated all of the decrees of the occupation. To the Haitians, foreign ownership connoted plantations, renewed serfdom, and a class of landless laborers. To Americans, alienation of land was essential if investors were to be attracted to Haiti. German merchants had evaded the letter of the Haitian law by marrying locally; Americans, particularly the representatives of syndicates, could hardly be encouraged to enter into such alliances. Nor would the Americans permit the Haitians to revise the proposed constitution to require a period of residence before purchase of land could be legal. Again, the Germans would benefit. When the National Assembly persisted, drafting a document of its own, Dartiguenave authorized its dissolution ("In case the President did not sign the decree," testified the Marine Corps commandant, "he was to be informed as coming from me, that I would suppress the National Assembly myself and would recommend the establishment of a military government"), a decision gleefully enforced by Smedley Butler.[28] (Haiti was given no second chance until 1929, when the election of another assembly was countenanced.)

In lieu of legislative approval, the Americans decided to permit Haitians direct democracy. The constitution was to be approved by the voters, 95 per cent of whom were illiterate and, according to a State Department memorandum, "ignorant in most cases of what they were doing," in the spring of 1918.[29] Beforehand the Gendarmerie gave receptions and barbecues to encourage a favorable response and, where necessary, used less tactful means. It distributed the ballots, supervised the actual polling places, and treated opposition as prima facie evidence of rebellion against authority. No matter how the American administration sought to explain it, the final vote (98,225 for and 768 against) tended to reflect the nature of the plebiscite's sponsorship. Sixty-seven of ninety-six

---

[28] Quoted in Douglas, "Occupation," 250. Butler's position is stated in Thomas, *Gimlet Eye*, 216–217.
[29] Quoted in Schmidt, "Occupation," 122. See also Buell, "Occupation," 349.

polling places cast no negative votes whatsoever. Later Josephus
Daniels, then Secretary of the Navy, told Roosevelt that, "in the
light of experience [I expect that] we both regret the necessity of
denying even a semblance of 'self-determination' in our control of
Haiti. . . ." [30]

Although Wilson was exceedingly embarrassed at the Paris
Peace Conference by Haiti's subject status and, from there, even
sought the immediate withdrawal of American troops, officials on
the spot argued forcefully and successfully for more rather than
fewer Marines to combat the *cacos*. They held the government of
Dartiguenave on an even tighter leash than before, having already
managed to assume control of many, if not all, of the important
functions of his government. They gave orders in routine as well
as policy matters, even directed Haitian personnel, and denied
Dartiguenave the weapons of patronage and the right to dispose at
will of funds collected locally. The financial adviser — who from
1919 to 1922 was John McIlhenny, a friend of Roosevelt's from
Louisiana who seems to have been more concerned with making
successful personal investments than in developing Haiti — insisted on supervising the disbursement of all local funds, including
some not covered by the treaty. Americans directed the appointment and removal of ministers of finance, prepared the budgets,
and told the Banque Nationale when and when not to give monies
to the government. Whenever he deemed it necessary, the minister in charge of the United States legation peremptorily directed
American officials to disregard new legislation enacted by the
council of state. He and the financial adviser also withheld the
salaries of individuals, including the president, when they wished
the council to enact laws to which Haitians might raise serious objection. The ability to exert this kind of pressure proved important when the National City Bank desired to obtain complete control of the Banque Nationale and a more favorable and flexible
rewording of its charter. It proved valuable during the renegoti-
ation of Farnham's concession for the generally useless national

30 Daniels to Roosevelt, July 15, 1933, quoted in E. David Cronon, *Josephus Daniels
in Mexico* (Madison, 1960), 68. Many of the criticisms of the plebiscite, with supporting testimony, were contained in a long speech given in the Senate by William
E. Borah of Idaho, June 19, 1922, *Congressional Record*. For excerpts from the
1918 constitution, see Millspaugh, *Control*, 222–225.

railway.[31] The Americans in charge further ignored or refused to permit the execution of decisions of the Haitian courts which, as British colonial governments in Africa were wont to declare, were repugnant to natural law and justice — or simply inconvenient. Instead, the occupying forces brought offenders and cases before its own courts, or even detained them without trial, procedures which Haitians naturally feared and resented. Finally, when even Dartiguenave could stand no more, and procrastinated more than before (the immediate issue was the authorization of a Haitian-backed National City tendered loan for the financially questionable purpose of external debt-consolidation and a proposal to give the Banque a monopoly on the importation of foreign currency)[32] the Americans in 1922 simply replaced him with Louis Borno.

The accession of Borno coincided with the appointment of an American high commissioner with authority over all officials of the occupation. It also inaugurated what one of the treaty officials subsequently called the Americo-Haitian joint dictatorship.[33] Brigadier-General John Henry Russell, a Georgian who had commanded the Marines in Haiti during the war against the *cacos*, became the first high commissioner despite a widespread assumption in Washington that the assertion of civilian authority was desirable.[34] Russell was untrained in the arts of colonial rule and had little experience of the worlds of finance, business, and civil administration. He also represented "all that the *élite* had found distasteful in the first phase of the intervention." [35] But he was upright, honest, and direct. And the treaty and the constitution notwithstanding, he ruled (the word is not too strong) Haiti with the firm, unyielding hand of a practiced disciplinarian who cherishes each measure of authority.

The 250 Americans of the treaty services, although employed by,

31 For the scandal, see Douglas, "Railway," 60.
32 Sténio Vincent, *Outline of the Financial History of the Republic of Haiti* (Port-au-Prince, 1939), 17–21; Marc E. Malval, *La Politique Financière Extérieure de la République d'Haiti depuis 1910: La Banque Nationale de la République d'Haiti ou nos Emprunts Extérieurs* (Paris, 1932), 99–101.
33 This is the phrase of Arthur C. Millspaugh (*Control*, 107). Millspaugh was the financial adviser from 1927 to 1929.
34 Nothing in his daughter's book (Brooke Russell Astor, *Patchwork Child* [New York, 1962]) clarifies the decision-making process involved. Nor does she possess any of her father's papers.
35 Montague, *Haiti*, 239.

paid by, and responsible to the government of Haiti and its various ministries, were all directly answerable to Russell. Nothing was done by them, even if commanded by Haitians, if Russell disapproved. Only he could correspond, for example, with Washington or the president of Haiti. At the same time, if the president of Haiti ordered one of his American employees, the commandant of the Gendarmerie for example, to act, the commandant knew better than to obey without the express sanction of his high commissioner. Russell also drafted all Haitian legislation, negotiated contracts with foreign (especially American) companies, took charge of all educational, agricultural, and sanitary matters, constructed the roads, and collected the revenues. He was omnipotent, a dictator constrained only by harassed officials in the State Department (it is an axiom that men on the colonial spot are at a considerable advantage; the bureaucrats at home can only hesitate, never initiate without the cooperation of their commissar) and the degree to which he relied for political reasons upon the talents of President Borno.

Like his predecessor, Borno was a mulatto. A poet, he had served as Dartiguenave's minister of foreign affairs and minister of finance. He was, moreover, an ideal choice as chief executive during the heyday of American rule, for, viscerally and intellectually, he believed in the authoritarian rule of the wise. For him, dissent was divisive, and the presence of the Americans was welcomed as a means of ensuring the suppression of the popular will — to the extent that it could be expressed in Haiti — and support for the ascendancy of the light-skinned bureaucratic aristocracy.[36] For these as well as personal reasons, Borno agreed to become president despite the fact that no national elections had been held in Haiti since 1917, and the president would be selected by the council of state, an appointive body unusually responsive to the occupiers' will. The same council, loyal to Borno (who packed it with supporters) and the commissioner, reselected Borno as president in 1926. He apparently enjoyed being a creature of the Americans, showing few overt signs of hostility. "Mr. Borno," wrote an American visitor of unquestioned integrity, ". . . avers that the situ-

[36] See Borno, quoted in Davis, *Democracy*, 250; Borno, quoted in Schmidt, "Occupation," 254; Buell, "Occupation," 387. But see Bellegarde, *Résistance*, 60–61.

ation calls for a dictatorship under us and him, and quite openly defends it. He impressed me as being a highly cultured, vindictive, patriotic, personally ambitious, shrewd, and dictatorial man, lacking in balance." [37] Occasionally, when Borno failed to cooperate with alacrity, the financial adviser simply brought him to heel by expediently withholding his pay. It was this kind of behavior which epitomized the joint dictatorship; the high commissioner ruled and the Haitian president, perhaps less supinely than he might, acquiesced.[38]

It was during the tranquil, comparatively prosperous era of the joint dictatorship (Russell misleadingly tried to compare his governing of Haiti to Lord Cromer's activities under the Anglo-Egyptian condominium) that Americo-Haitian efforts were devoted as never before to the amelioration of Haitian life. Any assessment of the impact of the American occupation depends largely upon an appreciation of what the northern modernizers sought to, could, and did achieve in terms of material and societal betterment. In turn, no appreciation is possible without an understanding of the profound, self-imposed, financial constraints within which the occupiers opted to act. In common with other colonies of the day, Haiti could look to its temporary rulers for no direct budgetary or developmental support. Aid was not then in vogue, and metropolitan treasuries expected their off-shore dependencies to finance improvements out of locally generated, but better managed, revenues. Deficit spending was almost unknown and almost never approved.

In Haiti's case, the United States admittedly did pay the salaries of a peace-keeping force, and of advisers seconded to the Gendarmerie (after 1928, the Garde), and the treaty services. But the total salary bill was small, and further sums, amounting to about 13 per cent of local Haitian expenditures on wages and salaries, were paid out of Haiti's income to Americans (many of whom received two monthly checks). This last was by no means the most significant non-developmental drain on Haiti's limited monetary resources. Much more influential were the external debt repay-

[37] Clarence K. Streit, "Haiti: Intervention in Operation," *Foreign Affairs,* VI (1928), 626.
[38] Millspaugh is otherwise critical, but he still asserted (*Control,* 107) that Borno was "far from being merely a politician or a puppet."

ment policies established by the American financial advisers. The
United States, according to the Roosevelt corollary to the Monroe
Doctrine, had already promised to be garnisher to the world, and
American economic operations in Haiti completely fulfilled the
spirit as well as the letter of President Theodore Roosevelt's
intent. Between 1922 and 1929, before the world economy fell dramatically, the American advisers managed to produce yearly budgetary surpluses by drastically reducing local expenditures and collecting customs and other revenues efficiently. Naturally, the
curtailing of local expenditures limited the funds available for developmental purposes, but even more damaging was the insistence
that the repayment of external debts should have priority over all
other possible uses for Haitian funds. This dictum was adhered to
rigidly by a succession of financial advisers, all of whom had previously served in a similar capacity in other parts of the underdeveloped world; their extremely conservative policies were directed to
the rapid amortization of the debt, most of which was held by
Americans. They even used the accumulated budgetary surpluses
to retire the debt far in advance of what was required and, in terms
of more modern notions of debt management, desirable. In 1927,
for example, of the annual expenditures of about $7 million,
nearly 40 per cent was devoted to servicing the debt, about 20 per
cent to the Gendarmerie, and about 21 per cent to public works.
Public health, agricultural, and educational services divided the
remainder. Large cash reserves were also built up for debt repayment — in anticipation of the lean years that eventually did come
— which enabled Haiti (supervised by Americans until 1947) to
continue paying off its bonds while all other Latin American nations defaulted. As the leading adviser admitted in a fit of candor,
satisfying external creditors starved Haiti of capital improvements.
An American presidential commission came to the same conclusion: "It might have been better to have reduced the taxation, especially the export tax, and left the debt to work itself out during
its normal term, thus keeping more money in the country where
experience had shown it was badly needed." [39]

---

[39] Report of the Forbes Commission, 1930, quoted in Schmidt, "Occupation," 218,
where supporting data for much of the discussion of debt repayment will also be
found.

If funds for modernization were scarce, at least the Americans used the few resources that were available with imagination and reasonable efficiency. Although the *corvée* had resurrected a number of French-built roads and transformed deteriorated bridle paths into vehicular ways between the towns, the provision of a basic infrastructure was, as late as 1922, still an obvious necessity. By the end of 1923 the Department of Public Works had linked all of the major towns except Jacmel to Port-au-Prince. By the end of 1924, 650 miles of major roadway (from Ouanaminthe to Cap Haitien to Port-au-Prince to Cayes, with a spur from Port-au-Prince to Belladère on the Dominican border) were being maintained and, by the end of 1929, 1600 miles (mostly gravel) had been completed. Fifteen steel, 68 concrete, and 127 wooden bridges had also been erected, these improvements together contributing to the ease with which peasants could market their crops and, in time, desert the rural for the urban areas of the country. In 1929 about 3000 automobiles and numerous buses were registered in Haiti. Pan American Airways also began flying from Miami to Bowen Field in Port-au-Prince.[40]

There were other improvements and innovations for which the Americans were responsible, not least of which was the telephone system, with its two automatic exchanges (the first in the hemisphere), 22 other exchanges, 1205 miles of long distance telephone cable, and, by 1929, 1200 subscribers. Irrigation canals also had been constructed, although the project to irrigate the Artibonite Valley (as the French had done) had faltered and only 206,000 acre-feet of water were being delivered to 8000 farms. Wharves and lighthouses, school buildings, Gendarmerie outposts, barracks, hospitals, a courthouse, and a college were also constructed, and clean water was supplied to 10 towns and 64 villages.[41]

The period of the American occupation was by and large a prosperous one for Haitian exports, but the prosperity was due almost entirely to very favorable movements in coffee prices. From 1910–14 to 1924–28, the purchasing power of exports (in 1957–59 dol-

[40] U.S. State Department, Division of Latin American Affairs, "Report Covering Haiti" (January 1, 1930), mimeo. 69–70; Douglas, "Occupation of Haiti," 376; Millspaugh, *Control*, 158–159.
[41] State Department, "Report," 68–70; Millspaugh, *Control*, 159. For the comparable 1960's figures, see above, 6.

lars) rose from $21.94 million to $33.96 million, or, in per capita terms, from $12.30 to $15.76. But the quantity of exports rose only 5 per cent, a small decline in coffee being offset by an increase in cotton and the reappearance of sugar in the export lists.

"From sheer necessity," reads an official report, the occupation also assumed responsibility for hygiene and sanitation.[42] There were a few understaffed and poorly maintained hospitals, no systematic program of preventive medicine, and a number of endemic diseases, the most important of which were tuberculosis, malaria, yaws, syphilis, and hookworm. By the end of 1929, the Haitian Public Health Service, organized and directed by medical personnel from the U.S. Navy, employed more than 2000 doctors and technicians, 37 of whom were American and 66 French (nearly all nuns). Thirteen modern hospitals (the largest with 400 beds) and 153 rural clinics were staffed and, with the assistance of the Rockefeller Foundation but against the vehement opposition of the Haitian elite, the National School of Medicine was reorganized and a few Haitian doctors encouraged to obtain advanced training in the United States. " 'Almost overwhelming' is the only term to aptly describe the mass of people frequently crowding their way through the clinic gates," reported one of the energetic American directors.[43] In addition, swamps were drained, streets cleaned, garbage collected, dogs and humans inoculated, abattoirs policed, public and private latrines constructed, and an attack begun on major diseases and the general ignorance which had contributed to their spread.

The quality and direction of education were of concern to Americans despite the failure of the treaty of 1915 to sanction an advisory or supervisory role in this sphere. The Haitians recorded some 46,000 students in all schools in 1913, only slightly more than the previous peak in 1895, but considerably more than in 1905. The last few years before 1913 had witnessed considerable increases in budgets for education, and during 1913–15 these averaged about $400,000.[44] (How much was actually spent on education during these tumultuous years is another question.) During

---

42 State Department, "Report," 73.
43 Captain Kent C. Melhorn, report, quoted in Millspaugh, *Control*, 140.
44 U.S. Commission on Education in Haiti, *Report* (Washington, 1930), 45.

the entire period of the occupation, this allocation to the Haitian-controlled Department of Public Instruction remained about the same, even though prices and population increased substantially. Yet the Haitian-run schools still managed to increase enrollments, both from 1913 to 1920 and from 1920 to 1930, as is shown in Table 2. As always, the enrollment statistics for rural public schools were open to serious question.[45] Particularly noteworthy in Table 2 is the expansion of private schools and national religious schools (which charged a substantial tuition to the students in addition to receiving money from the state), and the decline in public secondary enrollment. These changes, plus the rise in urban primary enrollment, attest to the strong desire of Haitian parents to educate their children and the willingness of those with money to pay for private instruction.

Table 2

Enrollments by Type of School, 1920–30
(Figures in thousands of students)

		1920	*1930*
I. Urban Schools			
A. Publicly Supported			
1. Lay Public — Primary		21.9	27.2
2. National Religious — Primary and Secondary		7.7	12.9
3. Lay Public — Secondary		2.0	1.3
B. Private — Primary and Secondary		9.2	13.6
(Private Secondary)		(2.9)	(4.2)
C. Vocational (Service Technique)		0	2.4
II. Rural Schools (all publicly supported primary schools)			
A. Lay Public		22.0	27.3
B. Presbyteral		4.8	9.6
C. Service Technique Schools		0	6.9
Total		67.7	101.1
Total supported by Haitian Department of Instruction		58.5	78.3

Sources: 1920 data from Leyburn, *People,* 282–283, and Edner Brutus, *Instruction Publique en Haiti, 1492–1945* (Port-au-Prince, 1948), 480. 1930 data from Commission, *Report,* 8–9.

[45] Leyburn, *People,* 282–283.

Rather than bolster the Haitian-run system, which the Americans deemed (with some justice) corrupt, inefficient, and misguided, they preferred to emphasize and support vocational and agricultural instruction. They scorned formally educated, Francified blacks, presuming that a distaste for manual labor was revolutionary in intent. The American director of the Service Technique de l'Agriculture et d'Enseignement Professionel, which was established in 1923, sought, like Booker T. Washington in the United States (and but a few Haitians), to train men to appreciate the dignity of honest toil: "The strong, steady, and skilled hand is the first and primary requisite of all industry," he said. "Give us men who know labor. Give us men who are not ashamed of honest toil." On another occasion Freeman made it clear that he wanted to try to turn young Haitian minds toward industrial production and cause them "to think of that phase of [their] life rather than to keep before [their] mind[s] always the possibility of going to the city and taking . . . a 'white collar' job." [46]

The educational branch of the Service Technique (which was created in 1923) received (after 1925) substantially more money than the Haitian Department. Many of the funds were used for school construction — by 1929 there were eight urban vocational schools (with new buildings and equipment) and sixty farm schools (most with new buildings),[47] but the operating expenses were also many times higher than in Haitian-run schools, largely because the salaries of the American and Haitian teachers in the Service were much higher than in the other branch.[48] Annual operating expenses per pupil in 1930 were 392 gourdes in the Service's industrial (vocational) schools, and 97 gourdes in its rural schools; for the Haitian-run schools, the figures ranged from 44 to 4.9 gourdes (see Table 3). (The 4.9 gourdes for the rural public

[46] Speeches of George Fouche Freeman, March 25, 1925, quoted in Schmidt, "Occupation," 243; in Schreadley, "Intervention," 250. For American scorn, see John Henry Russell, quoted in Charles E. Chapman, "The Development of the Intervention in Haiti," *Hispanic American Historical Review*, VII (1927), 315. Haitians also claimed responsibility for initiating the vocational program of the Service Technique. See Brutus, *Instruction Publique*, 498–499; Joseph Justin, *Etude sur les Institutions Haitiennes* (Paris, 1894–95), 2v.
[47] Commission, *Report*, 9, 31.
[48] Logan, "Education," 443–444.

Table 3

Budget Allocations and Expenditures per Pupil, 1930
(Figures in thousands of gourdes; thousands of students)

	Lay Public	Nat'l Relig.	Serv. Tech.	Total
I. Primary Schools				
A. Urban				
Expenditure	378	567	946	1891
Pupils	22.8	12.9	2.4	
Expenditure per Pupil	16.6	43.9	392	
B. Rural				
Expenditure	134	58	666	858
Pupils	27.3	9.6	6.9	
Expenditure per Pupil	4.9	6.1	97.1	
II. Secondary Schools (all urban)				
Expenditure	344	98	0	442
III. Higher Education				
Expenditure	50		900	950
Expenditure (under I-III)	906	723	2512	4141

Sources: Expenditures were calculated from Commission, *Report*, 48. For pupils, see Table 2.

schools tells us much about the quality of education being dispensed there. The rural religious schools, it must be remembered, received additional funds from the church.) Even allowing for high start-up costs for the Service's industrial schools, the disproportion in the budget allocations is striking.

Although the schools of the Service Technique were not in operation long enough (total enrollment was 825 in 1925, 5000 in 1927, and 8300 in 1930) to give the "vocational education theory" a thorough test, it seems likely that the students in the American-run vocational schools learned little that was economically useful beyond reading and writing. Despite the literary and classical orientation of the Haitian curriculum, probably a great deal more for Haitian education could have been done by putting the Service Technique's educational budget (around $600,000 annually in the late 1920's) into the Haitian-run school system. But in 1929 all educational expenditures were still only 11 per cent of the total budget, as against 38 per cent in Puerto Rico;[49] the latter island, with half of Haiti's population, was spending $4 million to Haiti's $1 million.[50] On this kind of budget, no educational transformation was possible.

The central school of agriculture at Damien — a miniature Tuskegee — was undoubtedly the Service Technique's most useful and lasting educational accomplishment. Haitian students were trained in modern techniques, and, despite the difficulty of teaching elite students to work with their hands, agricultural science as a discipline has in Haiti today a prestige which owes much to the Service Technique.

The Service Technique also attempted to modernize Haitian agriculture directly. By sponsoring the first soil and geological surveys, it provided a firm basis for subsequent experimentation. It encouraged the cultivation of Virginia tobacco and, behind a hastily erected tariff barrier, Haiti by 1928 was self-sufficient and entertained expectations of becoming an exporter. The Service's five experimental stations (there also were a model dairy, a cattle breeding station, etc.) investigated the potential of vine rubber (particularly during World War II) and maize, played a prominent role in the development of the world's most extensive sisal plantation near Fort Liberté on Haiti's northern coast [51] and, on demonstration farms and in the field, used a variety of means (including an extension service) to bring about the improved care of coffee trees. The Service sponsored legislation designed to standardize the grading of coffee beans, and hence their marketability. (Private investors meanwhile were active in the promotion of sugar, pineapple, castor oil, and cotton production, and each received assistance from the Service.) In cooperation with other American-run treaty agencies, it also examined the problems posed for peasants by insecurity of tenure and excessive fragmentation of holdings. A cadastral survey was begun. But at no point did the

49 *Ibid.*, 440–441; Montague, *Haiti*, 258–259.
50 Inman, *Through Santo Domingo*, 76.
51 See Robert L. Pettigrew, *The Story of Fort Liberty and the Dauphin Plantation* (Richmond, 1958), 86–145ff; below, 298.

Service really find means to bridge the vast gap between American and Haitian technology. They adapted only partially to local conditions, and made the usual assumptions of indigenous ignorance which, as in Africa and Asia, were self-defeating. Culturally, they took too readily as given that Western incentives would easily motivate peasants whose whole way of life had been predicated on an escape into isolation. There is a further factor that limited the effectiveness of the Service Technique: much of its research and experimentation presumed the investment of large sums of private capital, and the establishment of plantations. But only a very few Americans were, in fact, induced to invest in the land, and the onset of the Depression discouraged additional investments (except in bananas in the north where the Standard Fruit and Steamship Company obtained a monopolistic concession).

Of all the factors that vitiated the accomplishment of American ameliorative agricultural, educational, and medical objectives in Haiti, prejudice probably proved most damaging. Its existence alienated and hence forfeited the cooperation of the elite without gaining the support of either the upwardly mobile blacks or the peasants. That the discrimination inherent in life in the United States should have been extended to Haiti occasions no surprise, but the fact that Southerners predominated in the ranks of the treaty services (leading officials were from Mississippi and Louisiana) and were present among the officers of the Marine Corps (and, conceivably in larger numbers, among enlisted personnel)[52] would only have accentuated the extension of Southern stereotypes and values to Haiti. An early commandant of the Marine detachment in Haiti set the tone of the occupation when he described the local elite as "real nigger and no mistake — There are some very

[52] It has been demonstrated that the percentage of Southerners in the total United States population (1916–32) was greater than the percentage of officers of Southern descent in the Marine Corps and the percentage of Southern-born officers serving in Haiti, but nothing is known of the origins of the enlisted men who, as officers in the Gendarmerie, were in the vanguard of Americo-Haitian relations. These conclusions are based on Ann Hurst, "Southerners to Handle Haitians?" unpub. undergraduate paper (Wellesley, 1964), as cited and discussed in Hans Schmidt, "The United States Occupation of Haiti: Racial and Cultural Antagonisms," 16; Robert Debs Heinl, Jr., "Haiti: Impacts of American Occupation, 1915–1934," 1, both unpub. papers presented at a Center for Haitian Studies colloquium (Cambridge, Mass., April 1969).

fine looking, well educated polished men here but they are real
nigs beneath the surface." Another commandant ascribed to the
elite the "general characteristics of such people the world over —
vain, loving praise, excitable, changeable, beyond belief illogical,
and double-faced." They were men whose "sincerity must always
be doubted . . . [for] no matter how much veneer and polish a
Haitian may have, he is absolutely savage under the skin and
under strain reverts to type." [53]

The prejudice implied by the above extracts was institutionalized in Haiti by the erection of a color bar. After white American
women arrived in the dependency in 1916, social contact between
Americans and Haitians decreased markedly and the hotels, restau-
rants, and club catering to Americans became off limits to Haitians. Even Haitian presidents were excluded from the American
club, and only male Americans attended ceremonies in the presidential palace. Military personnel made a fetish of segregation,
while businessmen were more relaxed; but Americans of any per-
suasion who persisted in fraternizing openly with Haitians were
ostracized and vilified.[54] Yet Americans, like fellow Anglo-Saxons
in Africa, took Haitian mistresses, were responsible for the growth
of prostitution in Port-au-Prince and Cap Haitien (where the Marines were garrisoned), and appeared uncultured and boorish to
the Haitian elite; as the crowning insult, few spoke French flu-
ently, or even cared to learn. There were some Americans, admittedly, and a number in the upper ranks of the administration, who
endeavored to dismantle racial barriers and cement cultural ties.
But their efforts were for the most part viewed as idiosyncratic exceptions.

Haitians of nearly all classes came to resent the occupation, a
sentiment which was hardly modified by the failure of the Americans to prepare either Haitians or Haiti for the occupiers' departure (due in 1936, according to the amended treaty, but clearly

53 Colonels Littleton Waller Tazewell Waller and Eli K. Cole, quoted in Schmidt,
"Antagonisms," 17–18.
54 See Edna Taft, A Puritan in Voodoo-Land (Philadelphia, 1938), 94; Seabrook,
Magic Island, 127–134, 145–149, 155–156, 166–167; Addie Hunton and Emily Greene
Balch, "Racial Relations," in Balch, Occupied Haiti, 115–117; Gruening, "Haiti
Under American Occupation," 837.

capable of being delayed). Russell, the high commissioner, maintained to the end of his tenure a stern, unyielding, essentially narrow-minded approach to his clients. They were to be administered, not involved. He made no attempt to broaden the political base. Consensus was not something a colonial administrator, in Africa or in Haiti, knew how to seek. Despite pressure from the State Department, no attempt was made to welcome Haitian participation in the political process, nor in the preliminary planning (what little there was) for the resumption of *de facto* Haitian sovereignty. Neither the treaty services nor the leaders of the Gendarmerie had begun training their replacements — as in most of Africa, whites demonstrated no inclination to make indirect rule effective. Where elections had been held in the communes they had been rigged by the Americans, the ballot was still denied on a national level, and the president continued to rule by fiat and to act as a foil for the occupation. Censorship of the press, and of incoming and outgoing telegrams, was heavy-handed, and at any one time several editors were apt to be languishing in jail.[55] By 1928, no one in authority was paying even perfunctory obeisance to the original lofty moral justifications for the American intervention. As tutors, the Americans disillusioned those Haitians who had hoped to learn and angered the vast, cynical majority.

With a share of power, upward mobility, and affirmation of dignity denied to all but Borno's clique and other sycophants, disillusion inevitably hardened into despair when Russell began to entrench rather than uproot American authority. In 1927 the joint dictatorship proposed to amend the constitution so as to permit the executive to abrogate the life tenure of members of the judiciary and replace them (during a twelve-month period after the passage of the amendment) at will. Other amendments would have permitted Borno's presidential term to be extended from four to six years (the State Department later refused to let Borno continue), allowed the council of state to regulate the press and trial by jury, reduced the term of office of senators from six to four years, and sanctioned the levying of taxes on communes without their con-

[55] See Georges Sylvain, *Dix Années de Lutte pour la Liberté, 1915–1925* (Port-au-Prince, 1925), II, 197–207.

sent. Despite the unwillingness of the occupation to hold legislative elections — "the masses of voters are still too ignorant and too much out of touch with the world" [56] — these amendments were submitted in 1928 to another farcical plebiscite and approved 177,436 to 3799. As an American wrote sarcastically, "to be constitutionally inconsistent was better than to be consistently unconstitutional." [57] A year later, after the occupying forces had continued to repress dissent and deny Haitians any sense of political or social involvement, fear of defeat induced the government to postpone the legislative (and hence the presidential) elections which had been promised for early 1930. Taxes had also been increased despite the hurricane of 1928 (and the resultant poor coffee crop). And then the world economy collapsed, dooming the export of coffee in 1929–30.

In Haitian eyes, the American occupation had become morally and politically bankrupt. At the same time, the administration of President Herbert Hoover had begun to implement its Good Neighbor policy toward Latin America, and officials in the State Department had on several occasions cautioned Russell against overdependence upon martial solutions to political problems. Whether Haitians knew that Russell was under pressure from the United States is unclear, but the combination of internally and externally generated dissatisfactions was sufficient to bring about the first large-scale manifestations of disaffection.

The students at the Central Agricultural College were the first to challenge the legitimacy of the occupation when they quit classes in October 1929 by way of protesting a reduction in scholarship stipends. (The students apparently felt that the funds saved by the reduction would be used to pay the salaries of American experts who would, in turn, fill the positions for which the students were being trained.) They also stoned the home of the much despised head of the Service Technique. Medical and law students struck in sympathy, and then students in urban secondary

56 Dana Gardner Munro (head of the Division of Latin American Affairs, U.S. State Department) to Francis White (Assistant Secretary of State) April 23, 1929, quoted in Schmidt, "Occupation," 254.
57 Millspaugh, Control, 116.

schools, and eventually rural primary schools, joined what had become a general strike of the protoelite.[58] In turn, displeasure with the educational system under the occupation was transformed by mid-November into a more widespread criticism of the policies of the Borno-Russell administration. Even Borno's disavowal of his candidacy failed to defuse the continuing discontent and, in December, a strike of customs employees turned into a more general uprising. There was tumult and rock throwing in the capital, in Cap Haitien, in Jacmel, and in other towns. Russell declared a curfew and martial law, which only goaded the crowds, and then, in Cayes (to which region a large number of Haitian cane cutters had been repatriated from Cuba), a group of twenty inexperienced Marines fired into a crowd of 1500 hostile peasants, killing at least five and possibly more than twenty, and wounding several score.[59] Subsequent restraint on the part of the Marines, the return to work of strikers in Port-au-Prince and Cap Haitien, a reaffirmation of Borno's withdrawal by the State Department, and the appointment by an alarmed President Hoover of a commission of inquiry calmed the immediate situation. But it was clear, to the Americans anyway, that the occupation had suddenly proved too embarrassing to be continued.

The withdrawal was effected with haste. Hoover wanted out, his commission, after hearings in Haiti, ratified this political judgment and, despite the imprecations of Russell and other treaty advisers and the marked reluctance of Borno, the Americans began the virtually unconditional (the rights of American bondholders would still need to be protected) and painful process of extrication. Russell was recalled and Borno was ousted. (Borno was described by William Allen White, the editor and a member of the Forbes Commission, as "thin, tall, toothy, and most disagreeable" — a man who "lives entirely apart from reality [and] has a little sneering laugh." "I kept pinching myself," White wrote. "It just did not seem possible that any man should be so patent a stage villain." [60])

[58] For blow-by-blow details, see State Department, "Report," 183–196; Logan, "Education," 460.
[59] L. J. de Bekker, "The Massacre at Aux Cayes," *Nation*, CXXX (March 12, 1930), 308.
[60] Quoted in Walter Johnson, *William Allen White's America* (New York, 1947), 421.

An interim government under President Eugène Roy was installed until the election of deputies and senators could be held in October 1930. The election, with the Marines confined to their barracks and other American influence held to a minimum, was reported to have been the fairest Haiti had ever known. All pro-American and pro-Borno candidates suffered resounding defeats, and Sténio Vincent, the leader of the Senate, a mulatto, and a man with acceptable patriotic credentials, became president (his "non-renewable" term extended until 1936). He and Dana Gardner Munro, the former chief of the Latin American division of the State Department who had replaced Russell, were concerned primarily with ousting the Americans, and Munro was also concerned with the improvement of Americo-Haitian relations, so the apparatus of dictatorship fell into desuetude, and Haitians once again began to give meaningful orders.

Secretary of State Henry L. Stimson instructed Munro to "withdraw from any participation in the internal affairs of Haiti at the earliest moment when such withdrawal can be effected with a reasonable hope that there will be no return to the conditions which compelled [our] intervention in 1915." [61] This enunciation of principle was, however, inherently self-contradictory. If the political and economic state of Haiti had not already been altered by the course of the occupation, then, politically, it was long past time. Haitianization of the upper layers of the treaty services and the Gendarmerie had made derisory progress, and accelerated promotion could hardly substitute — as the Belgians subsequently discovered in the Congo — for the gradual transfer of the administrative skills and attitudes of another culture. Even Russell realized that no progress had been made in training Haitians for self-government on the American model. "Our treaty officers," remarked one percipient visitor, "explain that there is 'so much to do' that they have 'no time to waste in debating or explaining matters to the Haitians' — especially as an 'interpreter would usually be necessary.' . . ." [62] The Americans had refused, until the riots

[61] Stimson to Munro, October 18, 1930, quoted in Schmidt, "Occupation," 291. See also Ulysses G. Weatherly, "Haiti: An Experiment in Pragmatism," *American Journal of Sociology*, XXXII (1926), 365.

[62] Russell to W. Cameron Forbes, March 13, 1930, quoted in Schmidt, "Occupation," 286; Streit, "Intervention in Operation," 623.

of 1929, to appreciate the finite quality of time. The reality of withdrawal at all, and particularly in 1936, had been accepted only by a few and, even by those, only fitfully. The policy of the American occupation had not been one of training Haitians in the arts of self-government or of strengthening the representative institutions upon which, said a critic, "both their republic and ours are founded. Nor has it even been calculated," he observed, "to leave Haiti with any sort of government strong enough to maintain itself without us." [63] Furthermore, even after withdrawal was assured in 1930, the administrators of the treaty services tried to avoid Haitianization.

The State Department and Munro hoped to train and promote Haitians somewhat more speedily, but still deliberately. They envisaged an ordered withdrawal. But this well-meant attempt to beat a seemly retreat and simultaneously to Americanize Haiti's political posture was thwarted by Vincent and the Haitian government. He and his colleagues would brook no delay, and each concession extracted from the harassed representatives of the United States naturally encouraged yet further attempts to accelerate the pace of devolution. The threat of renewed disturbances (Jacmel, Port-au-Prince, and Cap Haitien had experienced severe dislocations in 1930) and the unwillingness of Hoover's government to contemplate the use of force or to accept (or to understand) the logic of its colonial obligations, quickly brought about the abandonment of its hopes for a measured disengagement and, thereby, any possibility that the balance sheet of the occupation would work out positively. Early in 1931 the United States conceded immediate Haitianization of the Department of Public Works and rapid promotion within the Garde, and later that year concluded a formal Haitianization agreement which permitted the United States to exercise control only within freshly circumscribed fiscal and medical spheres. [64] The United States simultaneously began running down its own activities in Haiti and withdrawing from financial entanglements with the National City Bank and other American enterprises. Once arrangements had been made for continued, if limited, American supervision of Haitian customs collection and

[63] Russell to Forbes, March 13, 1930, quoted in Schmidt, "Occupation," 286.
[64] For the text, see Millspaugh, *Control*, 250–252.

debt repayments (the Banque Nationale was subsequently sold to the government of Haiti), the Americans could at last conclude arrangements for their departure. The occupation ended, two months ahead of the accelerated schedule, in August 1934.

In retrospect, it seems that American ideas and actions deflected more than they shifted the direction of political development in Haiti. Nineteen years might conceivably have proved sufficiently long to have demonstrated the efficacy of Anglo-Saxon political institutions and approaches and the utility of their application and the assumptions which undergirded them. Given the presence of evangelically minded individuals, American tutelage could have wrought impressive, and more than cosmetic, changes in the methods of Haitian administration and government. Haitians could have been reminded of the importance of "the public interest," the advantages of conciliation and tolerance, the possibilities of pluralism, and the value of creating consensus. At the most general level, the Americans might have been expected (unlike other colonial powers) to have introduced more of the matter of politics into the Haitian equation. But they in fact did not, thinking that such considerations could, and should, be avoided. That the Americans failed to change Haiti fundamentally is hardly surprising; that the initiatives that they took proved politically and socially sterile, if not also counterproductive, is more startling.

The United States intervened in Haiti without having articulated medium- or long-range goals, and proceeded to rule within a colonial context without elaborating a program for the attainment of the conditions which would have obviated the necessity for that arrogation of *de facto* suzerainty. Furthermore, by ruling arbitrarily — more openly but in the manner of previous Haitian dictators — and by failing to involve Haitians in any significant way, the Americans offered them no model of political responsibility. The level of indigenous political participation was exceedingly low, especially during the absence of a legislature, and very unrepresentative, so that Haitians could justifiably claim that they were ruled less representatively and democratically than the American dependencies of Puerto Rico and the Philippines. As far as the majority of Haitians was concerned, a new clique had merely replaced the old. Power, as they had long known, gave license, corrupted morally if not also economically, produced authoritarianism, and was the main ingredient of success. To govern was to have power. To govern was to benefit the ruling clique only. Politics was, strictly speaking, a struggle between cliques. And nothing in the character of the American occupation, except possibly its willingness to dissolve itself and its emphasis upon probity and efficiency, altered these basic preconceptions of Haitian life. As tutors, the Americans reinforced a set of unfortunate and retrogressive stereotypes.

Reducing the results of the occupation to a set of value-laden expressions is obviously unjust. Nevertheless, as the Americans failed adequately to prepare the Haitians for majority rule and the resumption of self-government, so they also re-emphasized the importance (and the stigma) of color. By favoring mulattoes over black members of the elite, they revived class antagonisms. By unambiguously stressing the worthlessness of men of color they also unwittingly encouraged some black intellectuals, including Duvalier, to seek psychological reassurance by reaffirming their African roots and emphasizing the essential integrity and dignity of Haitian ancestry. The establishment of *Les Griots,* a group and journal which focused attention on the African bases of Haitian culture, was but one manifestation of this new concern with *négritude;* Duvalier was to capitalize upon it politically, and to use black power as a rallying cry for his subsequent mobilization of non-elite support.[65]

Otherwise, the lasting achievements of the occupation were few. The Americans constructed roads and bridges, installed a telephone system, and provided a number of similar material improvements which Haitians enjoyed until, from lack of maintenance, they no longer functioned. But such material benefits ceased with the end of the American occupation; no one had been trained to maintain the improvements. No cadre of modern-thinking, self-confident civil servants existed. Only in a minor way, for example in agriculture, had the Americans managed to modify Haitian administrative methods and attitudes. A visitor in the late 1920's ex-

[65] See below, 160–161.

pressed the anxieties of his fellow critics: "The machine runs beautifully now while we are at the controls, but how will it run when we step out in 1936 and the man who all the time has been on the donkey steps in to fly alone? Then will come the real test of everything we have done and of everything we have left undone." [66]

Only the Garde had been reformed and modernized; outgoing Americans hoped that the hastily promoted leaders of the Garde would, like the officers of the constabulary in the Dominican Republic, in Cuba, and in Nicaragua, check the excesses of the political cliques in ways which could not be expected from the judiciary or the legislature. It was soon realized, however, that this was an illusory hope, for the American occupation had failed completely to cure the fundamental structural malaise of Haitian political life. Nor had it managed to set the republic on a profoundly new economic road. Instead, the Americans had prepared Haiti for a continuation of authoritarianism and a renewal of instability.

[66] Streit, "Intervention in Operation," 619.

V

The Coming of Duvalier

DESPITE THE INTERVENTION of the Americans, a deep-seated malaise continued to inhibit orderly political development in Haiti. Between 1915 and 1934 the occupying forces had treated a variety of national complaints without noticeably understanding their etiology. The American diagnoses were superficial and did not immediately contribute to a cure for the disease that had overwhelmed an impoverished and insecure nation. In the manner of earlier Haitians, the Americans responded to particular symptoms and prescribed remedies for parts of the whole. They introduced improved political and technological processes. But no simple surgery or symptomatic drug was sufficient. Haiti suffered from more than a century of complex decay, and, although it was then apparent only to a few, arresting the disease presupposed an imaginative transformation of the basic structure of Haitian society rather than any essentially cosmetic application.

Haiti was a sick society which had never recovered from the excesses and isolation of its nineteenth-century crucible. The American interlude had re-established order, cleansed the economy, and provided a modicum of stability without removing the conditions which had paralyzed the republic in former times. Poverty, ignorance, illiteracy, social antagonism, class conflict, suspicion, distrust, fear, greed, paranoia, intolerance, and the absence of a sense of deferred gratification were among the constant components of the national malady. Together they constituted the matrix of politics from the late nineteenth century through the mid-twentieth century, the actions and character of the government of Sténio Vincent, who ruled Haiti throughout the 1930's, and the governments of his successors reflecting the strength of these factors, the changes wrought by the American occupation (especially the professionalization of the Garde and the elimination of the *cacos*), and international developments over which Haiti had virtually no control.

The structure of society had hardly changed since the era of Boyer. In the 1930's the elite maintained its customary ascendancy. Its membership was still recruited more by ascription than achievement, and lines between the elite and the masses were strongly etched and only rarely crossed. Members of the elite and light-skinned foreigners dominated all activities in the republic; commerce, the civil service, banking, the professions, the army, and politics were in their hands. Not all representatives of the elite were light-skinned, however, as blacks from the north, especially from Cap Haitien and Port-de-Paix, had long before penetrated the ranks of the ruling class. Nevertheless, color, wealth, literacy, fluency in French (as well as in Creole), and educational attainments were attributes and distinguishing characteristics of this class. Its members disdained manual labor of any kind, and many among them preferred bureaucratic to mercantile employment. Investment in property and education and a degree of ostentatious consumption took priority over investment in business and modern agriculture. Politics was their primary avocation.

Under Vincent the elite was composed of 30,000 heads of families and their dependents — about 150,000 persons or 5 per cent of the population of about 3 million. They constituted the rural and urban leadership, but fewer than 2000, and perhaps as few as 300, actually ran Haiti.[1] They formed the cliques which fought for the spoils of the presidency and either backed or schemed against the incumbent. Although family, sectional, and color distinctions and antagonisms were important, the elite thrived upon and was therefore rent dramatically by constant political competition. Victory in this sphere provided a share of the power without which many members of the Haitian elite (or at least the ruling segment of that

[1] George Eaton Simpson, "Haiti's Social Structure," *American Sociological Review*, VI (1941), 640. See also John Lobb, "Caste and Class in Haiti," *American Journal of Sociology*, XLVI (1940), 25–28.

elite) felt themselves impotent and humanly destitute. This was the arena of their most impassioned displays of prowess. For them, power was sufficient reward, conceivably because of the paucity of other spheres within which human ability and aggression could be tested.

Although a middle class had emerged as a result of the occupation, its membership was neither distinct nor functional, consisting for the most part of the less successful urban-based aspirants for inclusion within the elite category. Furthermore, the number of such aspirants was limited, the impact of the occupation having failed to ease the social acceptance of upwardly mobile achievers or to create a differentiated role for this group. In the 1930's, as in the 1950's and 1960's, the middle class was embryonic, politically and socially unimportant and, in a society historically sharply separated by language, culture, the way of life and its rewards, and exposure to change, essentially anomalous. At the end of the American occupation, as before, Haiti continued to lack a distinctive buffer group between the elite and the masses.

The cleavage between these two classes was formidable. The predominantly rural masses have always constituted between 90 and 95 per cent of the population of Haiti; their urban segment included no more than about 5 per cent in the 1930's. During modern times, as in the past, they have been separated from the elite by illimitable social distance sanctified by objective distinctions of language, occupation, religion, recreation, family life, income, education, mobility, and political power, and by their mutual social heritage of superordination and subordination.[2] In significant respects the life of a Haitian peasant had hardly changed since the colonial period; in the 1930's he followed the identical daily round, ate his meals at the same hours as had his enslaved ancestors, and tilled his fields in a manner hallowed by time.[3]

With the exception of those very few peasants who had extricated themselves from the parochiality of their rural surroundings,

[2] George Eaton Simpson, "Haitian Peasant Economy," *Journal of Negro History,* XXV (1940), 499. See also Mabel Steedman, *Unknown to the World, Haiti* (London, 1939), 61; Maurice de Young, "Class Parameters in Haitian Society," *Journal of Inter-American Studies,* I (1959), 451–452.
[3] See Herskovits, *Haitian Valley,* 68.

the masses were spatially immobile — in the 1930's, 80 per cent of
one sample resided where they had been born. In the rural areas
fierce individualism and a striking absence of any division of labor
were normal. Educational opportunities for peasants were virtually non-existent, nearly all upper primary schools being situated
in a commune (where the living expenses would have constituted
too great a drain on peasant resources). Medical facilities were
equally scarce, peasant life being characterized by malnutrition
and endemic illness. Politically, the masses were still inarticulate.
In the 1930's the peasants were reported to "have no conception of
political issues and [to] . . . have almost nothing to do with the
government. Some of them vote, but this means nothing. . . ." [4]
Or, to quote another observer: "The fact is that Haitian peasants
take the elite and its government largely for granted. *Aprè Bô-
Dié, sé Léta,* they say in Creole — 'Right after God comes the
state.' " [5]

Ignorance, disease, and political apathy characterized peasant
life in post-occupation Haiti. As conditions, they reflected the destructive poverty of rural and lower-class urban existence. In the
first place, peasants were ubiquitous: In the 1930's Haiti boasted
an average density of nearly 300 per square mile, three times that
of the Dominican Republic and twice that of Cuba, and, because
such a small proportion of Haiti is arable, the effective density approached 900 or 1000 per square mile. The sugar industries of the
Dominican Republic and Cuba had each attracted 80,000 Haitians
before 1935, but there was very little other permanent net emigration. Similarly, the urban areas of Haiti could not begin to provide employment opportunities for the increase in the rural population. Conditions in Port-au-Prince and other coastal communes
were unattractive to families who could, if they remained at home,
at least be assured of a tiny plot of land in the mountains or, if they
were fortunate, in some reasonably fertile valley. Even in those
regions where the land had been subdivided beyond the point
where it was feasible to fragment holdings further, or where the

4 Simpson, "Social Structure," 645. For immobility, Simpson, "Economy," 515.
5 Jean L. Comhaire, "The Haitian 'Chef de Section,' " *American Anthropologist,*
LVII (1955), 620.

land had become virtually valueless, peasants somehow managed to lay claim to a tiny pocket of soil and, with great ingenuity, reap crops on which they could subsist.

Haitian peasants could rarely escape from the vise of desperate poverty. Their methods were primitive, the plow being disdained.[6] Too much or too little rain, and the occasional hurricane, could eliminate an annual crop, and even the poorest Haitian depended (much more than a comparable African or Asian) upon products supplied by the wider cash economy. If peasants were fortunate they ate one or two meals a day of red beans and rice, yams, and bananas. Although each family might own a goat or pig, few ever ate any meat, preferring to save their animals to sell when desperate for cash. Their days were thus spent trying to extricate themselves from the consequences of a never-ending crisis of impoverishment — not with politics — and attempting to amass capital (in order to buy land and animals) by successfully growing marketable cash crops.

During the 1930's the external environment was especially hostile to the Haitian peasant. Of Haiti's leading export commodities in this period, coffee (51 per cent of the total by value in 1938–39), cotton (12 per cent) and bananas (7 per cent), on behalf of the Standard Fruit Company, were peasant-grown, sisal (7 per cent) and sugar (13 per cent) being harvested on American-owned plantations.[7] Coffee, entirely the product of smallholdings, was the mainstay of the economy — as it had been since 1820. The government obtained most of its revenues from an export levy on coffee, and speculators and foreign-born exporters all took a portion of the return. Before the Depression the average annual value of the crop was about $10 million, but between 1931 and 1936 the annual crop, nearly all of which was sold in France, fetched about 40 per cent less. In 1936, however, the Third Republic renounced

[6] For two fortuitous introductions of the plow, see Charles John Erasmus, "Agricultural Changes in Haiti: Patterns of Resistance and Acceptance," *Human Organization*, II (1952), 23–26.

[7] Simpson, "Economy," 507–508. In 1932–33, coffee supplied 77 per cent of Haiti's exports by value. For these figures and detailed discussion of crops, particularly bananas, see Louis R. E. Gation, *Aspects de l'Economie et des Finances d'Haiti* (Port-au-Prince, 1944), 57 and *passim*.

its existing tariff agreements with Haiti, raised the duties on Haitian imports, and effectively barred access to the market to which Haitian production had been geared for more than a century. Belgium, Italy, and Scandinavia took up some of the shortfall, but only the American market held out any long-term allure. Funds were therefore devoted to the improvement of harvesting, drying, decorticating, and grading procedures in order to satisfy the higher standards of this market, and in 1939 the United States was purchasing more than 30 per cent of Haiti's coffee exports. By then, however, Brazil had abandoned coffee valorization, and Haitian coffee prices fell again.

The social and economic conditions already outlined constituted the general context within which the government of President Vincent found it necessary to function. From its inauguration in 1930 to its demise in 1941, and particularly after the American withdrawal in 1934, Vincent's administration was able to draw upon a fund of legitimacy derived almost entirely from its vigorous antagonism to the American occupation. Vincent consciously proclaimed himself responsible for the second rebirth of an independent Haiti.[8] A visitor tartly observed that Vincent had "fabricated a conqueror's role for himself and struts as the second deliverer of Haiti. . . . He goes about it by having himself photographed with the frowning mien of a conqueror and looking for all the world like a ferocious rabbit." [9] Upon Vincent's election in 1930 he had vowed to "pursue the Liberation of our territory." He had also promised to "be an intractable defender of the material and moral interests of the Republic," a statement that was obviously subject to continuous reinterpretation.[10] At the time, however, it implied that Vincent would continue to defend the democratic, representative, and progressive ideals for which he had long fought. The American critics of the occupation welcomed his accession to power and presumed, as did many leading Haitians, that the stability provided by the reform of the Garde and of the repub-

[8] Of innumerable speeches, see the one at Cap Haitien, November 27, 1934, in Sténio Vincent, En Posant les Jalons (Port-au-Prince, 1939), III, 77–80.
[9] Zora Neale Hurston, Tell My Horse (New York, 1938), 107.
[10] Quoted in Hogar Nicolas, L'Occupation Américaine d'Haiti: La Revanche de l'Histoire (Madrid, 1956), 256.

lic's finances would permit the Vincent regime to make of Haiti a model, liberal oasis in the Caribbean. Rafael Leonidas Trujillo, an American-trained soldier, had already — in the wake of the American occupation — seized power in the Dominican Republic, but with Vincent in command of the revitalized nation and Démosthènes Pétrus Calixte, a well-mannered colonel, in command of the Garde, it was widely assumed that Haiti could avoid the Scylla and Charybdis of military dictatorship and anarchy.

These expectations were in fact realized in a manner peculiarly Haitian. From 1934 to 1950 it was the threat of renewed American intervention and the quality of the local men of power, more than any newly discovered national genius for political compromise, which prevented Haiti from following the lead of the Dominican Republic or from lapsing into a phase of behavior reminiscent of the events of 1900–15. Yet power, especially the securing and maintenance thereof, was no less a fundamental aspiration than it had been previously. The base of political participation had not been broadened to any significant extent and, despite the Americans, the same types of cliques operated as they had always done, and for roughly the old kinds of rewards. For example, Pamphile Charmeur, a once wealthy senator, had "backed the wrong presidential candidate." Since that time Charmeur had "lived in pinching poverty." [11] Certainly the Americans had provided no strikingly new models, authority having remained as centralized and unresponsive to the commonweal during the occupation as before. The masses, as has already been indicated, played no greater role under Vincent than under Soulouque. When the Americans left, corruption, nepotism, and favoritism of all kinds reappeared. Indeed, it is arguable that Vincent maintained himself in office because he distributed financial largess widely, and without necessarily depriving his immediate backers of their own rewards.[12]

Like states of similar political and economic fragility, inexperience, and size which had traditions of intolerance, deep rifts among

[11] Taft, *Puritan,* 96.
[12] For examples, see Démosthènes Pétrus Calixte, *Haiti: The Calvary of a Soldier* (New York, 1939), 65–66; Montague, *Haiti,* 282–283.

the elite, and severely circumscribed spheres of achievement, Haiti could hardly be expected to perform politically as if it had magically been translated into a middle-class democracy. And from the start of his rule Vincent sought to transform the "joint dictatorship" of Russell and Borno into a purely Haitian institution. Despite his previous protestations to the contrary, he almost immediately began gathering the strands of power into his own hands. By 1933 the Senate had refused to continue eroding its own power and in 1934, following the formal departure of the Americans, Vincent moved to consolidate his growing control over all aspects of Haitian life. By means of a referendum, an instrument originally employed by the Americans, in 1935 he obtained the consent of those who cast ballots (by 454,357 to 1172) for the transfer of authority over all economic matters from the legislature to the executive. Shortly thereafter he interpreted the successful outcome of this referendum as a sufficient mandate for the ouster of the eleven senators (including eminent scholars like Jean Price-Mars) who had opposed him in 1934. Next, he decided that a new constitution (to replace the constitution of 1932 which had been modeled upon the constitution of 1889) was needed to provide a firm basis for the continuation of the leadership of the president. In the manner of the nineteenth century, a committee of deputies and senators obediently drafted and subsequently sanctioned this new document of government which, according to Vincent, would "guarantee the sovereignty of the country and . . . be suited to the needs of the people." On a later occasion he said that "unlike the previous ones . . . [the new constitution would be] based on the will of the people." [13] According to its clauses the president became the "personification of the nation" with power to dissolve the legislature at will, to reorganize the ranks of the judiciary, to appoint ten of the twenty-one senators (and to suggest the other eleven names to the Chamber of Deputies). The judiciary and the legislature were declared to exist wholly in order to serve the executive. Between sessions of the assembly, a permanent committee of six deputies and five senators would assist Vincent in making decrees which had the effect of legislative acts. The constitution also praised the pres-

[13] Vincent, speeches to the Assemblée Nationale, April 8, 1935, and at Cayes, July 21, 1935, Posant les Jalons, III, 146–154, 192–193.

ident, by name, for his efforts, and extended his term (due to expire in 1936) by a further five years.

No president could have asked for a more painless transformation from representative to dictatorial government. The maneuver had even been accomplished with a façade of legality. That Vincent was considered personally indispensable was confirmed overwhelmingly by another national plebiscite, and, from 1935, he was virtually free to act decisively without consulting persons outside the ranks of his own clique of merchants and officers. (This was a small group which, others said, by 1936 completely controlled Vincent, using him as a "front.") His view, and the view of presidents before and since, was simply that "the Government makes the Constitution, the Laws, the Regulations and Agreements; that such instruments could not handicap its activities and that it must dispense with them, whenever such measures as were deemed necessary for the maintenance of the Government rendered such a decision necessary." [14] And the president, who personified the will of the people, embodied the government. It followed that Vincent reintroduced censorship, jailed editors without trial and suppressed their publications, ended what little independence had been exercised by judges, and resumed the Haitian practice of arbitrary arrest and indefinite detention without trial. One impartial observer noted that "people fear to be too friendly with those out of favor with the Power." Professional men paid a heavy price for opposition to the president. "These individuals may or may not have been candidates for elective or appointive offices but in case they were candidates, they have lost not only the hoped-for offices but much of their practices as well." [15] Without too much difficulty Vincent overcame his opponents, made mockery of the remaining constitutional and legal safeguards, enforced obedience to his person and, with a flourish, in 1939 obtained another near-unanimous mandate from the voters to do away with their prerogative of directly electing the president and amending the constitution. He did not permit Haiti to "waste valuable time holding popular elections." [16]

[14] Calixte, *Calvary*, 84, 107.
[15] Simpson, "Social Structure," 641.
[16] From his speech at the town hall in Les Cayes, December 18, 1938, Vincent, *Posant les Jalons*, IV, 193. For details of the 1939 changes, see *ibid.*, 262–278.

It is instructive to ask how Vincent managed so easily to reassert the pre-eminence of the executive. The existence of unsettled market conditions argued for continuity of office, and it is probable that the resident American financial adviser gave Vincent encouragement and support of importance. Sidney de la Rue, the adviser, had no stated power and no longer possessed immediately available Marine backing, but until about 1941 the presumed ability of the adviser to recall American troops or somehow to block the channels of finance inhibited Haitians from ignoring his advice. There were, in any event, no obvious alternatives to Vincent; no one then possessed his degree of legitimacy, or his ability to act decisively. It is also true that few Haitians expected their presidents to behave any differently from Vincent. The masses were uninvolved and constituted no part of the political equation, while the elite, although riven by factional disputes, were in part reconciled to and in part frightened of Vincent's administration. Positively, too, Vincent had proved himself an energetic, free-spending modernizer. He sponsored the construction of schools[17] and dispensaries in the rural areas, established a teacher-training college, conscientiously strove to maintain and improve the American roads, initiated the construction of irrigation and drainage works, promoted the granting of the Standard Fruit export concession which dramatically stimulated the growing of bananas in Haiti, actively encouraged the modernization of the coffee industry, saw the possibilities of tourism, and negotiated favorable commercial treaties with the United States. He was not opposed to excluding foreigners from certain branches of Haitian commerce — a policy that endeared him to the elite — and tirelessly exhorted his people to "work, not talk."[18] Whether or not he obtained outrageous rewards for himself, he was seen to be active on behalf of Haiti and, most meaningfully, sought to enhance the esteem of its people. This last quality, and a pronounced ability to project himself,

17 But see Steedman, *Haiti*, 82–83.
18 For example, his letter to the Secretary of State for Agriculture of March 20, 1938, Vincent, *Posant les Jalons*, IV, 96. Vincent's achievements are catalogued and discussed in his *Efforts et Résultats* (Port-au-Prince, n.d. but 1939), *passim*. For an idolatrous panegyric of Vincent's virtues, see Gérard de Catalogne, *Haiti Devant son Destin* (Port-au-Prince, n.d. but 1940), 115–159.

doubtless increased his acceptability and, to some extent, vitiated his castration of the democratic process.

Even Vincent's manipulative skills would, in the absence of any increased level of political participation, have proved ephemeral without the acquiescence and, after 1938, the positive support of the Garde. Technically a constabulary, the Garde was the most formidable military force post-revolutionary Haiti had ever seen. Although it was composed of fewer than 4000 officers and men (plus another 1100 paramilitary rural assistants), the Garde possessed modern weapons and an efficient communications system, and had been well-trained by the Marines. It possessed a degree of discipline that was rare in the civil service, and its officers, who had all passed through the Ecole Militaire in Port-au-Prince, were — like their African counterparts during the 1960's — among the best-educated and most able Haitians of their generation. If these young leaders of the Garde had not been so thoroughly drilled to eschew anything that connoted interference in politics, it is likely that Vincent's government would have proved short-lived. Instead, Calixte, whom an American described in 1938 as a "tall, slender black man around forty with the most beautiful hands and feet that I have ever beheld on a man," hewed very closely to the traditional American line and, if his own testimony can be believed, also adhered to the canons of accepted Western military behavior by executing presidential decrees with which he disagreed, and which he also believed to be unconstitutional. The American reported that he was "truly loved and honored by the . . . men under him." [19] Calixte steadfastly tried to keep the Garde out of politics even after it was clear that the president was intentionally subverting Calixte's authority and supporting a pliable subordinate. The loyalty of the Garde to the office of the executive even survived the president's refusal to permit its field units to practice with the light artillery and automatic field weapons supplied to the battalion attached to the palace (and stored there), and to transfer soldiers from the palace to the frontier in the face of Dominican maneuvers. The loyalty also survived the Garde's impotence and the failure of the president to order retaliation after

[19] See Calixte, *Calvary*, 29–30; Hurston, *Horse*, 110.

Trujillo's massacre of about 20,000 Haitian cane cutters in the western provinces of the Dominican Republic in 1937.[20] To be sure, by this time Trujillo had begun interfering in Haiti. He had succeeded in suborning Calixte and other Haitians, like the future president Elie Lescot. By means of flattery — in 1936 he nominated Vincent for a Nobel Prize — he had also tried to turn Vincent into a lackey. Trujillo backed the abortive coup by younger officers of the Garde which led to Calixte's dismissal. A purge of the better-trained officers (Duvalier was frequently to use this technique) followed. They were replaced by younger, less experienced men who were expected to be loyal to Vincent and his ruling clique. By 1939 the Garde had undergone a thorough politicization and, thereafter, it played a role analogous to the military machines in the neighboring republics of the Caribbean.

While Vincent and his cohorts were consolidating their control of Haitian life (and largely by way of reaction to their exclusiveness), a few darker-skinned intellectuals began to challenge domination by a light-skinned elite in a manner that was to have exceedingly important consequences for the political development of the republic. The specter of a Haiti occupied — of an intensely proud people humbled and reminded of their seeming inability to govern themselves effectively — had already compelled Haitian intellectuals to re-examine the problems of their country and to search for new and imaginative solutions to the series of hoary national insecurities which had so bedeviled their country. There were other causes for the intellectual ferment of the 1920's and 1930's, pre-eminent among them being the growth in educational and other opportunities, the general and intangible broadening of horizons, and, for one group, a new awareness of Africa which was derived from anticolonial writings and agitation, and contact with

---

[20] A visitor wondered aptly whether Vincent thought "it better to allow the Dominicans to kill a few thousand Haitian peasants than to arm the peasants and risk being killed himself? Does he fear that if the stores of ammunition in the basement of the palace were issued to the army that his own days in the palace would be numbered? . . . Are his own people more to be feared than Trujillo?" Hurston, *Horse*, 109. For the massacre see Robert D. Crassweller, *Trujillo: The Life and Times of a Caribbean Dictator* (New York, 1966), 154–156; Raymond H. Pulley, "The United States and the Trujillo Dictatorship, 1933–1940: The High Price of Caribbean Stability," *Caribbean Studies*, V (October 1965), 25–26.

Francophone Africans in Paris. Additionally, Haitians had some knowledge of the Harlem renaissance. *Négritude* was the product of the interaction of French-speaking West Indians and Africans in the 1930's; Haitians of a particular intellectual background were driven by some of the same emotions. For them the occupation constituted a colonial episode subjectively comparable to that endured by Africans.

Bereft of tangible moorings, dark-skinned members of the Haitian elite consciously looked to Africa and, ultimately, saw that their road to political salvation and cultural justification could best be traveled with the masses. In 1927, Jacques B. Roumain, a youthful member of the moneyed mulatto elite who had grown up in Switzerland and France and who had been stung to patriotism by the impact of the American occupation, established the short-lived *La Revue Indigène* with Normil Sylvain, Carl Brouard, Philippe Thoby-Marcelin, Emile Roumen, Antonio Vieux, and others (and, in 1941, the Bureau d'Ethnologie), in order to encourage the study and literate re-examination of Haiti's dominant heritage and forgotten majority. Then, in the next year, Jean Price-Mars, an older physician and civil servant, published *Ainsi Parla l'Oncle: Essais d'Ethnographie* (Port-au-Prince), a pioneering study of the way of life of the rural masses of the republic. Although this book (based on lectures given between 1920 and 1923), like the whole of Price-Mars' work, tended to romanticize the lot of his country's peasants, it proved unexpectedly influential and, for literate black Haitians, *Ainsi Parla l'Oncle* constituted a charter for research and a stimulus to identification. Essentially, Price-Mars criticized his countrymen for being ambivalent about and denying their African beginnings and for seeking to assimilate themselves to the dominant European-derived culture.

Roumain's novels, the first of which appeared in 1930, extended the thrust of Price-Mars' argument; he subjected urban mores to critical scrutiny, began to celebrate the folkways of the rural masses, helped to organize the Haitian Communist Party, and, because of his antagonism to the Vincent regime, was sent into exile. He studied anthropology in Paris at the Musée de l'Homme, retreated to Columbia University when the Germans reached Paris, and then returned home only to be sent by President Elie Lescot to Mexico City as the Haitian *chargé d'affaires*. It was during this period of quasi-disgrace before his death in 1943 at thirty-six that Roumain wrote *Gouverneurs de la Rosée,* a powerful novel of social protest written in Creolized French.[21]

By the early 1930's, a number of black and mulatto intellectuals had also begun to capitalize upon the initiative of Roumain and Price-Mars. Employing prose and poetry, they had commenced a frantic but serious re-examination of the Haitian dilemma while others, equally frenetic but less rigorous, simply tried to ride the sudden wave of enthusiasm for cataloguing the customs of the rural masses. These excited disciples of Price-Mars and Roumain developed what a contemporary has called a school of "emotional ethnography, at times frankly mystical, written in a rococo style and showing little or no capacity to grasp the overall problem" of the country.[22] In their hands "folklore" — the study and glorification of presumed cultural affinities with Africa, and their manifestations in modern Haiti — became a political weapon of some power and utility. It legitimized and gave a new thrust to the struggle of the black against the mulatto elite, and involved a new clientele — the urban masses and those peasants for whom the affairs of the state were not impossibly remote.

Of all of the products of the folklorique direction, the tireless advocates who constituted the Groupe des Griots, and who began publishing a weekly revue (*Les Griots*) in 1937 and a journal en-

[21] Roumain's novels were *La Proie et l'Ombre* (1930), *Les Fantoches* (1931), *La Montagne Ensorcelée* (1931), and *Gouverneurs* (1944) — all published in Port-au-Prince. The last, which followed his death by a few months, was translated by Langston Hughes, Mercer Cook, and an informal committee of Haitians as *Masters of the Dew* (New York, 1947). Edmund Wilson, *Red, Black, Blond, and Olive* (New York, 1956), 116, called it "an inevitable communist novel." For a general appreciation of the genre, see Murdo J. MacLeod, "The Haitian Novel of Social Protest," *Journal of Inter-American Studies,* IV (1962), 207–221; Jacques C. Antoine, "Literature: From Toussaint Louverture to Jacques Roumain," in Mercer Cook, *An Introduction to Haiti* (Washington, 1951), 93–120; Jean Price-Mars, *De Saint-Domingue à Haiti: Essai sur la Culture, les Arts et la Littérature* (Paris, 1959), 51–56.

[22] Rémy Bastien, "The Role of the Intellectual in Haitian Plural Society," *Annals of the New York Academy of Sciences,* LXXXIII (1960), 846. For a discussion of the cultural revival more generally, see Pattee, *Pueblo Afroantillano,* 373–391; Edith Efron, "The 'New Movement' in Haiti," *Caribbean Quarterly,* IV (January 1955), 14–31.

titled *Les Griots: La Revue Scientifique et Littéraire d'Haiti* in 1938, were the most influential ideologically and, in time, politically. Arthur Bonhomme, Brouard, Louis Diaquoi, Kléber Georges-Jacob, Lorimer Denis, and François Duvalier were among the early sponsors of the quarterly, the first issue of which also printed articles by J. C. Dorsainvil, Roumain, Marcelin, Jean Price-Mars, Horace Pauléus-Sannon, and other participants in the Haitian cultural renaissance.

Duvalier, neither the best known nor the most literary of these writers, was then a government-employed physician in Port-au-Prince. Although his family stemmed originally from Cayes, the future president's grandfather, a tailor, took the Duvalier family to Port-au-Prince during the reign of President Boisrond Canal (1876–1879). François's father taught in local secondary schools and subsequently became a *juge de paix* — a kind of municipal court judge — in the capital. François was born there in 1907, went to local schools, eventually completed his secondary education in 1928 at the Lycée Pétion — one of Haiti's better schools — and obtained his medical training at the Ecole de Médecine of the Université de Haiti. During the ten years after receiving his license in 1934, Dr. Duvalier worked for the government throughout the Département of the West, and particularly in Léogane and Port-au-Prince. In 1943 he became chief of a rural clinic near the capital and a member of an anti-yaws campaign team. In the next year, presumably at the behest of the American Sanitary Mission which was then directing the long-term programs of preventive medicine in Haiti, Duvalier obtained a fellowship from the United States Institute of Inter-American Affairs. The Institute sent physicians and engineers to selected schools of public health in the northern tier of the United States, and Duvalier was one among several Haitian students who enrolled in the School of Public Health at the University of Michigan. They were admitted — as were nearly all foreign students — as "non-candidates for a degree." But if a student acquitted himself well and attained the required academic average during the autumn term, he could be and usually was admitted to degree candidacy, which permitted the award of a master's degree in public health at the end of the second

semester. "Many of the Haitians," said an American who knew
Duvalier well during this period, "did qualify and have subsequently had responsible positions in all parts of the world with the
World Health Organization." But Duvalier failed to attain a passing grade in either public health administration or epidemiology,
two of the four core courses, despite his apparent eagerness "to
conform to the pattern of study which we had here at Michigan, a
most difficult pattern to follow on the part of some of the foreign
students." What another friend remembers was his inability to
understand English sufficiently — and his failure to overcome this
deficiency in the university's English language institute presumably contributed to his mediocre performance at the School. However, "My own opinion," said one of his teachers, "is that Duvalier,
despite his medical degree, was, academically-speaking, stupid."

Duvalier was not then visibly handicapped by any emotional
problems: several respondents recall him with favor. "He showed
no characteristics," said one, "which seemed to be leading toward
the many statements and episodes which have been attributed
to him." Another called him "companionable . . . genial, at-
tentive." He seemed, recalled a third, "quiet, pleasant, well man-
nered [and] friendly. He was reserved and dignified, but very
thoughtful and considerate. He seemed singularly non-aggressive
(especially in view of later history). . . . I detected none of the
characteristics that he must have needed to take him where he now
is [although he] was not easy to know well." Whatever the precise
reason for his lackluster performance, Duvalier was asked not to
register for the second term of the academic year 1944–45, despite
continued residence in Ann Arbor. Although President Duvalier
now credits himself in conversation with the Michigan degree, it is
a figment of his memory.[23]

Despite, or, conceivably, because of his failure at Michigan, the
Sanitary Mission subsequently sent Duvalier to Puerto Rico on a
practical short course in tropical public health procedures. He was

[23] Biographical information is derived primarily from a lengthy interview between
the author and Duvalier (November 11, 1968). I am also indebted to several of
Duvalier's teachers and acquaintances in Haiti, New York, Mexico, and at the
University of Michigan for further details of his life in writing and conversation.
None, however, wishes to have his name mentioned.

involved in a malaria control offensive in 1945–46 and then helped to organize what he now remembers — again erroneously — as a famous and very successful anti-yaws campaign which continued until 1948. Penicillin, the efficacy of which had been indicated during World War II, was not then widely available or sufficiently inexpensive for use in Haiti. Nevertheless it was during these years that he traveled on horseback throughout the country and gained an intimate knowledge of rural problems. According to Duvalier, he became widely appreciated as a benefactor and — the objective reality is now difficult to discern — something of a folk hero.

Meanwhile, in company with the other members of the Griots, and especially in collaboration with Denis, a severe-looking high school teacher from Cap Haitien who never appeared without a black hat on his head and an upright staff in his hand, Duvalier had begun to elaborate the ideological structure of black power upon which he was subsequently to base his claim to rule. Although it is unusually difficult to specify Duvalier's contribution — even where ostensibly attributed — to the mélange of doctrine that constituted the message of the Griots, he was an early and forceful critic of elite domination. He wrote of Africa and blackness in order to educate the elite and their American supporters who were wont to denigrate Haiti's heritage and, by extension, to castigate the ex-slaves who constituted the mass of the republic's population. One of Duvalier's earliest essays was a lengthy disquisition on Africa's history, racial composition, and social diversity.[24] It praised the accomplishments of the "Negro-African" civilizations and preached a gospel of profound racial pride. Turning to the Haitian revolution, Duvalier was unstinting in his acclaim for Dessalines — the great defender and "martyr of the masses," who overthrew the privileged class and became the first socialist premier of Haiti. "His life," wrote Duvalier, "filled with sacrifice, must serve as an example." Other black leaders of Haiti, especially President Salomon, who believed in unrestricted majority rule and

[24] "Les Civilisations Negro-Africaines et le Problème Haitien" (1936), *Oeuvres Essentielles* (Port-au-Prince, 1968; 2nd edition), I, 229–231. Earlier, with Arthur Bonhomme (later ambassador to Washington) and Lorimer Denis, he had written *Les Tendances d'une Génération* (Port-au-Prince, 1933).

sought the "regeneration of the masses," and President Soulouque, were equally celebrated by Duvalier.[25]

Throughout the late 1930's Duvalier struggled to help to create an awareness of the rich intellectual and moral content of the origins of the mass of Haitians as a counter to the doctrine of black inferiority; he listed black Francophone Africans who had made notable contributions to the arts and letters and, on occasion, adopted a note of aggressive cultural chauvinism. He urged Haitians to read their own authors. He advocated — as if mere advocacy could create it — the development of a truly national spiritual consciousness. Yet, despite the munificence of Haiti's heritage, Duvalier believed that the peoples of the republic lacked any sense of moral consciousness. The Haitian conscience was devoid of all ideas of traditional ethics. Haitians were, he said, opportunist and unconscionably pragmatic. And there was a lack of vigor in the collective personality.[26]

It was also true that popular culture contained more to value than to disavow. He was only one among many Haitian writers who rediscovered *vodun,* but his were among the more influential tracts and, in view of his later incorporation of *vodun* into the body of the state, it is relevant to note his early appreciation of its history and functions. *Vodun,* he reminded his readers, contributed to the achievement of national independence. It was the "supreme factor of the unity of Haiti." *Vodun* "came to crystallize, in the dynamism of its cultural manifestations, the past of the African on native soil, his martyrdom in the colonial hell, the heroism of the knights in realizing the miracle of 1804. And as this religion is a constant creation, it sublimates, in its perpetuation through the generations, the tragedy of . . . the Haitian masses." [27]

The rural masses, with their *vodun* religion, the psychology of the peoples of a forgotten continent, and their long tradition of

25 "La Tragédie des Protagonistes des Questions de Classes à Travers l'Histoire d'Haiti" (1948), *Oeuvres Essentielles,* I, 291; "La Vivante Continuité des Valeurs Spirituelles ou Nationales" (n.d.), *ibid.,* 429–442; "La Mission des Elites" (1949), *ibid.,* 396–397.
26 "Le Noir d'Afrique et la Civilisation Européenne" (1938), *Oeuvres Essentielles,* I, 130.
27 "L'Evolution Stadiale du Vodou" (1944), *ibid.,* 173.

developed Africanness, constituted the authentic population of Haiti. They, said Duvalier, embodied "humanism," a concept which encapsulated and affirmed the dignity of man, took account of his original grandeur, implied the possibility of man's perfection, and found its fullest flowering in individualism. For him, in 1939, humanism curiously could be recognized in a scientific and Roman Catholic mode as well as in a Communist or Hitlerist configuration. Humanism, he went on to expound in a typical formulation, embraced "the Haitian Man in the entirety of his characteristics, in his present and in his past, in the diverse historical milieux where he has evolved." He sought to establish the foundation of a "science of the Haitian Man." [28]

Yet merely being Haitian, Duvalier later indicated, was insufficient. Being black was pre-eminent, and by the late 1940's Duvalier (in company with Denis) was avowedly antimulatto in his writings and speeches, insisting that the blacks, who constituted the majority, had for too long been oppressed by the light-skinned elite. The blacks deserved to triumph because they were black, and more numerous, and because they had suffered at the hands of a local ruling class. Duvalier wrote of classes, and may have intended his interpretation of the Haitian dilemma to sound Marxist, but basically he offered no more than a simplistic redress of the racial balance. The mulattoes had sinned, and ought now to be deprived of power. They had denied educational opportunities and governmental power to the masses, and they had prevented the masses from sharing the fruits of freedom and independence. Mulattoes as a class were the incarnation of evil, being, he said, the descendants of pirates and corsairs. For many years mulattoes hid their true nature behind a façade of manners which had been learned from the whites; but now Duvalier had managed to unmask their pretensions. The future president also indicated that mulattoes could redeem themselves only by thinking black — by associating with and supporting the advancement of the masses. In turn, he predicted that the masses would gain and retain power if they could unite with the black middle class (in which category he presumably placed himself). If the masses were to be redeemed,

[28] "Pour un Humanisme Totalitaire" (1939), *ibid.*, 118.

they needed a leader like Toussaint, who constituted the collective will of the people — who knew better than they did what the masses thought and wished to believe. This leader would represent the influence of the generations of blacks and would synthesize the conscience of his race in the manner of Tiberius, Toussaint, and Kemal Ataturk. History, Duvalier also believed, was deterministic. A crisis would bring forth a leader who would redeem his people, establish a nation, and found empires.[29] This was the heroic role in which Duvalier was consciously to cast himself.

There is a further dimension of Duvalier's personality which can be traced in his writings. That he excoriated mulattoes, championed blacks, wrote mystically of the need for a blackened spiritual base, allied himself to *vodun,* and — not too clearly — believed at best in a rarefied conception of unrepresentative democracy is evident. His xenophobia, particularly his contempt for foreign-born Roman Catholic priests, followed and was associated with an expression of the most profound paranoia. In this latter regard, Duvalier may merely have been reflecting a national characteristic, but his own utterances certainly embodied such a response to perceived reality. He accused the French missionaries of systematically dehaitianizing the national soul, of persisting in a colonial mentality, and of having demonstrated their contempt for the value of an education based on Haitian history. He condemned Catholic priests for collaborating with the American occupation and directly contributing to the destruction of the Haitian soul by teaching distorted history in the schools. A leading priest had preached against the folklorique movement of which Duvalier was a leading member; of him and his ilk, Duvalier blustered: "Not being content to delay the moral unification of the nation by poor-quality instruction, not content to attack our principal cultural institutions, our traditions, they still extol the maintenance of our rural masses in their state of ignorance." [30]

Before the end of World War II the polemicists and thinkers of the Groupe des Griots affected and dealt with the masses not at all.

[29] Lorimer Denis and François Duvalier, *Le Problème des Classes à Travers l'Histoire d'Haiti* (Port-au-Prince, 1948), *passim.* This work, originally published as a pamphlet and manifesto, is also contained in Duvalier's *Oeuvres Essentielles,* I, 309–366.

[30] "L'Avenir du Pays et l'Action Néfaste de M. Foisset" (1948), *ibid.,* 407–408.

If their ideas percolated through the backwoods of Haiti, no one noticed. Similarly, although the ruling class remained fully aware of *Les Griots* and the burden of its message, the elite proved no more responsive than had its predecessors. Considering the state of the world and American markets, the government of Sténio Vincent cannot be said to have failed its constituents economically as much as it had left the country untouched and stagnant. The Vincent regime perpetuated the entrenched privileges of the elite and ignored the large reserve of legitimacy which would have permitted it to bring about basic reforms in the prevailing structure of Haitian society. It is easy to criticize Vincent and his cabal for lack of vision, but his government — alone of the administrations of twentieth-century Haiti — had the kind of backing which could have been mobilized in support of significant nation-building. Instead, there were no noticeable reorientations. The political base was, if anything, narrowed. Sectional and class distinctions were made more rigid, and the importance of color was re-emphasized. What Haiti had gained from apparent stability and financial (not economic) normalcy, it forfeited by entrenching the control of an unresponsive and authoritarian oligarchy. Haiti, despite — or because of — the American interlude, had not changed.

This lack of change, or any hope for positive improvements in the future, alienated the black elite and their supporters — an alienation which was reinforced as much by the way in which Vincent left office as by his methods while ruling. In 1941, despite the provisions of the constitution, Vincent was elected by the captive legislature to a third term. At this juncture the United States refused to sanction such a departure from legality and Vincent, with a farcical show of magnanimity, permitted the senators and deputies to elect senator Elie L. Lescot, Haiti's ambassador to the United States, to a five-year presidential term. The 56 to 2 vote was induced as a result, one participant reported, of beatings, electric shocks, and the liberal use of torture.[31]

Lescot was a distinguished Haitian of esteemed lineage, who had long served the state. His paternal grandfather had been a respected *magistrat* (mayor) of Cap Haitien, while Ovide, his father,

31 Max L. Hudicourt, *Haiti Faces Tomorrow's Peace* (New York, 1945), 11. Vincent died in 1959.

served as a judge for many years in Cap Haitien. On his maternal side, Elie Lescot was descended from a leading member of the court of the emperor Faustin I. He was born in le Cap in 1883, received his primary and secondary schooling there, and then joined an uncle who owned a number of export-import outlets in the Port-de-Paix region. In 1905 he entered the service of the state as an interpreter for the customs service in Port-de-Paix. Six years later he was elected to the Chamber of Deputies; in rapid succession he became the director of the main secondary school in Port-de-Paix, a justice of the peace, Haitian consul in Antilla, Cuba, judge of the civil tribunal of Port-de-Paix, and, after being invited to remain in Port-au-Prince, a member of the National Court of Cassation, minister of education and of agriculture, minister to the Dominican Republic, and, finally, ambassador to the United States.[32] By 1941, it seems evident, Lescot was a reasonably sophisticated, surprisingly well-equipped, and commendably experienced candidate for the presidency. He was also in the pay of Trujillo. In 1939 he had begged the Dominican dictator for funds, which were granted, with which to buy votes in the Haitian assembly. He purchased his election to the presidency with such tainted gourdes and during his years in office remained "bound to Trujillo by a golden cord, apparently beyond regret." But whatever qualities of judgment and statesmanship he may have possessed were — by the curious chemistry of Haiti's highest office — rendered irrelevant when he acceded to the presidency. In addition to his loyalty to Trujillo, he was transformed, like so many of his predecessors and successors, from a cautious diplomat into a megalomaniacal president; like Vincent, he regarded the occupation of Haiti's highest office as sanction for unbridled personal and presidential license, for authoritarianism and intolerance, and for a disregard of the constitutional stipulations to the contrary. He believed as devoutly as nearly all of the other Haitian presidents that "the chief of state is everything. Everything comes from him and everything returns to him." [33]

[32] Biographical details may be found in an otherwise much too sycophantic account, Alfred Nemours, *Les Présidents Lescot et Trujillo* (Port-au-Prince, 1942), 19–25.
[33] Quoted in George Eaton Simpson, "Haitian Politics," *Social Forces*, XX (1942), 488. For Lescot and Trujillo, Crassweller, *Trujillo*, 160–161, 224.

The reign of Lescot continued and accentuated the pattern of government reintroduced into Haitian life by Vincent. The masses were ignored; a clique within the elite ruled on behalf of and with the acquiescence of the leaders of the Garde. (Lescot assumed the command of the Garde and appointed his son as his principal assistant.) Corruption and nepotism were widespread. Lescot established a social security fund for the workers, but the advance deductions of 6 per cent of the salaries of all workers went, in the absence of any records, into his own pocket. Arbitrary processes led to the arrest and imprisonment of critical journalists and hostile deputies; Lescot silenced newspapers and the clergy and, despite a formal adherence to the Atlantic Charter, he denied basic rights and liberties to his subjects. "We have decided," he said in 1944, "to apply the four liberties only when the Haitian people know how to use them, and when the exploiters . . . have transformed them into true citizens conscious of their rights and duties." [34]

Lescot welcomed the creation of La Société Haitiano-Américaine de Développement Agricole, a private organization which attempted to assist the American war effort by growing vine rubber and oil palms in northern Haiti. The society, funded by an Export-Import Bank loan of $5 million, obtained a long-term monopoly on rubber production and jurisdiction over the 200,000 acres which it occupied. Lescot even permitted the society to oust large numbers of peasants from the concession area and to destroy their field crops in order to plant *cryptostegia* (hevea or vine rubber). By 1945, it was clear that the economic and productive results of the new scheme were chimerical, and that a vast area of Haiti had been not only ravaged, but that its development had been accompanied by untold peasant hardship.

The urge to obtain overweening power and succeed themselves by fiddling with the existing constitution was and is an occupational disease of Haitian presidents. Lescot, having already demanded legislation which gave him complete personal control over the Haitian budget, in 1944 — ostensibly as a security measure — appropriated all of the possessions of foreigners. In the same year

[34] Speech of May 15, 1944, quoted in Nicolas, *La Revanche,* 274.

he compelled the assembly to alter the constitution of 1935, as amended in 1939. He was empowered to fill vacancies in the two chambers without calling elections, which were not, in any event, to be held while World War II continued. The duration of the presidency was also extended retroactively from five to seven years (i.e., Lescot could continue in office until 1948). Of all of these changes there was growing criticism, but wartime powers enabled the president to repress hostility unmercifully until, the United States and the Dominican Republic having made their displeasure known, two young journalists took the end of the war as a signal for a new outbreak of resentment. In their newspaper *La Ruche*, René Dépestre (later a leader of the Haitian Communists in Cuba) and Théodore Baker urged the end of despotism, and specifically called upon Haiti to adhere to the principles of the Atlantic Charter. The issue of January 1, 1946, resulted in its ban and their own detention. "This," wrote one observer, "was the drop of water that overflowed the vase." [35] Students went on strike in Port-au-Prince, Lescot threatened to use troops to end it, civil servants joined the movement of protest, some blood was shed, the cabinet resigned, and an army triumvirate consisting of Colonel Franck Lavaud, Chef d'Etat-Major of the Garde, Major Antoine Levelt, the director of the Ecole Militaire, and Major Paul E. Magloire, commander of the palace guard, assumed power, ousted Lescot, and dissolved the assembly. For Haiti, it was a relatively painless and, considering the pretensions of the elite, fitting dénouement to a recurrent drama.

To label the demise of Lescot a dénouement is to employ the idiom of common speech. Strictly, there was no resolution of unfolded problems. There was no conclusion to the multi-act tragicomedy, no reprieve for the protagonists, and no opportunity for belated curtain calls. Indeed, after a brief change of scene — with the players assuming new guises — Haiti resumed her idiosyncratic, perverse, and singularly bloody peregrination across the boards of Caribbean history. The junta of 1946 hence proved a departure from the past only in terms of style. The ruling triumvirate repre-

---

35 *Ibid.*, 277. Trujillo's release of incriminating letters of fawning supplication from Lescot contributed significantly to the ferment.

sented several branches of the interlocking oligarchy; although it remained in office for seven months, it too faced angry mobs incited by would-be presidential aspirants in Port-au-Prince, was compelled to abandon an attempt to govern through a cabinet of national unity or a board of military officers, and, by May 1946, staged a comparatively clean election for the members of the legislative assembly. The assembly in turn selected a constitution from those of the past and, in August 1946, calmly elected Dumarsais Estimé president for five years.

Although black, of humble origins, and immediately hailed as the authentic redeemer of the Haitian masses, Estimé had long before achieved a secure place in the ranks of the national elite. He was born in 1900 in Verrettes, a small village in the valley of the Artibonite River. Orphaned, he was brought up by Estilus Estimé, an uncle who was the local *magistrat* and a member of the national Senate. With his uncle's support, Estimé attended school locally and in St. Marc, and completed his secondary education in Port-au-Prince. He received a license to practice law, and became a teacher of mathematics in the Lycée Pétion, where Duvalier was one of his pupils. He opposed President Borno, who retaliated by refusing him permission to teach. But from 1930, when Borno fell, to 1946, Estimé represented Verrettes in the Chamber of Deputies. For a time he was its president and, under Vincent, he became minister of education. In that position he managed to end the awarding of baccalaureate degrees without reference to merit, raised the salaries of teachers, curbed nepotism and corruption, tried to improve the examination system, and, overall, obtained a reputation for probity.[36] In the light of this background, it cannot be claimed that Estimé was himself an authentic representative of the masses; rather, his victory in the elections of 1946 over three other candidates, each of whom was equally black, and one of whom was Calixte, the favorite of the workers of Port-au-Prince, was the victory of the folklorique movement of black intellectuals — appropriately backed by Magloire and the Garde — who had

[36] For biographical details, see the partial account in Jean Magloire, *Dumarsais Estimé: Esquisse de sa Vie Politique* (Port-au-Prince, 1950), 14–43. See also Colbert Bonhomme, *Révolution et Contre-Révolution en Haiti de 1946 à 1947* (Port-au-Prince, 1957), 22–23.

long sought real political power. And it was these men, Duvalier
among them, who assisted Estimé's essay into mass leadership.

With the cooperation of these younger, reform-minded blacks of
modernizing mien, most of whom had grown up during the American occupation and its mulatto-dominated aftermath and had
been heavily influenced — like their African counterparts — by
the liberal rhetoric of World War II, Estimé launched a program
of unquestioned reform. He promised to respect the independence of the judiciary and the legislature, freedom of the press, and
the rights of political parties to exist and to criticize the government. He encouraged the formation of trade unions and rural cooperatives, expanded the national school system (Pierre Eustache
Daniel Fignolé, the idol of the masses of Port-au-Prince, and later
president, was then minister of education), increased the salaries
of employees of the central government, combated the exploitation of laborers by contractors, and began bringing more and more
non-elite blacks into the civil service. Duvalier, successively direc-
tor-general of the national public health service, under secretary of
labor, and secretary of state for labor and public health, played a
role in the elaboration and implementation of new social legislation and also continued (with the cooperation of the United States
Sanitary Mission to Haiti — the Inter-American Cooperative Public Health Service — and the Pan American Sanitary Bureau) to
wage a serious campaign against endemic diseases.

Both Estimé and Duvalier welcomed and encouraged such unusual and, for Haiti, radical experiments as the UNESCO-backed
pilot project in fundamental education, an attempt to transform
and ameliorate the life of Haitian peasants in the Marbial valley
near Jacmel. Beginning in 1948 with an ethnological survey of the
region, the project was intended to inaugurate a program of mass
literacy, to encourage improved agricultural methods, foster soil
conservation, sponsor small processing industries, introduce new
standards of preventive and curative medicine, and, in general,
demonstrate how techniques of community development could
raise the standard of living in a depressed, overpopulated, and isolated rural area.[37] By 1950, however, it was evident that the oppo-

37 The first phase of the project is described in a UNESCO pamphlet, *The Haiti
Pilot Project* (Paris, 1951); Conrad G. Opper, "Ataque Frontal Contra La Miseria:

sition of local notables, the unwillingness of the peasants to accept new or to alter their traditional methods without good reason, personal inadequacies and corrupt behavior manifested by the initial Haitian administrators and their employers, a shortage of funds, and the impoverished conditions of the location originally selected at the behest of local figures, would prevent the realization of these aims to any significant degree. It was the kind of defeat which Haiti was accustomed to administering.

Yet the government of Estimé was successful in initiating the kinds of changes which, in time, could have benefited the masses and, given a modicum of political tranquillity, radically altered the direction of Haitian political development. But Estimé was neither a Perón nor a Vargas. He was as bound as were his predecessors by the politico-social alignments which limited the ability of a president to initiate or to carry out social transformation. The political structure of Haiti also prevented Estimé from mobilizing the kind of popular support which could have sustained him during a struggle with the competing interests of opposing cliques. It also seems evident that Estimé lacked the ability to project a vision which could have stirred Haitians of all classes.

Estimé also made a number of blunders which forfeited the reluctant consensus — and particularly the support of the commercial classes and the army — which had been fully his in 1946 and 1947. For political reasons he broke up the Standard Fruit and Steamship Company's monopoly of bananas, dividing its concession into seven sections which were then granted to his loyal supporters. As a result, shipments of banana stems — in 1946 Haiti's second export crop — fell drastically, from nearly 500,000 stems in early 1947, to 259,173 in early 1948 and 134,257 in 1949, a 75 per cent decrease.[38] He concentrated new development projects, financed for the most part by the Export-Import Bank, in the Artibonite Valley (his home area), and paid comparatively little attention to the south and the north. He and his ministers intensified the growth of urban demand by initiating several questionable

Como se Lleva a Cabo una Campaña de Educacion Fundamental," *El Correo*, III, (1951), 5–7; *New York Times*, July 3, 1950; and several confidential reports. See also below, 315–316.
[38] *Hispanic American Report*, II (May 1949), 29.

projects, particularly in the capital; a largely externally induced
inflation created profitable opportunities for the in-group but created hardship for many others. Because of a shortage of governmental revenues and the falling off of banana and cotton receipts,
he attempted to impose heavy and unusual imposts on the internal
consumption of sugar. In March 1949 a law was passed that required each worker to invest 10 per cent of his salary (15 per cent
if more than $50) in national defense bonds, which would pay 3
per cent interest and mature in 1959. Workers began leaving their
employment in large numbers, particularly from the large plantations. A few months later the government announced a campaign
against immoderate profit-taking by textile merchants, a measure
that alienated the petty shopkeepers. Then he decided to attract
tourists by encouraging the construction of hotels and other facilities in the capital and by sponsoring an international exposition to
celebrate the bicentenary of the establishment of Port-au-Prince.
Vast funds — nearly $12 million (much of which was never ac-
counted for), thrice the original estimates — were devoted to this
poorly sited sixty-acre extravaganza, but, by the beginning of 1950,
it was evident that the resulting financial returns (plot rentals and
increased tourist business) would not begin to cover out-of-pocket
costs.[39]

This fiasco could have been excused, however, had Estimé, unlike so many earlier Haitian leaders, not succumbed to the national disease which afflicted most occupants of the presidential
office. In 1949 he began increasingly to emphasize his indispensability and to strike demagogic postures. He declared a desire,
despite the constitution, to succeed himself in office.[40] He became
more intolerant of the resultant dissent and paranoid in his response to the fulminations and plottings of Haitian exiles resident
in the Dominican Republic. (Estimé had tried to revive Haitian
claims to all of Hispaniola, and in 1948 Trujillo had begun backing exiles, most of whom were mulatto, in their attempts to overthrow Estimé by force.) Foiled assassination attempts, and cabals,
real or imagined, were announced with some regularity during the

39 *Ibid.*, III (May 1950), 18; (June 1950), 18; (July 1950), 18. See also the scathing
comments of Wilson, *Red, Black*, 91–93. *Time* (February 22, 1954), 45, reported that
the exposition had cost $26 million of which $10 million disappeared.
40 On the syndrome, see Bellegarde, *Dessalines à Parlé*, 115–123.

final months of 1949. Caches of arms were discovered, several alleged conspirators were shot, and a number of Haitians, including nearly one third of the officer corps of the Garde — most of whom were mulatto — were taken into custody. Local, non-Dominican-backed opposition was also curbed. Three political parties and eight newspapers were banned, and students and shopkeepers who went on strike were censured and attacked. There were the usual rounds of arbitrary detentions, and, by the beginning of 1950, Estimé had introduced martial law. Then, even more portentously, Estimé decided, despite the constitution and the rivalries of others, to go ahead with his plan to succeed himself and rearrange the relevant documents. After a rigged national election of senators and deputies early in 1950, he even sent a howling mob into the well of the Senate to impress the reluctant legislators with the gravity of their responsibilities. By so doing, however, he unleashed the kinds of countervailing forces which led rapidly to his own downfall, and to the ouster of his associates, including Duvalier.

Estimé failed the essential test of Haitian political life — the maintenance of legitimacy during periods of stress. Once it was generally realized that Estimé was, like all of his predecessors, a mere opportunist with no real love for or support from the masses, the disappointed students, workers, and merchants turned against him. "One does not achieve a popular movement like the one promised by 1946 only to obtain some more pseudo-bourgeois," explained a former member of his cabinet. "It is illusive social shifting, because in Haiti more than anywhere else one cannot shift class despite a new financial and political standing. The newly rich, rocketed up by the revolution, have forgotten too quickly the old song of the humble-hearted." [41]

The mercury of Haitian politics had once again found its level. The same junta that had encouraged Estimé's accession removed him — in order to end a state of incipient anarchy — in May 1950.[42] This time, however, the army was reluctant to hand authority back to incompetent civilians. In October, Paul Magloire

[41] Quoted in Jean-Pierre O. Gingras, *Duvalier, Caribbean Cyclone: The History of Haiti and its Present Government* (New York, 1967), 83–84.
[42] The proclamation of the junta is printed in Nicolas, *Revanche*, 290–291; Bonhomme, *Révolution*, 46. The latter also contains Senate resolutions against Estimé.

became the first president of Haiti to be elected directly by the people. By way of demonstrating the irrelevance of parties and partisan ideology in Haitian politics, he ran — unlikely as it later seemed — as a candidate of the Mouvement Ouvriers et Paysans, Fignolé's "party" (with which Duvalier had at one time also been aligned) and obtained 99 per cent of the votes cast (151,115 to 2000). His only opponent, who hardly campaigned, was a little-known follower of Estimé, an architect named Fénélon J. Alphonse. Despite the party affiliation, too, the triumph of Magloire was viewed incontrovertibly as a victory for the old elite — for the "enemies of the people" who would deny the gains which had been achieved on behalf of the black middle class and the mass of illiterate peasantry. Yet Magloire was as black as Estimé; what he lacked was any semblance of charisma or the kind of ability with words which would have enabled him to project a popular image of himself. In fact, Magloire was essentially a pragmatist who ruled, like his predecessors, in cooperation with and on behalf of a coterie of military and commercial supporters, none of whom was noticeably sympathetic to the folklorique movement of the black intellectuals. Magloire's elevation to the presidency signified a change in style and personnel more than any reversal of political direction.

Haiti's thirty-third president (and twenty-second soldier to become chief executive) was a scion of one of the leading *arriviste* families in Cap Haitien, where the name Magloire is common, and where blacks had always been counted among the elite. His grandfather had farmed a small plot of land in Quartier Morin, near le Cap, and his father, Eugène François, had risen through the ranks of the army to become a general under President Nord Alexis. Paul Eugène was born in 1907 and attended local schools and Lycée Philippe Guerrier in Cap Haitien, where he taught for a year (1929–30) before beginning a two-year course at the Ecole Militaire. He emerged a sous-lieutenant in late 1931 (he later took a law degree at the university) and served successively as aide-de-camp to President Vincent, adjutant to the commander of the Artibonite, Northwest, and Northern Provinces, in the civil prison in Cap Haitien, and as governor of the national penitentiary in Port-au-Prince. In 1944, he assumed control of the palace guard.

Later in the same year he accompanied Lescot to the United States and, in 1946 when strikes paralyzed the capital, he and the two other officers (Lavaud and Levelt) intervened politically to preserve order and prevent bloodshed. The alternative, he later reported, was to use the troops against the strikers, and Magloire temperamentally and strategically was opposed to the employment of such tactics on behalf of a regime which had hitherto neglected blacks.[43] After a brief period as minister of the interior, Magloire returned to his position as commandant of the palace guard under Estimé until the president, incited (according to Magloire) by Duvalier and Louis Raymond, his minister of the interior, justice, and national defense, began killing mulattoes indiscriminately. These actions — the attempt to perpetuate Estimé's term in office, illegally, and the intimidation of the Senate — finally turned Magloire against the regime. He was the strongest member of the junta that succeeded Estimé, and "because I had no choice" Magloire agreed to become president in 1950.[44]

By this time Duvalier, who bitterly opposed the Magloire coup, had achieved a certain prominence. In addition to his position as minister of health and labor, he had begun building a constituency of his own among the workers of Port-au-Prince. In particular, he derived some support from the taxi, truck, and bus drivers of the capital, the best organized body of workers in the country. He was also assisted by his alliance with Fignolé and the successful party which had been set up by Fignolé.

Magloire, who knew Duvalier throughout the period of Estimé's presidency, reported that his character was then "incomprehensible," i.e., inscrutable. A number of foreign visitors who dealt officially and informally — in several cases very closely — with Duvalier during this era also reported that the future president appeared to be an able, comparatively competent, seemingly honest, shy, and not particularly impressive minister. One visitor found him distant, mild-spoken, and not very communicative, but

[43] These and other matters were discussed during the course of a lengthy interview between the author and President Magloire, April 21, 1969. Biographical detail may also be found in Service d'Information, *Les Etapes d'un Relèvement: Le Président Magloire au Service du Peuple* (Port-au-Prince, 1956), vii–xii.
[44] Interview of April 21, 1969.

pleasant and — in negotiations — more to the point than many of his colleagues. To a second he was gentle and considerate. Certainly he then betrayed no megalomaniacal qualities — a point that was also made by a number of his teachers and fellow students at the University of Michigan. Another foreigner who talked at length with Duvalier immediately before the coup in 1950 recalled an impression "of a man under considerable tension who was very nationalistic in his attitude." [45]

When Magloire became president Duvalier resumed his position as a paid consultant to the American Sanitary Mission's anti-yaws project. At the time nearly 80 per cent of the rural population of the republic suffered from yaws, the earlier eradication schemes having proved ineffective, largely because they depended upon painful, difficult, and long-term treatments of arsenic, bismuth, and mercury. By 1950, the efficacy of penicillin had been demonstrated, although no large-scale eradication schemes had been organized. Between 1951 and 1956, however, Drs. Guillermo Samamé and Sascha Levitan of the Pan American Sanitary Bureau yaws eradication team, in cooperation with the American mission and a number of Haitians (among whom Duvalier was not prominent) devised and administered a house-to-house program of injections which virtually eliminated the menace of yaws. Magloire's Haiti paid about $200,000 a year for this program, although the initial negotiations had been conducted by Duvalier under Estimé's government. It was continued, after the successful completion of the phase of eradication, throughout the 1950's and, by way of a follow-up program, until 1964. As early as 1954, however, Duvalier had severed his connections — as inconsequential as they may have been — with the United States mission and, fearing Magloire's wrath, had gone into hiding (where he read Niccolò Machiavelli's *The Prince*) from which he emerged only shortly before the fall of the Magliore government.

One of the Americans who worked with Duvalier between 1951 and 1954 later realized that during this period he had completely masked his political pretensions. Yet his assessment of Duvalier's

---

[45] For obvious reasons, each of the respondents quoted or alluded to wishes, for the present, to remain anonymous.

personality jibes with that of the Haitians and foreigners who knew the future president at Michigan and during his tenure as minister of health. "I recall Dr. Duvalier," he wrote, "as an extremely quiet, serious appearing individual. He was soft-spoken and appeared unwilling to disclose his thoughts and opinions to others, except for a few trusted Haitian associates with whom he talked freely. Even though he was generally non-communicative, it was usually quite obvious that his mind was not idle. Strangely enough, the majority of the educated local employees in the office seemed to be completely unaware of his political aspirations or the methods he would employ to pursue them. I mention this to point up the fact that he is an extremely difficult person to know, even by those with whom he is closely associated."

The yaws program was but one example of the way in which Magloire concentrated, pragmatically — as might be expected of a Marine-trained soldier — upon the improvement of Haitian life. The efforts of the American financial advisers had long before helped to achieve economic and fiscal stability. Vincent and Lescot had paid only passing attention to development, and Estimé was only slightly less concerned with stability at all costs. (Haiti regained full control over its bank only in 1947.) Throughout this era of relative political stability the country's economy had for the most part remained stagnant, however, and deforestation and soil erosion, increasing population pressure, the collapse of the banana and cotton crops, and fluctuating markets for coffee and sisal implied the possibility of continued stagnation and, indeed, negative growth. Under Magloire, what can be called economic development for the first time received attention. Hitherto, there had been no planning of any systematic kind. There had been no centralized determination of priorities, the yearly budget consisting generally of rough estimates of probable returns from customs revenues (then 70 per cent of the receipts), income taxes (fewer than 3000 Haitians were affected in 1950–51; they contributed 8.4 per cent of receipts), and several kinds of property tax, none of which put a premium on the productive use of land holdings. Budgeted expenditure estimates consisted almost entirely of a list of salaries paid to employees of the central government, each department presenting an unchecked roster of names and a general synopsis of proposed project expenditures.[46]

Magloire fully appreciated the developmental potential of foreign investment. His government consequently spared no effort to attract foreign firms. It continued Estimé's attempt to encourage the establishment of new industries by offering tax concessions of some magnitude (but by no means so lavish as Puerto Rico's), and also sought in numerous informal ways to provide the kind of political and economic climate which businessmen would appreciate. In early 1951, Magloire banned both Fignolé's Mouvement, the party which had backed him for president, and the Communist-oriented Popular Socialist Party, because they had "plotted to sabotage foreign investments." In the same year Magloire welcomed the formation of a national labor federation, but within a few months it became clear that trade unions that attempted to resist management or government domination would be persecuted. The right to strike existed in reality no more under Magloire than under his predecessors, and, in later years, whenever strikes were attempted, Magloire simply jailed those who withheld their labor.

With equal energy he sought foreign assistance. A Point Four general agreement was concluded with the United States for the development of dairy and cattle farming, soil conservation projects, the improvement of sanitation, and new drainage facilities. Magloire also negotiated an expansion of Estimé's poorly thought out and badly executed Artibonite River project — a dam to be constructed at the Peligre narrows and intended to irrigate 100,000 acres and supply hydroelectric power for industrial development. Originally estimated at $6 million, a revised project of $20 million was decided upon in 1950. Work was halted after $40 million had been spent without installing any electrical generating equipment. The newly dug canals irrigated only a disappointing total of 50,000 acres.[47] Even with adequate implementation, the project would, in view of the soil salinity and severe drainage problems in large parts of the Artibonite basin, have been a very dubious venture.

[46] See Moore, "Monetary-Fiscal Policy," 237–248. Moore was a United Nations financial expert on loan to the Haitian government.
[47] Moral, *Paysan*, 325–329.

Foreign advisers and the Magloire government realized that the country lacked the kind of basic infrastructure which would enable Haiti to make the fullest use of its resources. At the end of 1951, only seventy-five miles of paved arteries existed (only twenty-two miles having been constructed during the year). Magloire undertook a major program of trunk and feeder road construction; the main route from Port-au-Prince to Cap Haitien, and from le Cap to Fort Liberté, was surfaced for the first time (in 1969 hardly any of this asphalt remained), and a new route was provided to Christophe's Citadel, the country's main tourist attraction. One of the earliest projects authorized (and completed in 1953 at a cost of $7 million) was that for improvements to the port and wharfage facilities in Cap Haitien, the president's home. In the north, too, a small dam provided water for the region of St. Raphael. Electricity was supplied to the small town of Léogane, in the south. And officials of the U.S. Customs Bureau began revamping Haiti's methods of administration.

These varied activities would have been impossible without the extremely favorable coffee prices in the first half of the 1950's. While non-coffee exports declined substantially, total export earnings (with almost unchanged quantities of coffee exports) rose from $30.9 million in 1946–50 to $46.1 million in 1951–55. In 1957–59 dollars, these figures are $37.9 and $49.1 respectively. Higher export incomes, a modicum of political stability, the road construction, and the energetic wooing of capital by Magloire and his associates led to a certain amount of import-substituting industrialization. In 1952 a number of Haitian firms joined forces to establish a sack, rope, and twine factory at Miragoâne, and Haitian businessmen began a plastics factory in Port-au-Prince. In 1953 Delta Airlines considered the organization of a Haitian airline, a project that came to naught. Other investments that were realized, however, were a hosiery mill and factories for the manufacture of iron nails, carbonic gas, aluminum utensils, and flour. Foreign capital was also interested in export industries. Cubans, in cooperation with the government, constructed a sugar grinding mill near Cayes. In 1953, Reynolds Mining Corporation, a subsidiary of Reynolds Metals Company, prepared to exploit the extensive bauxite deposits near Miragoâne.

Many of these projects were envisaged in the five-year plan of 1950 and the overambitious and never significantly implemented six-year public works plan of 1954; in addition, Magloire built fifteen model villages with new houses, clinics, and schools, cleared a slum and constructed Cité Magloire — with new housing for workers — near the capital, and presided over a rapid growth in the tourist industry. By the end of the 1953–54 season, three times the number of tourists were registered (in comparison with 1950–51) in addition to regular calls of ships of the U. S. Navy.[48]

The world economy was kind to Haiti. Although Haiti's cocoa fetched consistently less than it had, and the prices of locally grown bananas, cotton, edible oils, and sugar remained low, sisal benefited marginally from the dislocations caused by the Korean War, and coffee, still Haiti's mainstay, steadily increased in value by about 20 per cent yearly until Hurricane Hazel, in October 1954, struck hard at Cayes, almost totally destroyed Jérémie and several small towns, and denuded about 40 per cent of Haiti's coffee trees of their cherries; it also uprooted 50 per cent of the trees bearing cacao.[49] Fortunately, the tourist industry, rice and cotton, and the main sisal plantations were largely unaffected, but coffee prices slumped from their 1954 peak, the unusual level of prosperity which had been achieved by the Magloire government being curtailed throughout 1955 and 1956. By then, the annual budgets had risen to about $36 million. Of this amount, the interior ministry absorbed nearly 25 per cent, education 14 per cent, public health and preventive medicine 13 per cent, and foreign affairs 11 per cent. The remainder was allocated in small amounts to public works, and the other administrative departments. In 1954–55, $3 million was allocated to hurricane relief. Salaries, however, still comprised most of the expenses.

Magloire's regime had a distinct economic impact on Haiti. But the fruits of development, as might have been anticipated, were enjoyed unequally. To be sure, certain groups of peasants benefited from improved transportation facilities, irrigation water, and the opening up of new overseas markets for their produce, while the urban masses clearly shared some of the return from the expanded

48 *Hispanic American Report*, VIII (May 1954), 20.
49 *Ibid.* (January 1955), 20.

tourist trade, new industries, and ancillary service opportunities. But the regime's projects, many of which were located in urban areas, provided little benefit to the great mass of peasants, whose welfare was in any case of little concern to the Magloire government.

In the absence of either a broadened political base and equitable distribution of the new wealth, or the inculcation through oratorical means of a sense of meaningful participation or sacrifice for an ongoing national enterprise, discontent was bound to arise. The gap between the emerging city proletariat and salariat and their leaders seemed to them to be widening; a sense of relative deprivation accompanied the new prosperity, as it nearly always does. The bribery and corruption which had regularly been prominent in Haiti flourished (as it does under Duvalier). It was widely known that contracts and concessions to foreigners or Haitians would be granted only in exchange for appropriate individual rewards (sometimes partnership) to the ministers, military officers, and others who occupied positions of influence. Magloire also controlled the soap, sisal, and cement monopolies.

As many previous occupants had demonstrated, succession to the presidency implied a license to make money. Magloire and Marcaisse Prosper, his chief of police, made no secret of their intentions. They lived ostentatiously, built grand and expensive mansions, and projected playboy images. An "amiable, hard-drinking, pleasure-loving officer," Magloire was frequently seen in the nightclubs of the capital, "his bodyguards and the bearer of his private bottle standing at attention behind him." [50] Few observers doubted that Magloire and Prosper dipped their hands deeply into the national till. "The scandals caused by the misappropriation of hurricane relief funds by military and government officials, for their plantations or villas in the cool and pleasant hills surrounding Port-au-Prince, brought about the final discrediting of the Magloire regime." [51] There were limits, even in Haiti, and by 1954 Magloire had begun to exceed them rather blatantly.

[50] Herbert Gold, "Caribbean Caudillo: Magloire of Haiti," *Nation*, CLXXX (February 5, 1955), 119. For a discussion of corruption in Haitian society, see Bellegarde, *Dessalines à Parlé*, 345–346.
[51] Leslie F. Manigat, *Haiti of the Sixties, Object of International Concern* (Washington, 1964), 40–41.

The legitimacy of a Haitian executive is, for historic reasons, notoriously fragile. During 1954 Magloire made it clear that his government would respect the civil liberties of its subjects no more carefully than had earlier governments. The usual mechanisms of repression were employed with the exception that Magloire personally was not bloodthirsty. In early 1954, the police broke up and carried away the printing press and type of the daily *Haiti Démocratique,* arrested Fignolé, the editor and deputy, and his employees and friends and, within a few days, had rounded up 171 persons, 17 of whom were members of parliament theoretically immune from arrest. All of those detained were accused of fomenting revolution on behalf of Fignolé and his Mouvement. The police claimed to have discovered large quantities of firearms and seditious propaganda in the homes of the accused. Persons acquainted with them took refuge in foreign embassies; Senator Marcel Hérard, for example, had himself smuggled into the Mexican Embassy rolled up in a rug. But by April, Magloire — "in compliance with a petition presented to him by the Haitian Congress" — granted an amnesty to everyone, even Fignolé, who had been involved in the conspiracy against his regime.[52] Others, on different occasions, were less fortunate. He closed schools that were considered to be centers of subversion, and — like all of the other Haitian chief executives — muzzled the press. He also closed the faculty of medicine and dissolved its student association, ended the chauffeurs' union and detained many of its members.[53] Criticism was hardly welcomed, even when it emanated from outsiders. When a visiting American was quoted in the local press as having referred approvingly to Montaigne's dictum that "all culture comes from the people," he was warned that "further statements of this sort" would result in his expulsion from Haiti.[54]

The catalogue of arbitrary abuses is endless, and characteristic of Haitian dictatorships, particularly once they begin to lose their precious and limited reservoir of esteem and good will. Like some

[52] *Hispanic American Report,* VII (May 1954), 19; *Le Nation,* January 12, 1954, quoted in Bonhomme, *Révolution,* 85–86.
[53] An imposing list of transgressions was offered in a radio speech by Victor Nemours Constant, December 19, 1956, quoted in Bonhomme, *Révolution,* 64–67.
[54] Gold, *Happy Problems,* 175.

others, too, Magloire saddled his citizens with *ad hoc* extra taxes for this or that supposedly noble or necessary purpose, without the precise uses of the special imposts readily becoming apparent. And he apotheosized his own regime, distributing official photographs which named him as the apostle of national unity. Finally, Magloire, the inheritor of the incapacitating malaise of most Haitian executives, indicated that he might try to avoid vacating the presidency when his term expired. Under one interpretation of the constitution, the term should have been concluded by May 1956, by another in December 1956, and by Magloire's (correct) reading of admittedly conflicting and ambiguous articles, in May 1957.[55] When he failed to step down in May 1956, Senator Louis Déjoie, a wealthy, vocal sixty-year-old mulatto agronomist and businessman from the south, and Clément Jumelle, a husky black who was educated at Fisk and Chicago universities and was Magloire's minister of finance, both of whom had recently announced their candidacies for the soon-to-be-vacant position, focused the already existing opposition to the president. Secondary-school students and chauffeur-guides (organized by Duvalier) went on strike in Port-au-Prince, Cayes, and Jacmel, many prominent men and several editors were arrested, and there were battles with the police which resulted in numerous injuries. Martial law followed, with the president striking an even more authoritarian posture than usual. A period of tense calm lasted until early December, when Magloire banned political meetings and partisan radio broadcasts, and jailed Déjoie and 146 others. An impassioned "Protestation" signed by Déjoie, Duvalier, Marceau Désinor, Justin Latortue, and nineteen other candidates for the presidency denounced this unfair limitation of their political rights,[56] and, within hours, Magloire decided to surrender his mandate. The president and the members of the Court of Cassation, each of whom was in turn constitutionally obliged to succeed to executive office, were unsure of military support and each refused Magloire's gavel. At this juncture, with a show of phony dismay meant conceivably to disarm the opposition, the

55 The contrasting opinions are set out with the contemporary analyses in Bonhomme, *Révolution,* 96–99.
56 Text in *ibid.,* 107.

Garde requested Magloire to "place himself once more at the service of the nation." [57] The legislature was dissolved.

But Magloire's mandate as dictator was soon lost. A passive general strike paralyzed nearly 90 per cent of Port-au-Prince on December 10. Government offices, buses, taxis, and businesses were stilled according to a plan coordinated by Duvalier and backed by a number of the younger military officers. Magloire later blamed the disaffection of the officers on unusually slow promotions which had been their fate during the 1950's, and the growing antagonism within the army between black and mulatto officers. Certainly, by this time there was a sizable faction loyal to Duvalier.[58] After two days of this strike, Magloire — who confessed to like the good life too much to fight back against difficult odds — retired for the second time and, with some dignity, took his family to Jamaica and on to France and Brooklyn.

Magloire had presided over a vast accumulation of power and wealth — contemporary estimates ranged between $12 and $28 million — much of which he lived to enjoy overseas. By his manner, especially his cynical disregard for maintaining even a façade of political justification, as much as his blatant peculation, he discredited the highest office. His very success also excited potential rivals. But of more long-term significance was the inability of this representative of the army, and its other commanding officers, to demonstrate that the military could ensure Haiti's adherence to constitutional forms and provide for orderly presidential succession. The "illegitimate" usurpation of power by the army simply ended its effectiveness in the face of the determined deployment of the alienated citizens of the capital and, later, a determined and canny dictator. The fall of Magloire marked the end of the successful manipulation of the complex formulae of cronyism and interlocking cliques that had dominated Haitian politics for at least a century.

As if catharsis were required before Haiti could resume its search for a fitting destiny, Magloire's final resignation signaled the start

---

57 *Ibid.*, 111.
58 Interviews with Magloire, April 21, 1969; Col. Jacques Laroche, January 1 and June 11, 1969; Duvalier, November 11, 1968.

of the kind of indescribable turmoil and chaos which had racked the republic before the American occupation. Taken together, the events of the next eight months — above all the failure of any set of norms to win widespread acceptance and the inability of the usual mechanisms to achieve a lasting consensus — illumine the character and vagaries of Haitian politics in a microcosm. Essentially — and it is almost impossible to simplify and epitomize the ensuing political cataclysm in the course of which there were five weak, querulous and inherently unstable governments, thirteen bitterly antagonistic contenders for the presidency, bloody strife between political partisans, and armed clashes between factions of the Garde and the police — the north and the southwest virtually seceded from the capital, the army refused and, for a time, proved unable, to maintain order, Port-au-Prince was paralyzed by a series of general strikes on behalf of one or another of the candidates, there was an almost total breakdown of the country's economy, and interethnic, class, and color rivalries were unleashed on a scale which surprised even experienced Haitians. Throughout, Duvalier schemed cleverly and mordantly, using the months of disorder to extend the tendrils of his influence into unexpected sectors of Haitian life and thereby to lay the kind of supporting grid which would make his victory, when it came, total.

The search for order and direction began calmly and hopefully enough with the installation of Joseph Nemours Pierre-Louis, then fifty-six years old and the chief justice of the republic's highest court, and a member of the International Court at The Hague, as provisional president until the elections which were scheduled for April. His cabinet included two other justices and Jean Price-Mars, the doyen of Haitian intellectuals, in an attempt to provide an impartial caretaker administration. But, despite its ostensibly non-political character, everything in Haitian life hinged on power, which is the essence of politics, and the members of the Pierre-Louis cabinet soon mirrored the factions of the nation. There was intense disagreement about the kinds of support and covert advantages which should be given to particular presidential candidates and sufficient internal dissension to make day-to-day administration impossible; on February 1 the cabinet resigned. It

was feared throughout the capital that Pierre-Louis, who had refused for procedural reasons to dismiss Magloire's legislature, favored a return of the recently ousted dictator or, at the very least,
wanted to back Jumelle. Because of these anxieties, the resignation of the cabinet was immediately followed by a general strike
called by Déjoie and Duvalier, both of whom sought to prevent the
rise of Jumelle and were prepared to cooperate in order to eliminate his rivalry. Déjoie also hoped to capitalize on a provision in
the 1950 constitution which stipulated that the next acting president should be a justice of the Court of Cassation; in this case the
eligible justice, Jean-Baptiste Cinéas, was an avowed ally of Déjoie
and his administration and could — given the character of Haitian
politics — presumably ensure Déjoie's election.

The general strike of February 2, 1957, brought Port-au-Prince
to a standstill.[59] It also brought about the resignation of Pierre-
Louis on February 3. The army, under General Léon Cantave,
had remained neutral throughout the strike. After Pierre-Louis's
resignation, however, Cantave summoned seven of the twelve candidates — including Duvalier; Jumelle, a leading lawyer, jurist,
and journalist; Alfred Viau, recently in exile in Mexico; and Julio
Jean-Pierre Audain, formerly in exile in Santo Domingo — to a
meeting in the military headquarters in order to discuss the ways
in which the provision of central authority could best be maintained. Déjoie, who presumed that Cinéas would take over, boy-
cotted this meeting and, as a result, lost a measure of prestige and
popularity by his obstinacy. The other seven contenders, however,
were themselves unable to choose a presiding official. They turned
the problem over to the National Assembly, which, after much
weighing of the advantages of backing this or that candidate, and
perhaps instructed by Cantave and mercantile interests, on February 6 named Franck Sylvain president until the elections. Meanwhile, the economy had begun to collapse in the face of a total
withdrawal of tourism and the coincidental failure of the coffee
crop. Money circulated less freely than usual; the central govern-

[59] The reconstruction of the events of this turbulent period was derived from the
pages of the *Haiti Herald* and the *Hispanic American Report*, and the documen-
tary accounts in Bonhomme, *Révolution*, and Clément Célestin, *Compilations pour
l'Histoire* (Port-au-Prince, 1958 and 1959), 3v.

ment tilted precariously on the edge of bankruptcy, its credit having become exhausted.

Throughout the remainder of February and the first weeks of March, economic, political, and social conditions worsened — at least in Port-au-Prince, the nerve center of the nation. It was during these difficult days that Fignolé's star came to shine more and more brightly. A quondam "professor" of mathematics in a local lycée and an emotional journalist, he had unsullied credentials as the champion of the urban masses of the capital and the straightforward, honest intellectuals of the elite and petit bourgeoisie. Born in the southwest, he attended schools in the capital, lost his teaching position after criticizing Lescot, then formed the Mouvement, served as a cabinet minister under Estimé (who also imprisoned him briefly), and was a member of the National Assembly from 1950 to 1955. His politics were vague but exciting; he espoused "renovating nationalism" à la Ataturk, and a kind of Perónist "justicialism." He later described himself as an "advanced democrat." [60] But his ideology mattered far less than the excitement and urgency of radical reform which he generated in his audiences. He was by far the most effective stump orator Haiti had seen since the days of the revolution. His mastery of Creole and his trenchant, biting criticisms of the establishment delighted the crowds. He had long been the favorite of the longshoremen and laborers of the city. (In 1949 he had organized and obtained wage increases for employees of the Haitian-American Sugar Company.) For the first time he began to make a national impression. But — to anticipate — Fignolé was an individualist who had no organizational flair and delegated responsibility erratically. He spent too little time creating confidence among the military, and recruited too few operators into his genuinely populist movement. He could command too few disciplined divisions. What he possessed in time of crisis — and what made him feared by the other candidates — was charisma sufficient to inflame mobs and destroy the capital.

By the end of March 1957, the shifting alliances of candidates

[60] Robert I. Rotberg, "Fignolé Derides Haiti Vote Plan," *New York Times,* August 14, 1957.

had turned on Sylvain. He was widely (and probably correctly) believed to be favoring Duvalier; and, since Haitians habitually distrust each other when power and the resolution of what we have earlier supposed might be basic oedipal conflicts are at stake, and have paranoid delusions during the calmest of times, it is hardly surprising that Sylvain's caretaker government was denounced by nearly all of those opposed to Duvalier. Fignolé, Jumelle, Déjoie, and Audain, despite their internecine antagonisms (supporters of Fignolé and Déjoie had killed one another only a few weeks before), declared that Sylvain's cabinet was composed exclusively of Duvalierists. Simultaneously adding to the tension, the employees of the Haitian-American Sugar Company and the Banque Nationale went on strike — but for non-political reasons — and the Banque closed in mid-March. Then, after Sylvain had refused to accept the resignation of his cabinet during the last week in March, a general strike again brought business and administration in the capital to a halt. By way of coping with the strike, Sylvain and his police raided and destroyed a local radio station which had broadcast the appeals of the Youth Association for the Defense of Citizen's Rights and made wholesale arrests of private citizens after disrupting a demonstration and motorcade in support of Jumelle. (By this time Jumelle was in hiding from Sylvain's police.) A bomb exploded, injuring several soldiers, and, at this point, Cantave intervened — claiming that Sylvain (others accused Duvalier) was attempting to seize power in the wake of outbreaks of violence — and forced the acting president to resign.

Two acting presidents had failed to move Haiti beyond the square in which it had been left by Magloire. Cantave again called a conference of the contenders. It lasted three tumultuous days, by the end of which only five of the candidates — Duvalier, Déjoie, Fignolé, Métrius Bonaventure, and Auguste Fauché — were still talking to one another and the general. An executive council of thirteen representatives of these five was installed to prepare the country for elections, but the members of the council worked together only until the end of April when Duvalier's three supporters resigned, crying foul. Duvalier declared that the other contenders were scheming against his candidacy. During the course of an impassioned broadcast, he tarred his opponents unmercifully

with the elitist label. This speech, as a sample of his brand of dem-
agoguery, deserves to be quoted in part:

> My message today will be short. It will be a precise and calm de-
> nunciation of the mad coalition which, under the pretense of govern-
> ing, is busying itself on our political scene.
>
> Having agreed to collaborate with our equals on the Executive
> Government Council in preparing honest public elections, the very
> first day we came up against a curious and almost pathological su-
> periority complex.
>
> Falsely and ridiculously accused of organizing official elections in
> the interest of the majority . . . they have taken the success of a
> coup d'état to be a demonstration of power.
>
> . . . In their egocentric exaltation and in their total lack of ability
> to analyze the situation they have confused all meanings of the event;
> the rapport of the other forces at work, the role played by the Army
> in the events, the limits imposed on the political coup by the actual
> electoral position — all this disappeared in the euphoria of having,
> through a coalition of indigestible contrasts, overthrown Sylvain,
> stopped the course of our victory, and forced the parties to a new
> wait-and-see electoral policy. . . . Subsequently we were conde-
> scendingly offered a small place in the Government, rather as a poor
> relation is offered a stool in the circle of a prosperous family. And
> they intended to make us realize that we had no more say in the
> matters at hand, under the pretext of administrative purification,
> and substituted an electoral plan which was to serve their interests
> alone and to be to the detriment of those of their competitors.
>
> . . . They have gone mad. Happy and congratulating themselves
> on being at last all reasonable men together, all civilized men, all
> refined men, and being at last rid of the "rurals" which we are.
> . . . They have gone mad.
>
> They dare to keep Duvalier, the most popular of the candidates,
> in the outer darkness like a punished child. They have gone mad.
>
> People of the North-West, of the North, of the Artibonite, people
> of the South-West, people of the Grande Anse, middle classes of
> Port-au-Prince, intellectuals, masters of the mind and of the arts,
> professors, teachers, students: they have decided to ignore you. They
> have gone mad. . . . The mad coalition has decided that you and
> I have nothing to say. It is going to decide for us. It is going to
> fabricate elections. It is going to give us a leader.
>
> Men and women, supporters of Duvalier, you, my thousands and

my dozens of thousands, you from the heroic North, brave people
from Dérac, Phaeton and Maribaroux, you from Vallière and from
Mombin Crochu, you from Cap, Fort Liberté, Ouanaminthe, valiant
heroes from Limbé, thousands from the North-West, you from Port
de Paix, Môle, Jean Rabel, unconquered and unconquerable armies
of the Artibonite, and all of you from Belladère, Hinche, Mirebalais,
Lascahobas, oh, my cohorts; still unsubjugated Marigot, Cayes-
Jacmel, Côtes-de-Fer, appropriately named Jérémie which adorns for
ever the poem of steel made by the love of Estimé, Dame-Marie, Anse
d'Hainault, lucid South of Cayes, of Cavillon and d'Anquin, lucid
South of Nippes and of the Coteaus, have you understood? They
want to decide without us. They have gone mad.[61]

At this confused juncture, Cantave proposed that a three-man
military junta should rule, but Déjoie and Fignolé strenuously opposed such a solution (Duvalier approved of it). There was yet
another general strike, instigated by Déjoie and Fignolé, and the
capital began to lose all of the attributes that made life there in any
way worthwhile. Finally the supreme court, backed by Cantave,
ruled that the council should continue, nay, had to continue, to
govern the country until the elections despite the resignation of
Duvalier's men. The commencement of voter registration, which
followed, was the signal for Duvalier, Jumelle, and three minor
candidates to join forces in opposition to Déjoie and Fignolé, who
they claimed had seized control of the administrative machinery
and electoral organization of the country; they threatened to boycott the elections while Déjoie and Fignolé explained that they
were simply dismantling the electoral machinery which had been
rigged by Sylvain to favor Duvalier.

The council decreed the end of public discussion of the elections. It prohibited broadcasts of any kind and closed down the
main stations in the capital. But this action provoked new disorders. Upcountry, in St. Marc, 10,000 farmers armed with knives
prevented food supplies from being taken to Port-au-Prince and set
up a committee of public safety to rule the port. In Cap Haitien a
cabal of five pro-Duvalierists established another committee of
public safety to control the affairs of the republic's second city
until such time as a provisional government responsive to "the will

61 Celestin, *Compilations*, I, 301–302.

of the people" should be established in the capital. There were similar secessionlike activities in Jérémie, Cayes, and Jacmel in the south. On May 18, a major public holiday, police fired on an anticouncil demonstration of many thousands in front of the cathedral, killing two and wounding others. Backers of Fignolé also used clubs and rifle butts on these and other demonstrators. The judges and the bar went on strike, schools and stores remained shut, and the army maintained its posture of neutrality. Two days later, however, the council tried to replace Cantave with Pierre Armand, the police chief, because of the army's refusal to move on St. Marc.

Once again the army, under Cantave, ousted the council and took control. At least it attempted to do so. Cantave banned all political meetings and proclaimed a modified form of martial law. But a new strike was the response of the urban population. Cantave, who blamed it upon the machinations of Déjoie and Fignolé, was unable to cope; he was unsure of his men, none of whom had been nor could be paid while the Banque remained on strike. There was a day or two of drift, at the end of which Duvalier, who had contributed to disorder by withdrawing his support from the council, decided that the time was propitious to resume his participation in the politics of conference and confrontation. Cantave asked the council to recommence its sittings, in the midst of which Armand — conceivably backed by Déjoie — and his contingent of soldiers declared war on Cantave and began several hours of shooting (one bomb was dropped) in the vicinity of the national palace. Duvalier supported Cantave. On the same day, May 25, mobs raced through the streets of the city, overturning cars, stoning, and looting in a manner that had become customary. The climax of this circus of contention was the decision of Duvalier, Jumelle, and Fignolé — the three darkest-skinned candidates — to join forces in an anti-Déjoie coalition, which had the effect, as a gesture of reconciliation, of bringing about the immediate resignations of both Cantave and Armand.[62]

[62] There was a government inquiry, the transcript of which was published as *Minutes d'une Commission de Recherches Réunie au Quartier-Général du Département de la Police de Port-au-Prince d'Ordre du Chef d'Etat-Major de l'Armée d'Haiti pour Enquêter sur les Évènements du Samedi 25 Mai 1957* (Port-au-Prince, 1958).

Fignolé, who on May 28 became president at the head of a cabinet consisting of five of his own supporters, four of Duvalier's, and three of Jumelle's, had fallen for Duvalier's carefully laid trap. Déjoie, who still could marshal impressive support in the cities and in the south, was effectively sidetracked, Jumelle had ceased to pose a major threat and, as Duvalier probably reckoned, Fignolé's image of incorruptibility would be compromised by the exercise of power, particularly in an impossible political situation. In General António Kebreau, who replaced Cantave, Duvalier also could count on a strong supporter.

For nineteen days Fignolé labored energetically to restore stability to Haiti. There was widespread hunger and the threat of famine because of a breakdown in communications and distribution, monetary disorder, and the paralysis of will that accompanies fear. Nevertheless, Fignolé continued his campaign against Déjoie, his sometime ally, tried both to purge and to bribe (with pay increases) the army, and, at the end of his first week in the presidency, summoned 1000 political partisans of all persuasions to exchange views on democracy in the presidential palace. He put his case for liberal democracy persuasively and generally appeared, by the middle of his second week, to have accomplished far more than would have seemed possible. His very success alarmed the other candidates, many of whom circulated rumors about an impending coup that would make Fignolé a permanent president. Whatever the precise etiology of his downfall, by June 15 Fignolé had played out the rope on which he had unwittingly been strung by Duvalier. A predawn raid by Kebreau and the army ended Fignolé's presidency and ushered in a new wave of disorder. Fignolists, employing the *tenèbres* method of passive resistance, banged rocks against steel drums and lampposts and wailed throughout the night in the crowded districts and shantytowns of Port-au-Prince. The army sent in its tanks, which sprayed houses with machine-gun fire. The mobs responded by stoning the army and burning and looting parts of the city. After several days of this kind of disorder the army triumphed; 50 were dead and more than 250 wounded. Fignolé was hustled off to New York. And then tanks were used to force shopkeepers to open up their commercial establishments and to bring about the arrests of supporters of Déjoie and Jumelle.

The army ruled decisively throughout the summer. It outlawed strikes and the closing of stores on any pretext, curbed the press, radio, and speech, and generally used the existing state of siege as an excuse to clamp down on all political activity not favorable to Duvalier. When the electoral legislation was promulgated by the junta in August, it included provisions which, because he was in exile, effectively disqualified Fignolé, and made the candidacies of Jumelle and Déjoie marginal. In an interview from exile in Manhattan, a forlorn and realistic Fignolé charged that the military was determined to stage elections which would put "a tool of the army" in power.[63] According to the electoral procedures announced by the junta, voters, who would, incidentally, include women for the first time, were expected to prepare their ballots beforehand — an open invitation to fraud — and then to deposit them at the polls on the appropriate day. Thirty-six hours before the election, Jumelle withdrew his candidacy because a Duvalierist had been appointed attorney general; his office was responsible for announcing the official returns. This left only Duvalier and Déjoie in the race, and by September 22 Duvalier had captured the allegiance of the army, which appreciated his sobriety and seeming honesty. The younger officers in the army, after all, had "suffered the Magloire regime without supporting or benefiting from it." [64]

The army presumed that Duvalier was close to the Americans, without whose assistance Haiti's economy was almost certain to suffer a massive seizure. Duvalier's other widely accepted qualities also contributed to his victory. He was closer to the people than Déjoie, he had a reputation as a thinker and sociologist, he appreciated the importance of *vodun,* and as a minister under Estimé he had sponsored social legislation and been associated — the stories were greater than the reality — with the successful anti-yaws campaign. He had also nurtured support in the rural areas, particularly among some of the more important peasant leaders and *houngans,* or *vodun* priests. The United States may also have seen

63 Rotberg, "Fignolé."
64 Manigat, *International Concern,* 47.

in him — as did many outsiders — the best hope for stability and decent government.[65] Fignolé had never trusted him, but few members of the Haitian elite, and fewer outsiders, trusted Fignolé or Déjoie. From Duvalier, there was a hope of honest, competent, if — and this was the prevailing opinion — uninspired rule. On September 22 — for all of these reasons, but mostly because the army organized the election and assisted illiterate peasants to cast their ballots — more than 900,000 Haitians, of 1,600,000 registered, voted overwhelmingly in favor of Papa Doc (and 23 of 37 of his followers seeking seats in the Chamber of Deputies) and against continued chaos. The official tally was Duvalier, 679,884, Déjoie, 266,993.[66]

[65] "People say we put Duvalier in power," later wrote an influential American, "which is not wholly true. When he was running for office in 1957 our astute ambassador, Gerald A. Drew, had serious reservations but was unable to keep an uncritical AID director from ostentatious support of the Duvalier bandwagon, a factor which very likely carried the election." Robert Debs Heinl, Jr., "Bailing out Duvalier," *New Republic*, CLVI (January 14, 1967), 15.

[66] Bernard Diederich and Al Burt, *Papa Doc: The Truth about Haiti Today* (New York, 1969), 10.

VI

The Personalization of Power

THE ACCESSION of Duvalier was widely welcomed, especially outside Haiti. His record — aside from the questionable machinations of 1957 (about which few knew much in detail) — was remarkably uncompromised for a man who had been involved in Haitian politics for so long. As a physician and a cabinet minister, he had assumed an enlightened attitude toward the peasants, he had not noticeably used his positions of public trust in order to enrich himself, and, to the extent that his network of acquaintances has been charted, he had long associated with the promoters and articulators of a Haitian intellectual and cultural renaissance. Although he rode into office on the shoulders of the soldiers, Duvalier's credentials were sufficiently good and — for Haiti — sufficiently unusual to persuade knowledgeable observers that under his leadership Haiti would at last have an opportunity to emerge from the political and social dark ages. He was expected to possess the vision and the ability to overturn the traditional stereotypes of Haitian politics in order to modernize, develop, and transform a system (more accurately, a mode) of political, economic, and social response whose antique mores made it peculiarly self-insulating and resistant to change. Hope of progress, in other words, was embodied — not unreasonably — in Duvalier, supported by the army, and aided and abetted by young and energetic representatives of the predominantly black, socially conscious, middle class.

But the progressive social revolution never occurred. Instead Haitians experienced tyranny, rapacity, and an all-encompassing, disfiguring dictatorship which has surpassed all of its Third

World counterparts in singlemindedness of purpose, tenacity, and lack of redeeming social and economic features. Duvalier chose to concentrate on the retention rather than the mobilization of power, on repression rather than elevation, and on oratorical flourishes rather than meaningful advances in national well-being. That he was able to do so and to survive for so long is a measure of his success, and equally of the extent to which the years of Duvalier have radically altered the accepted canons of Haitian political life. Before his assumption of the presidency, no ruler since Dessalines, except possibly Soulouque, had so thoroughly personalized the state and nullified the effective influence of the traditional repositories (institutions and informal groups) of countervailing power. No previous ruler had so neatly and traumatically divided his citizens into warring camps, so dramatically revived basic (oedipal?) tensions and fantasies, and so hypocritically maintained the rhetoric and trappings of parliamentary democracy while blatantly and with impunity flouting the constraints of constitution and custom. It has been said that no ruler in Haiti's history so deserves the opprobrium which has been heaped outside his palace door. None has been so canny, so calculating, so ruthless, so self-serving, and so successful (or lucky) as he. Before examining the present, discussing the possibilities for change and modernization, and scrutinizing the future, it is necessary to analyze the elaboration of Duvalier's dictatorship over time.

1. Toward Absolutism

During the months before he became president Duvalier promised, if elected, to eliminate all forms of oppression and abridgment of liberty and to campaign vigorously against hunger, poverty, illiteracy, and injustice. Democracy, he pronounced, "is the best form of government"; dictatorship was finished. He pledged himself to maintain the "great traditions" of the Haitian army. "The Army," he declared, must remain "a healthy and pure power, an immaculate sword in the service of Democratic Civilization." He refused to fight except with ideas: "I appeal," he said, "to every Haitian to behave better than he ever has before." He asked the electors of Gonaïves to consider all that he had achieved as a sociologist, doctor, and member of the government — "when all of my efforts were directed toward helping the people"; he would provide honest and peaceful government, and guide Haiti along the path of liberty. Above all, he planned to unify the country, for Haiti should belong to all, not just to the people of one class or color. Finally, after criticizing the selfish governments of the past, Duvalier asked the electors to choose between continued and increased servitude, or even regression, and the democracy of well-being.[1] During a press conference after his victory at the polls, Duvalier made renewed pledges of a similar nature, and in the same spirit of compromise and benevolence: "My Government will guarantee the exercise of liberty to all Haitians and will always give them the necessary protection in that exercise for their well-being. It undertakes to maintain that liberty for all without governmental pressure on anyone, and to preserve that Haitian-American unity which is for the mutual benefit of the two peoples, the two oldest democracies of the Western Hemisphere." Duvalier also promised to frame a new constitution which would "embody the principles which define revolutionary societies and which will give an historic interpretation to the social development of this country."[2] These electoral appeals and promises may now seem deliberately mendacious and specious, but at the time that they were uttered Duvalier may have intended them as more than mere mouthings of the hustings; in a manner different from that of his opponents and predecessors, he actually campaigned in all parts of the country, perhaps as much to persuade the army, wealthy merchants, and foreigners of his liberal intentions as to extract votes from a benumbed populace.

Duvalier, even more so than many other rulers, is capable of

[1] The above quotations and sentiments are taken from Duvalier's speeches throughout 1956 and 1957, as reprinted in his *Oeuvres Essentielles: La Marche à la Présidence* (Port-au-Prince, 1968), II. The dates on which the speeches were originally printed in various Haitian newspapers and the pages in *Oeuvres Essentielles,* in order of appearance above, are September 15, 1956 (5–6), September 7–8, 1956 (4), February 26, 1957 (268), February 21, 1957 (15), December 23, 1956 (33), February 2, 1957 (101), March 21, 1957 (138).
[2] *New York Times,* October 23, 1957.

compartmentalizing his ideas and actions.[3] If his triumph had been widely hailed, it is at least arguable that he would have developed the apparatus of merciless oppression more gradually and governed, for a time anyway, with some regard for the niceties of representative democracy. But these conditions were never even approximately realized, Duvalier's ascendancy being challenged from the start by Fignolé, Déjoie, Jumelle, and their partisans. Duvalier also could not have helped but be apprehensive about his ability to avoid the fate of Estimé, Lescot, and Magloire — or any of their nineteenth-century forebears — if he adhered too slavishly to decidedly un-Haitian postures of political behavior and notions of executive responsibility. If he believed at all in the authenticity of his own emergence as a national savior and regenerator, in his personal indispensability, and in the extent to which his own destiny was inextricably Haitian, then he was bound to justify the use of any and all means to achieve self-sanctified goals. He later became visibly megalomaniacal and, although both casual and clinical observations are lacking for the period before 1957, it is probable that close observation would have revealed the tendencies which were to become so apparent after Duvalier's accession to the presidency. (In this last connection, it is not frivolous to wish that we knew far more about Duvalier's early relations with his parents, and their methods of child rearing.) In retrospect, however, his subsequent responses to opposition were foreshadowed in his speeches only by revealing understatement: "I have no enemies except the enemies of the Nation." [4]

When Duvalier formally assumed power in October 1957, Haiti's treasury was virtually empty — exports having declined $14 million in value (coffee production fell 43 per cent) since 1956 and tourists having almost vanished — while several important United States aid programs had been suspended because of Hai-

3 This is not, however, the "compartmentalization" of Erika E. Bourguignon, "Class Structure and Acculturation in Haiti," *Ohio Journal of Science*, LII (1952), 318. She uses compartmentalization to "characterize individuals of all classes who are currently exposed to acculturative pressures." For her it is a "mode of dealing with materials derived from different cultural contexts." In the sense used above, Duvalier is simultaneously able to pursue two parallel, even divergent, paths of action. See also the discussion of Duvalier as a schizoid personality, below, 348–351.
4 *Oeuvres Essentielles*, II, 303 (May 15, 1957).

ti's failure to pay its share of their joint expenses. There was diplomatic hostility with the United States because the local police had murdered a prominent manufacturer who carried American citizenship, and martial law had been declared. Citizens had been authorized to shoot "enemies of the state" on sight. Duvalier naturally began operating on the assumption that he could govern only after his grip on the state had been strengthened, his opponents crushed, and nodules of potential future discontent dispersed. Before the end of 1957, he had thus made good use of the kinds of offensive tactics which were, with variation and some change of pace, to serve him effectively throughout the first twelve years of his regime. Within weeks of his inauguration he had declared an amnesty for political prisoners (it mainly benefited his own partisans) and had begun a systematic purge of the followers of Déjoie. Déjoie's political party (L'Alliance Démocratique d'Haiti) was said to be Communistic, and several of its officers were arrested. By December about one hundred suspected opponents had been jailed without trial, another hundred or so had gone into hiding, and several of the more prominent Haitians had begun to seek asylum in foreign chanceries. During the same month the leader of the transport workers' union was imprisoned without charges or a trial and, in the new year, the Union Nationale des Ouvriers d'Haiti, an embryo trade union federation, was banned and its general secretary detained. (Later he was banished to a village in the interior.) The roster of cabinet ministers was reshuffled within six weeks of its installation, and two of Duvalier's strongest supporters were dropped while others were assigned to new positions. A large loan, supposedly for the planting of bananas, but in reality a bribe to encourage Duvalier to oust exile plotters from Haiti, was accepted from Batista's Cuba and several well-placed Americans were retained as public relations advisers in order to counter criticism of a general kind in Washington. Early in 1958 the first foreign correspondent was expelled for "biased" reporting; and taxi drivers, backed by the government, demanded that the better-class stores in the capital should pay them a percentage of the purchases of the remaining tourists. These events were symptomatic, in their different ways, of Haiti's des-

perate plight. Even more discouraging to outside investors was
the atmosphere of tension and instability which permeated the
capital. In late February, therefore, both in order to improve the
economic prospects (and spoils) on which his own future depended and in order to flush out those opponents who had escaped
police dragnets, Duvalier persuaded Déjoie to emerge from hiding and to meet with him. In exchange the president proclaimed
another amnesty and emptied the jails. But he refused to lift the
ban on strikes or to restore freedom of speech, press, and radio. [5]
Indeed, it was soon clear that the amnesty marked but a strategically astute pause in Duvalier's drive for all-out power. And it
was the perpetuation of power for its own sake that mattered most.

Duvalier's policy was comparatively elemental, but surprisingly
effective for being so unexpected and resolute. He began to attack
on all fronts; moreover, where his predecessors or rivals would
have tried simply to eliminate their antagonists, Duvalier knew
that friends were potentially even more dangerous. Supporters
could turn against him at critical junctures, and, even more
importantly, no one — no matter how loyal — could be allowed
to develop separate, and potentially fissiparous, sources of political
or economic strength. First he turned to the army in order to
forestall the emergence of another Magloire. Without the tacit
cooperation of General António Kebreau, Duvalier would never
have gained the presidency or weathered the turmoil of his first
hundred days in office. Kebreau's loyalty was also unquestioned,
but he had been talking and acting as if he wanted the army
to maintain a posture of and a capacity for independent action.
It was widely, and probably correctly, assumed that Duvalier
continued to rule only with Kebreau's support. A weaker, less
audacious, and less wily ruler would have sought to conciliate the
general, but Duvalier, because he knew that he could rely upon
the backing of many of the most ambitious younger officers, refused to retreat. In early March he declared that he, not the
army, made all of the decisions in Haiti. Less than a week later,

5 Throughout this chapter, unless otherwise noted, the record of the period is de-
rived from contemporary accounts in *Le Nouvelliste, Le Nouveau Monde,* and *Haiti
Herald* (all newspapers of Port-au-Prince), *The Times, New York Times,* and
Hispanic American Report, and from subsequent interviews with participants.

he transferred twenty officers, including Kebreau's closest friends and potential allies, to various remote rural posts. Two days later he dismissed Kebreau (who fled to the Dominican Embassy), appointed Colonel Maurice Flambert (the commander of the Dessalines battalion) to a six-year term as his successor, and set about removing all of the army officers whose loyalty was unproved or, if loyal, whose strength of character might subsequently serve as a focus for discontent. This action, like the many later purges, also permitted younger officers to be promoted more rapidly than they could otherwise have been, and enabled the president to begin introducing black semiliterates from the ranks into important positions.

That officers should be loyal to him alone, and not to their commanders, soon became apparent, and well-rewarded. He "undermined any potential cohesiveness based on esprit de corps between high-ranking and intermediary officers." [6] In the same way he insisted upon personally appointing *chefs de section*, the rural administrators of Haiti who had hitherto always been nominated by the army chief of staff. With an astuteness that became characteristic, he also redirected the other chains of military command. The chief of the Dessalines battalion (a role Magloire had played under Estimé), the head of the central garrison of the capital, began to report directly to Duvalier without going through the normal military communications links and the chief of staff. The president also began to concentrate all of the country's modern small arms, machine guns, cannon, and ammunition in the lower basements of the palace (a process he completed in 1964), the better to oversee its use and disposition.

The press was next. There were then six or seven prominent daily newspapers in the capital, none of which had a circulation larger than 3000 or 4000, and each of which was backed by the government or conflicting interest groups. Several were unabashedly pro-Déjoie or doggedly independent and therefore implicity opposed to Duvalier's regime. Furthermore, dictators

[6] Manigat, *Haiti of the Sixties*, 50. The Dessalines battalion, so called because it was quartered in the Caserne Dessalines behind the national palace, was properly called the Département du Palais National. But this is not the "palace guard" of Duvalier.

abhor dissent; if tolerated, it tends to encourage those who would aspire to overthrow the regime. Its articulation also often serves to arouse new discontent and expectations of change. But in Duvalier's Haiti, where subjectivism and egocentricity had been elevated to the level of policy, criticism in print, or even a lack of lavish obeisance, derogated the president's otherwise self-fulfilling vision of himself and his actions. If it were more important to reign and rule than to preside over the rejuvenation of Haiti — and by the end of Duvalier's first six months in office a qualitative shift of this kind had been discerned — then it would be essential, no matter the cost, to crush disaffection, however timorous, wherever and whenever it might appear.

When the *Haiti-Miroir* wrote of the growing climate of terror, and specifically of the intimidation of prominent but defenseless citizens of Port-au-Prince, its publisher and leading columnist were arrested. The editor of the *Indépendance* was detained when he complained about Duvalier's interference with the press and, so that the lesson would be driven home, the plants of both dailies and *Le Matin,* another antagonistic newspaper in the capital, were destroyed in midnight raids. A few weeks later *Le Patriote,* a fourth Port-au-Prince paper partial to the growing forces of opposition, was persuaded to suspend publication after its offices were bombed and members of its staff seriously injured. (A spokesman for Duvalier claimed that these "outrages" had been perpetrated by unknown "fanatics" partisan to Déjoie.)[7] Later, *La Phalange,* the widely read Catholic-supported daily, was harassed and, when Duvalier felt himself strong enough, suppressed. But, with this last exception, from about mid-1958, none of Haiti's many newspapers or radio stations dared to criticize or offend the regime. Destruction, detention, and torture were seen to provide little recompense for bold adherence to the traditions of independent journalism. Moreover, Duvalier held each of the proprietors in thrall by virtue of discreet subsidies, control of access to electricity and labor, the supply of officially written editorial matter which the newspapers were compelled to print as their own, and the forcible addition to their staffs of writers em-

7 Clément Barbot, quoted in the *New York Times,* January 22, 1959.

ployed by and obviously loyal to the ministry of information. Outgoing press cables, personal telegrams, some telephone calls, and the mails were also censored, if sometimes haphazardly and inefficiently.

By mid-1958 the usual Haitian intolerance of criticism and dissent had been reinforced by the elaboration of new techniques and weapons of repression. Individual disloyalty and disaffection were discouraged by the planting of informers, nighttime raids by masked men supposedly called *cagoulards* (after the French Fascist organization of the 1930's) — the modern version of Soulouque's *zinglins* and the forerunners of the *tonton macoutes* — detention for weeks or months without charges or trial, torture, and the mysterious disappearance or death of those most vocally alarmed by the trend of events. Terror of this kind is truly effective only if it is wildly arbitrary and capricious, if explanations are never more than implications, and if the low-level operatives do not themselves comprehend the overriding motives and are actuated by more base and easily aroused animosities of their own.

In all of these particulars Duvalier had begun to achieve signal success by the beginning of his eighth month in office. He was attacking on nearly all fronts, immobilizing and demoralizing the normal forces of local opposition: the army, the press, merchants, and individuals, especially the Port-au-Prince elite. Among the arrests in the last category was that of the country's leading poultry raiser and his pregnant wife, both mulattoes, who were seized in the middle of the night. (They may have favored Jumelle.) And when a brave deputy in the assembly dared demand an explanation of the arrests and terror, he too was taken into custody despite his parliamentary immunity. (Duvalier, who blandly denied any knowledge of the arrests, said that the deputy had been plotting to overthrow the government.) In May, after bomb explosions in the capital — probably detonated on Duvalier's orders — had provided him with the necessary excuses, the subservient National Assembly voted the president extraordinary powers (he was frequently to rule by decree in the years that followed), formally suspended civil liberties, and declared a state of siege. The government also imposed a curfew. Quickly Duvalier decided that

Déjoie and his partisans were responsible for the disturbances, and for the subsequent wave of unrest in the capital. Déjoie was outlawed. At first he hid in the open country near Port-au-Prince. Then he wandered around the countryside during the day and, after the vigilance of the army relaxed, Déjoie, dressed as a woman and with his face and arms blackened, entered the city each night to converse with political allies. Eventually he fled into the Mexican Embassy, and, after the ambassador refused Duvalier's request to release Déjoie as a common criminal, the Haitian guard around the embassy was withdrawn and Déjoie flew to Mexico before going on to the United States and the Dominican Republic. "For the last six months," Déjoie told reporters upon his arrival in Mexico City, "I have not had one night of uninterrupted sleep. There has not been a night when I was not aware that I might be either betrayed or executed or assassinated." [8] Almost simultaneously, Duvalier began to search for Clément and Ducasse Jumelle, both of whom had gone into hiding with prices on their heads.

The atmosphere of repression was heightened after the failure of the first of the five invasion attempts which were to punctuate twelve years of Duvalier's rule. Following a pattern that was later to become familiar, a tiny group of exiles and mercenaries — in this case three ex-army officers who had been purged by Duvalier and five Americans (including two deputy sheriffs from Dade County, Florida) — hired a launch near Miami, sailed to Haiti, and found, to their dismay, and perhaps contrary to what they had been led to expect, that the populace was not ready to rise up on the appearance of such a body of armed men. (Another airplane load of sixteen men and munitions was prevented from departing by American customs officials in Miami.) Most of the later groups were, in supposed emulation of Fidel Castro, to land on the isolated northern or southern shores of the republic. But in 1958 the cabal was particularly bold: after landing near Déluge, south of St. Marc and fifty miles north of Port-au-Prince, and shooting the local military commandant, they drove to the capital and took over the Caserne Dessalines without a fight. Had they gathered

8 *New York Times*, July 13, 1969. Déjoie died in New York on July 11, 1969.

any support from the soldiers in the barracks and kept the paucity of their numbers secret, they conceivably could have attacked the palace, next door, where Duvalier had moved all of the army's weapons, and quickly ousted Duvalier. Instead they chose to take a stand in the Caserne, which soldiers and *macoutes* soon stormed. All eight of the rebels were killed. [9]

The abortive *coup* played into Duvalier's hands. From the National Assembly the president received new "extraordinary" powers to govern by decree for six months; he made plotting against the security of the state and attempts to assassinate the head of state, government officials, or army officers punishable by death, and promulgated a new code according to which persons spreading rumors or "false news" would be shot. This latter legislation was made retroactive to mid-1957. He also promoted Flambert to major general. His police and *macoutes* meanwhile made more than one hundred political arrests and, said one report, shut down forty-six newspapers throughout the country. Displays of loyalty were also solicited, especially from wealthy businessmen, who made the first of many special contributions to the defense of the realm. Deputies donated one month's salary and Flambert collected nearly $17,000 from his fellow army officers. All radio transmitters, many of which were in missionary hands, were confiscated, and, for seventeen nights, a dusk-to-dawn curfew remained in effect. During these post-invasion days of rising tension, the secret police also discovered Clément Jumelle's two brothers, Charles and Ducasse, in a car. Both, handcuffed, were shot "while resisting arrest." [10] Foreigners, whose elimination would have involved Haiti in interminable complications with their various mother countries, were expelled on a few hours' notice. Some, like a French priest who had lived in the republic for twenty-nine years and a British garage-owner who had resided there almost as long, were suspected of disloyalty to the regime. All residents and passing tourists, whatever their background, also were subjected

[9] The fullest contemporary account of this invasion is contained in a speech by Thomas P. Whitney to the Overseas Press Club of the United States, August 13, 1958, reprinted in *Haiti Herald*, November 2, 1959. See also Diederich and Burt, *Papa Doc*, 113–120.
[10] *Hemispherica*, VI (October 1958), 2.

to rough searches in Port-au-Prince and the suburbs of Carrefour and Pétionville. Roadblocks were set up in various sections of the urban area, and all cars — even those of daily commuters — were searched thoroughly. In time, the *tonton macoutes* manning the barricades regularly demanded "tolls" from the occupants of each car, a practice which continued, more or less on a free-lance basis, until 1964. Later in the year — to choose one from among the many other indications of the arbitrary exercise of power — a distinguished leader of the Haitian bar was jailed when he labeled a series of military courts unconstitutional. In order to prevent merchants from provoking strife by closing down their establishments, Duvalier prohibited the declaration of commercial default or bankruptcy without prior permission. And Déjoie, the archenemy, was sentenced to death *in absentia* by one of many drumhead trials held by hastily convened military courts.

Without the acquiescence and support of a significant proportion of the military, the newly raised paramilitary, and the civil service, Duvalier could hardly have crushed his opposition so easily and effectively. The force of his own personality — what might be called charisma if he had ever tried after the election to appeal to the masses — his unquestionable personal ruthlessness, and his masterful ability to make the most of the vanities and weaknesses of foes and followers alike enabled him to make others do his bidding. But this was, in any event, the Haitian pattern; it may well be that Duvalier filled some deep subconscious longing. That he could manipulate and control is established, but how he gained such a hypnotic hold over his subordinates is less clear. Some of the illiterate men of the country who served in his bodyguard accorded him the awe and respect which worship of the *vodun* gods had taught them to render to a leader who seemed, and perhaps claimed, to be in touch with the supernatural. Duvalier's somber dress (he can resemble the Baron Samedi of *vodun*) and patterns of speech impart an aura which is effective in such contexts. Even more evocative is and was his mysterious manner, deviousness of mind, and willingness to take advantage of the superstitions of his less sophisticated fellow countrymen. Duvalier was never loath to associate himself with the powers and ritual of *vodun,* the better to impress his allies and intimidate his enemies.

In secular contexts, too, Duvalier began during 1957 and 1958 both to try to revive his country's listless economy and to prepare a program of action for the future. Only by making or promising improvements in the former sphere could he provide the prospect of the kind of reward which has generally attracted support in Haiti. The function of a program of action was analogous; plans (the more elaborate and grandiose the better) and planning gave hope and encouraged Haitians, or at least those Haitians who were sufficiently involved to care, to accept the rhetoric and delusion of deferred gratification. Instead of an ideology, which was never developed and which was foreign to his approach, Duvalier attempted to provide bread (but no circuses) and the promise of jam. It was also essential, as much for psychological as for the obvious economic reasons, for Duvalier to regularize his relations with the United States and obtain financial assistance therefrom. Haitians still believed that their presidents rose and fell largely at the behest of the great North American uncle; if, during his first few months, Duvalier had been unable to demonstrate that he was blessed by firm American backing, then he might have forfeited his claim to leadership — which he had otherwise justified. Aid, and talk of aid, were of course prime indicators of his place in the pantheon of American interest, and new contracts with commercial firms from the United States were nearly as useful in the unremitting psychological wars between a Haitian head of state and those of his citizens who could make or break a regime. To this end, the willingness of the American Export-Import Bank, which had already lent Haiti $24 million for the still unfinished Artibonite Valley project, to permit Haiti to draw the remaining $3 million of its credit despite the failure of Haiti to keep up its repayments, was exceedingly helpful. (The International Monetary Fund allowed Haiti to use a $5 million standby credit.) The International Cooperation Administration provided Haiti with about $2 million in aid, $400,000 of which was allocated primarily to the irrigation of the plains of Quartier Morin in the north and Cayes-Torbeck in the south. Early in 1959, again, the United States

lent Haiti a further $4.3 million for the completion of the Arti-
bonite irrigation scheme begun during the Magloire administration,[11] and agreed to provide $3.5 million immediately in order to
help the government balance its budget and relieve its crippling
shortage of foreign exchange. Apparently the United States was
motivated to assist Duvalier's Haiti so munificently because it was
convinced that only he could provide the necessary stability.
From 1959 fear of the spread of Castroism from Cuba to Haiti and
then to the Dominican Republic also seems to have been influential. The State Department and the International Cooperation
Administration chose to ignore Duvalier's methods and concentrate on his role as a force for continuity and anti-Communism.[12]

Duvalier was equally active in encouraging the inflow of private
capital. By means of presidential decrees he gave concessions for
mineral and petroleum exploration and exploitation, the construction and operation of television stations, the planting and
processing of kenaf, sesame, and ramie, the processing of guano,
the manufacture of chocolate, a fertilizer industry, the development of casinos and hotels, the construction of a sugar factory, the
improvement of the telephone system, etc. A contract was signed
with a Florida-based company for the redevelopment of an odious waterfront slum in the capital, the costs to be shared (nominally, anyway) by the government and the American promoters.
Haiti gave the Standard Commercial Tobacco Co., Inc., of New
York an exclusive right to export and import tobacco, the government itself retaining the exceedingly lucrative local monopoly not
only of cigarette sales, but also of matches. (Proceeds from this
monopoly were to have gone into a nonfiscal account which could
be employed for extrabudgetary expenditures such as security.)[13]
To a Virginia company Duvalier gave the exclusive privilege of
producing and buying bananas for export. A Japanese fishing corporation planned to establish stations on the Haitian coast in order
to exploit the surrounding waters of the Caribbean. However, not
all of these relatively large-scale enterprises actually commenced

---

11 See above, 180.
12 *New York Times*, February 28, 1959.
13 For a further discussion of nonfiscal accounts and their uses, see 273, below.

operations; nor were their contributions to the gross domestic product all quantifiable. Yet each, the numerous minor ones, and the resumption of activity at the Texan-owned Caribbean Flour Mills (import) and Haitian-American Meat and Provision Company (export to Puerto Rico),[14] added in measurable ways to Duvalier's ability to maintain himself and his retinue during the difficult first eighteen months of his tenure.

Projects with a wider appeal were also articulated by Duvalier during the critical opening months of his regime. He has always appreciated the importance of image and has never been reluctant to coat the pill of dictatorship for (largely) external consumption. He introduced legislation that provided that literates would each be required to instruct at least one illiterate to read and write Creole and that foreigners would also learn Creole or pay $2 a month into a fund for teachers of illiterates. A detailed five-year program for the construction of rural schools was introduced, with fanfare. The president was also busy, during mid-1958, ceremoniously inaugurating projects of unquestioned social value: the scheme for rehousing the slum-dwellers of La Saline; a new livestock market in Croix-des-Bouquets, the important entrepôt in the Cul-de-sac plain; a shopping center; a mortgage bank; and the proposed new jet airport. He also welcomed social security regulations which applied for the first time to employees of commerce and industry, and which depended partially on a state subsidy. His minister of health outlined the government's impressive plans for new hospitals, laboratories, and clinics in the rural areas. The minister of public works promised to electrify all of Haiti within a very few years, to reopen and maintain roads long closed, and to reduce unemployment by constructing

---

[14] The Haitian-American Meat and Provision Company, owned by Clint P. Murchison, was later linked to Robert G. Baker, the onetime U.S. Senate aide who was convicted of using his political influence for improper private gain. He arranged the relaxation of American veterinary requirements and a juggling of the quota on beef and pork imports so that the Haitian factory could ship its tinned products to the lucrative American and Puerto Rican markets. Baker received a fee of 1 cent per pound on the meat sold in the United States. He was paid at least $20,000 before other activities brought him to the attention of the Senate Rules Committee and the U.S. courts. See *Hispanic American Report*, XVII (March and April 1964), 40, 134; *New York Times*, July 18, 1969.

a variety of necessary public works. Some of these early initiatives, like the airport and the social security reforms, were eventually realized, and many of the slum-dwellers were transferred to slightly better quarters, but new rural schools and hospitals have always been conspicuous by their absence, and there was far more talk, in the manner of earlier epochs in Haitian history,[15] than concerted action. Few of the projects, wrote a foreigner then resident in Haiti, "have ever gone beyond the paper stage; they appear to be dummy operations set up for the benefit of promoters and their friends in office." [16]

One handicap was always the shortage of funds for development; so much was siphoned off in salaries or supplementary payments to unnamed individuals that little was left for actual projects, some of which, even when they were occasionally begun, were soon abandoned after financial resources were exhausted. Another was the chronic lack of administrative follow-through. To take one example, in about 1962 the statistical service, which lacked trained manpower and had not published a set of annual statistics since 1958, divided an annual budget of about $100,000 among eighty employees, leaving about 10 per cent for operations. Thirty of the employees apparently never appeared in the office, and there was an item of $4000 in the budget to pay the wages of the service's five chauffeurs. But the service possessed only one automobile, which usually lacked fuel.[17] Most important, however, was Duvalier's reluctance (a reluctance which he has shared with most of the previous rulers of Haiti) to ameliorate the conditions of Haitian life. Haitian governments have long believed that the rural areas were best left to themselves. The provision of educational and medical services to peasants could well invite trouble. And roads and other public works, although useful for purposes of security, might encourage mobility and the introduction of new ideas into comfortably isolated and (from the point of view of the ruling elite) happily backward parts of the republic.

15 See the comments by Hesketh Prichard, 3, above.
16 Lynn Grossberg, "Haiti: The Explosive Buffer," *Nation*, CXCI (August 20, 1960), 84.
17 Berkeley Rice, "Haiti: Last Act of a Tragicomedy," *Harper's Magazine* (May 1963), 73.

During the first year of Duvalier's rule it became apparent, despite the heady rhetoric of uplift and the promise of reform, that he was interested in gaining power more for the sake of power than for using that power to transform the state. There was much talk of social revolution, of the rehabilitation and advancement of the black middle and lower classes, of a cultural renaissance which would stress the African heritage of the majority of Haitians and eradicate any lingering traces of inferiority, of a Haitian "Operation Bootstrap," and of what was called a new nationalism. He did provide opportunities for poorly educated Haitians by creating new security services and altering the composition of the army. He also eliminated any remaining preferences for mulattoes in the civil service, recruiting and promoting blacks much more liberally than before. But these shifts in the complexion of patronage and followership were meant to serve ends more political than social. Furthermore, had the proceeds of the special, often *ad hoc,* and highly irregular "taxes" which were imposed on merchants and the affluent been devoted to social change and relieving the lot of the poor, then the claims of the Duvalier regime to be revolutionary could have been advanced. Instead, Duvalier, and the essentially urban and largely black bourgeoisie with which he shared (or ostensibly shared) the responsibilities, burdens, and spoils of office, behaved from the start as Haitian ruling oligarchies have always behaved. They preyed upon the less fortunate — whoever was out of favor and, on the Sicilian model, could claim no protector — jealously guarded their "territory" insofar as they could gain marginal degrees of autonomy and, together, perpetuated the neglect to which the underprivileged in Haiti had long been accustomed.

Insecurity plagues and obsesses dictators of every circumstance, station, and psychological composition. From the first, Duvalier was sufficiently well schooled in Haitian history to appreciate how thoroughly his countrymen would abhor radical deviations from the island's political norms. Since — even for a Haitian — he was also unusually prone to paranoia, his concern for security would have been heightened. Strictly on commonsense political grounds, too, Duvalier understood and chose to guard against his ex-

treme vulnerability. His manner of coping with insecurity has
already been indicated; what was unusual and what proved so effective, however, was Duvalier's masterful sense of timing and his
ability to keep both opponents and supporters continually off balance. He would strike without warning, willingly sacrificing the
loyal with the potentially disloyal, sometimes because a man or a
group was developing — possibly divisive — sources of strength
or presuming or talking too much, sometimes because the president's sensitive antennae detected troublesome resonance emanating from only vaguely located quarters, sometimes because he
wanted to reward particularly loyal subordinates, sometimes because it was the moment to shake the bag of tricks, and nearly always — and with frequency — in order to show, again and again,
who was boss. In late 1958, for example, he reshuffled the cabinet
for the second time within a year and, then, in December
dismissed the entire general staff of the army (two generals,
ten colonels, and forty lieutenant-colonels), replacing the recently
promoted Major General Flambert by Colonel Pierre Merceron,
formerly the police chief of the capital, and began the process of appointing younger, darker, presumably more loyal, officers — men
who had been trained after the end of the occupation — to the
vacant positions. (Merceron and his deputy, however, were mulattoes.) Flambert and his predecessor, Kebreau, were sent overseas as ambassadors. At roughly the same time (the scheme was
first broached in 1958), Duvalier devised a neat method of further
insulating his 5100-man army from politics and simultaneously
adding to his own prestige and security; he invited the United
States Marines to send a small mission to Haiti for the purpose of
retraining the Garde, originally a creation of the Marines, for internal security and public service. In January 1959 about eight
(later sixty-four) Marine, Coast Guard, and Navy personnel under Colonel Robert Debs Heinl, Jr., arrived and set about trying
to operate in what proved the most impossible and contradictory
of situations: "My job," wrote Heinl, "was to help the Haitian
military do [its] jobs better and at the same time get them back
into trim as a force capable of holding off coups at home as well
as adventures by Premier Fidel Castro." Duvalier, however,

"wanted us only as a show of US support for his regime. As soon as he found that I would not allow American military aid to be misused to enhance his personal power and that we were bent on rebuilding his army around a professionally trained corps of honest, patriotic young officers and NCO's, his interest cooled. . . . I felt like a doctor transfusing blood into one arm of a failing patient while another MD — Dr. Duvalier — had a suction pump on the other." [18]

Duvalier presumably saw the purges and Heinl's retraining and re-equipment exercises (the United States supplied Haiti with matériel in 1960 and 1961) as complementary facets of the same process. Without Heinl, regular purging could only have drained the Haitian armed forces (and the army was also the police, the coast guard, and the air force according to a reorganization which dated from the 1920's) of their morale and ability to resist internally and externally generated threats to the regime. But because he and Clément Barbot, a black, and his closest and toughest adviser during 1958–59, still feared the army, and because the Garde Présidentiel (the palace guard which was established in 1959) was worried about Heinl's mission and the attitude of the United States, Duvalier needed a cadre of thugs to run the kinds of errands which no American-advised army would have been permitted to handle. He had — in the *cagoulards* — a body of men already devoted to the regime and willing, if turned loose, to sell their services to an opposition, so they evolved the organization which became known as the *tonton macoutes* or, more politely, the *Milice Civile* (until 1962) and, since, the *Volontaires de la Sécurité Nationale*. (A *macoute* is a special kind of bag or sack, *Ton Ton* means uncle, and, by extension, the *tonton macoutes* — the bagmen — are bogeymen who dispatch their victims.) Although Barbot claimed in 1959 to have 25,000 such men under arms, it is unlikely that the *macoutes* ever numbered more than 10,000 and, during the early years, not more than about half that number. The hard core, moreover, was composed of about 2000 toughs based in the capital.

[18] Robert Debs Heinl, Jr., "Haiti: A Case Study in Freedom," *New Republic*, CL (May 16, 1964), 15.

The *macoutes* were distinguished from the army, and from private citizens in or out of the government, by the freedom with which they used their guns and by their unswerving loyalty to the president. He alone enrolled a *macoute* and granted him permission to carry a gun. Tacitly, he also gave the *macoutes* (only their trusted elite were paid) the privilege of extorting and corrupting, and of interfering with and ignoring all of the usual liberties and rights enjoyed by citizens. In turn they reported directly to him, only the very lowest ranking and most rural channeling their accounts through intermediaries. The *macoutes* with bases in the countryside were distinguished from those of the urban elite by their affecting of a uniform — usually of faded blue denim — their use of old Springfield-type rifles (they were usually seen encumbered by bandoliers of cartridges), and their recruitment from the traditional leadership structure. Often local leaders of the *macoute* were *vodun houngans* or priests, or *chefs de section*.

In the cities, especially in Port-au-Prince, the *macoutes* were recruited from tougher stock — from the paracriminal element or from among the newly migrant, slum-dwelling classes of the capital. They served as a security force and a secret police — as shock troops and intimidators. In a manner reminiscent of Prohibition-era gangsters, they dressed in shiny blue-serge suits, and tucked their revolvers into belts or armpit holsters. They picked fights and settled grudges in the streets, and left their victims to lie all day in the sun in order to indicate their strength and disdain for the normal processes of justice. For Duvalier, they were the embodiment of terror and power, a ruthless extension of the personalized, predatory state. From behind their dark, steel-rimmed glasses they could observe the army, civil servants, journalists, tourists — almost anyone. And they knew that their arbitrary actions — however reflexive in origin — would be well rewarded. Because of the structure of their loyalty, the lack of any institutional *esprit de corps,* and their fundamental vulnerability as individuals who derived their strength solely from him and his license to carry arms, Duvalier could control them, dividing and conquering, and purging as the occasion demanded. He used them, and they were his creatures.

Barbot, more than any single figure since 1960, was responsible for helping Duvalier to shape and elaborate the machinery of repression. Nominally the president's private secretary, Barbot may be more accurately described as Duvalier's only trusted troubleshooter. In this capacity he performed effectively, transmitting orders to the ministers and the *macoutes*, dealing with foreign figures of importance — like Heinl — and, conceivably, even influencing the content of the president's short-term policies. Barbot's printed calling cards at one time identified him as the chief of Haiti's secret police, but he later declared that the cards had been "wrongfully printed" and had been "recalled." [19] Barbot, from Gonaïves, was five feet eight inches tall, had accompanied Duvalier into hiding between 1954 and 1956, and was — according to those who knew him well — utterly ruthless, terribly vindictive, very nationalistic, and unceasingly bitter about his own childhood treatment at the hands of the Roman Catholic Church (he was whipped by priests for suggesting in school that Dessalines was a patriot). But he was not a "doublecrosser" and he conceivably believed sincerely in the various reforms that Duvalier professed to support.[20] During the unusually troubled months of 1959, and especially during May and June of that year when Duvalier was incapacitated by a serious heart attack, Barbot was exceedingly influential — even dominant. With the *macoutes*, he dispersed violent, antiregime demonstrations by the slum-dwellers of the capital, victimized minor opponents in petty, bullying ways, intimidated shopkeepers, hunted down followers of Déjoie within weeks of an official amnesty which applied to him and them, and which was obviously intended — once again — simply to flush out into the open known opponents of the government (four prominent backers of Déjoie were among those killed; another twenty-nine fled to foreign embassies), and, despite the serious threat of famine in the northwest due to drought, relentlessly concentrated on defending the regime against enemies real and imagined.

The bizarre side of Duvalierism was demonstrated with some

19 Interview with Barbot by Peter Kihss, *New York Times*, January 22, 1959.
20 Interview with Colonel Robert Debs Heinl, Jr., July 22, 1969.

force shortly afterward, in April, when Clément Jumelle, aged
forty-two, who had been hiding for twenty-one months in peasant
huts and holes in the ground, staggered, gravely ill with uremia,
into the Cuban Embassy and died. Because of *vodun* — ostensibly
a religion ordering the relations between the living and the dead,
in practice it defines a formal set of relationships among the living
themselves, especially those involving the question of power —
and the respect and fear customarily accorded the deceased, the
proper interment of the dead is obligatory and important in Haitian life. But the *macoutes* and the police interfered with Jumelle's funeral procession; as the coffin started out toward its last
resting place, Duvalier's men forcibly hijacked the hearse, sped to
St. Marc, and buried him there.[21] Believers in *vodun* assumed
that Duvalier wanted to transform Jumelle into a *zombi* and use
him, and his essential organs, in order magically to strengthen the
dictatorship.[22] Others supposed that Duvalier simply feared disturbances during and after the burial services or, with a juvenile
vindictiveness which is psychologically understandable and hardly
unknown in Haiti, simply wanted to heap the last possible degra-
dation upon the Jumelles as punishment and as a warning to potential dissidents.

Although there were signs of unrest before, the president's
heart attack in 1959 — as always when a strong man is temporarily or possibly permanently removed from the scene — caused
acute tension, aroused renewed enthusiasm among the oppressed,
and provoked the kinds of incidents that can lead to a general
uprising. Bombs went off in a variety of places — in a nightclub,
near another, near the home of the head of the army, amidst a
religious celebration, in a theater, and randomly throughout the
capital. Jean Magloire, the minister of the interior and national
defense, was wounded by a grenade. A senator even dared verbally to attack the regime vitriolically. Then, after Duvalier had

21 This incident obviously provided the basis for the interrupted funeral in
Graham Greene, *The Comedians* (Harmondsworth, 1967), 119–126. The fullest account of the actual incident is in *The Haiti Herald*, April 19, 1959.
22 For the use of magical powers, see Rémy Bastien, "Voudon and Politics in Haiti,"
in Harold Courlander and Rémy Bastien, *Religion and Politics in Haiti* (Washington, 1966), 60; Huxley, *Invisibles,* 43.

recovered and airfields and even the flat roofs of Christophe's lofty and inaccessible Citadel had been strewn with old petrol drums to prevent airplane landings, the presidential palace had been sandbagged and ostentatiously prepared for attack, and several hundred Haitians had been arrested — including a number of mulattoes — and scores had been tortured and beaten, thirty-one men, nearly all of whom were Cuban (a similar invasion in April had been thwarted by the Cuban coast guard), landed near Les Irois on the distant southwestern coast of Haiti opposite Jamaica. But this invasion attempt was as forlorn as the others. The Haitian army, airlifted there and advised throughout by Heinl's mission, soon killed twenty-six and captured five; devoid of logistic support from without or a network of dedicated *maquisards* within, they represented a puny force around which few peasants would rally. The several prisoners who were later brought to the capital said that they had been told that 100 armed Haitians were already fighting the government and that 5000 or more Haitians would revolt after learning of their landing. They said that they were shocked to find no revolutionary fervor among the Haitian peasantry. But Haiti was not Cuba, and the peculiar terrain and human complexion of the Sierra Maestra were lacking everywhere in Haiti. Nor were the invaders led by men of resource and dedication like Castro and Ernesto Ché Guevara.

Duvalier recovered from his illness with surprising alacrity and, as far as could be discerned subsequently, with little observable damage. It is not known precisely when Duvalier's diabetic condition was diagnosed, but the mild diabetes with which he is afflicted often becomes apparent during middle age. By 1959, anyway, he was being treated with injections of insulin (a hormone produced in the pancreas which has the effect of lowering the blood sugar level). The president's cardiac arrest in May therefore could have been produced by a true heart attack (myocardial infarction) or as a result of metabolic imbalance secondary to his diabetes. Whatever the precise etiology or the exact diagnosis of his attending physicians, his condition was made more critical by the amount of insulin with which he was immediately injected. In 1959 insulin, which is lethal in high doses and which is difficult to measure in the blood stream, was in some Latin American circles an accepted treatment (but usually in lower doses) for heart attacks. It was believed to have a stabilizing effect on the injured heart muscle, but an overdosage of insulin can cause low blood sugar which, in turn, can result in dysfunction of the brain temporarily or permanently. In any event, Duvalier was in a coma for nine hours. American specialists, rushed to Haiti by the U.S. Navy from Guantánamo Bay on Heinl's initiative, eventually resuscitated the president, however, and assisted his recovery.

There is no doubt that Duvalier's will to regain the summit of power was great and, by mid-1959, successful. Yet physicians assert that since diabetes is a metabolic disorder which is often accompanied by and accelerates the progress of arteriosclerosis, a diabetic who has had a cardiac seizure (which could be a by-product of this disease) is apt to have a more limited life expectancy than otherwise. He might be prone to renewed heart attacks and, almost certainly, circulatory deterioration which might affect the functioning of the legs and brain. It would also not surprise most medical practitioners if the combination of cardiac arrest, insulin shock, and coma had affected Duvalier's mental processes. Yet the extent of any change or deterioration was not immediately noted, except by Barbot and one or two casual amateur observers, and any attempt to link the president's subsequent mental excesses with his heart attack and coma must be regarded as lacking in evidence.[23] Furthermore, in Haiti the level of repression and the scale of ruthlessness were as high before as after the period of illness in 1959.

Illnesses and invasions, or merely an apparent relaxation of vigilance, can imply weakness. In the aftermath of a dangerous summer, Duvalier predictably moved to reaffirm his personal rule by attacking real and imagined enemies. In September the Senate, under duress, again declared a state of siege (in order to combat a putative Communist conspiracy) and gave Duvalier power

23 But Herbert Morrison, who worked for Duvalier as an adviser and who may have been using an alias, believes that the illness marked a turning point. "From that moment on he started to disintegrate right in front of my eyes. He started going mad." Quoted in Trevor Armbrister, "Is There Any Hope for Haiti?" *Saturday Evening Post,* CCXXXVI (June 15, 1963), 80.

to rule by decree and suspend parliamentary immunity. He used this power almost immediately to impeach six of the country's twenty senators who had taken advantage of his illness to criticize Jean Magloire and had subsequently questioned the manner in which state funds were being disbursed. (They sought refuge in foreign embassies.)[24] A mock election was held so that more tractable senators could be chosen by the people. Shortly afterward he reshuffled the cabinet for the fourth time. Meanwhile, he resumed the reign of terror which had abated while the invaders were being pursued and captured. A prominent writer, to take one example, was arrested when he went to police headquarters to receive an exit permit so that he could attend a literary conference in Switzerland. He was accused of plotting against the state. The major in charge of the army's transport network was suddenly detained on a similar charge. A middle-aged man was arrested and fatally beaten when the police failed to find his son-in-law, who was suspected of destroying a gas station. And so on.

But Duvalier, who had humbled the press, emasculated parliament and the judiciary, and debased the army, reserved his most powerful ammunition for the Catholic church, the only remaining locally based institution of any potential for meaningful opposition. In other Latin American countries the church had played a noticeable role in tumbling dictators. Haiti was a Roman Catholic country and, in theory, the vast majority of its inhabitants, and nearly all of the urban elite, were adherents. Yet, because of *vodun,* the church was weaker than in Mexico, Colombia, or the Dominican Republic. Its hierarchy was largely of French origin and had supported Déjoie; it was also renowned for its conservatism, the gradualness with which it promoted indigenous clergy (although there was a Haitian bishop),[25] and its hostility to the folklorique school of which Duvalier had been a prominent member.

By attacking the church Duvalier and his government risked excommunication — but he had taken more dangerous risks before — and the alienation of a section of the elite which had, however, probably already been alienated from his regime. By

24 Grossberg, "Explosive Buffer," 84.
25 In 1963, of 416 priests only 113 were Haitians. There were 180 French clergy.

doing so he could gain popularity in the countryside where the church had long been viewed as alien and somewhat oppressive, he would gain the approval of the *vodun* priests and adepts, a not inconsiderable force, he would warn and silence resident foreign critics (missionaries — especially Protestant — were and are numerous), and he would demonstrate to those of his people who still feared him too little that he could take on and destroy large external sources of power as well as those of Haitian size. In August 1959 his police arrested and expelled the French rector of the republic's largest Roman Catholic secondary school and a popular small-town priest, also French. When about a thousand worshippers gathered in the Notre Dame Cathedral in Port-au-Prince to pray for the priests, Barbot and troops equipped with M-3 submachine guns routed them, wounding several in the process. Archbishop François Poirier and the other local bishop immediately denounced the president's actions, and a warrant for the French-born archbishop's arrest was stayed apparently after warnings from the Vatican. Only in 1960 did Duvalier feel sufficiently confident to complete his attack on the church: Poirier was deported on short notice (he left without funds or baggage). Rémy Augustin, the Haitian bishop who was named to act for Poirier and who, according to the regime, was a "servile element of token indigenization," was arrested and expelled; in early 1961 ten French and Canadian priests were deported and, despite a declaration of the Sacred Consistorial Congregation of the Vatican that anyone who had anything to do with the expulsion of the archbishop or bishops would be automatically excommunicated *Latae Sententiae,* Bishop Paul Samson Jean-Marie Robert of Gonaïves, who had served thirty-nine years in Haiti, was ousted from his diocese along with his Haitian curate. The church warehouse in Gonaïves and churches elsewhere were looted, and the papal nuncio was withdrawn.

Simultaneously Duvalier packed the parishes with his own supporters, often with men "whose personality and even morality were not above reproach." [26] In 1961 he even managed an audacious inaugural celebration and Te Deum mass for himself in the

26 Manigat, *Sixties,* 53.

capital's cathedral. In 1962 seven priests working in the Artibonite were ejected for failure to offer prayers for Duvalier (they were relieved of $1200 and their cameras), Robert was deported, and Father Jean-Baptiste Georges, a Haitian priest who had cooperated with the regime and even served as minister of education in one of the early cabinets, was arrested (and allowed to leave the country). Then in 1964 all of the members of the Society of Jesus active in Haiti were sent home to Canada, and, for protesting too openly and too courageously, the American bishop of the Haitian Protestant Episcopal Church — who was well known for his patronage of indigenous art — was deported at gunpoint after twenty-one years in Haiti.

2. Fashioning the Predatory State

Dating the phases of Duvalierism can conceivably be construed as an exercise in the categorization of phenomena which defy rational arrangement, but it is useful to divide the era into three. The first stage, during which (as has already been indicated) Duvalier, essentially by trial and error, fashioned a personalized apparatus of control and terror which succeeded in rewriting the long understood rules of Haitian political and social existence, lasted until late 1959. By 1960 it was clear that the consummation of Duvalierism was sheer power, and would not, once enemies had been eliminated, result in the spread of social justice, economic development, or any kind of national cleansing and widespread modernization. Duvalier had consecrated himself — like presidents before him, if never previously so singlemindedly and ruthlessly — to the gods of destruction, brutality, and sadism. The years from 1960 through 1964 (the second stage) would mark the further employment and skillful perfection of Duvalier's techniques of tyranny. The rhythm of repression which had been introduced between 1957 and 1959 was maintained and elaborated; the leveling of excrescences of potential dissidence was to continue and be paralleled by the steady raising up and glorification of the supreme leader. During this central stage of consolidation and triumph, Duvalier's strength came fully to be appreciated. Unlike nearly all of his predecessors and most Latin American dictators, he had none of the usual personal foibles. The accumulation of corrupt resources was desired only insofar as it added to the strength and security of the regime. For Duvalier, unlike Magloire, wine, women, and song were largely immaterial. (Although Duvalier has seemed suitably paternal to his daughters and son, his relationship with his very upright-appearing, light-skinned wife has never been characterized by associates as warm. Nor can Duvalier be said to have other obviously significant and durable bonds of personal affection. He is not a man with revealed interests outside the politics of power and squalor.) He demanded but did not court the adulation of the masses or, particularly, world opinion. More and more his became a self-contained, self-justifying world where, as in eighteenth- and nineteenth-century Sicily, the hunchbacked was straight, the devious normal, and the corruption of daily interaction widely accepted. The third stage began in 1965. By then the body politic was weary, the internal battles had all been won, and the instruments of terror needed no more than slight adjustments to maintain their tone and effect. Having endured and succeeded, Duvalier could relax, if warily, and de-escalate verbally if not in fact. A new, lowered plateau of normalcy and, to be sure, stability was possible. By the third stage, the man had fully become the state, and it was fully responsive to his will.

During the second stage Duvalier relentlessly eliminated anyone, especially erstwhile supporters, who could possibly develop a separate and challenging base of power. He reshuffled the cabinet six times between 1960 and 1964, retaining throughout this period and, in a few cases, until the present only the most subservient and feeble of his ministers. Some of the more dynamic, like Clovis M. Désinor, in 1969 minister of finance, were dropped and even exiled for periods of time. The cardinal principle was that no one was indispensable except the president. He ousted respected directors of quasi-governmental institutions like the Banque Nationale (twice in one year) and the university, installed weak and ineffectual but loyal substitutes, and then purged them whenever they had grown comfortable and reasonably secure. In this respect his rule was even more unsettling than that of Hitler or Stalin, and far more quixotic than that of Trujillo or Batista. He also continued his policy of retiring generals and colonels whenever they tried to command their troops or otherwise assert themselves as a separate force. In 1961 General Merceron, who had retained his position as chief of staff for a remarkably long three years, and who Duvalier said "merited a rest in a temperate climate," [27] was replaced by Colonel Jean-René Boucicaut, the commander of the Dessalines battalion. At the same time Major Claud Raymond was removed as commander of the same battalion and assigned to the military academy as its commandant, and Colonel Daniel Beauvoir, the chief of police in Port-au-Prince, was retired, as were the eight colonels in charge of military posts in the provinces. Less than a year later, after a captain and a colonel had been sentenced to death for plotting Duvalier's assassination and Boucicaut had tried to support Heinl's opposition to the *macoutes,* he fled with his wife and four children into the Venezuelan Embassy. Duvalier announced that Boucicaut, then forty-four, had reached the age of retirement; the chief of the army quartermaster corps, an undistinguished and poorly educated sybaritic colonel, Gérard Constant, replaced him as chief of staff and, although subsequently there were frequent shifts of lesser-ranking officers in the army (in 1963, for example, an American-trained colonel was shot while trying to escape and five other officers fled into foreign embassies, perhaps after plotting against the regime, sixty men — one-third of the officer corps — being dismissed in consequence), he has since maintained that position, but not the influence that previously had been attached to it.[28]

In Haiti, where suspicion and mistrust can be said to be imbibed with mother's milk, the pinnacle of power was the seat of loneliness. There, nearly everyone aspires to be boss. Duvalier knew that those closest to him could prove the most dangerous. In 1960,

---

[27] Quoted in *Hispanic American Report,* XIV (November 1964), 793.
[28] Constant was rewarded for the assistance which he gave to Duvalier in Jacmel during the campaign of 1957.

when Barbot was publicly being called the chief of the *macoutes* and was obviously riding the crest of his fortunes, Duvalier unceremoniously placed him, and ten associates, under arrest. (Barbot had secretly been negotiating for assistance and future recognition from the United States and Trujillo.) For eighteen months Barbot rotted in Fort Dimanche, the republic's notorious torture chamber and political prison near the capital, before being released.[29] Duvalier offered him a new sedan to indicate that "no hard feelings" remained, but Barbot found that his wife had been under house arrest for several months and that a son had suffered a mental breakdown and been refused medical assistance. After a few weeks at home and in a Jesuit retreat, he disappeared, pledging to overthrow Duvalier. The president in turn ordered that Barbot be killed on sight. During the spring of 1963, the forces that Barbot had gathered around him shot it out on a number of occasions with the *macoutes*, in one engagement killing forty-five in an ambush. A few weeks later they managed to contact and threaten the president by telephone, thereby throwing him into a frenzy. It was also rumored that Barbot had been wounded and twenty or so physicians were arrested on suspicion of having treated his wounds. His brother Ernest, an official in the ministry of education, was arrested, and Clément Barbot's wife and family obtained asylum in the Argentine Embassy. A priest, subcabinet ministers, and wives of former ministers were likewise arrested. By the end of May Barbot was hiding in the capital, regularly taunting Duvalier, and skirmishing with *macoutes* in the streets. Had the United States government supported Barbot with arms, Duvalier might have been toppled. But, in July, Clément and his brother Harry Barbot, a physician, were betrayed and cornered in Cazeau, five miles east of the capital. Captain Gracia Jacques of the palace guard and his soldiers set fire to the sugar

---

[29] According to one account — given by Colonel Heinl in an interview with the author on July 22, 1969 — Barbot was spared death only because he had taken the precaution to disinter the skull of Duvalier's father, with which he made an *ouanga* or fetish. It is not known whether Duvalier ever recovered the components of the *ouanga*. The disinterment is also mentioned in Huxley, *Invisibles*, 83. Diederich and Burt, *Papa Doc*, 148, refer to the removal of a heart rather than a skull. For Barbot and Trujillo, see Crassweller, *Trujillo*, 353.

cane surrounding their small hut and gunned down the Barbots and nine others as they stumbled through the flames.

The dismissal of Barbot in no way moderated the reign of terror or diminished the activity of the *macoutes*. If anything the second stage of Duvalier's dictatorship was marked by unbridled bullying of defenseless Haitians throughout the republic, by the elevation of torture and bestial brutality to astounding levels, and, in Port-au-Prince alone, conservatively by at least 2000 killings, only a few of which were premeditated or, in any normal sense, necessary for the defense of the realm. The essence of terror is its unpredictable arbitrariness, the absence of explanation, the lack of any means whereby wrongs can, even theoretically, be redressed, and the inculcation of a widespread feeling of mental impotence. The *macoutes* satisfied these general criteria and, it can be said confidently, omitted few of the requirements of the theoretical model of enforcement terror.[30]

A very few largely authenticated (fully satisfactory authentication is impossible for obvious reasons) specific, but randomly chosen, examples — in addition to the ones already mentioned — may suffice. In 1961, four U.S. Marines on liberty in the capital and a Haitian citizen were picked up at gunpoint at night — conceivably because of an altercation over girls — taken to the palace, manhandled, and eventually released only because of Heinl's vigorous intervention. Resident foreign businessmen were requested to contribute to various "projects" of the regime — particularly Duvalierville, a new town sixteen miles outside of Port-au-Prince; if their offerings were deemed inadequate, they were beaten. In 1960 Cromwell James, a sixty-one-year-old black Grenadan who ran a store outside of Port-au-Prince, was taken into custody and died from injuries and gangrene poisoning received in Fort Di-

---

30 "Enforcement terror" is the functional opposite of "agitational terror," distinctions employed by Thomas Perry Thornton, "Terror as a Weapon of Political Organization," in Harry Eckstein (ed.), *Internal War: Problems and Approaches* (Glencoe, 1964), 72. He also defines terror sensibly in a way that would be appreciated by Duvalier and the *macoutes*: "Terror is a symbolic act designed to influence political behavior by extranormal means, entailing the use or threat of violence" (73). Eugene Victor Walter, *Terror and Resistance: A Study of Political Violence* (New York, 1969), concentrates on the use of terror by authority, which he calls a "regime of terror," the opposite of a "siege of terror" (7).

manche. In 1962 a night watchman working for the Public Works Department in Port-au-Prince refused to give *macoutes* equipment from a warehouse, was bound in barbed wire, hung from his office door, and left to bleed to death. Another night watchman in Pétionville was crucified. In 1963, after the clandestine distribution of anti-Duvalier leaflets, thirty students and their relatives, including several distinguished professors at the university, were tortured. Six teen-age boys who put down-with-Duvalier signs on the wall of a church were promptly executed. A government spokesman explained that they were probably Communists. A businessman told an American reporter: "You must not come here again because if [the *tonton macoutes*] have some reason to hate you they may take it out on me. I can walk out of this office to the corner and just disappear. No one will ever hear of me again. It happens every day." [31] In a border town the Dominican consul-general's throat was cut as a warning to persons assisting Haitians to escape eastward into the neighboring republic. And the regime even televised an execution. Indeed, during 1963 the *macoutes* became responsible for so many acts of depredation that two gangs, one from Gonaïves under Zacharie Delva and another from Port-au-Prince, fought what amounted to a mini-civil war, with the men from Gonaïves proving victorious on their own turf. According to one account, after the losers had been shot, their mutilated bodies were left on the steps of the local Catholic church with genitals stuffed in their mouths.[32] This was the era when a "morals squad" appointed by the president cruised the streets of Port-au-Prince arresting prostitutes, homosexuals, and innocent couples making love.

That year, too, after shots had been fired at the president's twelve-year-old son Jean-Claude and fourteen-year-old daughter Simone, François Benoit, a lieutenant who was suspected of complicity in the attack simply because he was the army's best marksman, reached asylum but five members of his family were machine-gunned and their houses burned. "Duvalier was taking no chances," wrote a journalist who was then visiting the capital. "Haitians who walked anywhere near the . . . presidential pal-

31 Sidney Lens, "The Frightened Land," *Progressive*, XXVIII (February 1964), 29.
32 Armbrister, "Any Hope," 79.

ace . . . had to hold their hands over their heads. Nervous soldiers put up roadblocks . . . [At one] the private police stopped an American businessman. As one of them emptied his pockets, another held a machete poised above his neck. Downtown, an uninvolved Haitian . . . drove slowly along Rue St. Cyr. Suddenly and without any provocation, an army sergeant opened fire. As [the man] tumbled from the car, gravely wounded, two doctors rushed out into the street to help. The sergeant whirled, pointed his submachine gun at them and told them to mind their own business. Then he walked over and administered the *coup de grâce*. . . ." A mulatto jewelry manufacturer was killed for no apparent reason. A Haitian working for the American Embassy went home for lunch one day and disappeared. Even an American diplomat and a commercial attaché were stopped and searched at gunpoint. The observer quoted an American nun who had long lived in Haiti: "One day last week a man stole some milk from our school because his children were hungry. The Tontons caught him, and when he wouldn't share the milk they put him in jail. The moment I heard about it I went to ask for his release. He was all right, and the men said they would release him if I came back in three hours. By the time I returned, the man's hands and arms had been broken and his back was a mass of raw flesh." [33] Meanwhile, at the behest of the regime, Haitians were still in the midst of celebrating the month of "National Gratitude and Indefectible Attachment to President Duvalier."

When a five-member committee of the Organization of American States arrived in Haiti to investigate the carnage, Duvalier, who speaks French well and English passably, refused to speak to them in anything other than Creole. However, the members of the committee understood that he would agree to cease harassing foreign embassies (Haitian soldiers had invaded the Dominican chancellery and had attempted to storm the residence of the Dominican ambassador, where Benoit had taken refuge) [34] and

[33] *Ibid.*, 78–79. For the killing of the family of Lieutenant Benoit, see Roland Wingfield, "Haiti, A Case Study of an Underdeveloped Area," unpub. Ph.D. thesis (Baton Rouge, 1966), 245; Diederich and Burt, *Papa Doc*, 204–209.
[34] President Juan Bosch of the Dominican Republic prepared to go to war over this "outrage." See his *The Unfinished Experiment: Democracy in the Dominican Republic* (New York, 1965), 185–186.

begin honoring the Latin American tradition of asylum. But no
sooner had the committee departed than absolute martial law was
declared (the state of siege had never really been lifted since
1958), a curfew was imposed from which not even members of the
diplomatic corps were exempt, and the president moved about
escorted by the army's two half-track troop carriers (its five tanks
were immobilized). During May 1963, 196 identified Haitians
were supposedly killed by the *macoutes*, 103 Haitians sought asylum in embassies, and hundreds fled across the border to the Dominican Republic. In order to halt the exodus, the *macoutes*
cleared an area along the border from two to ten miles deep, de-
molishing border homes and shooting anyone who tried to gather
crops in the cleared zone. "Travel on the island," wrote Graham
Greene after a well-timed visit, "is almost at a standstill. The
roads were always a deterrent, but now there are roadblocks round
Port-au-Prince to the north and controls at every small town to
the south. Within a circuit of a few kilometers from Port-au-
Prince I was searched four times, and it took me two days at the
police station, where the portrait of the Doctor is flanked by snap-
shots of the machine-gunned bodies of Barbot and his compan-
ions, to gain a two-day permit for the South." [35]

As Duvalier's *macoutes* made anachronistic even Haitian notions
of personal liberty and freedom, so the head of state made mockery of the political process, constitutional constraint on executive
power and, again, the widely accepted and rather loosely construed definitions of proper Haitian presidential behavior. Duvalier's object, during the second stage of his dictatorship, was to
complete a process begun during the first: to entrench himself
in power by any and all means, to quell even the most vestigial
parliamentary opposition, to put himself above the state and
any lingering appeals to natural law, and, largely in order to enhance the successful accomplishment of the last objective, to glo-
rify his person. In 1958 and 1959 parliament or the Senate, not
without a certain degree of reluctance and intimidation, had
granted Duvalier special powers to rule by decree. From 1960

[35] Graham Greene, "Nightmare Republic," *New Republic*, CXLIX (November 16,
1963), 19.

through 1965, and again in 1968, the legislators similarly effaced themselves. For six months at a time (in 1968 for a year) they let him make whatever he wished of their own constitutionally ordained powers. Sometimes the ostensible precipitating factor was an invasion or an economic crisis (and in 1961 and 1962 his special powers were supposedly to be used for economic legislation only), with the concurrent need for the president to be in a position to act swiftly and unhampered by the idiosyncrasies of deputies. But, since parliament acted only on draft bills submitted by Duvalier, had learned not to voice dissent, and had voted immediately and obediently whenever asked, and since nearly all of the deputies resided in the capital (even when parliament was not in session), rule by delegated fiat merely avoided a requirement of form and, literally, a few hours' delay. Duvalier's object in requesting special powers, however, was not to expedite the conduct of official business — all decisions were in any event made by him directly irrespective of whether or not parliament was sitting, and public questioning of the regime or its officials was never tolerated after 1958; it was to humble all men and institutions which might be thought to challenge the eminence of his rule and to crush any pockets of independent and constructive thought wherever and whenever they appeared.

In order to tighten his grip that extra notch, Duvalier in 1961 suddenly dissolved parliament two years before its legal mandate expired. Since the twenty-one-member Senate had been less acquiescent in 1957 and 1958 than had the thirty-seven-man Chamber of Deputies, he decreed the end of Haiti's bicameral legislature. Henceforth, *pace* the then still-existing constitution of 1957, Haiti would have a unicameral Chamber of Deputies of fifty-eight members, the elections for which were held in late April. All of the candidates were nominated by the president (there has never been a real Duvalierist political party) and, for reasons which were not immediately clear, every ballot was headed with the name of the president. Was he merely signifying his formal approval of the candidates? Or did he have other, typically mysterious, purposes in mind? His term as president was not due to terminate, according to the constitution, until 1963, and, whether or not he hoped to run early, the constitution explicitly forbade a second term. Yet Duvalier knew that his four immediate predecessors as full-term presidents, and a number before the American occupation, had been overthrown precisely when they attempted to amend the constitution so as to permit an otherwise illegal extension of their mandate. For obvious reasons, attempts to prolong a presidency had historically crystallized existing opposition, provoked riots, and, on occasion, invited outside intervention. Therefore Duvalier astutely avoided these complications by joining his name to those of the various candidates for deputy.

On election day "Army troops stalked the capital's polling places. . . . Some of them guided the people brought into town from outlying areas in government trucks to vote, while others reminded all government employees that, though it was Sunday, they were ordered to work — and vote. . . . From Cap Haitien came word that Army men with guns forced everyone emerging from church to go to the polls. . . . All were handed the ballot of just one candidate and informed that the . . . others had been jailed the night before." [36] This kind of procedure was usual in Haitian elections, and no one was particularly surprised that the government claimed that each of the Duvalier-backed deputies had been elected by overwhelming margins to four-year terms. Although only about 100,000 persons voted, the announced total of 1,320,748 ballots bemused few. Duvalier introduced a new, ingenious, and audaciously farcical category into Haitian electoral lore, however, when he blithely indicated his pleasure at being reelected by the people to a new term of six years. Since his name had been on the top of the ballot papers, the people had voted for him, Q.E.D. "His enemies," said the president, "could only reproach him with one crime, that of loving his people too much." Also, "as a revolutionary," he had "no right to disregard the voice of the people." [37]

The new parliament, as one man, wholeheartedly resolved that

36 Alida L. Carey, "Our Choice in Haiti: Duvalier or the People," *Commonweal*, LXXV (March 2, 1962), 588.
37 First quotation by an anonymous special correspondent in "The Agony of Haiti," *The New Statesman*, LXII (December 29, 1961), 988; second quotation in Armbrister, "Any Hope," 80.

Haiti's government was "revolutionary and progressive; representative, not dictatorial," and supported by a "large but indeterminable" segment of the population.[38] Later, Duvalier began to be referred to as "The Pacifier," "The Renovator of the Nation," and "The Object of Absolute Confidence" largely during a phase when he was attempting, rather unsuccessfully, to identify his regime of "black power" with the new states of Africa (Haiti opened diplomatic relations with Dahomey, Mali, and the Ivory Coast, having had them for some years with Ethiopia and Liberia); the example set by Kwame Nkrumah — "the Osagyfo," or redeemer — was never far from his mind. Duvalier had also become the only president of Haiti ever to have a town named after himself during his term of office.

Toward the end of 1963 he declared himself the embodiment of everything that had ever been glorious in Haitian history: "I am the Revolution and the flag," he declared on every suitable occasion. The neon lights near the capital's central common began blinking a similar message: "Je suis le Drapeau Haitien, Uni Indivisible. François Duvalier." Pronouns referring to him or his office henceforth were capitalized. Photographs of the dictator, already in all stores and offices, began to appear prominently in private homes. A government-supported newspaper in Port-au-Prince featured, on its front page, a two-column montage of Christ with his hands on the shoulders of Duvalier. The legend read: "I have chosen him." This incipient cult of personality was, however, never carried to its Nkrumahist extremes; no statues of the dictator were erected and, unlike Nkrumah, Jomo Kenyatta of Kenya, and Dr. H. Kamuzu Banda of Malawi, his head appeared only on coins (the medium of peasant exchange) and never on bills (the smallest paper denomination, 1 gourde, is worth 20 cents). And homage was, except during much of 1963 and 1964, paid to him only in comparatively limited amounts, largely because he tended more and more to avoid public displays, mass rallies, and the kinds of occasions for which the upwelling of adulation and reciprocal manifestation of charisma would have proved efficacious. Yet, the glorification of 1963 was but a way of preparing

[38] Quoted in *Hispanic American Report,* XV (October 1962), 712.

the people for the ultimate entrenchment of Duvalier's regime.

In April 1964, completing the process that had been started in 1961, he declared himself — in response to "popular demand" — president *Ad Vitam Aeternam*. "It is not easy," he explained, "to find a man who has complete confidence in himself, and in his country, and who decides to maintain its dignity and its prestige; such a revolutionary is found only every 50 or 75 years." He knew that he would go forward because he was a revolutionary. "For many years I have . . . been reading the pages of history because I knew that I had to fulfill a holy mission, a mission which will be fulfilled entirely." [39] The Chamber of Deputies and the army endorsed this declaration, 6000 or more *macoutes* and villagers demonstrated in his favor, a new constitution was approved by the legislature and, with a flourish of legality in a situation that was no less droll than that of 1961, the constitution was overwhelmingly accepted by the nation's voters after a plebiscite in June. (The official totals were 2,800,000 "yes" and 3234 "no," individuals having been allowed to cast as many ballots — all marked *oui* in advance — as they wished.) Henceforth Duvalier was "Le Président à Vie." In the cities and villages signs sprouted with the legend "Doc à Vie," and letters from the president carried "à vie" as a handwritten endorsement. It marked the beginning of a new era, the constitution, in a calculated way, making no provision for succession.

The transformation of the state into a personal fief, the subordination of a natural ethos to an individual will, and the elimination of any Haitian or foreigner, or institution, capable of detracting from, minimizing, or holding out hope against the perpetuation of dictatorship — these were all standard and well-tried Haitian (and authoritarian) techniques of maintaining one-man rule simply carried to, and, in some aspects, well beyond, the previously conceivable or experienced parameters. But internal preeminence and security were, in Haiti, rightfully seen as an insufficient guarantee of longevity and continuity. Throughout Haiti's modern history foreigners had always played a major role in shaping its destiny. They had helped to seat and unseat presi-

[39] Quoted in *Le Nouveau Monde* (April 5, 1964).

dents, sponsored revolutions, and intervened martially, and — especially in the case of the United States — were believed still to be willing quickly to snuff out governments in the Caribbean that were offensive. Recent episodes in Guatemala and the Bay of Pigs (and the Cuban missile blockade) were as salutary to Haitians as the occupation and its aftermath in their own past. Throughout his years in office, particularly during the second stage of consolidation, Duvalier therefore had to fashion a policy of ambivalence: he desperately needed financial aid and the spiritual shelter of Uncle Sam, but he could ill afford to prostrate himself before Washington or forfeit the gains to be made by awakening his people's residual (but easily aroused) abhorrence of American or other interference. Furthermore, if Papa Doc could manipulate and in any way humiliate Uncle Sam, then it would further enhance his own self-propagated image of invulnerability. Because of the peculiar psychology of Haiti, successful harassment of the United States would also weaken the resolve of his enemies and contribute noticeably to his security.

Duvalier was not necessarily the master of events (the shift from Eisenhower/Dulles to Kennedy/Rusk *et al.* and the ebb and flow of larger and more important world affairs obviously impinged from time to time on his own rocky shores), but from 1959 to 1963, and in many ways through 1969, he managed both to display enmity toward foreign benefactors and shamelessly to take advantage of their generosity. He played on American sensitivity toward Communism, and instinctively knew that he could do better by being difficult, and by behaving irascibly, recalcitrantly, and unpredictably. But above all he wanted to win favor and yet be his own master, a duality of policy which proved unsuccessful thanks to circumstance (largely corruption) and a curious lack of ultimate subtlety.

A recurring problem in relations between the United States and Haiti concerned the way in which funds borrowed from America or granted by agencies of the United States government were disbursed. To take a typical example, in 1960 work was suspended on the Artibonite Valley irrigation scheme because the Duvalier regime — not for the first time — was employing and discharging engineers and administrative officials without American approval. The project was jointly controlled, but when the Haitians dismissed a well-qualified engineer and hired two men, one of whom had been arrested for peculation in 1958, the Americans saw their funds being drained away, as they had been under Magloire, for purposes of patronage. The differences between the American aid mission and the Haitian government were ironed out, however, and work resumed on the project. In succeeding months American loan funds were committed for a survey of a much-needed paved road from Port-au-Prince to Cayes (presumably the likelihood of receiving fat commissions persuaded the Haitian Senate to authorize a costlier survey by a private American firm instead of a less expensive one offered by the World Bank) and the expansion of a sisal plantation and processing plant near Cap Haitien — a total of $800,000. In addition, the United States began supplying equipment for the modernization of Haiti's military establishment and underwrote a major portion of the recurrent budget deficit. In 1960 the United States supplied $11 million to Haiti and in 1961 $13.5 million, then slightly less than half of the $30 million total of Haitian public expenditures. An Acting Assistant Secretary of State for Inter-American Affairs, testifying in 1961 before the Senate Foreign Relations Committee, maintained that the United States had "no other alternative [than Duvalier's tyranny] and that we ought to try and elevate the standard of living for the people and raise their level of civilization." But at this same hearing Senator J. William Fulbright called the Assistant Secretary's testimony "very unsatisfactory"; American aid simply shored up a tottering and odious regime. Senator Hubert Humphrey argued that "the Haitian government is frightful, and I think that all the members of our government know it." Why, he then asked, "are we supporting it?" [40]

After the Balzackian "re-election" of Duvalier in 1961, the United States in fact began noticeably, if tentatively, to moderate its diplomatic support. Ambassador Robert Newbegin was instructed to be cool and correct, and for the next two years American representatives ostentatiously absented themselves from

[40] Quoted in *Hispanic American Report*, XIV (September 1961), 607.

functions commemorating Duvalier's second inauguration and, in general, operated at lower and lower temperatures as Duvalier became more and more of an embarrassment and a trial. For a time, however, financial assistance continued and the military mission remained (although the relationship between Heinl and Duvalier had become strained). President Kennedy definitely wished to rid the Western Hemisphere and the Haitian people of Duvalier, but, after the Bay of Pigs fiasco, he and his closest counselors could devise no way of deposing Duvalier which would involve only minimal visible American participation, which would be foolproof, and which — the constant dilemma of all students of contemporary Haiti — would result in a regime markedly less repulsive.[41] After Duvalier began attacking the United States in early 1962 (he echoed criticisms of 1960) for being both "interventionist" and "indifferent" to his nation's economic plight, the State Department replied with equanimity and, at the O.A.S. meeting of foreign ministers at Punta del Este, even agreed to be blackmailed (the price: a hospital and a jet airport) in exchange for a critical, pro-American vote for sanctions against Cuba.[42]

Conditions inside Haiti grew so loathsome, and Duvalier's attitude toward other states became — for the political reasons already enumerated — so antagonistic, however, that a further deterioration in relations could not long be avoided. The ambassadors of the major Western countries represented in Haiti had already protested on a number of occasions against the extortion and harassment of their nationals by the government and its *macoutes*. This was a trial of strength for Duvalier and, in early 1962, he requested the recall of the British ambassador. The United Kingdom reduced its regular representation to the *chargé d'affaires* and, in time, to the consular level. There were continuing difficulties with the Latin American embassies over asylees, and Venezuela and the Dominican Republic regularly withdrew ambassadors and

41 President Kennedy could naturally devote only a minute portion of his time to considerations of Haiti, but Arthur Schlesinger, Jr., Ralph Dungan, and Richard Goodwin were all concerned with Haiti from time to time.
42 See Arthur M. Schlesinger, Jr., *A Thousand Days: John F. Kennedy in the White House* (Boston, 1965), 782–783. Because of a worsening in relations neither the airport nor the hospital was built with American funds.

other officials.[43] American frigidity had not as yet affected economic planning, for the people would suffer, or so it was explained; and in early 1962 the Agency for International Development allocated $7.25 million for economic and technical assistance and promised to lend a further $3.4 million for the southern highway, actions which again aroused congressional ire. Senator Stephen Young deftly pointed out that "Intervention may be an offensive word in our Hemisphere, but we are already intervening on behalf of Duvalier instead of the people of Haiti." [44]

It was less these political reasons than purely technical ones — a matter not of principle but of practice — which led first to a suspension of aid in late 1962 and finally, with President Kennedy's explicit approval, to a formal curtailment of all assistance in 1963. Agency for International Development inspectors had long been worried about the return on funds granted and lent to Haiti; by 1962 it was realized that the $18.5 million which had been spent in Haiti since Duvalier's accession had largely found its way into the hands of the regime. Of $3.4 million supplied for roads, the only visible result was a repaved main boulevard in downtown Port-au-Prince. There had been corruption on a grand scale, the government of Haiti had almost always defaulted on its obligations to pay its small share of projects, and Haiti refused haughtily to allow the United States to oversee the payment, employment, and discharging of all Haitians associated with American-aided projects. In 1962 Heinl also sought to cut off military aid for the same kinds of reasons — especially the diversion of funds and resources to the *macoutes*. After the suspension was made permanent in late 1963 (a situation still theoretically in effect as late as 1969) only the antimalaria program, surplus food distribution, and small grants to Haiti made through international organizations, remained. Furthermore, Ambassador Raymond L. Thurston had been withdrawn as a sign of American displeasure before Duvalier unceremoniously declared him *persona non grata* and refused even to let him return to the embassy to put his family

43 For the war that almost was, see Robert D. Tomasek, "The Haitian-Dominican Republic Controversy of 1963 and the Organization of American States," *Orbis*, XII (1968), 294–313.
44 Quoted in *Hispanic American Report*, XV (July 1962), 416.

affairs in order. Since Colonel Heinl had for many months made no secret of his dislike of Duvalier's machinations, in particular objecting to the transfer of army equipment and funds to the *macoutes*, his recall was demanded and, subsequently, the Marine advisers once again marched out of Haiti. The Air Force mission followed.

The diminution of American aid (and the failure of either France or Czechoslovakia — with whom Haiti negotiated — to begin writing large checks), when coupled with a faltering in the republic's economy because of a slump in coffee and sisal prices, the hesitant response of American travel agents and tourists (a response encouraged by the U.S. State Department), and a general decline in local commercial activity, intensified Duvalier's need for cash. Yet straitened circumstances only encouraged the further fabrication of ingenious devices designed to make the most of Haiti's limited fiscal resources.[45] Increases in export duties for coffee and sisal, on imports, and even of postal rates (the last theoretically for a literacy campaign) were imposed although they proved regressive and entrepreneurially inhibiting. Peasants purchased large quantities of vegetable oil; the government made its distribution a monopoly without lowering prices. Foreign-owned companies and men of wealth with important stakes in the country shared the burden; they were encouraged to contribute to the stability of the regime by subscribing to national bonds, government lotteries, the construction of capital improvements, etc. In 1960, for example, Oswald G. Brandt, a textile and coffee magnate and reputedly Haiti's wealthiest private citizen (although he held British and then Jamaican citizenship), purchased an entire issue of bonds — $1 million worth — supposedly secured by increases in the gasoline tax. Import firms also "received special treatment from the customs office. Its powerful employees diverted a part of the incoming orders, while invoices and notice bills registered the entire delivery. Soon, street vendors could be seen, calmly selling the diverted goods and products at low prices."[46] Throughout 1961 the *macoutes* openly extorted money

45 Cf. S. N. Eisenstadt, *The Political Systems of Empires* (Glencoe, 1963), 121–127.
46 Manigat, *Sixties*, 75.

from businessmen on behalf of Duvalierville. A compulsory national lottery began to flourish during the same year, grossing
$2.25 million, much of which was garnished from a portion of
every government salary check. There were small cash prizes, but
the winners were never too well known, and few Haitians waited as
expectantly as Bostonians do for the results of the Irish Sweep-
stakes. In October 1961, the beginning of the new fiscal year,
Duvalier announced the issue of "economic liberation" bonds:
this "funny money" would pay 5 per cent and be redeemable in
five years, and all wage earners were to be subjected to compulsory deductions from their pay packets. Insurance policies, imports, and exports would also provide new revenue through a 1
or 2 per cent tax on value. Vehicles would be inspected — for an
appropriate fee. "At the request of the users," the *macoutes*
would also begin collecting tolls on roads and bridges; this method
was easily adapted to private enterprise, and urban areas were
soon a maze of toll booths. An ingenuous official communiqué released in mid-1962 by the Mouvement de Rénovation Nationale
(the extrabudgetary organization charged with devising new and
varied means of extortion) informed residents of Pétionville that
they were no longer required to "pay the full amount of money"
requested of them for a new lycée and road repairs. The amount
of their contribution was now to be "left to their generosity." [47]
Later in the same year, the government fell behind in its payment
of wages, refused to distribute pensions, and even failed to provide the mandatory Christmas bonus. The regime's cement distribution monopoly had fallen more than $200,000 behind in
its reimbursements to manufacturers, so it increased wholesale
prices to distributors by 25 per cent.[48] The *macoutes* even tried to
"supervise" the distribution of American surplus foods.

It should be evident that little of this neatly extracted revenue
was being returned to the majority of Haiti's population in the
form of enhanced services or capital improvements which, over
time, could have a multiplier effect. Much — the proportions are

[47] *Haiti Herald,* July 29, 1962.
[48] See Richard Alexander, "The Hell of Haiti," *Nation,* CXCVI (February 2,
1963), 99.

impossible to discern or estimate even crudely — was finding its way into the pockets of lesser as well as commanding figures in the regime. The president was thought to be supplying cane cutters — about 30,000 a year — to Trujillo's Dominican Republic for capitation fees paid in advance plus 50 per cent of each worker's wages.[49] Duvalier purchased a large beachside house and one or two other establishments, gave large foreign automobiles to his daughters, and was said — in the usual way — to maintain bank accounts in Switzerland as well as in New York (ironically in the First National City Bank). Cabinet ministers and notorious *macoutes* were building fancy houses at salubrious elevations overlooking the capital, and there was an unusual demand for furniture from Italy, France, and the United States, a vogue for the latest in hi-fi equipment, and a craze for imported luxuries of all kinds. A minister of tourism in 1960 spent $350,000 developing his own resort for tourists in the Gulf of Gonave; the ministry of public works, where the fruit of corruption was extraordinarily ripe, was usually run by the president's favorite of the hour (one early incumbent was jailed for exceeding the bounds of decent avarice); the president called periodically for an end to corrupt practices in the ministry of justice; and the head of the Haitian Red Cross was a swaggering *macoute*. But even the degree of conversion of public funds was hardly unusual for Haiti (or similarly situated underdeveloped countries); only the rapacity and accompanying terror were new.[50]

None of the "austerity" funds was devoted to the alleviation of Haitian misery. The disastrous hurricanes of 1958 (Ella and Gerda), 1963 (Flora), 1964 (Cleo), and 1966 (Inez), and the floods of 1961, 1962, 1963, and 1968 were the occasion for inflows of foreign (mostly American) assistance and almost total neglect (certainly before 1966) of relief measures by Duvalier's government. In 1963, for example, when Flora engulfed the southern peninsula, leaving 5000 dead and 100,000 homeless, and destroy-

49 Gingras, *Cyclone*, 115–116; *Toronto Star*, July 4, 1967.
50 In terms of the definitions and discussion in Joseph S. Nye, Jr., "Corruption and Political Development: A Cost-Benefit Analysis," *The American Political Science Review*, LXI (1967), 417–427, the costs of Haiti's corruption exceeded its benefits for political development.

ing 95 per cent of the cattle and about half of the exportable coffee
crop, the United States Congress allocated $250,000 for relief,
U.S. naval units airlifted food, men, and equipment to the area,
and CARE, the Salvation Army, the American Friends Service
Committee, and the Church World Service hurried to assist while
the Haitian government did little more than declare a three-day
period of national mourning. In the aftermath of Cantave's in-
surgency,[51] its military forces remained near the capital lest exiles
take advantage of the tragedy in the south to invade from the
north or west.[52]

Other emergencies evoked similar responses from Duvalier's
government, and, even during times of tranquillity, the percentage of available funds devoted to the mass of the people was derisory. Despite large injections of American aid, no secondary
schools had been built by Duvalier by 1964, when only four of the
sixty-eight private and public high schools were in the rural areas
and a mere 19 per cent of the eligible pupils (16 per cent in 1967)
attended schools of any kind; throughout the school system there
were only 1200 teachers for more than 100,000 students; illiteracy
remained as high as or higher than before; electric power was
available only in the main cities, and there at best intermittently;
port facilities were decaying, and the Artibonite Valley irrigation
facility still remained unfinished; unemployment had increased
faster than the government's ability to inflate the already large
number of persons paid by the state; morbidity and mortality
rates remained unaffected by state action; in short, Duvalier's
dictatorship had brought most of his subjects negative returns.
The government was spending only $7 per head (61 cents on ed-
ucation and 65 cents on health) compared to $12 in Bolivia and
$500 in the United States. Haiti's per capita income had, if any-
thing, decreased as productivity had slumped; population growth
and natural disasters had taken their tolls, but more debilitating
than any other factor was the use of available resources for purposes of state security. About 65 per cent of all funds were devoted
to such ends. To take one minor example, in 1963 the members of

---

[51] See below, 245.
[52] *New York Times,* October 11, 1963.

the palace guard had each been issued smart blue uniforms (costing $150 each) and high leather boots (at $40 per pair). One investigator claimed to detect seventeen budgetary switches from ministries to the security forces in a single issue of the government gazette.[53]

It needs no imagination to suppose that the peculiar combination of terror, repression, anomie, and exploitation that was Duvalierism should have aroused intense dissatisfaction among the elite, mulattoes, intellectuals, students, and persons of sensibility who discovered that their meager ambitions would be thwarted by barriers of personalized rule. Many Haitians in modest circumstances, as well as large numbers of the apolitical educated classes, consequently voted with their feet and, ignoring the required exit permission, fled illegally to the Bahamas by sea and thereafter to the United States, moved across the border into the Dominican Republic, even sailed across the Windward Passage to Cuba, or endured protracted but eventually rewarding delays to obtain a visa to the United States. By 1963, 1000 Haitians were reported to be employed in the Congo (Kinshasa), and between 1960 and 1962 310 Haitian professionals began working in Guinée for President Sékou Touré or the United Nations. Emigration of trained Haitians was not new, but Duvalier's methods and the worsening economic conditions of their homeland drove this group away in increasing numbers. By the middle 1960's about 80 per cent of Haiti's most qualified physicians, lawyers, engineers, teachers, and other professionals had fled to the United States, Canada, or Africa. Duvalier was not sorry to see many of them go; they would obviously contribute to discontent if they stayed, while, from overseas, they would remit large sums of foreign exchange to their families in Haiti.

The ruthlessness of the *macoutes* and the police prevented nearly all except the most spontaneous and idealistic manifestations of internal discontent. In 1959 secondary school teachers in

[53] Lester Velie, "The Case of our Vanishing Dollars in Haiti," *Reader's Digest*, LXXX (March 1962), 125; Brand, *Impressions of Haiti*, 48–53. According to a 1962 report of the Inter-American Development Bank, of 700,000 children of primary school age, 641,000 had no schools available. Cited in *Hispanic American Report*, XV (August 1962), 513.

Port-au-Prince struck for four days in protest against the continued employment of one of their colleagues, an active informer,
and the government capitulated. In 1960, after their treasurer
had been jailed as a Communist, students throughout the nation
went on strike to try to call attention to economic stagnation and
to bring down Duvalier. It was a tactic that had proved effective
during the American occupation and the presidencies of Lescot,
Estimé, and Magloire, but although the boycott of classes lasted
about eighty-eight days and helped to bring about the release of
imprisoned students, it led to new decrees which made jail sentences mandatory for parents of rebellious students, placed the
university under total state control, introduced noxious loyalty
oaths for students and professors at the university, and helped to
strengthen the power of the regime. Aside from the battles with
Barbot in 1963 and desultory demonstrations in 1967, this was the
end of openly expressed dissatisfaction emanating from inside the
country.

The vast majority of Haiti's population was not ready for revolution. They had always known hard times, mean dictators, brutality, and deprivation. But they had endured, and for many the
degree to which Duvalier was more evil than his predecessors was
largely immaterial, for Haitians were accustomed to living in
peril. Some also swallowed his propaganda; he was, after all, the
big man — "the boss" — and they were merely little folk without
education or sophistication. Most of all, they had difficulty antici-
pating a beneficial return from their own actions of protest or
aggression.[54] "Duvalier," said a bitter Haitian, "has performed an
economic miracle. He has taught us to live without money and to
eat without food. . . . [He] has taught us to live without life." [55]
Haitians remained apathetic — and undernourished, disease-
ridden, poorly clothed, and illiterate. A large portion of the men
who might have been the natural fomenters of violently expressed
discontent had fled, together with the disgruntled elite. Few were
Communists, but all saw in the success of Castro the hope of over-
throwing Duvalier from without. The attempted invasions of

[54] For an analysis, see below, 366.
[55] Herbert Gold, quoted in Gingras, *Cyclone*, 128.

1958 and 1959 had proved abortive, but during the early 1960's Haitians in Montreal, New York, Miami, San Juan, and Santo Domingo (Cuba had seen the futility of backing random groups of Haitians) plotted, formed alliances of basically antagonistic exiles (which Duvalier's agents often managed to penetrate) — Fignolé, Déjoie, and Magloire formed umbrella organizations on several occasions — and raised funds for the purchase of airplanes, ships, and armaments. They had to bide their time — or at least they thought that it was essential to wait — until the American military missions had left the country, American moral support had been withdrawn, and Duvalier's minions were clearly on their own.

In August 1963, former General Léon Cantave, who had opposed Magloire and tried to preserve law and order during the hectic first five months of 1957, led about one hundred men — the largest number to invade Haiti since the beginning of Duvalier's regime — to Fort Liberté, in the northeast, and captured one or two villages as well as the town before troops airlifted from the capital repelled the insurgents and drove Cantave and many of his followers over the nearby frontier into the Dominican Republic.[56] During the next summer Father Georges and other exiles, apparently with Dominican encouragement if not backing, coordinated a series of landings and subsequent guerrilla activity new to Haiti. In June one fairly large group came ashore at Lagon des Huitre, east of Belle Anse, in the southeast and fought in the mountainous area of La Selle for three weeks before being subdued. Despite reprisal arrests in Jacmel and Port-au-Prince, the shooting of fifty political prisoners in Fort Dimanche (Duvalier was also credited with the execution of twenty-three suspected traitors in the palace basement), and the killing of the families of several ex-officers resident in New York, there was another landing in August on the western tip of the southern peninsula. At Petite Rivière de Dame Marie thirteen Haitians under ex-Captain Yvan D. Laraque tried vainly to arouse the local peasants and fought a series of engagements with the *macoutes* and the army

[56] For commentary and detail, see *Le Monde*, August 25, 1963; Diederich and Burt, *Papa Doc*, 251–261.

throughout the next three months (during which time there were new killings in the capital and in towns in the south, and a bullet-riddled decomposing body of one of the rebels killed at Grande-Anse was for days gruesomely propped up on a chair on the pavement near Bowen Field, the international airport) until eleven of their number were killed and two captured (and later executed). Once again exiles had tried to topple Duvalier from without despite the absence of secure lines of logistical support and pre-existing contracts with an efficient and exhilarated *maquis*. The social distance between the elite and the peasantry was too great, even had the countryfolk not been profoundly apathetic — and afraid. The invaders might fight, but the peasants knew that the avoidance of trouble was their only guarantee of continued existence in an environment as exacting as Haiti's. Duvalier had, indeed, succeeded, and the political system elaborated (however higgledy-piggledy) was equal to the kinds of challenges which it was asked to meet throughout the period from 1957 to 1964. From that point of view, Duvalier could well make himself president for life.

3. Perpetuating One-Man Rule

The predominant patterns of Duvalier's dictatorship had been laid down by the end of 1964. Repression had been etched in the face of the land; Haitians had been trained to respond, to flee, or to take the inescapable consequences. For the better part of the next five years Duvalier needed to do little more than to perpetuate the policies which had heretofore proved so salutary. Having subdued the state, eradicated foci of internal opposition, thwarted invading exiles, and ignored the displeasure of the United States, he could also begin paying at least some attention to the reconstruction of his impoverished and anxiety-ridden country. He felt secure and knew that some relaxation of oppression — not vigilance — and a degree of normalization were absolutely necessary if he were to continue to possess anything over which it would be worthwhile to rule. The test, in succeeding years, was how to foster a climate conducive to growth while continuing to discourage his enemies, and how to lower tension while ensuring his people's continued subservience. This was a balancing act which demanded poise and careful attention to the finer points of equilibrium. To falter was to fail, and Duvalier, because of the thoroughness with which he had cowed the country between 1957 and 1964 as well as his artistry and artifices as a politician, rarely faltered.

In a New Year's speech of January 2, 1966, Duvalier stated that he wished that day to be considered as the *"moment of the nation's economic consciousness. . . .* Today seems to Me the date, the day, the ideal moment for reclaiming your spirit and heart, your willingness and conscience in new action which will consolidate the political victory and definitive triumph of our Revolution in its economic organization. . . . The time has come to put an end to the explosive phase of the Duvalierist Revolution, a phase during which the essential administrative and institutional failures have been set straight through removals, purges, and further purges. . . . Everything involving the functioning and progress of any true Revolution effaces the political, social, and economic superstructure of the former regime. . . . The time has come to pass on to the phase of administrative organization in order to avoid losing or destroying the political victory of the Duvalierist Revolution, and I will undertake . . . to assume responsibility for the necessary changes because I have assumed for Myself the authority of the State and entire responsibility for the nation. . . ." [57]

This was the authentic voice of a victor seeking to chart a new path and, implicitly, to begin refurbishing both his image and the image of his state. He began to leash the *macoutes* and restrain the excesses of his entourage. The changed atmosphere was noticeable. The curfew was ended, roadblocks were removed from the cities, and armed civilians patrolled the streets less ostentatiously and less frequently. A veneer of calm was restored. The president even began to pay unusual attention to tourism. He appointed special commissions and sponsored promotional exercises, and for a time tried to remove the lamentable and very numerous beggars from the streets of the capital. He welcomed every conceivable

[57] Quoted in *Le Nouveau Monde,* January 9, 1966.

kind of American promoter who might have contacts, skills, or capital to contribute to the regime. He lowered his guard ever so slightly, but perceptibly, and more and more — since he could now afford it — cultivated an air of reasonableness, the better to impress foreigners and international agencies. By now, too, he had worn down the morally outraged; Americans, leaders of the Organization of American States, and representatives of the United Nations accepted the *fait accompli*. Duvalier was still there, still in charge, and was someone with whom it was essential to work if the great mass of Haitians were not to suffer further.

But only appearances, not methods, had changed. The dictator still ruled alone, and by decree; the Chamber of Deputies remained obsequious; the electorate trooped to the polls whenever requested (in by-elections and the legislative balloting of 1967), and, if permitted, made the necessary marks on official paper; the judiciary maintained a complaisant silence; cabinets were shuffled and reshuffled; new advisers were recruited from abroad and others dropped; and aid was solicited successfully from the Inter-American Development Bank (with U.S. acquiescence), the Food and Agriculture Organization, and voluntary agencies which disbursed official U.S. funds quietly. New international alliances were forged with Taiwan; in 1969 Haiti became the fifth state to recognize Biafra. Although a Roman Catholic bishop was arrested in 1965, peace was made with the church in 1966, when the president's excommunication was lifted and a papal nuncio dispatched to Port-au-Prince.[58] "In our prayers," the new French archbishop of Port-au-Prince addressed the president on his sixtieth birthday, "we will ask God that these wishes which we express today be realized. I assure you of our complete collaboration in the political, economic and social spheres."[59] President Lyndon B. Johnson instructed his ambassadors to think and act positively; the complications connected with the intervention in the Dominican Republic, the war in Vietnam, and anxieties in Europe put a premium on neutrality toward zones of apparent stability.

The exodus continued. In 1968 more than 3000 Haitians

[58] For interesting commentary, see the *Journal de Genève*, September 5, 1966. For Biafra, see below, 345.
[59] *Caribbean Monthly Bulletin*, IV (May 1967), 2. Duvalier again began deporting priests in 1969.

slipped into the Bahamas, there to embarrass the newly independent government.[60] In early 1969 the government of the Bahamas believed that approximately 11,000 Haitians were living in its islands.[61] Fewer Haitians sought employment in Africa than before, but by early 1968 there were more than 75,000 Haitians in the United States, many on the west side of Manhattan, about 10,000 in Canada, 300,000 in the Dominican Republic, and 50,000 in Cuba. There were nearly ten times more Haitian psychiatrists in Montreal than in Port-au-Prince, more Haitian physicians overseas than in Haiti, and more local economists working for the United Nations or the Organization of American States than for the government of Haiti. There were more Haitian nurses in Canada than in Port-au-Prince. In 1965 the United States consulate processed twenty-five visa applications every day, and most Haitians had to wait eight months before their names reached the top of the list.[62]

This brain drain was the result of economic as well as political factors, especially since the regime increased, rather than lessened, the tax burdens of businessmen and professionals after 1964. Supplementary imposts were levied, nominally for "street repairs," storm sewers, an institute of social research, and innumerable other transient, and, frequently, spurious, causes.[63] The state also gave itself a monopoly of the importation of fish and gave the Régie du Tabac exclusive control over the distribution of cotton, evaporated, condensed, and fresh milk and cream, butter, cheese, margarine, wine, champagne, whiskey, rum, perfumes, dental products, soap, bandages, air conditioners, automobiles, airplanes, and electrical appliances.[64] Needless to say the regime continued to grant lucrative concessions to individual private promoters, some of whom had unsavory foreign connections.

Extortion of foreign businessmen diminished, as the appropri-

---

[60] The Bahamanian authorities deported illegal immigrants with regularity, on at least one occasion to the accompaniment of bitter shipboard riots by repatriated Haitians. *The Times,* August 19, 1968.

[61] Letter from the Secretary to the Cabinet of the Bahamas, April 8, 1969. This is the official figure. It is likely that another 20,000 Haitians were in the Bahamas illegally.

[62] *Washington Post,* February 16, 1965. The lines became still longer in 1969.

[63] For a partial list see *Le Nouveau Monde,* January 2, 1966.

[64] *Ibid.,* September 19, 1965.

ation of goods and services produced by Haitians became regularized and customary. But the baleful *macoute* was still there, his
gun was loaded, and — although affrays in the streets tended to
become more infrequent — he still shot in anger. In 1965 a
"string of killings" culminated when a prominent *macoute* went
into a nightclub in search of a band leader who had complained
about the conduct of the *macoutes*. The band leader was not there
and the militia man fired a burst from a machine gun, killing a
former deputy and seriously injuring two others. In the same year,
in Cap Haitien, *macoutes* went on a rampage in a bar, killing
several respected residents for no apparent reason. In 1967 an
abusive *macoute* leader was shot to death by an enraged army
officer whom he had pistol-whipped; Duvalier attended the huge
state funeral and declared national mourning. (In other areas of
Port-au-Prince his death was the occasion for "wild celebrations"
which the government dared not suppress.) The *macoute* had
been an extortionist who made market women and small businessmen pay him protection money and operated a small bar and crap-
shooting establishment and a notorious brothel.[65] In early 1968
an elderly person from Cap Haitien began arguing with national
bank officials "who wouldn't cash his government check. Abruptly
he was seized, questioned briefly, tied to a tree and killed with four
rifle shots by members of the Ton Ton Macoute. . . . The crime:
'Economic Sabotage.' "[66] As late as 1967 a diplomat in Port-au-
Prince admitted to an American reporter that the *macoutes* made
him edgy. "I don't like sitting near the President at these functions because there are so many Ton-Ton Macoutes . . . with
drawn guns around him," he said. "Some even have their fingers
on the triggers and some day during real or imagined trouble one
of us . . . is going to get it."[67]

In fact, those who "got it" — literally or figuratively — were
the same persons as before, the ones who "reached above themselves," who thought that they could build a separate base of
power, or who, in Duvalier's eyes, had begun to adopt a threaten-

[65] Harvey Rosenhouse, "Come to Haiti and Meet Papa Doc's Police," *New Republic*,
CLVI (March 11, 1967), 10.
[66] Kenneth G. Slocum, "Papa Doc Holds On," *Wall Street Journal*, April 20, 1968.
[67] *Washington Post*, June 27, 1967.

ing posture. Clémard Joseph Charles, the president's wealthy personal banker and financial adviser, and a man who had received several lucrative monopolistic concessions including compulsory automobile and old age insurance, control over the capital's main wharf, and a bank — after smuggling aircraft from the United States to Haiti in 1964 — was in 1967 sent to Fort Dimanche after boasting too loudly that he was in line to succeed Duvalier. There may also have been a suspicion that he was cheating financially. He eventually emerged from prison rather chastened and devoid of his thirty-three businesses, property, and money. What the dictator gave, he retrieved.

Patterns varied while fates remained the same: Pierre Giordani, a Corsican who had lived in Haiti since his childhood and had become the "boss" of Cap Haitien as chief *macoute* and a deputy, and who had helped to cleanse the north of the dictator's opponents, fled into the Panamanian Embassy in 1967. The same year a former henchman of Rafael Trujillo, who had begun helping Duvalier to modernize the methods of the *macoutes,* disappeared and was believed to have been liquidated. Jean Tassy, who had replaced Barbot as the putative head of the *macoutes,* and whose reputation as a sadistic killer was widespread, made his way into the Brazilian Embassy (at one point in 1967 a refuge for forty-four Haitians) and thence to Rio de Janeiro. Even the sycophantic and studiously loyal Gérard de Catalogne, newspaper editor, director of tourism, and publicist extraordinary, a man who had survived the fall of one regime after another, lapsed into disgrace, temporarily, during 1967. There were others who vanished, and thirty-two soldiers, believed to be plotting against the president, were executed in 1966.

But a combination of military trifling with the favors of his daughters (Simone consorted with Captain Harry Tassy and had an abortion after Tassy refused to leave his own wife; Marie-Denise became pregnant and took Colonel Max Dominique away from his wife; and Nicole gave birth after sixth months of marriage to Luc-Albert Foucard) [68] and the discernment (or supposed dis-

[68] Norman Gall, "Duvalier's Latest 'Housecleaning' May be a Sign of Disintegration," *Philadelphia Bulletin,* September 10, 1967.

covery) of a plot against himself, led Duvalier in June 1967 personally to command the firing squad which executed nineteen army officers, including Harry Tassy. It was "not only a duty, but an obligation," he said.[69] The nineteen who died were apparently brought quietly together in small groups, and then dispatched. Colonel Dominique, then in charge of the Departement du Ouest, was allowed, however, to ransom his relatives and flee to Spain (with Marie-Denise), where he became Haiti's ambassador and, later, inspector of embassies abroad, before returning to Port-au-Prince in 1969. Dominique's chauffeur and two bodyguards fared less well; immediately after his departure they were taken into custody and shot. This was the old ferocity, but the occasions for its display were becoming less frequent.

Invasions of Haiti characteristically take place during the "dead season" — the end of the sugar-cane and coffee harvests, when people, particularly those connected with cutting and processing cane, are laid off for the summer and money in most pockets is in shorter supply than usual — on the assumption that oppressed peasants and workers will revolt when they are beginning to grow hungry. There was another[70] in May 1968. An ancient B-25 bomber of uncertain provenance dropped several bombs harmlessly near the presidential palace and on Cap Haitien after flying from an illegal airfield in the Bahamas. The same plane also landed at Cap Haitien (where it was eventually captured) while two other aircraft flown from the Bahamas deposited about thirty-five armed guerrillas there. The local army detachment defended the town — which was separated from the airport by a river and an easily guarded bridge — while the guerrillas dug themselves in at the airport. Some of the insurgents reached the town, and others

[69] Agence France Presse exclusive interview in *The Times,* April 7, 1968. In the same interview he defined his regime as one of "applied democracy."

[70] In 1967 Father Georges and Rolando Masferrer, a Cuban exile, assembled three airplanes, a shrimp boat, and smaller craft, machine guns, mortars, small arms, three tons of explosives and ammunition in the Florida Keys, recruited four dozen Haitian exiles, twelve American mercenaries, about two hundred Cuban exiles, and a Columbia Broadcasting System television crew, and prepared to surprise Duvalier. But before the filibustering expedition managed to board its various craft, agents of the U.S. Customs Service apprehended Georges, Masferrer, and seventy-one of their colleagues, many of whom were sentenced to jail. See Robert K. Brown, "The Plot Against Papa Doc," *National Review,* XIX (January 24, 1967), 91.

tried to use a powerful local radio station run by American evangelical missionaries. In a taxi four even attained the mission headquarters a few miles beyond Cap Haitien (and seven miles from the transmitter) and returned without being captured. But whatever the rebel plan may have been (a boat that was apparently intended to transport additional rebels from the Bahamas foundered before reaching Haiti), there was no rising in the town or the countryside where the inhabitants, however interested, remained cautious.[71] For a night and part of two days the insurgents held the airport and managed to kill one foolhardy Haitian officer, a Haitian vice-consul on leave from Miami, and his driver. The local *macoutes* were virtually useless. Only after Duvalier had dispatched troops under the command of Colonel Breton Claude from Port-au-Prince to Cap Haitien did the tide turn. The puny Haitian air force bombed and strafed, the coast guard effectively shelled the airstrip (nothing larger than a Constellation could land there), destroying a hut and a refrigerator, and units of the army finally killed five rebels, captured ten, and scattered the remainder.[72] Delva, the enigmatic *macoute* leader from Gonaïves, had meanwhile kept the 40,000 inhabitants of Cap Haitien in line, rigid censorship of press and diplomatic cables had been imposed, and even ordinary telegrams could not be sent without the signature of the president. Roads out of the capital and the other major cities were blocked, and, for the next six months, travel was permitted only under very special circumstances. The evangelical mission and its transmitter were closed for six weeks until the American head of the organization waited twenty-four hours in the palace, managed to see the president, and retrieved the keys to the station from his desk. In the aftermath of the invasion, which had been even more quickly crushed than its predecessors, Duvalier also obtained special powers to rule by decree from his obedient legislature.

There was a comic *coda,* too, when the South African-born di-

[71] The invasion was seemingly prepared hastily after the Bahamanian police had discovered the rebels' secret training camp. Seventy-eight Haitian exiles being trained by ex-Lieutenant Roland Magloire were imprisoned in the Bahamas.

[72] The above account is derived from the testimony of eyewitnesses independently interviewed in Cap Haitien.

rector of the Bahamas information office arrived in Haiti as a week-
end tourist, acted oddly, and asked a surgeon to carve a scar in his
cheek. Despite his innocence of any overt wrongdoing (the circumstances were curious, and are still incompletely explained) or
any connection with the Haitian exiles, his timing was incriminating, and the Haitian government spent the summer trying him for
espionage. He was sentenced to death but reprieved "generously"
by the president, and deported. More seriously, six prominent
businessmen, including Oswald Brandt, the seventy-six-year-old
millionaire who had for so long helped support the regime, his
nephew Clifford Brandt, the lawyers Georges and Jean Claude
Léger, and Robert Nadal, another wealthy head of one of the
country's best known import-export firms, were all accused of helping to finance the invasion; the real reason for their detention may
have been their failure to continue to provide Duvalier with the
monetary backing to which he had become accustomed.[73] Nadal
was released quickly, and, although the others were detained for
more than three months, they lived in comparative comfort in military barracks and were, in the end, reprieved. By autumn Duvalier was feeling less anxious and had begun to demonstrate to any
who would listen — especially foreign journalists — that he really
was a man of good will. He even remitted the death sentences
which had been meted out by a military court to the captured invaders.

"I hope that the evolution you have observed in Haiti," Duvalier said at the time, "will serve as an example to the people who
have the leadership in the free world. Where democracy is concerned, there must be evolution. There is nothing static about
democracy." [74] He had earlier criticized the men behind the invasion: They were "a small, pleasure-loving, grasping and lazy elite,
veritable leeches who do not want this country to progress. . . .
They want only power for the privileges that this power
brings." [75] This, the revealed truth of Duvalierism, was but another example of the kind of thought that has been called "pro-

[73] The two Brandts had been imprisoned in 1964, held for two weeks, and deported
to Jamaica. But within three months they were back, at the dictator's request.
[74] Quoted in *The Times*, August 21, 1968.
[75] *New York Times*, July 5, 1968.

gressive mystification." [76] Anna Freud would probably have related this and similar utterances to introjection that — in her terms — was related to paranoia.[77] Whatever, it was vintage Duvalier, the same man and dictator who deftly "forgot," in late 1968, to pay a month's wages to his employees and, at the same time, knew that every civil servant would want a copy of volume II of his own *Oeuvres Essentielles;* the equivalent of $15 was deducted from their wages in November in order to pay for copies of the fat volume of old speeches.

Duvalier, as he has told his people so many times, was "in control." A cabinet reshuffle in late 1968 and the retirement in early 1969 of Eloüs Maître, a leading *macoute* and bodyguard (after Duvalier had welcomed Dominique and Marie-Denise back from exile and installed the latter as his private secretary), made it clear that he had not lost his sensitivity or his ability to manipulate the matrix of Haitian politics to his own advantage. He claimed to have killed nearly one hundred Communist infiltrators in the spring of 1969, but observers saw few bodies, and none corresponded with those of the five known Communists whose names were released to the press. They might well have been killed, but months before, in Fort Dimanche.

At the beginning of the summer, the president also fell ill. He may have had a mild heart attack, or simply succumbed to circulatory difficulties arising from his diabetes. The Port-au-Prince rumor mill worked overtime, inventing a number of serious complications and, by way of wish fulfillment, there were earnest reports of his paralysis, derangement, and demise. Haitians everywhere were ambivalent. They feared that they might in fact soon be without a leader, a chief, a big boss. Losing a dictator is as traumatic as suffering one, and fears and anxieties intensified when an old Constellation dropped about eight incendiary bombs (kerosene drums filled with petrol) on the capital during three bombing runs one warm day in early June. (It had departed secretly from the Bahamas and of the ten men aboard when it ran out of fuel and landed at an American air base elsewhere in the Bahamas,

76 Manigat, *Sixties,* 60.
77 See above, 23.

two were Haitian exiles, one was a Canadian, and seven were
American mercenaries.) [78] There was some shooting the next week
by trigger-happy palace guards perhaps frightened by a low-flying
scheduled jet airliner, and a certain amount of added tension when
Duvalier taped a brief speech to the people but refused to appear
in public. Only his well-photographed appearance on July 1 with
Governor Nelson Rockefeller, President Richard M. Nixon's special envoy, dispelled the disquiet of his populace and the immediate hope of exiles.[79] Once again his triumph was complete.

The Renovator had continued to win the political and emotional battles, but, as is discussed in Chapter VIII, he was no nearer
to winning the critical economic battles than he had been in 1957.
Twelve years of despotism had done nothing to alleviate the national malaise. The purely economic decline is clear, but what is
equally certain, if far less quantifiable, is that there had been no
significant progress on any of a number of social fronts. There was
much talk of revolution, but little evidence of it — even since the
beginning of what Duvalier was wont to call his second decade of
development. More blacks from the lower — but not the lowest
— stratum of society had been given a stake in the perpetuation of
Duvalierism, and hence in the government of the day, but there
had been no broadening of the base of political participation, no
elaboration of a meaningful philosophy of social justice, no deep-
ening of a respect for a cultural heritage — in short, no transformation of society. The vaunted rearrangement of the class structure proved, on closer inspection, chimerical. The dictatorship of
Duvalier, it must be said, lacked any redeeming features except, in
its later years, stability. But the price paid for such a negative result had been unbelievably high, and the social and economic costs
astronomical. There was lamentation for the great opportunities
for political development which had been forfeited — perhaps for
years to come. Symptomatically, too, even after twelve years of the
revolution, Duvalierism lacked any meaningful ideological expres-

[78] *Miami Herald,* June 10, 1969. One of the Americans may have been an under-
cover agent.
[79] Aides to Governor Rockefeller reported that Duvalier looked frail, that he was
obviously still ill and weak, and that Governor Rockefeller had to support him on
the palace balcony.

sion. It was authoritarianism without justification, and, ground small, the essence of Duvalierism was power for power's sake. It had failed to foster progress. It was the most nakedly absolutist of the remaining regimes of dictatorial cast. Yet, this last condemnation simply demonstrates the extent to which the Duvalierist regime was truly Haitian. No less than its predecessors, it was a product and the embodiment of Haiti's own national structure, the constraints and deficiencies of which were abundantly, and ineradicably, reflected in the composition of Duvalierism.

VII

The Human Resources

HAITI'S HUMAN AND PHYSICAL RESOURCES are sufficiently impoverished to require a detailed discussion before returning to the analysis of political problems and prospects. Harsh demographical, epidemiological, and economic realities condition every aspect of the
republic's political development and effectively constrain the possibilities of both political and economic modernization. This
chapter deals with the first two areas, while Chapters VIII and IX
offer an analysis of the structure and developmental potential of
Haiti's economy.

In preindustrial societies such as rural Haiti, the birth rate tends
to be fairly constant and is determined primarily by how many
women are of childbearing age. The death rate and, in turn, the
rate of population increase fluctuate considerably each year and
depend upon three interrelated factors: climate, morbidity, and
food supplies. Nutrition is particularly critical in a subsistence
economy such as Haiti's because a man's daily output of work may
depend more on his intake of calories than on his years of schooling.

Most Haitians have a monotonous and meager diet. They rely
upon raw sugar cane, sorghum, maize, rice, cassava, red and black
beans, yams, plantains, and *rapadou* (a coarse brown sugar) for
the bulk of their food. They drink *clairin* (crude rum) and, when
they can afford to, eat salted fish, freshly slaughtered goat or pork,
rolls baked from white wheat flour, and, occasionally, eggs, beef, or
poultry. According to the region there may be citrus fruit, avocados, mangoes, and breadfruit. Rural Haitians rarely consume

milk, cheese, butter, or vegetable oils. This diet not only is poor but is also conducive to malnutrition.[1]

The nutritional state of a population everywhere, but particularly in Haiti, affects its health. Children whose deaths are ascribed to epidemic diarrhea, young women who succumb to tuberculosis, and middle-aged men who die of bacterial pneumonia may more properly be considered victims of starvation. Children between the ages of one and four are exceptionally vulnerable to diarrheal disease if they fail to receive an adequate supplementary diet during and after the process of weaning. In Guatemala and India, it has been demonstrated that during this period proper foods are more effective in preventing diarrheal deaths than piped water or concrete privies. Obversely, infections like measles or diarrhea, which exhaust the child's limited nutritional reserve, can transform mere undernourishment into a gross state of malnutrition.[2]

Because Haiti lacks reliable vital statistics such as age-specific death rates, the current state of the republic's malnutrition must be determined by sample survey methods. In 1954, an investigator noted a striking deficiency of both daily caloric intake — 2096 instead of a recommended average adult ration of between 2200 and 3200 — and protein — 45 instead of 75 grams.[3] In 1958, a second study observed a correlation between the level of daily wages and the number of meals eaten by families, the average daily calorie

---

[1] Carlos Boulos, "Une Enquête Alimentaire en Haiti," *Bulletin de l'Association Médicale Haitienne,* VI (1954), 186; F. W. Grant and D. Groom, "A Dietary Study in Haiti," *Journal of the American Dietetic Association,* XXXIV (1958), 711; W. H. Sebrell, Jr., *et al.,* "Appraisal of Nutrition in Haiti," *American Journal of Clinical Nutrition,* VII (1959), 551; Derrick B. Jelliffe and E. F. Patricia Jelliffe, "The Nutritional Status of Haitian Children," *Acta Tropica,* XVIII (1961), 23–24; Kendall W. King, *et al.,* "Food Patterns from Dietary Surveys in Rural Haiti," *Journal of the American Dietetic Association,* XXXIV (1968), 116.

[2] M. Behar and Nevin S. Scrimshaw, "Epidemiology of Protein Malnutrition," in I. Galdston (ed.), *Human Nutrition, Historic and Scientific* (New York, 1960), 257–273; H. A. Bruch *et al.,* "Studies of Diarrheal Disease in Central America," *American Journal of Tropical Medicine and Hygiene,* XI (1963), 579; Nevin S. Scrimshaw, "Ecological Factors in Nutritional Disease," *American Journal of Clinical Nutrition,* XIV (1964), 112–114, 116, 118; N. S. Scrimshaw, C. E. Taylor, and J. E. Gordon, *Interactions of Nutrition and Infection* (Geneva, 1968), 30, 250–252.

[3] Boulos, "Enquête Alimentaire," 186, 188. For the standard recommendations, see Jean Mayer and F. Stare, "Nutritional Diseases," in G. W. Hunter, W. W. Frye, and J. C. Swartzwelder, *A Manual of Tropical Medicine* (Philadelphia, 1966), 592.

consumption (from 980 to 2307, depending upon income group), protein intake (from 25 to 68 grams), fat consumption (from 27 to 94 grams), and the average expenditure on food per day per adult (from 5 cents to 25 cents). They confirmed the same relationships with respect to height and weight, the total male sample averaging 65 inches and the female 62 inches. (The average adult heights in the United States are four and two inches taller respectively.) Over half of the Haitian adults were 5 per cent or more underweight for their height according to the standard calculations of the Metropolitan Life Insurance Company.[4] An even more comprehensive survey of 300 Haitians found an average intake of 1589 calories and 37 grams of protein, only 22 grams of which came from animal sources. The average per capita expenditure for food was 8 cents a day. Mean adult stature was 66 inches for males and 62 inches for females, with a "striking frequency" of very short adults. Fifty-one per cent of the adults were 10 per cent or more underweight for their height. Only 4 per cent were 10 per cent or more overweight. A growth curve devised for children over five years old showed a pattern of development similar to that of Iowa school children, although the mean Haitian heights were retarded at every age. The pattern also suggested that puberty occurred at about the same ages in both groups, a finding which has since been confirmed by others.[5] It could be argued that the observed differences were due to hereditary factors, but another study demonstrated that Haitian school children from wealthy homes have a growth curve corresponding precisely to that of the Iowa grid.[6] These findings suggest that environmental, probably nutritional, factors are pre-eminent.

Wherever there is adult and adolescent malnutrition of this magnitude, the state of nutrition in infants is invariably worse. One survey of 1300 Haitian children aged one to three from

[4] Grant and Groom, "Dietary Study," 714. The U.S. height standards are taken from M. G. Wohl and R. S. Goodhart, *Modern Nutrition in Health and Disease* (Philadelphia, 1968), 567, 569.
[5] Sebrell *et al.*, "Appraisal of Nutrition," 551–553, 570–577. See also J. B. Romain, *Recherches sur la Puberté en Haiti* (Port-au-Prince, 1969), 1–7; A. Bordes and H. Titus, *Manuel de Puericulture* (Port-au-Prince, 1967), 16.
[6] Kendall W. King *et al.*, "Height and Weight of Haitian Children," *American Journal of Clinical Nutrition*, XIII (1963), 106–109.

twenty-six areas found 7 per cent with florid kwashiorkor, 60 per cent malnourished according to the Gómez criteria (a weight less than 90 per cent of the mean weight of a Jamaican infant of the same age), and 69 per cent with abnormally small arm circumferences — a measure which is an index of both nutritional and developmental status.[7] A more recent investigation has identified six months as the age at which Haitian infants begin to fall behind infants in more prosperous environments.[8] It confirmed that the Haitian newborns nourished by their mother's milk begin life normally and then, because of inadequate supplementary feeding at the time of weaning, later fail to thrive. Ninety-nine per cent of Haitian rural women breast-feed their infants for six months, but only 81 per cent continue to twelve and 50 per cent to eighteen months.[9] Furthermore, infants were customarily weaned to herb teas, starchy gruels, and similar foods from which protein was conspicuously absent. Such a regimen not only results in relative height and weight deficiencies but also increases vulnerability to diarrhea at a time when increased mobility makes ingestion of contaminated food and water more likely. Although diarrheal disease

[7] Jelliffe and Jelliffe, "Nutritional Status," 19–21; Derrick B. Jelliffe and E. F. Patricia Jelliffe, "Prevalence of Protein Calorie Malnutrition in Haitian Preschool Children," *American Journal of Public Health*, L (1960), 1357, 1362.

[8] I. Beghin, W. Fougere, and K. W. King, "Enquête Clinique sur l'Etat de Nutrition des Enfants Préscolaires de Fond-Parisien et de Gauthier (Haiti): Juin, 1964," *Annales des Sociétés Belges de Médecine Tropicale*, XLV (1965), 577. Representative results are expressed in the following table from 579:

Weight of Children of Different Ages
in Fond-Parisien, Haiti
(Expressed as a percentage of normal weight)

Age	Percent of Normal Weight
0–5 months	102.1
6–11 months	89.8
12–17 months	81.1
18–23 months	81.0
2–3 years	81.0
3–4 years	77.2
4–5 years	79.8
5–6 years	75.0
6–7 years	70.3

A similar trend was also observed by King, "Height and Weight," 108.

[9] Jelliffe and Jelliffe, "Nutritional Status," 26.

is a relatively minor problem for well-nourished infants, it is likely to be fatal for marginal ones.[10]

Relatively little is known about specific vitamin and mineral deficiencies in Haiti. According to one study, between 17 and 39 per cent of females displayed enlarged thyroid glands (a manifestation of iodine deficiency), 13 per cent were anemic (reflecting iron or protein deficiencies and/or blood loss due to parasites), and, whereas 8 to 81 per cent had the clinical stigmata of chronic vitamin A insufficiency, only 7 per cent demonstrated the lowered blood levels indicating an acute deficiency. This apparent inconsistency may well be explained by the availability of mangoes, a fruit rich in vitamin A, during the period of the survey.[11] Similarly, clinical findings of riboflavin and blood levels varied according to the seasonal presence of the avocado, a fruit rich in riboflavin. Unfortunately, both mangoes and avocados are unavailable for about six months of the year, during which time acute deficiencies are likely.

The 1969 population of Haiti was estimated to be 4,768,101 by the Institut Haitien de Statistique.[12] Plus or minus about 200,000, this is a reasonable figure; it is consistent with the number projected from the Haitian census of 1950 and the estimates of the Service National d'Eradication de la Malaria (SNEM), which has conducted a series of local censuses throughout Haiti.[13] In view of these figures and the comparative data on density and rural-urban ratios presented in Chapter I, no discussion of health conditions can overlook Haiti's demographic burden of tightly clustered rural residents practicing subsistence agriculture of the most basic kind.

[10] Scrimshaw, "Ecological Factors," 113.

[11] Sebrell et al., "Appraisal of Nutrition," 567, 568, 574. This same study also reported some scurvy, or vitamin C deficiency manifested by low serum levels of ascorbic acid and bleeding gums. F. A. Klippstein, I. M. Samloff, and E. A. Schenck, "Tropical Sprue in Haiti," Annals of Internal Medicine, LXIV (1966), 575, have noted vitamin B_{12} and folic acid deficiencies in the Artibonite Valley.

[12] Institut Haitien de Statistique, "Estimation de la Population de la République d'Haiti" (August 7, 1969), 5.

[13] The 1950 census exhibits many gross technical deficiencies, but it is Haiti's only census since the early nineteenth century. Jacques St. Surin, Indices Démographiques et Perspectives de la Population d'Haiti de 1950 à 1980 (Port-au-Prince, 1962), 5; U.N., Demographic Yearbook, 1967 (New York, 1968), 103; J. Mason, Development of the Haiti Malaria Eradication Programme (Washington, 1968), 1–24 passim; Censo de Recursos y Servicios en Salud, Oficina Sanitaria Panamericana (Port-au-Prince, 1968), 19–24.

Several Haitian censuses have also disclosed an apparent excess of females over age ten (because of undercounting, emigration, and higher death rates among men) and a marked youthfulness. Nearly half of the population is less than fifteen years old.[14]

By Western standards, family ties are loose. Less than a quarter of all couples are legally married, the remainder living in *plaçage*, or common-law relationships. Rural Haitian women, however, rarely enter into such arrangements prior to age twenty and, unlike their counterparts in the Anglophone West Indies, who begin reproduction earlier, usually do not begin childbearing until age twenty-one or later. Most, despite their delayed start, ultimately go on to bear children (88 per cent of women over twenty-five had borne at least one child in a recent rural survey), an indication that rates of voluntary and involuntary sterility are low.[15]

Haitian birth and death rates are virtually unknown, largely because the registration of such vital statistics since the only national census (1950) has been inadequate and incomplete. For example, during the first trimester of 1967, only 6475 births were reported of the 40,000 to 50,000 which probably occurred, and 4758 of the 20,000 to 30,000 deaths.[16] Such deficiencies force us to extrapolate from the few available figures: the birth rate can be approximated from the age structure of the population in 1950 as 35 per 1000, but because Haitians are reluctant (for fear of taxes and because of superstition) to report the presence of newborn children, that estimate may be low. Alternatively, we can utilize the concepts of stable and quasi-stable populations to compute a birth rate of 45.5 and a death rate of 25.5 per 1000 for the period between 1950 and 1955.[17] But the latter figures, especially the birth rate, are probably too high. A recent survey in rural Haiti has found birth rates of about 35 per 1000 and death rates (despite the obvious underre-

[14] For school enrollment and attendance, see below, 308–315; 394–395.

[15] Department of Population Sciences, Harvard University, unpub. field data (1969); J. Blake, *Family Structure in Jamaica* (New York, 1961), 12–17. The finding that only 12 per cent of rural women are childless does not support a favorite assumption of many in Haiti—that venereal disease is widespread.

[16] Institut Haitien de Statistique, *Bulletin Trimestriel de Statistique*, LXV (1967), 9–33.

[17] St. Surin, *Indices Démographiques*, 16. See also O. A. Collver, *Birth Rates in Latin America* (Berkeley, 1965), 132; E. E. Arraiga, *New Life Tables for Latin American Populations in the Nineteenth and Twentieth Centuries* (Berkeley, 1968), 145–149.

porting of infant deaths) of about 15 per 1000.[18] The difference
between these rates, or net increase, of 2.0 to 2.2 per cent per
annum is within the expected range. Life expectancy is about
thirty or thirty-five years, being depressed by the high rate of infant mortality — at least 150 per 1000.

Many reasons can be invoked to explain why the Haitian birth
rate is less than 40. The easiest (but least likely) is that many
births are unreported. Were this the only explanation, however, a
high child-woman ratio (children under 5 to women 15–49)
would be expected. Such is not the case. Data from the 1950
census indicate child-woman ratios of 457/1000 for Haiti,
556/1000 for Jamaica, and 749/1000 for the Dominican Republic.[19] It is more likely that a combination of somewhat delayed co-
habitation, conjugal instability, prolonged lactation, spontaneous
abortions, and high infant mortality are hindering effective Haitian fertility. Earlier in this chapter, the possibilities of delayed
puberty and frequent sterility as causes were rejected. Induced
abortions and folk methods of contraception may be operating, but
there are no authentic reports to support such hypotheses.

From the forgoing (and the data in Chapter I), it is evident that
the human resources of Haiti are poorly nourished, densely settled,
overwhelmingly rural, illiterate, predominantly youthful, and
characterized by flexible marriage ties, abundant fertility, and high
rates of mortality.

The diseases of the island were recognized early, malaria, ty-
phoid, and yellow fever being described by the middle of the eighteenth century and tetanus neonatorum soon after. Yaws was not
noted until 1909.[20] In order to make an accurate assessment of the
extent of these and other diseases in contemporary Haiti a thorough cross-sectional investigation of a sample of the whole population (rather than a mere listing of cases reported treated by
physicians or in hospitals) would be required, but this kind of investigation has never been undertaken. Limited surveys are available, however. They indicate that between 40 and 80 per cent of
all children are infected with intestinal parasites: ascaria, giardia,

18 Department of Population Sciences, Harvard University, unpub. field data (1969).
19 U.N., *Demographic Yearbook, 1965* (New York, 1966), 234.
20 R. Léon, *Les Maladies en Haiti* (Port-au-Prince, 1953), 10–15, 170; anonymous,
"Current Comment: Gangosa in Haiti," *U.S. Naval Medical Bulletin,* III (1909), 141.

trichuris, and hookworm.[21] Up to 30 per cent of rural newborn babies risk dying from tetanus during the first month of life.[22] Approximately 3 per cent of Haitians have active tuberculosis at any one time, most adults are tuberculin positive (an indication that they have been infected in the past), and 25 per cent of all deaths in one survey were related to this disease.[23] Fortunately, yaws and malaria, once the scourges of Haiti, have been attacked with vigor, and the lessons learned during those campaigns are applicable to future programs of preventive medicine in Haiti.

Yaws is a disease in which an organism similar to that which causes syphilis enters the broken skin and creates an ulcer. The source is either direct contact with other infected skin or indirect, such as via the feet of an insect. Ultimately one or more areas of the body may be covered with ulcers which erode the skin and the underlying tissue, including bone. Characteristically, feet, legs, joints, and face are affected, with resultant crippling, pain, and disfigurement. Afflicted persons are usually reluctant to appear in a public clinic for treatment, so medical facilities must be taken to the patient. When penicillin became available for general use, mass treatment became possible, and a successful eradication campaign (one-third of all Haitians had yaws) was begun. By 1954 nearly 90 per cent of the population had been treated by single injections of long-acting penicillin costing about 30 cents each.[24]

The elimination of malaria has proved more difficult because no single injection or spraying of infected houses or ponds is sufficient.[25] The type of malarial parasite may change and/or become resistant to insecticides, and geographical configurations may be al-

21 D. S. Polk, "Child Care in Haiti," *Clinical Pediatrics*, IV (1965), 298–304; Jelliffe and Jelliffe, "Nutritional Status," 31–35; Rockefeller Foundation, International Health Board, Annual Reports, 1924–1965, *passim*.
22 F. M. Marshall, "Tetanus of the Newborn," *Yearbook of Pediatrics*, XII (1968), 66–67.
23 H. M. Vandiviere *et al.*, "New Aspects of Mycobacterial Skin Tests," *Archives of Environmental Health*, XIII (1966), 72; Léon, *Maladies*, 184–185.
24 S. Christiansen, *Rapport sur le Projet d'Eradication du Pian en Haiti* (Geneva, 1966), 1–150; G. E. Samame, "Treponematosis Eradication with Especial Relation to Yaws Eradication in Haiti," *Bulletin of W.H.O.*, XV (1956), 897–903; J. H. Dwinelle, *et al.*, "Evaluation of Penicillin in the Treatment of Yaws," *American Journal of Tropical Medicine*, XXVII (1947), 633–641; above, 178.
25 For malaria in Haiti, see J. H. Paul and A. Bellerive, "A Malaria Reconnaissance of the Republic of Haiti," *Journal of the National Malaria Society*, VI (1947), 41–67; J. Mason and P. Cavalie, "Malaria Epidemic in Haiti Following a Hurricane," *American Journal of Tropical Medicine and Hygiene*, XIV (1965), 533–545.

tered by public works, new crops, floods, and hurricanes, each of which will ordain new spraying or drainage tactics. Even a *fête,* which inspires people to repaint their houses (neutralizing the insecticides) or cluster in the streets (during evening hours), may provide new opportunities for the transmission of parasites and undo months of careful control work. Before the national malaria eradication drive began in 1961, school children in some areas of Haiti had a malarial parasite rate as high as 66 per cent. At first SNEM attempted to limit mosquito transmission of malaria by spraying all residences situated below 500 meters, but by 1964 it was clear that the Haitian custom of eating outdoors and the tendency of the *Anopheles albimanus* mosquito to rest outside rather than inside a hut demanded new techniques. In malarious areas the entire population was given antimalarial tablets every three weeks. Ninety per cent of the rural population apparently took the pills, an extremely high rate of acceptance, and annual numbers of malarial cases fell from 10,000 in 1965 to 2559 in 1968. The costs of this program were, however, high — about $11 million through 1968 — and by 1969 it was not certain that eradication would in fact prove successful, given a recent increase in reported cases, a growing shortage of funds, and the tendency of malaria to flare up with epidemic force after remaining quiescent for several years, as has happened in Ceylon.[26]

Despite these relative successes, it would be unwise to conclude that all of Haiti's remaining health problems are susceptible to similar measures of preventive medicine. A smallpox vaccination program which was carried out with the yaws eradication scheme has been suspended and about half of the population remains unprotected. A plan to eliminate *Aedes aegypti,* the insect vector of yellow fever, stalled in 1958 and has not been resumed — a state of inactivity which is unique in the Western Hemisphere.

Tetanus neonatorum, a disease to which rural newborn Haitians are particularly susceptible, has also been relatively ignored. It is 100 per cent fatal if untreated and more than 50 per cent fatal even with optimal in-hospital management. Yet it is entirely prevent-

[26] A by-product of the malaria eradication drive is the availability of about 1000 persons employed by SNEM and capably trained in public health procedures.

able. After birth, during which the rural Haitian mother usually squats above a banana-leaf mat which rests upon the earth floor, the spores of tetanus gain entrance to the infant's body via the freshly cut umbilical stump, where they germinate into a lethal bacillus, the toxin of which is responsible for the disease. If the umbilical cord were not cut with scissors, an old knife, or a rock, the cord not bound with string, rags, wire, or grass, the stump not dressed with a septic poultice of dirt, herbs, powdered charcoal, or other ashes, and/or all young women were immunized with inexpensive tetanus toxoid vaccine (which can transmit immunity to the fetus during pregnancy), the disease could easily be eliminated. A national effort is necessary.[27]

Considering Haiti's overpopulation, poverty, and state of disease, family planning might make eminent sense. Unfortunately, Haiti's poverty of resources makes such a recommendation unrealistic except in the capital. Haiti lacks the very conditions which facilitate large-scale family-planning success: high rates of literacy, low levels of infant and child mortality, a high percentage of births in hospitals, and a high urban to rural population ratio.[28] Recently, however, several institutions in Haiti have begun to fit women with intrauterine devices, but acceptance rates have been modest. Approximately 10,000 women were wearing them in mid-1969 out of 750,000 women between the ages of twenty-one and forty-five. This indifference is probably more a result of limited education and high infant mortality than of the nominal Roman Catholicism of the country.

Haiti urgently needs an appropriately designed program of maternal and child care, as any examination of the life of a typical rural newborn infant demonstrates. He has an 80 per cent chance of surviving his first year of life, during which his chief hazard is tetanus neonatorum. After weaning begins, he is likely to become undernourished and protein-starved and often depends upon the

[27] Pan American Health Organization, *Annual Report to the Director, 1967, Official Document No. 86* (Washington, 1968), 8, 9, 210. Also see Marshall, "Tetanus," 69–7; K. W. Newell *et al.,* "The Use of Toxoid for the Prevention of Tetanus Neonatorum," *Bulletin of W.H.O.,* XXXV (1966), 863.
[28] In one study rural Haitians expressed little interest in family size. J. M. Stycos, "Haitian Attitudes Towards Family Size," *Human Organization,* XXIII (1964), 42–47.

meager leavings of the family cooking pot. He will suffer from diarrhea, during which his mother will give him dilute infusions rather than nutritious food and thereby loosen his precarious hold on life. His chances are slightly more than 70 per cent of reaching his third birthday and nearly 100 per cent of acquiring assorted intestinal parasites by mouth or through the soles of his unshod feet. He may well develop malaria. Because he will sleep in a hut tightly enclosed to prevent the spirits from entering, he will be infected by the viruses and bacteria, such as the tubercle bacillus, which are exhaled or coughed out by other members of the family. As younger brothers and sisters are born in the family, he may be transferred to another relative for care. By the time these risks are compounded, only 65 of every 100 children born in rural Haiti will be alive and living with their mothers when they reach the age of six.[29] Thereafter, the survivors' chances improve despite the fact that they are apt to be nutritionally dwarfed, host to intestinal and malarial parasites, and burdened with a focus of tuberculosis, the likelihood of which increases from 20 per cent at age five to 45 per cent at age ten and 90 per cent at age twenty-five.[30] But they will have survived the critical childhood years and demonstrated their fitness for the Haitian environment.

If rapid and widespread acceptance of contraception in Haiti is unlikely (even though family planning services may be considerably extended), it can be anticipated that the already high numbers of Haitians will, given a growth rate per annum of about 2.0 per cent, double every thirty-five years. There were about 1 million Haitians in 1860, 2 million in 1920, and 4 million in 1960. By 1980 there will be about 6 million. Indeed, this rate of increase may itself rise if the death rate declines as a result of badly needed maternal and child health programs, widened distribution of surplus food, or emphasis upon preventive medicine. But in the absence of a progressive development of rural health measures, little change is likely over the short term. Since birth rates are apt to be relatively constant, rates of natural increase will also remain the

29 Department of Population Sciences, Harvard University, unpub. field data (1969). Cf. the similar figure calculated for the Anglophone West Indies of the 1820's in G. W. Roberts, "A Life Table for a West Indian Slave Population," *Population Studies,* V (1952), 238.
30 Vandiviere, *et al.,* "New Aspects," 72.

same, and there will continue to be a high proportion of economically unproductive youths under age fifteen. The proportion will increase if infant mortality falls. This last factor will limit the accumulation of capital for industrial development.

Emigration could offer a safety valve to relieve population pressure, as it has throughout the Anglophone West Indies. But in Haiti prospects for such relief are not promising. About 7000 Haitians migrate annually to the United States, less than a tenth of the annual population increase, and, since the passage of new immigration legislation in 1968, it has proved even more difficult than before to enter the United States. There is little migration to the Dominican Republic and Cuba, although as many as can go to the Bahamas.[31] Those who do emigrate tend to be well educated, and the resultant drain of skilled personnel is particularly severe. In the medical field, for example, 500 Haitian physicians (200 of them in the United States) are believed to be abroad. In 1965, Haiti had the lowest ratio (7.6) of the number of physicians practicing in their own country to the number graduated in that year. (The ratio for Central America as a whole was 21.3.)[32] With so many demographic outlets closed, Haiti's only feasible option is to buy time by ameliorating the state of her nutrition.

To do nothing about the nutritional problems would fulfill the prophecies of Malthus but would limit population growth in a cruel and random manner. The application of such a remedy would, moreover, hardly enhance the quality of Haitian life now or in the future. Dependence upon massive shipments of surplus food from the United States is a short-term solution only for a fraction of the Haitian population. Agronomists can conceivably adapt fast-growing "miracle" rice or maize to Haitian needs but, if the Haitian government had the will and the administrative capacity, a better remedy would be based upon a long-term program of nutritional education. Haiti already has over thirty nutrition rehabilitation centers where mothers are taught how to nourish their children more effectively by carefully preparing blends of inex-

31 See above, 248–249.
32 *Health Conditions in the Americas, 1961–1964* (Washington, 1966), 121; *Migration of Health Personnel, Scientists and Engineers from Latin America* (Washington, 1966), 26. Another characteristic of Haitian physicians is their concentration in Port-au-Prince.

pensive, locally grown foods such as maize, millet, and red beans. A preliminary evaluation indicates that these centers, which have been carefully engineered both scientifically and socially, are effectively improving infant nutrition. Because this type of program is well suited to execution in rural Haiti, it could transform infant and child nutrition and lower death rates markedly, something which most of the current food distribution schemes, focused as they are upon hospitals, orphanages, schools, and food-for-work programs, are unlikely to achieve.[33]

Despite the enormity of Haiti's health problems, it is possible to set long-term health priorities. Haiti does not need doctors or even nurses to encourage rural families to boil water, feed their children properly, or build privies. Nor are sophisticated personnel necessary to make more hygienic the conditions which prevail during childbirth, to immunize against tetanus, diphtheria, and tuberculosis, or to complete the eradication of malaria. But there is a serious shortage of health manpower at the advisory, educator, and nurses' aide levels. Training such personnel and equipping them to carry out these measures is within the budget and capacity of the government. The effects would be sufficiently obvious to make the public receptive to additional programs, such as agronomy and family planning.

Any short-run prognostications must be pessimistic. For a decade, at least — whatever the state of the economy or the nature of the government — Haitians will remain underfed and diseased. Young children will die in large numbers. Manual laborers will be slight of stature and appear listless. Only in Port-au-Prince will Haitians be able to live hygienically. Major improvements elsewhere will depend upon gradual increases in educational and income levels, the introduction of responsible government, and massive shifts in rural mental attitudes. Only in the long run will Haiti be able to give its people a medically and demographically decent life.

33 J. M. Bengoa, "Nutritional Rehabilitation Programmes," *Journal of Tropical Pediatrics*, X (1964), 63–64; I. Beghin *et al.*, "Le Centre de Récupération," *Annales des Sociétés Belges de Médecine Tropicale*, XLV (1965), 557–576; Kendall W. King, *et al.*, "Response of Pre-School Children to High Intakes of Haitian Cereal-Bean Mixtures," *Archivos Latinamericanos de Nutricion*, XVI (1966), 53–64.

VIII

The Structure of the Economy

THE EXTENT of Haiti's poverty was indicated in the opening chapter of this book and has been implicit throughout the discussions of the republic's history, politics, and demography. As a leading foreign diplomat accredited to Haiti recently remarked, "If there is anything going for Haiti, I can't see it." With a per capita gross domestic product of around $70, Haiti is and has for long been one of the poorest countries in the world. As a result of the revolution, Haiti entered upon her independence with very few factors of production. Much physical capital had been destroyed by war and most of the educated people had been killed or had emigrated. Of greater importance, the highly organized and interdependent economy of Saint-Domingue had been based upon slavery. After Christophe's death, the society regressed to a form of economic organization involving less division of labor, and consequently much lower productivity. Furthermore, the harsh discipline of slavery shifted the people's preferences toward more leisure and less output.

1. The Factor of Governmental Quality

But the impact of the revolution alone cannot explain Haiti's failure to develop. Like the other former slave colonies of the Caribbean, prerevolutionary Haiti was highly stratified. Many of these islands also suffered from an increasing scarcity of agricultural land. But the major differentiation between nineteenth-century Haiti and the other island territories was political. The

French, Dutch, Danish, Spanish, and British islands all experienced a colonial rule which, with all of its deficiencies, at least provided a stable administrative framework for development. (The same conclusion may be drawn from the experience of African states during the twentieth century.) Haiti's governmental experience is identifiably the variable which accounts for its poorer economic record compared to other similarly situated states: successive regimes in Haiti have limited growth by failing to provide the goods and services normally furnished by public bodies, by plundering the private sector, and by wasting national resources.

Waste is the simple difference between what a government extracts from an economy in the form of taxes, inflationary finance, and irregular contributions, and the reasonable cost of the services which are provided by that government. Since the share of governmentally generated income is only around 12 per cent of GDP, waste cannot be more than about 10 per cent of GDP, and is probably somewhat less than that. But if the elimination or drastic reduction of waste were accomplished by cutting taxes while leaving the level of services constant, it would exert little impact on the rate of growth since the overall savings rate would not be greatly altered.[1]

More serious developmental consequences flow from the failure of Haiti's government to provide good quality and sizable quantities of public goods and services. As a result, the Haitian private sector (including the church) has provided an abnormally large share of total educational services, and private companies habitually maintain sections of the national highways. The supply of public goods and services has always been limited, and has helped to put a ceiling on development. At the same time, the government has plundered the private sector of the economy, particularly by exacting irregular contributions from companies or individuals with visible wealth. This mode of predation has always been practiced by the rulers of Haiti, but none more successfully than Duvalier.[2] When coupled with waste, and the failure to provide pub-

---

[1] For military spending, if we assume a negligible degree of transfer of skills, expenditures on defense and internal security are useless for purposes of development.
[2] For Duvalier's plunder, see above, 210–211, 240–241. The Haitian public accounts as reported by the Banque Nationale de la République d'Haiti are quite opaque as

lic services, such rapacity has made private investment in physical and human capital unprofitable. It is therefore scarce relative to the supply of unskilled labor.

The explanation of Haiti's stagnation in terms of the quality of her government may seem unduly narrow; many "obstacles to growth" can be listed for Haiti: a largely illiterate population, a peasant culture which resists most forms of economic change, and an urban society which despises manual work and holds the peasantry in contempt. The inhibiting influence of these factors on development is not denied. But these obstacles have been shared by most countries at very low levels of development, and some of these countries have nevertheless managed to develop. Why? In the case of Jamaica and several African countries which have made considerable progress, the quality of the government seems to have been a critical factor.

Haiti has for long been caught in a vicious circle of poverty; she stagnated not only because she was too poor to save or because population growth automatically absorbed increases in real income. Rather, Haiti failed to save because the quality of her government was poor, and, in turn, the extent of Haiti's poverty impeded the development of political institutions capable of maximizing the potentialities for economic growth.

Another major obstacle to development in Haiti was the apparent failure of the ruling elite to perceive its true interest. Its economic welfare depended upon marketable peasant output, always the major source of governmental revenues. Projects like the construction and maintenance of roads, the clearing of irrigation canals, and the distribution of improved crop varieties were in the economic interests of both the elite and the peasantry. But because of the tradition of administrative incompetence and paralyzing

---

to a meaningful functional breakdown of expenditures. The totals are probably fairly accurate for what we might call the "fiscal accounts." From 1965 to 1968, these were about $38 million. (Contrary to the accounting practices of the Banque, repayment of the principal of foreign loans is here included in total government expenditure.) Not included are the receipts and expenditures of the autonomous agencies, of which the most important is the Régie du Tabac. This agency has collected taxes not merely on tobacco and matches, but also on flour, sugar, dairy products, textiles, whiskey, and other products, and has retained the profits of the national lottery. The balances are kept not in the Banque, but in the Banque Commerciale, the accounts of which are not open to inspection by other government agencies.

corruption, the ruling elite preferred to use the financial resources of the state to retain political power (through bribes) and to augment personal wealth, rather than to carry out projects of interest to the elite as a whole.

The character of Haiti's present economic backwardness will become clearer if we notice the historical processes of growth, particularly in the initial stages, in Africa and Jamaica. Throughout nearly all of precolonial tropical Africa, productive techniques were primitive and technological change was gradual or nonexistent. There was no generally utilized written language, and markets played a minor role in resource allocation. Foreign trade was insignificant, usually involving products that could easily be gathered. When Europeans colonized Africa they ended interstate wars and began providing the elements of a physical infrastructure, both important changes from a developmental point of view. But the trend of development was nearly always to increase a colony's exports, and to divert them to the mother country.[3]

Among the factors that influenced the critical shift of resources in Africa from the subsistence to the monetized sector — and hence increases in income — the acquisition of new skills was critical. To this process of acquisition, formal education clearly contributed. Table 4 indicates (as accurately as the available and very inadequate statistics permit) the relationship of educational enrollment and incomes in Africa. It is clear that compared with the African countries represented in the table, Haiti's income is remarkably low considering its educational level. Or, to view the same figures from a different perspective, it is evident that many African countries were able in the 1950's to achieve levels of income substantially higher than that of Haiti despite low levels of educational attainment. The data also demonstrate that given other growth-producing factors — exploitable natural resources, a good infrastructure (provided by the colonial governments), competent administration, and conditions of stability — a country can push its per capita gross domestic product above $100 without widespread education.

[3] See Solomon D. Neumark, *Foreign Trade and Economic Development in Africa* (Stanford, 1964), *passim;* Hla Myint, *The Economics of Developing Countries* (London, 1964), 23–68.

The shift from subsistence to the monetary sector, and the way in which that shift was managed, were equally critical variables. In some precolonial African societies markets were unknown, and

Table 4
Incomes and Enrollment, Haiti and Africa

	GDP Per Capita, 1958 ($)	Enrollment Rates, 1950 Primary	Secondary
Haiti	82	15 (1950)	3 (1956)
Gabon	240	21	1
Senegal	174	7	1
Congo (Brazzaville)	157	24	3
Ghana	152	15	11
Liberia	146	11	0.7
Ivory Coast	131	6	0.7
Zambia	130	35[a]	0.6[a]
Cameroon	92	25	0.7
Central Afr. Rep.	90	7	0.8
Congo (Kinshasa)	87	33	1
Guinée	86	3	0.3
Kenya	76	26	2
Togo	71	17	1
Niger	69	1	0.1
Uganda	65	18	2
Dahomey	65	9	0.7
Sierra Leone	64	7	1
Mali	60	3	0.4
Chad	52	1	0.1
Nigeria	48	16	1
Upper Volta	37	2	0.1

[a] African only

In this table are included all the countries in West Africa and in Equatorial Africa for which data are available. Also included are Zambia, Kenya, and Uganda.

Sources: U.N., *Yearbook of National Accounts, 1967* (New York, 1968), 828; *UNESCO Statistical Yearbook, 1965* (New York, 1966), 117–121. Haitian data are from Tables 21 and 25 below. All GDP figures are at factor cost. Enrollment rates are not adjusted for the length of the school curriculum.

in only a few did markets play an important role in resource allocation. Commodity price movements did not induce substantial changes in production patterns.[4] Furthermore, the sale of com-

4 See George Dalton, "Traditional Production in Primitive African Economies," *Quarterly Journal of Economics*, LXXVI (1962), 360–378.

mercial crops or the acceptance of wage employment frequently interfered with traditional obligations. Finally, the major shift from the subsistence to the monetized sector took place in most parts of tropical Africa only in the present century. But Haitian peasants have been exposed to a cash economy since before the revolution.[5] Everyone either sells crops himself or knows someone who does. Everyone uses the same currency for all types of transactions. Factors of production are purchased and sold, and there are no traditional obligations restricting the reallocation of resources in response to market incentives. Admittedly, resources are not very mobile in Haiti's peasant economy,[6] but this is the result of difficulties posed by technical obstacles to change rather than societal or religiously based resistance to innovation. Haitian peasants are adept at commerce, and their practices (and presumably those of agricultural producers, too) by and large do not conflict with the basic rules of economic rationality.[7] In comparing developmental procedures in Africa and Haiti, we can thus count the long experience of Haitians with the market mechanism as a definite asset, but it is impossible — because of the lack of comparative data — to decide the relative importance of this asset.

The case of Jamaica, Haiti's neighbor, is also illustrative. Table 5 shows that Jamaica's per capita income since 1832 has been substantially larger than that of Haiti; in the mid-1950's, for example, when Haiti was relatively prosperous and her per capita income about $82, Jamaica had a per capita income between $215 (1953) and $305 (1958) — 2.6 and 3.7 times that of Haiti.[8] Since then,

[5] Sidney Mintz, "A Tentative Typology of Eight Haitian Market Places," *Revista de Ciencias Sociales,* IV (1960), 15–57.
[6] See below, 278–279.
[7] Sidney Mintz, "The Employment of Capital by Market Women in Haiti," in Raymond Firth and B. S. Yamey (eds.), *Capital, Saving and Credit in Peasant Societies* (Chicago, 1964), 256–286; *idem.,* "Standards of Value and Units of Measure in the Fond-des-Nègres Market Place, Haiti," *Journal of the Royal Anthropological Institute,* XCI (1961), 23–38. For the agricultural producers, however, cf. Sidney Mintz, "Introduction," in Leyburn, *People,* xxviii.
[8] The Haitian figure is slightly higher than the $75.9 usually cited, but for purposes of comparison we have converted this figure by correcting for the change in the purchasing power of the dollar between 1955 and 1957–59. It is evident, too, that Haitian per capita income in constant prices changed little during the 1950's, $82 being a reasonable figure for an average year. See *Report to the Government of Haiti,* Mission of the Organization of American States, the Inter-American De-

Table 5

Per Capita GDP: Jamaica

(Figures in U.S. dollars at 1957–59 prices) [a]

1832	$201.60	1938	180.10
1850	157.50	1950	171.50
1870	153.80	1953	215.60
1890	160.20	1954	235.50
1910	177.00	1958	304.70
1930	202.90		

[a] The 1832–1930 series is taken from Gisela Eisner, *Jamaica, 1830–1930* (Manchester, 1961), 289, who gave the figures in pounds at 1910 prices. This was used as an index of GDP. The 1910 GDP in current pounds was converted to dollars at the 1910 rate of exchange (£1 = $4.84) and converted to 1957–59 dollars by using the U.S. wholesale price index. The series starting in 1938 is from Alfred Thorne, "Size, Growth and Structure of the Economy of Jamaica," supplement to *Social and Economic Studies,* IV (1955), 92, and Jeanette Bethel, "Some National Income Aggregates for Jamaica, at Constant Prices," *Social and Economic Studies,* X (1961), 138. These series were expressed in pounds in 1956 prices. This was used as an index of GDP. The 1954 GDP in current pounds was converted to dollars at the current rate of exchange (£1 = $2.80) and converted to 1957–59 dollars by using the U.S. wholesale price index.

Haiti's per capita income has declined in real terms, while Jamaica's has risen rapidly.

2. Agriculture and Rural Commerce

Haitian peasants are desperately poor, and the output per man and per acre of their tiny plots is low when compared with nearly all other Latin American and Asian countries. Yet there are techniques capable of yielding markedly higher outputs per unit of input than those obtained by most Haitian peasants. But these techniques are not widely adopted, and it is important to ask why,

velopment Bank, and the Economic Commission for Latin America (Port-au-Prince, 1962), mimeo., 1–155, and the *Annex on National Accounts,* 1–76 and Tables 1–50. (These will be referred to hereinafter as the *Tripartite Mission Report* and the *Annex.*) The per capita income figures are discussed in the *Report,* 3–5. International comparisons of income levels should employ purchasing-power parity exchange rates rather than official exchange rates. It is known that purchasing power parities can deviate substantially from official rates, even in the absence of trade restrictions (see Bela Balassa, "The Purchasing-Power Parity Doctrine: A Reappraisal," *Journal of Political Economy,* LXXII [1964], 584–596).

particularly since Haitian peasants are not economically irrational or uninterested in profit-making and accumulating capital.

Studies elsewhere indicate that peasant producers make decisions to plant one cash crop rather than another in accord with relative price changes in the market.[9] This is not to imply that peasants quickly accept or adopt technical improvements, but it is clear that they will shift quickly among crops with which they are familiar in an attempt to earn greater amounts of cash. Peasants also understand their natural environment and in most areas have made their agricultural practices conform to it.[10] But this appreciation in no way implies that peasants will adopt new techniques that have been proved superior elsewhere, i.e., on demonstration farms. To a considerable extent, this rejection of innovations is based upon common sense.[11] First, techniques designed to enhance productivity can rarely be introduced singly. If one change is made, others must follow. The introduction of the plow, for example, requires the purchase, care, and feeding of draft animals, and often the planting of a fodder crop. New cash crop varieties may require different methods of cultivation which are vulnerable to pests and thus require the use of insecticides or fungicides. Fertilizer frequently does not raise the yields of traditional varieties because they have been selected by farmers in the absence of fertilizer. Hence the introduction of fertilizer often requires the simultaneous introduction of new crop varieties. In addition, single applications of fertilizer in poor soils may prove uneconomic; annual applications over a considerable period of time may be required in order to make the practice advantageous. Equally, if peasants attempt to improve their livestock by importing new breeds, they may discover that the new beasts require different and more intensive care than the old. Examples of this kind could be multiplied; it is evident that the introduction of a new technique

9 Walter Falcon, "Farmer Response to Price in a Subsistence Economy: The Case of West Pakistan," *American Economic Review*, LIV (1964), 580–591; Robert Stern, "The Price Responsiveness of Primary Producers," *Review of Economics and Statistics*, XLIV (1962), 202–207.
10 For Haiti, see Harold A. Wood, *Northern Haiti: Land, Land Use, and Settlement* (Toronto, 1963), 146.
11 See Theodore W. Schultz, *Transforming Traditional Agriculture* (New Haven, 1964), *passim*.

brings about multiple changes in agricultural (or other) practices, and the risk of failure increases proportionally. On a demonstration plot, agronomists can deal with problems or failures. But peasant farmers cannot cope as readily with unexpected difficulties. It requires no excessive risk avoidance for marginal farmers to refuse to innovate when the consequence of failure may be starvation, loss of land, and downward social mobility.

If changes are to be made in the traditional peasant economy, then ways must be found to introduce changes in techniques which are immediately within the peasant's grasp, and which can be introduced piecemeal. If such techniques can be evolved, they will be employed more generally and effectively on medium-sized and larger farms because of the economies of scale in technical change. In Haiti, agricultural experimentation is thus particularly hindered by the very small size of nearly all of the farms.[12]

The willingness of peasants to make risky investments in new techniques is also influenced by the security of their tenure on the land. The Haitian census of 1950 reported that 85 per cent of cultivators were "owners," the remainder being classified as occupiers of state lands, renters, sharecroppers, and cultivators of unknown tenure.[13] But virtually none of these "owners" had or has a registered title to his land, and the predominant impression of observers is that the tenure of most farmers in Haiti is (as it is not in Africa) highly insecure.[14]

Given all of these considerations, it is not surprising that Haitian peasants resist change. But there are a number of other relevant factors: Haitian peasants have short time horizons and cannot

[12] The information cost of the acquisition of new knowledge, for one, is the same for the small and the medium-sized farm, but the potential benefits increase with the size of the farm. For the medium-size farmer the money cost of experimenting with new techniques also frequently represents a smaller share of income, and therefore a smaller risk. Marc A. Holly, *Agriculture in Haiti* (New York, 1955), 247, suggests the creation of a class of large-scale peasants. See also Arthur Mosher, *Technical Cooperation in Latin American Agriculture* (Chicago, 1957), 93.

[13] Gérard Pierre-Charles, *L'Economie Haitienne et sa Voie de Développement* (Paris, 1967), 68, shows that the number of cultivators counted corresponds to only about half of the rural population, so there must be a substantial number of peasants without land.

[14] See Brand, *Impressions*, 35; Schiller Nicolas, "Deboisement et Reboisement en Haiti," Service National de Production Agricole et Education Rurale [SNPAER] *Bulletin*, 16 (1938), 62.

always gauge the long-term return of new techniques, like soil conservation. They seem to have a high preference for leisure along
with a willingness to work extremely hard. They use the most
marginal cultivation techniques and almost everywhere refuse, for
example, to prune their coffee trees or remove shade.[15] They in-
dulge in "institutionalized envy" — the use of gossip, witchcraft,
and force to restrain nontraditional or socially unacceptable activities.[16] One observer noted the intensity of a "jealousy pattern" in
isolated areas of Haiti.[17]

Peasant progress and agricultural productivity are also influenced by the availability of rural credit and the character of rural
markets. It is axiomatic that capital markets are poorly developed
in preliterate rural societies, and Haiti is no exception. Credit is
bought and sold, but interest rates are so high that a substantial
fraction if not all of the interest represents a risk premium rather
than a return on capital. Capital consequently is rarely allocated
productively. Peasants can often obtain credit for a single crop season, but not for the longer periods which may be required for substantial improvements. They are frequently in debt to the purchasers of their crops or the vendors of their consumer goods and
peasants often feel that they can never be released from debt.
They are thus discouraged from making any great efforts to increase their production: when they produce large quantities, creditors merely retain extra fractions. Peasants also borrow at usuri-
ous rates of interest and are swindled by money-lenders.

These very real problems are not peculiar to Haiti. In other
countries, governments have established rural credit banks and cooperative credit societies in order to help satisfy the intense need
for credit among farmers who are experimenting with new techniques. But the case for governmental intervention rests on the
assumption of competence. Even under the most favorable circumstances, however, a government agency is apt to lose money
because of the extensive paper work involved in granting small
loans, a cost that local moneylenders avoid by knowing their clients

15 Moral, *Paysan*, 189, 268–269, 277, 280, 304, 308.
16 For the concept, see Eric R. Wolf, "Types of Latin American Peasantry: A Preliminary Discussion," *American Anthropologist*, LVII (1955), 461–463.
17 Erasmus, "Agricultural Change," 23.

personally. In many countries it is possible for government extension programs to be devoted to medium and large farmers only, but in Haiti nearly all farmers can be classed as very small.

Aside from the extremely high transport costs, which are due to the state of the roads, the Haitian marketing system is not so inefficient as is frequently alleged.[18] To be sure, a great many people are employed in marketing. But they represent a highly efficient substitution of labor for capital. To cite one example, commodities are sold in very small units — lard by the spoonful, kerosene by the tiny bottle, and matches by the stick — because consumers are willing to take extra trips to market and to pay higher unit prices in order to avoid tying up capital. Market women substitute abundant labor for scarce capital in innumerable other ways, too, thereby maximizing social efficiency within the traditional economy.[19]

The multiplicity of traders is explicable in part by the rudimentary state of the market for capital. Commerce in the rural markets is conducted with credit being extended from one exchange partner to another, and since each trader has but limited credit, he is able to do business only with a limited number of partners. Traders may borrow capital, but in the absence of enforceable contracts, not only is the trader's borrowing ability restricted, but his desire to lend to many other customers is also curtailed. A wise trader will lend only to persons whom he knows well and with whom he has a working relationship — he builds "a personal niche within the arena of exchange." [20]

If the rural exchange system is efficient within the traditional economy, it may still constitute a barrier to improvements in the quality of peasant-produced goods for export. The first step in the improvement of the quality of these goods is the establishment of a proper grading system, but doing so requires an investment by an exporting firm capable of being repaid only over time. Until pre-

[18] Moral, *Paysan,* 247; Pierre-Charles, *Economie,* 93–94.
[19] Mintz, "Market Women," 261, 268–269, 285; *idem,* "Fond-des-Nègres Market," 35–36.
[20] Mintz, "Market Women," 261; Barbara E. Ward, "Cash or Credit Crops? An Examination of Some Implications of Peasant Commercial Production with Special Reference to the Multiplicity of Traders and Middlemen," *Economic Development and Cultural Change,* VIII (1960), 148–163.

miums can be charged in foreign markets, the exporter must pay
more than the locally prevailing prices in order to bid high quality
goods away from competitors. In Haiti, where peasants often have
long-standing credit and personal ties to middlemen and exporters,
the quality-conscious firm might need to offer substantial premi-
ums, and such investment could prove unprofitable. Or the various exporting firms — in Haiti three control about 45 per cent of
the coffee market — could establish a common grading system; but
the resistance of Haitian peasants to quality improvement, the numerous middlemen through whom standards of quality would be
mediated, and perhaps distrust among the exporting houses themselves have militated against the development of common grading
practices.

Given the generalized nature of the several obstacles to rural economic development, it will be useful to discuss six specific examples of introduced change:

1) Governments of Haiti have long tried to raise the yields and
improve the quality of peasant-produced coffee.[21] After France denounced her commercial treaty with Haiti in 1936,[22] the government of President Vincent sought to promote a washing process in
order to gain entry for Haitian coffee into the American market.
The administration constructed a number of concrete drying plat-
forms and disseminated propaganda favorable to improved preparation of coffee cherries. An earlier law, which set up a grading
system based upon incentive rates of taxation, was reactivated.
Demonstration farms were established in order to show peasants
how to prune, weed, and space their trees. They were asked to thin
the shade above their coffee. Seedlings of new varieties were distributed without charge. Yet all of this activity did little to improve the yields and quality of Haitian coffee. Peasants continued
to cultivate their coffee in time-honored ways, and new varieties

---

21 Material on Haitian coffee is derived from Moral, *Paysan*, 263–280; William B.
Gates, Jr., "The Haitian Coffee Industry," unpub. typescript (Williamstown, 1959),
1–58; John M. Street, "Historical and Economic Geography of the Southwest Peninsula of Haiti," (Berkeley, 1960), mimeo., 250–260; Marcel Monfils, "Amélioration de
la Préparation et de la Présentation du Café Haitien," SNPAER *Bulletin*, 5 (1935),
1–52.
22 See above, 151–152.

accounted for only a tiny fraction of the trees. The percentage (including that of the few plantations) which was washed grew from about 3 in 1929 to an average of 9 in the 1950's, and 12 in 1967.[23] Yet in Jamaica the shift to washing took place rapidly after 1942 when the colonial government assumed control of all but the very best brands of coffee. In 1965 about 95 per cent of all Jamaican coffee was washed.[24]

If the Jamaicans could begin to wash their coffee, why — despite the various inducements — has it proved so difficult to persuade Haitian farmers to do likewise? The tax incentives were there, but they were cancelled out by high transport costs. If they are to be washed properly, coffee beans must be brought to the washing plant immediately after they are harvested. If the peasant chooses to retain the dried beans himself for a time, he holds a form of liquid savings — a feature particularly appealing to the peasant if credit is difficult to obtain. Furthermore, the *speculateurs*, or middlemen, whose position was threatened by the washing plants, opposed them vehemently, and the peasants may have been reluctant to break with the *speculateurs*.

The success or failure of other aspects of the quality improvement program should be reflected in a longitudinal series of coffee price statistics (Table 6). These pass elementary tests of consistency and can be compared with the two standard grades of Brazilian coffee most frequently quoted (Santos no. 4 and Rio no. 7). In an attempt to decide whether Haitian coffee — washed, unwashed, or combined — has increased its price relative to these standard grades (a meaningful question because Haitian unwashed is not a standardized grade and might be affected by governmental efforts to enhance quality), three comparisons with Brazilian coffees are shown in Table 7. None gives any indication of improvement in the quality of Haitian coffee and, indeed, they demonstrate its de-

[23] Figures from Robert F. Martin, "Improvements for the Haitian Coffee Industry," *Tea and Coffee Trade Journal,* LVII (1929), 290; Gates, "Haitian Coffee Industry"; Office du Café, "Documents sur le Café" (Port-au-Prince, 1967), mimeo.
[24] Figures from *Annual Reports* of the Jamaican Coffee Industry Board. See also Clive Thomas, "Coffee Production in Jamaica," *Social and Economic Studies,* XIII (1964), 188–217. The Jamaican yields are about 600 pounds per acre compared to Haitian yields of about 200 pounds per acre (Moral, *Paysan,* 277).

Table 6
Haitian Coffee Prices
(Figures in U.S. cents per U.S. pound)

| | Unit Values | | Quoted Prices, New York | |
	Haitian Statistics[a]	U.S. Statistics	Unwashed	Washed
1913–14	n.a.	9.43	10.33	14.71
1913–18	n.a.	n.a.	9.90	12.97
1924–28	19.47	22.16	n.a.	23.16
1936–40	6.75	6.24	n.a.	8.78
1955–58	48.91	43.26	50.02	58.16
1959–63	31.65	29.24	32.50	n.a.

[a] The Haitian (Benoit) unit values are from the official export figures and represent the entire crop. The United States unit values are from U.S. import figures and represent only that portion of the crop sold to the U.S. Both sets of figures are f.o.b. Haiti.

There are quoted prices available for "Haitian unwashed" and "Haitian washed" coffee on the New York market. The annual averages are averages of monthly quotations. The quoted price figures are probably more reliable than the unit value figures, since the former specify the grade and are less likely to be subject to misreporting. Unfortunately the series on unwashed coffee is incomplete, and for this reason some use must be made of the unit value figures.

Aside from the anomalous U.S. unit value for 1924–28, the U.S. unit values are below the N.Y. spot price of unwashed coffee. This probably reflects transportation costs. The U.S. unit values are also slightly below the Benoit unit values, except for the anomalous U.S. figure for 1924–28. (The peculiarity of this figure may be related to the fact that only a small percentage of the Haitian crop was sent to the U.S. in 1924–28. In any case, no further use will be made here of the U.S. unit values.)

Sources: Pierre Benoit, *Cent Cinquante Ans de Commerce Extérieur d'Haiti*, 25; Institut Haitien de Statistique, *Guide Economique de la Républic d'Haiti* (Port-au-Prince, 1964), 42–45; *Foreign Commerce and Navigation of the United States*, 1913 to 1940, various years; Bureau of the Census, *U.S. Imports of Merchandise for Consumption*, FT 125, 1955–63. Quoted prices: 1913–18: Unwashed, Lloyd Shaulis, "Prices of Tea, Coffee, and Cocoa," *War Industries Board Price Bulletin*, 18 (Washington, 1919), 12–13, 15. 1913–18: Washed, and 1924–28: Colombia, Federacion Nacional de Cafeteros de Colombia, *Boletin de Estadistica*, V (1936), 86, 96–97. 1936–63: Pan American Coffee Bureau Statistics.

terioration (although little reliance should be placed on small changes in percentages). Thus the quality improvement program has had little impact.

2) Two American botanists employed by the Service Technique in 1927 started selectively to breed varieties of Haitian cotton. Within two years they had developed a number of successful strains — collectively, Forbes-Barker cotton. These new varieties

gave higher yields on demonstration plots and their quality was deemed good by foreign purchasers. They were perennials, seeds

Table 7
Comparison of Haitian Coffee Prices
with Standard Brazilian Grades
(Prices in U.S. cents per pound)

I.	Haiti Unwashed	Rio No. 7	Ratio, Haiti/Rio
1913–18	9.90	9.10	1.087
1958–60	37.17	35.92	1.034

II.	Benoit Unit-Values	Rio No. 7	Ratio, Haiti/Rio
1924–28	19.47	17.33	1.123
1936–40	6.75	6.42	1.051

III.	Haiti Washed	Santos No. 4	Ratio, Haiti/Santos
1913–18	12.97	11.18	1.160
1924–28	23.16	21.74	1.065
1936–40	8.778	8.526	1.029
1947–49	29.12	28.51	1.021
1955–58	58.16	55.13	1.055

Note: The 1936–40 prices of Haitian coffee may be somewhat depressed relative to other grades of coffee by the French renunciation of the Franco-Haitian Treaty in 1936.

of the new varieties being distributed to peasants from 1929 to 1935 together with sizable subsidies to farmers employing the new seeds and prepared to follow the advice of the Service.[25]

In order to qualify for the subsidy, peasants had to plant entire

25 The distribution in thousand kilos by year was:

1929	1930	1931	1932	1933	1934	1935	1936
12	4	16	12	28	40	60	0

From André Audant, "Le Charançon du Cotonnier en Haiti," SNPAER *Bulletin,* 16 (1938), 64–90. H. D. Barker, "L'Amelioration du Coton Haitien par la Selection," Service Technique, *Bulletin,* 25 (1931), 38, gives the average yield of the new varieties on the demonstration plots at 750 pounds of ginned cotton per acre. The peasant, with his traditional varieties, obtained then and probably still obtains a yield in the vicinity of 100 pounds per acre. (From a typed manuscript of René Leveille, 1954, cited by William B. Gates, Jr., in "The Haitian Cotton and Cotton Textile Industries," unpub. ms. (Williamstown, 1959). Moral, *Paysan,* 303, gives the peasant yield around 1959 at about 130 kilos per hectare, which is 114 pounds per acre.

fields in cotton and to separate the different varieties and remove impurities. The available statistics do not reveal the extent of the new acreage devoted to Forbes-Barker varieties, but the increased production of cotton was probably due to an expansion of the area cultivated rather than to higher yields due to the employment of new strains.[26] Very little Forbes-Barker cotton was sold, but the Service claimed that the dissemination of seeds and the grading program had definitely improved the quality of local cotton.[27] Nevertheless, it seems that little change was wrought in peasant techniques of production.[28] By 1934, only 500 acres had been subsidized, and few of the farmers were peasants. Moreover, whatever progress had been made was halted by the arrival of the Mexican boll weevil in 1935. The planting of annual varieties of cotton (as in the United States) eliminates the boll-weevil problem, but when an attempt was made in the mid- and late 1930's to persuade Haitian peasants to plant annual varieties of cotton — which require intensive care — it was rebuffed.[29]

3) The rapid development of the banana industry was the result of the signing in 1935 of a contract between the government and the Standard Fruit and Steamship Company.[30] The company obtained exclusive buying privileges in Haiti in return for a commitment to develop the industry and purchase all of the marketable bananas offered for sale. The bulk of the crop was produced on peasant farms after the company had distributed planting stock, extended credit to producers, and set up buying stations. It also established a few plantations of its own in the Artibonite Valley,

---

[26] As a result of favorable prices in the 1920's, cotton production rose substantially even before the new seeds were distributed. The following table shows five-year averages of exports in millions of French pounds. (In this period virtually all production was exported.)

1917–21	1922–26	1927–31	1932–36	1937–41
2.49	3.90	4.68	5.88	4.10

From Gates, "Haitian Cotton," who obtained his figures from the official export statistics.

[27] SNPAER, Bulletin, 4 (1934), 43.

[28] Holly, Agriculture, 76.

[29] Audant, "Le Charançon," 91.

[30] See above, 137, 156. For bananas in Haiti, see Moral, Paysan, 301–313; Street, "Geography," 280–285; Holly, Agriculture, 67–70.

but found it difficult to acquire land.[31] Peasants accepted the new crop with alacrity, particularly in those regions where the government constructed systems of irrigation and there were modern roads.[32] They had long grown plantains for local consumption, and the exportable variety of banana needed only to be picked at the correct time and handled carefully on its way to the buying station. The swift growth of banana exports, and their equally precipitate decline, can be seen in Table 8. In 1943 other companies were permitted to grow bananas in Haiti, and in 1946, after the government of Estimé deprived Standard Fruit of its monopoly, it withdrew.[33] A number of locally owned groups continued the exportation of bananas, but their methods of handling the fruit were

Table 8
Growth in Banana Exports
(Figures in millions of stems)

1933	*1934*	*1935*	*1936*	*1937*	*1938*	*1939*	*1940*	*1941*	*1942*
.03	.27	.52	.60	1.3	1.4	2.0	2.3	3.3	1.9

1943	*1944*	*1945*	*1946*	*1947*	*1948*	*1949*	*1950*	*1951*	*1952*
.6	2.9	4.0	5.9	7.3	3.5	2.2	1.8	1.3	.6

Source: Benoit, *Cent Cinquante ans,* 48.

poor and, before long, Haitian bananas were thoroughly discredited on the American market. The peasants, disappointed and defrauded by local companies, simply ceased growing bananas.

4) Examples of highly directed rural change are the irrigation and mechanization schemes undertaken after World War II, either by the American Aid Mission itself or with the technical and financial assistance of the Mission.[34] In the Artibonite Valley, the Cayes-

[31] Giles A. Hubert, "Some Problems of a Colonial Economy: A Study of Economic Dualism in Haiti," *Inter-American Economic Affairs,* III (Spring 1950), 3–30.
[32] A major reason why Jamaica successfully developed bananas in the nineteenth century was that she had good transportation, in the form of a railroad network.
[33] See above, 173.
[34] The sources for this section are Street, "Geography," 326–329; Mosher, *Technical,* 73–99; Holly, *Agriculture,* 94–99; Pierre-Charles, *Economie,* 149–151; Charles Antoine, *Quelques Considérations sur le Milieu Rural à Deseaux: Une Expérience de Développement Communautaire dans la Vallée de l'Artibonite* (Port-au-Prince, 1959), 1–59.

Torbeck plain, and at San Raphael, heavy equipment was used to clear the land and prepare it for cultivation, and the services of the tractors were sold to peasants. The extension service organized the periodic cleaning of the irrigation and drainage canals, and distributed new varieties of rice. The combined effects of these technical improvements were to raise rice yields (on irrigated land) from 1200 or 1400 pounds per acre to 3600. The program survived a serious invasion of rats in the Artibonite Valley in 1957 and 1958 (with the help of the U.S. Mission and the U.N. chemical poisons and traps were utilized to bring the rats under control), but it could not survive the termination of U.S. aid in the early 1960's.

5) The Institut de Développement Agricole et Industriel, Haiti's development bank, has operated a program of supervised credit since 1966. In the Cayes region, where the program has made significant progress, the peasants are wealthier than the average, much of their land is irrigated, tenure is more secure, and many of them have been influenced by the ideas of migrant laborers repatriated from Cuba. They seem more receptive to change. Furthermore, the area has a comparatively new sugar factory and is the center of the country's production of essential oils.[35] Throughout Haiti only about $150,000 was expended during fiscal 1969 by the supervised credit program. Some $30,000 to $40,000 of the total was distributed in the Cayes region, where loans were made for rotations of corn, millet, and beans. The number of borrowers for each crop varied from 100 to 160, and the maximum number of acres involved was 400 (for corn).

The bank's thirteen agents in the Cayes area carefully screen loan applicants, all of whom must agree to follow the bank's advice. The agents insist that soils must be prepared properly by plowing behind draft animals, chemical fertilizers used, and improved varieties of corn sown. Plots of the traditional millet and beans are also supposed to benefit from the good soil preparation and fertilization. In order to facilitate the learning of new techniques, the agents have not only operated demonstration farms but

[35] This section is based on interviews with Haitian officials in Port-au-Prince and Cayes during February 1969. See also Garvey Laurent, "Etude Socio-Economique de la Vallée de Camp-Perrin: Plaine des Cayes — Haiti," *Bulletin Agricole*, V (1956), 1–63.

have even borrowed patches of their clients' land for similar purposes. But the change in techniques which the agents are asking the peasants to perform is great. Although the Cayes region is one of the few in Haiti where the plow is used at all, the total number in the region is minimal — perhaps 250 at most. Experience with this difficult technique is not widespread. Furthermore, the use of fertilizer requires a long, sustained effort, and often produces uncertain results. Since small applications of fertilizer are unprofitable because the heavy rains quickly wash them away, the bank has begun a program of "renewal fertilization": the application of large amounts of fertilizers over many years is designed to build up organic material in the soil and to increase its ability to retain new fertilizing elements. But the economic profitability of this scheme is still questionable. The bank scheme may or may not be economically sound but, even if it is, the program is highly *dirigiste* and depends upon continued governmental support (which is always problematical) over a number of years before the peasant borrowers will be sufficiently experienced and well endowed to continue without assistance.

6) Haiti has known rural cooperatives of various kinds since the late 1940's, when private religious bodies began to organize credit unions. (There were five unions in 1950.) Then, in 1951, the Service Coopératif Inter-Americain de Production Agricole, a bilateral agency staffed and financed jointly by the United States and Haiti, busily began establishing more credit unions. By 1952 there were 47; in 1956 the number was 60.[36] The promoters expected these credit unions to form the nuclei of more ambitious forms of cooperatives. The unions themselves merely acquired the savings of their members, but credit from outside was not pumped into a rural area through the union. By 1956 only one credit union had been transformed into a producers' cooperative; left to themselves, 41 of the other unions were dissolved by 1962 (in some cases because of embezzlement) and only 28 remained. By then, too, Duvalier's government had begun forming producers' cooperatives.

---

[36] For details about cooperatives, see Georges Mouton, *Crédit Agricole et Coopération en Haiti*, U.N. Report TAA/HAI/8 (1956); Marie-Thérèse Vallès, *Les Idéologies Coopérativistes et leur Applicabilité en Haiti* (Paris, 1967).

There were 210 in 1963 (see Table 9 for their composition) containing 28,500 members, but their numbers have since declined
drastically because of governmental neglect.[37] It is clear that the
cooperatives were almost all formed from above, and — being government institutions — were of little immediate use to most peasants.

One of the few successful cooperatives is situated in Fermathe,
near Port-au-Prince, and has been in existence since the early
1950's. An agronomist from the development bank at first met
weekly with several dozen peasants in order to impart the method-
ology of modern agriculture and cooperation. There was a small
demonstration plot, where the peasants themselves practiced the

Table 9
Cooperatives in Haiti, 1963

I.	Credit Unions	28	
II.	Artisan Coops	2	
III.	Agricultural Coops		
	Stores	4	
	Production	78	(17 for vegetables, 13 for coffee and cacao)
	Stock-raising	14	
	Fishing	4	
	Irrigation	21	(mostly construction and maintenance of canals)
	Sale of Agr. Products	55	(31 for coffee and cacao; 20 for sugar)
	Electrification	10	
	Community Works	23	(construction and maintenance of roads, buildings)
	Total, Part III	209	
IV.	GRAND TOTAL	239	

Source: Vallès, *Idéologies Coopérativistes*, 53–54.

new techniques. The agronomist introduced imported potato
seeds, insecticides, and fertilizer; then four of the farmers used the
new methods on their own plots and obtained good yields. The
agronomist marketed the potatoes in the capital, returning the
proceeds to the astounded peasants. In 1953, the first year of cultivation, the peasants produced 1600 pounds of potatoes. In 1954

[37] Pierre-Charles, *Economie*, 235.

they grew 60,000 pounds, opened a special stand in the Port-au-Prince market, and properly established their cooperative society with fifty-three charter members. By 1956, as a result of the suggestions of agronomists and loans from the bank, all of the cooperators were using selected seeds, natural fertilizers, insecticides, and new tools. Seven (in 1958, 90) had constructed cisterns for the collection of rain water.[38] In 1969, it was evident from personal inspection that progress had continued: there were improved cisterns and dry walls and terraces to combat erosion, and the cooperative purchased seeds, chemical fertilizer, and insecticides from an import house in Port-au-Prince. It was no longer dependent upon the government, and the incomes of its members were considerably higher than the peasant average.

The success of Fermathe, however, will be difficult to duplicate elsewhere. The proximity to Port-au-Prince conferred two important advantages not available in more distant regions: low-cost access to a large market and the possibility of frequent and regular visits by agronomists. Fermathe is also situated high in the hills, where fruits and vegetables which are much in demand in the capital can be grown fairly efficiently. Finally, Fermathe seems to have benefited from a fortunate combination of sensitive agronomists, good advice, and peasants receptive to change.

From a consideration of the results of the six cases we can conclude that peasants were able in some fashion to respond to attempts to alter their behavior. In the majority of the instances they merely adopted a single crop or a solitary idea without accompanying changes in general cultivation practices. Yet most of the projects failed, and not because the peasants were unresponsive. Either governmental efforts were interrupted or some external factor — like the boll weevil — attacked the projects before they were sufficiently strong to endure such intrusions. Haitian peasants were partially able to overcome fear of risk, community pressures against change, insecurity of tenure, short time horizons, and suspicion of outsiders. But even in those cases they could not sur-

---

[38] Details in Mouton, *Crédit Agricole*, 34–45; René Laroche, "Situation de l'Agriculture Paysanne Haitienne: Perspective d'Avenir," *Revista de Ciencias Sociales*, **IV** (1960), 166–168.

mount administrative incompetence and corruption — the con-
stants of Haitian life.

Any discussion of the problems of agricultural development in
Haiti must consider soil erosion. The mountains of Haiti show
their "knee-bones." [39] Whereas an aerial view of the Dominican
Republic discloses predominantly green forest, in Haiti there are
large areas devoid of vegetation and every hillside is scarred by gul-
lies. Severe population pressure results in the continued removal
of forest cover from steep slopes, rain water consequently rushing
down the mountainsides, denuding the freshly cleared land, and
aggravating erosion on farms downslope. Many acres once cultivated are now useless.[40]

The reactions of peasants and woodcutters constitute an excel-
lent example of external diseconomy which occurs when the
actions of an individual inflict direct losses on others, i.e., those
persons who cause the erosion do not necessarily suffer the unfortunate consequences. They do not own the land on which the
trees are cut and are unaffected by the faster runoff downslope.
The removal of forest cover and the resulting erosion contribute
to the rapid runoff of water during the rainy season, and consequent flooding. During the dry season, streams which were once
full no longer flow, and where they still carry water the increased
seasonal variation makes them less satisfactory for purposes of irrigation. Erosion can also cause a storage reservoir behind a dam to
silt up, thereby reducing the useful life of the dam (as at Peligre).
The deforestation of the hillsides overlooking Port-au-Prince,
when combined with no longer adequate storm sewers, in 1969
filled the streets of the capital with mud whenever there was a tor-
rential rain. Finally, more rapid runoffs may contribute to climatic
changes which accentuate the differences between rainy and dry
seasons.

[39] Moral, *Paysan*, 114.
[40] Unfortunately there are few reliable data on the number of hectares affected. In
1938 a Haitian agronomist estimated that more than 210,000 hectares of land once
cultivated had been abandoned. Of this figure, 90,000 were lands in the plains
rendered unproductive by lack of drainage, and 20,000 additional hectares in the
plains had been covered with rocks and sand. He judged that at least 100,000
hectares in the mountains had been abandoned. The 210,000 hectares are 7.8 per
cent of the total land area of the country, and 20 to 30 per cent of the area then
being cultivated. See Nicolas, "Deboisement et Reboisement en Haiti," 32–63.

Peasants could contribute to the control of soil erosion by planting along the contour and constructing contour drains, diversion channels, graded drains, stone walls, and earth embankments, by planting tree crops instead of the usual ground crops, by strip-cropping, and by the establishment of vegetative barriers — the appropriate practices varying with soil quality and the slope of the land. But in Haiti few peasants do so: they are shortsighted and ignorant of the proper methods. But they are also aware that because of backward transportation and marketing services, lack of access to credit, and insecurity of tenure, some soil conservation techniques (such as fertilizer application) are individually unprofitable. It should also be appreciated that some erosion may be justified economically: in a given country mining the soil (i.e., erosion) may permit the accumulation of other forms of wealth. Whether mining the soil is economically rational, however, depends upon the social costs and benefits of soil conservation practices, and these costs and benefits are determined by, *inter alia*, the ratio of population to available land. In view of the very high population density of Haiti, optimal resource allocation — which implies good extension services, transport and marketing facilities, fertilizer distribution systems, and easy credit — would undoubtedly include substantial soil conservation efforts. But where all of the other services are lacking, the benefit-cost ratio of soil conservation projects is questionable.

Neither in Jamaica nor in Haiti have extension services been able to combat soil erosion successfully, perhaps on account of the cultural barriers between agents and peasants. In both societies, peasants appear to have discounted future benefits at a particularly high rate.[41] Governments, however, can combat erosion directly by undertaking schemes of reafforestation, controlling cutting, subsidizing alternative sources of fuel, or insisting upon individual employment of conservation techniques. But in Haiti neither the substitution of other fuels for wood nor the supervision of tree fellings is apt to meet with success. The great bulk of wood consumption takes the form of peasant cutting for rural use, and the taxation or regulation of such consumption would hardly prove administratively feasible. Table 10 indicates that about

41 Edwards, *Small Farming*, 260.

Table 10
Uses of Wood in Haiti, 1953 and 1968

I. Composition by Value	1953	1968
SHADA timber	7.5%	
Other registered timber	11.0	
Peasant homes	4.4	
Other non-fuel	1.6	
Fuel (charcoal and firewood)	75.4	
	100.0	n.a.

II. Fuel Consumption[a]		1953		1968
	Urban	Rural	Total	Total
A. By Households				
Charcoal	1116	900	2016	2200
Firewood	103	5805	5908	11,300
B. By Factories			464	n.a.
(essential oils)			(12)	(49.5)
Total			8388	n.a.

[a] In thousands of cubic meters of wood. It is assumed that one meter of charcoal
requires four meters of firewood.

Sources: Part I, *Tripartite Mission Report. Annex*, tables 20 and 21. Part II, "Les
Combustibles en Haiti," *Bulletin Trimestriel de Statistique*, 11 (1953), 7–10. Per-
sonal interview with Joseph Wainwright of the Haitian Department of Agriculture,
February 1969.

three-fourths of all trees felled were used for firewood and charcoal. (The government now requires the use of petroleum rather
than firewood in all essential oil distilleries, but these factories consume only .5 per cent of the wood consumed for fuel.) It is clear
that the lack of official interest in the problems of rural Haiti, the
government's own lack of feeling for the future, and the absence of
an administrative apparatus which could be directed to the control
of erosion will make impossible any short-run changes in the continued waste of Haiti's most vital natural resource.

3. Visible and Invisible Exports

The visible per capita exports of Haiti are no higher today than during the mid-1920's and lower than they were during most of the nineteenth century.[42] The major source of variation in export

Table 11
Purchasing Power of Exports, 1924–65
(Figures in millions of U.S. dollars or in actual U.S. dollars)

	Exports in Current Dollars	Exports Deflated by U.S. WPI[a]	Per Capita Exports (Deflated)	Per Capita Exports Deflated by Import Price Index[b]
1924–28	18.36	33.96	15.76	12.53
1934–38	8.56	18.60	7.15	7.78
1946–50	30.90	37.94	11.66	9.87
1951–55	46.14	49.10	13.73	13.08
1956–60	37.78	38.10	9.70	9.63
1961–65	38.02	37.70	8.73	n.a.

[a] WPI = wholesale price index. 1957–59 = 100.
[b] Import price index based on 1957–59 = 100. The Tripartite Mission's index ran from 1950 to 1960. Benoit's index ran from 1924 to 1952. The two indexes were spliced for 1950–52.

Sources: Benoit, *Cent Cinquante Ans*, 79; *Tripartite Mission Report, Annex*, tables 41–43.

	1821–25	1838–42	1859–61	1888–92	1910–14
Per capita exports in 1957–59 dollars	26.40	16.80	19.80	33.10	12.30

earnings has been the changing price of coffee. Table 12 gives the ratio of Haitian coffee prices to the U.S. wholesale price index; it shows a striking correlation between this ratio and the purchasing

[42] Table 11 lists the visible exports of Haiti in current and constant prices from 1924 to 1965. Exports in current prices were deflated by the U.S. wholesale price index (1957–59=100) and by an index derived from Haitian sources of the unit value of imports. Both provide roughly similar results. For the nineteenth century, we list the per capita exports for selected periods in 1957–59 dollars. (The figures in 1910–14 dollars were multiplied by the rise in the U.S. wholesale price index from 1910–14 to 1957–59—from 100 to 267.)

power of exports. The ratio of coffee price to the index has also shown enormous variation but no secular trend.

The composition of Haiti's visible exports has changed substantially since 1924. Cotton rose from about 10 per cent of the total value of exports in the 1920's to more than 15 per cent in the mid-1930's, and has since virtually disappeared. Bananas were a negligible factor until the mid-1930's, rose to between 15 and 20 per cent (except for the years of shipping shortages in 1943 and 1944) from 1940 to 1947, and then disappeared.[43] Sisal was insignificant in 1930, reached 10 per cent in the late 1930's and a peak of

Table 12
Ratio of Haitian Coffee Prices to U.S.
Wholesale Price Index, 1821–1965
(1956–60 = 100)

1821–25	98.1	1934–38	43.9
1838–42	54.8	1946–50	67.0
1859–61	42.2	1951–55	129.8
1890	121.8	1956–60	100.0
1910–14	56.1	1961–65	76.9
1924–28	84.8		

Sources: Coffee price: 1924–65 from Haitian export unit values; 1924–50 from *Tripartite Mission Report, Annex*, tables 42–43; 1961–65 from C.I.A.P. Report on Haiti (Dec. 1966), 29. Coffee prices 1821–1914 from U.S. import unit values (from *Foreign Commerce and Navigation of the United States*).

about 30 per cent in the early 1950's, and then declined gradually — to about 5 per cent in 1969. Sugar contributed only about 5 per cent of exports by value in the 1920's, rose to 10 per cent in the late 1930's, had several good years during World War II, and has since fluctuated around an average of about 10 per cent.[44] Bauxite exports began in 1957, attained 9 per cent in 1960, and have remained roughly at that level. Copper exports, appearing for the first time in 1961, have averaged about 6 per cent of the total in the 1960's.

Visible exports by commodity and quantity are shown in Table

[43] See above, 173, 287.
[44] The Haitian sugar quota (for 1968 and 1969) was 30,300 metric tons, up 4500 tons from 1967. In 1968, as in numerous previous years, Haiti failed to fill her quota.

Table 13
Export Quantities
(Figures in millions of kilograms unless otherwise stated)

	Coffee	Cotton	Sugar	Sisal	Bananas[a]	Cacao	Bauxite[b]	Logwood[b]	Copper[b]
1910–14	34.54	2.02	0	0	0	2.4	0	3.82	0
1924–28	33.14	4.24	7.89	0	0	1.9	0	2.80	0
1934–38	27.80	5.46	31.34	6.00	.81	1.5	0	1.28	0
1946–50	25.12	2.36	25.89	25.52	4.14	1.6	0	.15	0
1951–55	26.24	1.02	25.42	26.48	.52	1.9	0	*	0
1956–60	25.62	.44	19.68	33.10	0	1.8	21.27	*	0
1961–65	24.18	0	30.00	16.54	0	1.8	42.54	*	1.27

[a] Million stems.
[b] Ten million kilograms.
* Not treated separately.

Sources: 1910–14 from footnote 50 (on export quantities and prices, 1821–1914) in Chapter III, above; 1924–50 from Benoit, *Cent Cinquante Ans*, 22, 32, 36, 41, 48, 51, 55; 1951–60 from Institut Haitien de Statistique, *Guide Economique de la République d'Haiti*, 42–45; 1961–65 from C.I.A.P. Report (December 1966), 29.

13. It is more useful to construct a quantity index, however, which reflects changes in relative prices and the relative gains to Haiti of exporting different commodities. The results of assigning price weights from some period in each decade are embodied in Table 14. (Exports of commodities not listed in the tables were calculated as a percentage of the total exports of each period, the per-

Table 14
Indices of Export Quantity

	1910–14 prices	1927–29 prices	1934–40 prices	1947–49 prices
1910–14	83.7	84.6		
1924–28	88.8 a	88.8	86.5	
1934–38		100.0	100.0	100.0
1946–50			123.6	135.3

	1947–49 prices	1956–60 prices
1946–50	100.0	100.0
1951–55	85.5	86.8
1956–60		91.8
1961–65		107.1

a 1924–28 set at 88.8.

Sources: See Table 13.

centage being added to the index of the quantity of the listed products in order to obtain an index of total exports.) From it we see that exports between 1924 and 1928 were only about 5 per cent higher by value than during the period from 1910 to 1914. There was an increase of about 12 per cent to 1934–38, and another ranging from 24 to 35 per cent to 1946–50. This was a peak period for exports; they then fell by 15 per cent in the early 1950's, rose by 5 per cent to the end of that decade, gained substantially at the beginning of the 1960's, and finally settled at a level about 7 per cent above that of the late 1940's.

The composition of the increases in Haiti's visible exports is also revealing. Coffee and cacao, produced mainly by peasants, belong in one category, the other containing everything else — cotton, sugar, sisal, bananas, bauxite, and copper. Cotton and bananas were and are produced largely by peasants, but those were and are crops of the plains, where peasants are more susceptible to the propaganda and extension efforts of the government or foreign firms. Table 15 displays the components of the increases in exports: in the prices of 1910–14, total exports rose from 100 to 106.1 in 1924–28, the two categories of exports being expressed as percentages of the 1910–14 exports. Coffee and cacao thus declined from 83.3 to 79.0 per cent of the 1910–14 total while all other exports rose from 16.6 to 27.1 per cent. (The two figures of 79.0

Table 15
Components of Export Increases

I. *1910–14 prices*	*Total Index*	*Coffee and Cacao*[a]	*All Other*[a]
1910–14	100.0	83.3	16.65
1924–28	106.1	79.0	27.1
Percentage Change		−5.2%	62.6%
II. *1927–29 prices*			
1924–28	100.0	78.7	21.3
1934–38	112.6	65.9	46.7
Percentage Change		−16.2%	119.4%
III. *1934–40 prices*			
1934–38	100.0	53.9	46.1
1946–50	123.6	48.9	74.7
Percentage Change		−9.2%	61.9%
IV. *1956–60 prices*			
1946–50	100.0	58.2	41.8
1951–55	86.8	61.1	25.7
1956–60	91.8	59.6	32.2
1961–65	107.1	56.4	50.8
Percentage change 1946–50 to 1961–65		−3.1%	21.4%

For explanation see text.
[a] These are expressed as percentages of total base period exports.

Sources: See Table 13.

and 27.1 equal 106.1, the total increase.) The line in the table labeled "percentage change" quantifies the upward or downward movement of each component, coffee and cacao declining by 5.2 per cent and the "all other" category rising by 62.6 per cent. It is evident that this latter group of exports increased its share of the total substantially from the 1920's to the 1930's, and from the 1930's to the 1940's. In each period the rise was about 25 per cent of base period exports, and was even greater if 1947–49 prices are used to measure the increase between 1934–38 and 1946–50. There was a decrease in the percentage increase of exports during the 1950's, when the quantity of total exports fell very sharply and coffee and cacao showed a slight increase, which was retrieved only in the 1960's, when bauxite and copper entered the list of exports and a number of minor commodities — mainly manufactured goods and essential oils — began to be exported in significant amounts.[45]

The manufactured exports are of particular interest, since the sharp growth from $4 million in 1967 to $8.6 million in 1969 provides one of the very few hopeful signs on the Haitian economic horizon. It would be useful to be able to predict the character and quantity of these exports in the future, but doing so is difficult in the absence of standard forecasting techniques for light manufactured exports. The factors of production are available in perfectly elastic supply: capital can be supplied from overseas, an enormous amount of unskilled labor is available in Haiti, and many of the finished products rely upon imported raw materials. For almost all of the products, Haiti's share of U.S. imports is tiny, and nothing prevents new goods from entering the trade. (The exception is softballs, Haiti supplying about half of U.S. imports in 1968. At the same time, the Haitian share in the total U.S. softball market is very small.) The more Haiti exports light manufactures, the more attractive it will become as a place of investment. The existence of a larger number of exporting firms will lower the costs of ancillary services, create a pool of skilled labor, and bring about other economies of agglomeration. Haiti's ability to export many items cheaply by air also gives it an important advantage over

---

[45] Haiti also exports small amounts of castor oil, goatskins, molasses, wheat offal, orange peels, honey and beeswax, rum, and logs.

Asian countries in those lines where frequent changes in product specification require continuous communication between producer and buyer.[46]

Trends by product group in Haitian manufactured exports are shown in Table 16. They are significant because the net foreign exchange earnings are considerably less than the gross for products composed of imported components and growth prospects are much greater for precisely the same products since they will be unaffected by bottlenecks in Haiti's agricultural sector. Exports of products made from locally produced material in 1969 were at the same level as in 1962. This category includes binder twine (made from sisal) which declined and has now regained its earlier level, carpets and leather manufactures, which have shown declines, and made-up textiles, art works, and wood manufactures, which have increased. Meanwhile, all products manufactured from imported components have shown substantial gains.

The level of United States tariffs influences prospects for Haitian growth in the manufactured sphere. The Kennedy Round tariff cut of approximately 50 per cent will benefit most of Haiti's leading export lines (see Appendix C), with the important exceptions of clothing and travel goods. Binder twine is already free of duty. Note, however, that these are nominal rather than effective rates of tariff. The effective tariff rate is designed to measure the protection afforded to the value added in manufacturing a product from its components.[47] Although we lack the data necessary to calculate the effective rates for Haiti, the results of the Kennedy Round will be substantially to reduce the effective rates on Haitian manufactures.

The United States Tariff Schedule also provides (Section 807)

---

[46] See Raymond Vernon, "Problems and Prospects in the Export of Manufactured Goods from the Less-Developed Countries," *UNCTAD Proceedings*, IV (1964), 200–209.

[47] Although the concept of effective protection is subject to some criticism, it is particularly useful in those cases where Haitian exports are made from imported raw materials which account for a substantial proportion of the product's value. The conventional formula for the effective rate is $f = \dfrac{t - qr}{1 - r}$, where f is the effective rate of the tariff, t the nominal rate, q the rate of duty on components, and r the proportion of the final product represented by imported or importable components. Charles P. Kindleberger, *International Economics* (Homewood, 1968), 111.

Table 16
Trends in Haitian Manufactured Exports, by Product Category
in Thousands of Dollars

		1962	1963	1965	1966	1967	1968	1969
I.	**Products made of locally produced components**							
655	Binder twine[a]	1917	2439	715	47	387	1459	1220
656	Made-up textiles	170	137	39	37	161	347	392
632	Wood manufactures	71	51	92	84	103	172	204
896	Art works	15	43	24	31	37	164	230
657	Carpets	182	90	81	62	50	51	45
612	Leather manufactures	136	231	162	177	136	47	168
	Above total	2491	2991	1113	438	874	2240	2259
	Others	274	169	168	151	121	98	269
	Total, Group I	2765	3160	1281	589	995	2338	2528
II.	**Products made of imported components**							
8944	Sport goods	176	199	319	574	695	1331	2160
841	Clothing	155	233	283	129	407	850	1326
851	Footwear	558	438	179	90	712	759	950
831	Travel goods	2	28	5	59	286	427	620
897	Jewelry	7	5	41	41	10	227	19
	Above total	898	903	827	893	2110	3594	5075
	Others	68	106	228	298	194	498[b]	718
	Total, Group II	966	1009	1055	1191	2304	4092	5793

Note: The division of products into Groups I and II was made in 1969 by David Raynolds of the U.S. Embassy, Port-au-Prince. Groups I and II do not add up to total manufactured exports, because S.I.T.C. group 990 (items under $251) was not allocated between I and II.

a Includes about $50,000 of hat bodies.
b Includes transformers, telecommunications, and miscellaneous metal products, all of which were negligible before 1968.

Sources: Bureau of the Census, *U.S. Imports of Merchandise for Consumption*, FT125, 1962–66; Bureau of the Census, *U.S. Imports for Consumption and General Imports*, FT135, 150, 1967–69.

for a reduction of duty on articles assembled abroad from components produced in the United States. This rate is applied not to the entire value of the article, but to that value less the value of the components obtained from the U.S. (It thus converts the nominal into the effective rate.) After the enactment of Section 807 in 1965, imports under it grew rapidly, especially from Mexico. American trade unions have, however, expressed dissatisfaction with this rapid growth in imports, and restrictions may in future be placed upon its applicability.[48] Three categories of electric

Table 17
U.S. Imports from Haiti under Section 807, 1968
in Thousands of Dollars

T.S.U.S. No.		Total Imports	Imports under Section 807	
			Total Value	Dutiable Value
734.56.20	Softballs	1298	142	52
700.55	Footwear	745	0	0
389.60	Misc. textile articles	273	112	58
740.38	Misc. jewelry	225	1.2	0.4
657.20	Misc. iron and steel products	72	72	11.6
685.90	Switchboard panels	117	117	31
686.10.60	Resistors	45	45	11.2
685.20.40	Misc. T.V. parts	36	36	6.2
—	Clothing	850	214[a]	118[a]
—	Travel goods	427	n.a.	n.a.

[a] Value of Section 807 imports under four leading T.S.U.S. categories. There may be additional Section 807 imports in the clothing group.

Source: Bureau of the Census, computer print-out on Section 807 imports.

products and the category of iron and steel manufactures all entered the United States under Section 807. (The ratio of value added in Haiti to total value is very small for these products.) Substantial fractions of the imports of clothing, softballs, and miscellaneous textiles were also brought in under this section. Since

[48] Table 17 gives an indication of the amount of imports from Haiti under this section. It gives the value of those imports, and their dutiable value, which is the value added abroad. U.S. trade statistics do not make total imports by country under Section 807 available in a convenient form. The data have therefore been presented for some leading Haitian exports.

Haiti, along with the other Caribbean countries, has a clear cost advantage over the United States in unskilled assembly operations, the provision of this section could represent an important future stimulus to manufactured exports from Haiti.[49]

In Haiti itself, legislation is extremely favorable to industrial investment. Manufacturers do not have to pay duties on imported materials or on the goods they export. There is a full income tax exemption for the first five years of operation, and only a gradual elimination of the exemption during the second quinquennium.[50] Another reason for optimism about the growth of manufactured exports is that they depend in no significant way upon governmental increments to the existing infrastructure. (The airport already exists.) Better vocational training in Haitian schools might be desirable. Most important of all is whether the government will avoid extorting from and otherwise interfering with exporters.

Most of the islands of the Caribbean have by now diversified their hitherto overwhelmingly agriculturally based economies by encouraging the inflow of tourism. Haiti is no exception; it offers an exotic culture, an appealing climate, several eighteenth- and early nineteenth-century edifices, high quality cuisine, low prices, and bizarre politics. The available figures for this source of invisible export earnings are set out in Table 18.[51] By 1968, after a

---

[49] A Haitian manufacturer of television parts reported in an interview (December 5, 1968) that for his product American workers averaged about 6000 pieces in 7.5 hours, but his Haitian workers managed 10,000 pieces in 8.5 hours, wages in Haiti being paid by the piece. The Haitian parts showed a somewhat higher rejection rate, but the plant had been in operation for less than a year.

[50] The extent to which this exemption encourages American investment is reduced by the tax credits provided for taxes paid to foreign governments by branches or subsidiaries of American corporations. See Lawrence B. Krause and Kenneth W. Dam, *Federal Tax Treatment of Foreign Income* (Washington, 1964), 8.

[51] Haiti apparently counts as tourists all visitors by airplane who stay at least one night, plus all visitors by ship, even though the vast majority of the latter spend only an early evening in Haiti, returning to their cruise ships for the night. In the 1950's, three surveys of air tourists found that on the average they remained in the country from two and a half to three days and spent from $35 to $40 a day. ("Dépenses des Touristes en Haiti," *Bulletin Trimestriel de Statistique*, 25 [1957], 29–34.) The ship-borne tourists, on the other hand, probably spend only an average of around $10 in an evening. Changes in the total number of tourists, then, give quite a misleading impression of changes in their total spending. Failure to separate air and ship tourists in estimating earnings may also account for the inconsistency in the official statistics. The department of tourism estimates of earnings show an

Table 18
Number of Tourists Visiting Haiti, 1950–68
(Figures in thousands)

	By air	By ship
1950	10.2	1.8
1956	29.4	36.4
1960	25.6	53.7
1961	18.8	72.2
1962	17.4	69.0
1963	7.3	38.0
1964	6.1	17.3
1965	9.9	16.6
1966	12.0	23.0
1967	15.0	31.7
1968	23.1	51.1
1969	—a	—

a In the first five months of 1969, air tourists were up 18 per cent over 1968.

Sources: Figures collected by the Department of Tourism. 1950–60: reported in *Tripartite Mission Report*, 44–46. 1961–68: from the U.S. Embassy, Port-au-Prince.

precipitous fall, tourism had recovered to the level of the early 1960's — a recovery which probably was assisted by the completion

Table 19
Tourist Expenditures in Haiti
(Figures in millions of U.S. dollars)

	1960	*1961*	*1962*	*1963*	*1964*	*1965*	*1966*	*1967*	*1968*
Calculated Tourist Expenditure	3.61	2.98	2.78	.76	.90	1.35	1.67	2.12	3.28
Dept. of Tourism Estimatesa	7.4	8.0	6.0	2.1	0.9	1.4	1.7	2.1	n.a.

a Source: C.I.A.P. Reports, 1968, 48; 1969, 60.

enormous decline from $8 million in 1961 to less than $2 million in 1965–67. Yet if the numbers of tourists are multiplied by $120 and $10, for air and ship tourists respectively, the total comes to only $3 million in 1961 and the decline is much less precipitous (see Table 19).

in 1967 of an international airport capable of handling the largest
jet aircraft, an ostensible political relaxation and lowering of tension in Port-au-Prince, and a rise in the level of American dispos-
able incomes. But even at the 1968 level, tourist receipts are only
9 per cent of commodity export earnings. And a substantial fraction of all tourist expenditures is for imported goods, especially
food.[52] There is excess capacity in hotels catering for tourists, even
in season, and — given political stability — there is no reason why
Haiti, now a laggard in the Caribbean competition for tourists,
should not increase its share of this growing business.

4. The Monetary System

Mention should be made of Haiti's monetary system, not because it affects its long-term development significantly, but because
it has been the object of considerable controversy.[53] The Haitian
gourde has been pegged at the rate of five to the dollar since 1919,
when an accord was signed with the United States. American
paper dollars have been legal tender and have circulated freely in
the country since that date (American gold coins and other foreign
coins circulated during the nineteenth century). They are now
estimated to total about 10 per cent of the currency in circulation.
The Banque Nationale was brought under the full control of the
Haitian government only in 1947; prior to that time, there was
no attempt by the Banque to moderate economic fluctuation
through monetary policy.[54] By the 1950's, however, the Banque
regulated the emission of gourdes and the level of demand deposits
and could in principle employ monetary policy to stabilize the
economy. So far as stabilization is concerned, the physical circulation of dollars in the country adds no complications beyond those

52 Although there is no information on the import component of tourist expenditure in Haiti, a study of Antigua in 1964 revealed that it amounted to about 40
per cent. Carleen O'Loughlin, *Economic and Political Change in the Leeward and
Windward Islands* (New Haven, 1968), 146.
53 Pierre-Charles, *Economie*, 176–181; Joseph Chatelain, *La Banque Nationale*
(Port-au-Prince, 1954), 193–202, 233–243.
54 See above, 144.

involved in a system of free exchange markets, provided that the exchange rate remains fixed.

The gourde is tied to the dollar by Haitian law, by agreement with the International Monetary Fund, and by the amount of dollars in circulation. But none of these constraints would inhibit a Haitian government from devaluing the gourde if it so wished.[55] (The dollar circulation merely implies that part of the windfall profit from devaluation would accrue to the private sector, instead of exclusively to the government.) In fact, Haitian governments have not wanted to devalue, a situation explicable in part by governmental pride in maintaining a stable exchange rate. The government's unwillingness to allow the rate to change naturally sets definite limits on the use of monetary and fiscal policy.

What are the economic effects of this exchange system? First, by refraining from inflationary financing the government is denying itself a source of revenue, one which nineteenth-century Haitian governments employed freely. Second, the fixed nature of the exchange rate subjects the whole economy to fluctuation as exchange earnings fluctuate. Third, the complete freedom of the exchange market permits the easy expatriation of capital, although it also encourages foreign investment by guaranteeing the absence of limitations on profit remissions abroad.

What can be said for alternative systems? The freedom of the exchange market is highly desirable in Haiti, since exchange controls lend themselves to corruption and inefficiency even in the hands of relatively honest governments. There is little to be gained by inflationary finance, since this is an inefficient way of raising revenues. (To be sure, *if* the proceeds of inflationary finance were put to productive use, the benefits would outweigh

---

[55] There is a further possible constraint in the curious fact that the notes issued by the Banque bear the words: "This bill, in conformity with the Convention of April 12, 1919, is payable to the bearer in legal money of the United States of America at the rate of five gourdes to the dollar." The Convention of 1919 no longer binds the Haitian government to maintain this parity, but the fact that these words appear on the banknotes would make it embarrassing for the government to devalue; the elimination of the words on new bills might also disturb the exchange market. Nonetheless, a government of Haiti could perfectly well couple a devaluation with a reminder to the public that the 1919 Convention is not binding in this respect.

the costs, but there is no reason to make this supposition.) Some advantages can be claimed, however, for greater exchange-rate flexibility.

There are two basic variants of exchange flexibility that are worth considering: a fluctuating exchange rate and an adjustable peg. A good case for a fluctuating exchange rate can be made in an economy with highly volatile foreign exchange earnings, for fluctuations in the exchange rate tend to moderate the effects on the domestic economy of externally induced disturbances. (The argument assumes that foreign exchange speculation would on the whole be stabilizing.) But it is not at all clear that the postwar variations in Haiti's export earnings have been violent enough to justify the use of a fluctuating rate. It would seem that a fixed rate would be appropriate for normal times (which would include the entire postwar period), but that if export earnings ever underwent a prolonged and sharp decline, such as occurred during the 1930's, a change in the adjustable peg would be preferable to intensive deflation.

The fixed exchange rate regime has served Haiti reasonably well, at least in the postwar period. There is the possibility that a fluctuating rate could prove desirable, but, even if it were preferable, it would make little difference to Haiti's long-term development because fluctuations in economic activity, which flexible rates are designed to moderate, are not one of the major obstacles to Haiti's escape from poverty and underdevelopment.

5. The Place of Education

The importance of education in economic development is well established, and for Haitian planners changes in the percentages of literacy and growth rates of education are among the most critical variables. Table 20 gives the enrollment in urban primary schools from 1920 to 1967.[56] Tables 21 and 22 display figures for rural

56 The data on the lay public schools are reasonably reliable, and those on national religious schools, which receive subsidies from the state, are almost as good. The statistical coverage of the nonreligious private schools clearly varies from year to

Table 20
Pupils in Urban Primary Schools, 1920–67
(Figures in thousands of students)

| | Public Schools | | | | |
	Lay Pub.	Nat'l Relig.	Total	Private Schools	Total
1920	21.9	7.7	29.7	9.2	38.9
1930	27.2	12.9	40.1	9.4	49.4
1938	21.0	21.5	42.5	10.3	52.7
1943	17.7	15.1	32.8	10.2	43.1
1950	29.6	19.9	49.5	12.3	61.8
1955	45.9	21.9	67.8	26.0	93.7
1961	n.a.	n.a.	88.0	44.6	132.6
1963	n.a.	n.a.	96.5	43.5 [a]	140.0
1967	72.8	39.1	112.0	42.5 [a]	154.5

[a] This decline in private enrollment is probably due to reporting failures.

Sources: 1920 data from Edner Brutus, *Instruction Publique en Haiti, 1492–1945* (Port-au-Prince, 1948), 480; Leyburn, *People,* 282–283. 1930 data from Commission on Education in Haiti, *Report,* 8. 1938–55 data are from *Bulletin Trimestriel de Statistique,* 23 (December 1956), 9. 1961–67 data are from *Tableaux de l'Ecole Haitienne* (Port-au-Prince, 1967).

enrollment and national (urban and rural) enrollment rates respectively.[57] In order to obtain some rough estimates of enrollment by age group, we can assume that the age distribution of all urban students is represented by the sample of lay public and national religious schools, and that the distribution of all rural students is represented by the sample of rural public schools. Table 23 states

---

year, however, and these figures must be used with caution, enrollment in such schools probably always being underreported. Thus the table provides only a minimum estimate of the share of private schools in total enrollment — between a fifth and a third throughout the entire period. It must be noted, too, that all of the figures are for enrollment, not average daily attendance, which is much lower.

[57] The conventional base — the population aged five to fourteen — has been used in order to calculate the rates of enrollment. They show an increasing enrollment rate for both urban and rural schools and overstate the population of children aged five to fourteen who are in primary school; some are younger and some older. (The data include preschool enrollments.) In the mid-1950's, the percentages of children outside the base were lay public (urban), 14.6; national religious (urban), 5.5; and rural public, 21.0. ("Evolution et Caractère de l'Enseignement Primaire Haitien," *Bulletin Trimestriel de Statistique,* 24 [December 1956], 40.)

Table 21
Pupils in Rural Primary Schools, 1920–67
(Figures in thousands of students)

	Public Schools	Church Schools	Total	Protestant Missions	Grand Total
1920	21.8	5.5	27.3		
1930	34.2	9.6	43.7		
1938	27.0	n.a.	n.a.	n.a.	n.a.
1944	38.6	14.2	53.0	n.a.	n.a.
1950	52.4	16.3	68.7	n.a.	n.a.
1955	74.7	21.0	95.7	18.4	114.1
1963	100.8	21.1	121.9	n.a.	n.a.
1967	98.2	20.6	118.8	12.9	131.7

Sources: 1920 data are from Brutus, *Instruction Publique*, 480. 1930 data are from
U.S. Commission on Education in Haiti, *Report*, 8–9. 1938–55 data are from *Bulletin Trimestriel de Statistique*, 23 (December 1956), 11. 1963–67 data are from
Tableaux de l'Ecole Haitienne.

Table 22
Primary Enrollment Rates, 1920–67
(Figures in thousands of students)

	Percentage of Population that is Urban[a]	Enrollment Rates[b] Urban	Rural[c]	Total
1920	n.a.	8.0	5.6	13.6
1930	n.a.	8.6	7.6	16.2
1938	n.a.	8.0	n.a.	n.a.
1943	n.a.	5.9	7.2	13.1
1950	12.2	7.2	8.2	15.4
1955	n.a.	10.2	10.4	20.6
1961	13.7	13.1	11.4	24.5
1967	n.a.	13.4	10.3	23.7

[a] Brand, *Impressions*, 30.
[b] Ratios of urban and rural pupils to entire population of primary school age, i.e.,
ages five through fourteen.
[c] The Protestant Missions have been omitted.

Note: Enrollment data are from Tables 20 and 21. The rural enrollment dates do
not always match the above dates exactly.

the results: there is an overall enrollment in the five to fourteen
age bracket of 17.2 per cent, the maximum of 20.3 per cent occurring at ages nine to ten.

Haitian pupils, like those in the new African states, are concentrated in the lower grades.[58] The ratio of pupils in a given grade to an arbitrarily defined population of a corresponding age (letting 1956 figures stand for 1967 and assuming that lay public and national religious distributions equal the national sum of urban pupils and letting rural public stand for all rural schools) is, for example, 15.2 per cent of the fourth grade; 75 per cent of the pupils who reach the fourth grade do so in urban schools. Since repetition of grades is frequent in Haiti, the first percentage also means that only 15 per cent of all Haitian children will ever attain (not finish) the fourth grade. (Table 24 gives the relevant

Table 23
Percentage of Children in School, by Age Groups, c. 1955

Age Group	Urban[a]	Rural	Total
5–6	7.7	5.6	13.3
7–8	10.0	7.4	17.4
9–10	10.9	9.4	20.3
11–12	9.2	9.8	19.1
13–14	7.1	9.4	16.5
5–14	9.0	8.2	17.2

a Urban pupils in age group as a percentage of country's population in that age group.

Sources: Table 22; *Bulletin Trimestriel,* 23 (December 1956), 40.

percentages.) The literacy rates by age group in the 1950 Census can be used as a check on these primary enrollment rate calculations.[59] By and large the two sets of data are consistent, with one rather surprising exception: the enrollment rates would lead one to expect a sharp increase in the literacy of school-aged children

---

58 Haitian schools begin with Enfantin I and II, the equivalent of kindergarten, the vast majority of the students being in II, presumably having skipped I, at least in urban areas. Then students enter Preparatoire I and II and go on to Elementaire I and II and Moyen I and II. After these primary years, they enter a seven-year secondary school, sixth class down to second class, plus rheto (first class) and philo. However, here we use numbered "grades" to indicate the post-kindergarten years. The source for urban schools is *Bulletin Trimestriel de Statistique* (December 1956); for rural schools, *Tableaux de l'Ecole Haitienne.*
59 Solon Mirville, *L'Ecole Primaire* (Port-au-Prince, 1959), 10–18.

Table 24
Primary Enrollment Rates by Grade, 1967

Grade	Urban	Rural	Combined
All Primary[a]	19.4	14.9	34.3
Kindergarten	43.8	56.8[b]	100.6
1	25.2	17.9	43.1
2	20.0	10.4	30.4
3	14.6	6.4	21.0
4	11.6	3.6	15.2
5	8.7	2.2	10.9
6	6.0	1.1	7.1

[a] Primary enrollment as a percentage of population aged seven to thirteen.
[b] This figure is affected by the fact that in rural areas the legal cycle stipulates two years in kindergarten. (See Brand, *Impressions*, 48.)

Note: The enrollment rate for a given grade is 100 times the ratio of the enrollment in that grade to the population of the corresponding age. The rate may exceed 100 because some students are required to repeat grades.

Sources: *Bulletin Trimestriel,* 23 (December 1956), 46–47.

under the American occupation, followed by a decrease in the 1930's. The literacy rates by age group in 1950, however, fail to show the expected bulge, which may reflect the financial starvation of the Haitian school system during the occupation.

Secondary school enrollment figures for the period from 1930 to 1967, which are far less reliable than those for primary grades, are given in Table 25. Numbers of students in private schools are probably underreported, and some of the secondary school enrollment statistics are in fact for schools (particularly those which are church-run) with a sizable proportion of children in pre-secondary classes. Nevertheless, the table shows a genuine and striking rise in public secondary school enrollments and in the public share of total post-primary enrollments.[60] Enrollment tends to be concentrated in the lower grades, but not to the same extent as displayed in the statistics for primary schools. We can calculate the distribu-

[60] The enrollment rate for secondary schools has again been calculated in the conventional manner, using a population base aged fifteen to nineteen. The resultant figures are somewhat high because of the inclusion of nonsecondary students, but the increase in the rate seems to be correct. (Cf. the puzzling figures in the *UNESCO Statistical Yearbook, 1965,* 123.)

Table 25
Secondary School Enrollment, 1930–67

	Public	Private[a]	Total	Enrollment Rate[b]
1930	1309	4218	5527	2.3
1943	1353	3514	4867	1.6
1953	4684	2163[c]	n.a.	n.a.
1956	6168	5503	11,671	3.0
1961	7647	7449	15,096	3.6
1967	11,710	9296	21,006	4.45

a Includes national religious in most cases.
b Enrollment as a percentage of population aged fifteen to nineteen.
c Probably too low, because of underreporting.

Sources: See Table 20.

tion of secondary school pupils by grade only for public schools in 1967 (Table 26), the rate declining to a very low level, 0.70 per cent, in the last year.

Table 26
Enrollment Rates by Grade, Secondary Schools, 1967

Grade	Rate	Grade	Rate
All	3.17[a]	3	2.92
6	6.18	2	1.89
5	4.30	Rheto	1.98
4	3.66	Philo	.70

a Enrollment in public and private secondary schools as a percentage of the population aged fourteen to twenty.
Source: *Tableaux de l'Ecole Haitienne.*

Vocational education could be important in a country like Haiti, and the relevant statistics are contained in Table 27. (The usual qualifications apply to private school data.) In 1961 there were 27 schools, of which 10 were private (teaching typing, stenography, and accounting). Of the 17 public schools, 4 were prevocational (i.e., primary), 3 concentrated on crafts, 1 was a technical school, and 6 were vocational schools proper.[61] Six years later

61 Brand, *Impressions*, 53.

Table 27
Vocational Education Enrollment

	Public	Private[a]
1930	2416 [b]	n.a.
1942	1368	n.a.
1945	758	447
1952	1665	849 (1951)
1955	2287	649 (1956)
1961	3387	n.a.
1967	4372	1673

[a] These are commercial schools.   [b] Day enrollment only.

Sources: 1930: Commission on Education in Haiti, *Report*, 8–9; 1942 and 1945: Mercer Cook, *An Introduction to Haiti* (Washington, 1951), 46; 1952 and 1955: George A. Dale, *Education in the Republic of Haiti* (Washington, 1959), 84; 1961 and 1967: *Tableaux de l'Ecole Haitienne*.

there were 15 public schools with 4372 pupils, 1410 of whom were in the primary schools. Of the remaining 2962, 362 were enrolled in four all-female home economics schools. It is clear that the vocational schools are unusually heterogeneous, and that the available statistics do not permit a meaningful breakdown of enrollment. Moreover, if vocational education is properly the training of technicians and skilled workers for industry, then only two schools qualify — the J. B. Damier technical school and the Ecole National des Arts et Métiers run by the Salesian Fathers. In 1967 these schools had 196 and 124 pupils respectively. Damier takes students who have completed five years of the seven-year secondary school cycle. The students then follow a four-year course in order to qualify as a general or automobile mechanic, cabinetmaker, mason, electrician, metal-worker, or plumber. One-third of those entering receive their diplomas, the students being strikingly overeducated for their respective occupations. But successful completion of the program facilitates entry into the United States; between 1964 and 1969 about 80 per cent of the graduates emigrated thither. The Ecole, however, takes pupils with a primary education and trains them for four years. They, too, go to the United States in number.

Table 28 provides enrollment figures for the publicly supported

Table 28
Higher Education Enrollment, 1930–67

	1967	*1956*	*1945*	*1930*
Science and Surveying	99	96	81	25
Medicine and Nursing	400	229	103	89
Pharmacy and Dentistry	55	72	35	18
Agronomy	40	31	31 ⎫	
Normal Schools	72	62	47 ⎭	207
Total, Scientific plus Normal	666	490	297	339
Law	549	327	192[a]	196
International Relations	55			
Administration	55			
Theology	46	30		
Ethnology	156	19		
Total	1527	866	489	535

[a] Enrollment in three law schools outside of Port-au-Prince was estimated by the author at 57.

Sources: 1930: Commission on Education in Haiti, *Report*, 23; 1945: Cook, *Introduction*, 57; 1956: Dale, *Education*, 104; 1967: *Tableaux de l'Ecole Haitienne*.

university by subject. It is clear that the expansion of higher education in Haiti has taken place primarily in areas of marginal utility for purposes of national development, i.e., in ethnology, law, international relations, and theology.

There is less known about the nature and rate of Haitian literacy than about the various percentages of pupils in the country's schools. But the overall rate is only a little higher than the rate of sixty years ago — about 8 per cent.[62] For some contrasting figures for rural and urban areas, see Table 29, where the range of literacy in 1950 was from 2 per cent in Marbial to 57 per cent in Port-au-Prince.

There have been a number of adult literacy campaigns, the first of which lasted from 1943 to 1951.[63] About 13,000 people then received certificates of literacy, and more than 40,000 were said to have learned to read and write Creole (Laubach method), without

[62] For the early period, see Logan, "Education," 434, whose estimate of 8 per cent for 1914 is borne out by the 1950 census statistics on literacy by age group.
[63] See Edward Paul, *L'Alphabétisation en Haiti* (Port-au-Prince, 1965), 25.

Table 29
Proportion of Illiterates in Population Aged 10 and Over

	Total	Men	Women
Port-au-Prince, 1949	43	33	49
Dessalines-St. Marc, 1950	83	80	88
Miragoâne, 1950	89	84	94
Marbial, 1950	96	93	98

Source: *Bulletin Trimestriel de Statistique*, 2 (October 1951), 14.

receiving certificates, in about three months.[64] (The government, it should be said, opposed this largely Protestant effort because the Laubach method did not facilitate the learning of French.) During the 1950's literacy campaigns were limited because of the lack of an agreed orthography, but the two small government programs which were in operation (and which used different Creole orthographies) resulted in about 14,000 new literates.[65] Under Duvalier, however, an orthography was accepted which facilitated the transition to French. In 1961 the official Organisation Nationale de l'Education Communautaire launched an adult literacy drive which is still in operation. According to the Organisation, about 66,000 persons (2.5 per cent of the population over fifteen years of age) received certificates before 1965.[66] There seem to be no figures available for the period since 1965, which may mean that the number of certificates earned has declined. There are also fewer literacy classes. The benefits of the program have probably greatly exceeded its costs, but it seems that literacy campaigns as presently organized are unlikely substantially to increase the percentage of the population made literate by primary education. Teachers serve on what amounts to a voluntary basis. (They are paid $5 a week — about 12 cents an hour — approximately the minimum hourly wage of unskilled workers.) It is particularly discouraging that the government has failed to give sustained support to such an inexpensive and worthwhile program.

[64] George Dale, *Education in the Republic of Haiti* (Washington, 1959), 101.
[65] *Ibid.*, 99; Paul, *Alphabétisation*, 51.
[66] The gross figure is from the 1968 report of the Inter-American Committee on the Alliance for Progress, mimeo., 89.

IX

Policies for Economic Development

SINCE DUVALIER'S RISE to power, Haiti's traditional social and economic elite has partially been replaced by a new political and economic elite. By any definition, however, a cleavage still separates the elite and the masses.[1] Its existence must be taken into account when designing strategies for economic growth, and proposals which benefit the ruling class and persons of privilege must be distinguished from those which are directed primarily toward the raising of the per capita incomes of the poor, either rural or urban, or both. A strategy devised for the elite would concentrate, for example, on increasing governmental revenues, which provide the largest proportion of its incomes, and broadening opportunities for this group in commerce and industry. If the production of taxable agricultural and manufactured commodities increased, then the government's income would also grow. But to expand the production of crops grown and consumed in the rural area — which are difficult to tax — would benefit the elite little. They would, however, profit from the encouragement of foreign private investment in mines and plantations producing for export and from public expenditure on urban physical infrastructure to promote import-substituting industrialization and industrial exports, farm-to-market roads, some agricultural extension directed toward the largest and most progressive farmers, irrigation works for taxable crops, and education in the urban area. It is true that at a later stage in development local businessmen might gain economically from the exclusion of foreign capital but, at Haiti's current level of development, infusions of foreign capital for export pro-

[1] See above, 273.

duction, and probably also for the local market, would enhance the
profitability of local businesses.

1. A Consideration of Strategy

International agencies like the Organization of American States,
the Inter-American Development Bank, the World Bank, and the
various branches of the United Nations are concerned with the
welfare of the Haitian people as a whole, but their policies toward
Haiti reflect an assessment of the ability of the government in
power to absorb financial assistance. If, as seems sensible, we assume that only moderate improvements in political mobilization
and administrative capacity are possible in the short term, then
even if international agencies can persuade Haitian governments
to employ economic assistance for rural betterment most conceivable regimes are apt to be uninterested and to lack the administrative capacity to make such peasant-directed schemes prosper. For
these and other reasons, we suggest that external assistance will
have a greater chance of promoting the welfare of all Haitians if it
is aimed at the elite as well as the peasants.[2]

Since the prospects for development in Haiti — even given
a more promising political environment — must be regarded as
bleak, modest goals are the only ones worth setting. International
agencies should avoid the most difficult problems and devise a
simple, gradually ameliorative strategy within the capabilities of
any likely Haitian government. The alternative, an all-or-nothing
approach based on the premise that substantial economic advance
is necessary if acceptable governments are to emerge, presumes the
dubious existence of a sharp discontinuity in the favorable effects
of economic progress on political development and population
control. It is possible to imagine ambitious development schemes
stressing the galvanizing effects of interdependency — where the
optimism of the whole encourages the managers of various sectors
to redouble their efforts — but in an environment like Haiti's they

[2] Admittedly, an international agency could itself organize and staff peasant-directed
programs, as does the Food and Agriculture Organization at Cayes. But doing so
forces the abandonment of one of the favorite precepts of all international organizations — that technical assistance should be self-liquidating.

can easily intensify inefficiency. Over-optimism also generates cynicism and loss of confidence in government, particularly in Haiti, where governments have always been grandiose in their planning.[3]

During the past two decades four knowledgeable economists — Friedmann, Moral, Pierre-Charles, and Young — have proposed comprehensive development strategies for Haiti. Young assumes that given Haiti's factor endowment — a great deal of unskilled labor, not very much good land, and a low capacity to generate the savings out of which physical capital can be created — productivity can be increased by governmental research and extension activities directed at the promotion of labor-intensive crops (such as cassava), the use of chemical and animal fertilizers, the introduction of improved varieties of inexpensive tools, and improved cultivation practices. Young is critical of irrigation projects and animal-drawn plows.[4] He seeks to show that small-scale labor-intensive cultivation is basic to Haitian culture. He believes that the introduction of capital-intensive techniques will fail because they are unfamiliar to Haitian peasants, inappropriate to the country's factor endowment, and less economic than labor-intensive projects. Like so many analysts of agricultural change in underdeveloped countries, he is concerned with economic efficiency. Political constraints are ignored. Instead he looks at the productive factors of the endowment and searches for the most efficient means of increasing production. But this kind of approach, and the literature in general with its emphasis upon supervised credit, rural education, fertilizer sales, new crop varieties, rural cooperatives, and community organizations, implicitly assumes that governments are interested in rural development and that they possess the administrative capacity to implement programs selected by experts.[5] Recommendations based upon such assumptions are clearly of little strategic value for the Haitian case.

Friedmann also recommends a peasant-directed strategy, but he

[3] For example, see Marian Neal, "United Nations' Technical Assistance Programs in Haiti," *International Conciliation,* 468 (1951), 81–118.
[4] Maurice de Young, *Man and Land in the Haitian Economy* (Gainesville, 1958), 2–3, 57, 64–73.
[5] The literature includes Herman M. Southworth and Bruce F. Johnson (eds.), *Agricultural Development and Economic Growth* (Ithaca, 1967); Max F. Millikan and David Hapgood, *No Easy Harvest* (Boston, 1967); John W. Mellor, *The Economics of Agricultural Development* (Ithaca, 1966).

pays explicit attention to the organizational requirements. He
states what has since become a fairly standard community development philosophy: Most important is the creation of rural community organizations with active local participants. A variety of tasks
are suitable for such groups: "reafforestation, local roads, erosion
control, local flood control works, community centers and schools,
and public health measures." [6] Again, the concern is with efficiency in producing "real" economic development which, according to his definition, is equated with a sustained increase in per
capita production.[7] He is aware of the usual barriers to the successful creation of community organizations and one peculiar Haitian obstacle — the absence of village communities with their long-
sanctioned social bonds.[8] But because a peasant-directed strategy
will economize on scarce resources, especially administrative skills,
Friedmann believes that it is the only one that can possibly work in
modern Haiti. In the absence of governmental initiative and ability, only local participation can maintain roads and clear irrigation
canals. In short, his is a strategy of self-help. Unfortunately, however, the implementation of such proposals also depends upon the
cooperation of the ruling elite. Friedmann hoped that if shown
how they "might assume the active leadership in raising national
culture to higher levels of self-awareness . . . [and] become the
vanguard of a dynamic movement of national progress," the elite
could prove responsive.[9] But without major short-run changes in
the configuration of the Haitian social and political ethic, strategies based on pious pleas for change are bound to prove illusory.

Moral is another believer in a peasant-directed strategy. He cannot, however, be accused of over-optimism. He is pessimistic about
the efficacy of supervised credit, fundamental education, technical
assistance in agriculture, and rural cooperatives.[10] Nevertheless, he

6 John Friedmann, "Development Planning," 48–49.
7 The favorable effects on income distribution are an additional reason for Friedmann's support of this approach, but he makes his case primarily on the grounds
that it is the only strategy which can be effective.
8 See also Sidney Mintz, "The Caribbean as a Socio-Cultural Area," *Journal of
World History*, IX (1966), 932–933.
9 Friedmann, "Development Planning," 43.
10 Moral, *Paysan*, 331, 335, 337, 338–339. Moral makes a very interesting criticism
of the idea of development through rural cooperatives. If one is really interested

feels that Haiti's only hope is the stimulation of change at the level of the family enterprise, which will accompany mass politicization.[11] But, as he realizes, this is an ideal solution, and one which can hardly be realized except in the very long run.

Similar peasant-directed strategies of economic development have been proposed by Bastien, Laroche, and Gates, but, like Young, Friedmann, and Moral, they presume totally unreal political contexts for development in Haiti.[12] In our view, there can be no immediate mobilization of new groups and only very moderate advances in administrative techniques. It therefore follows that peasant development must carry a low priority and that such rural projects as are undertaken should be concerned primarily with agricultural production. Rural health and education could come later. The total strategy should also be designed to avoid the unfortunate consequences of deficient administrative skills. Thus, logically, the encouragement of private sector industrialization is developmentally optimal. International agencies could also tolerate prestige investments (airports, hydroelectricity, and fancy irrigation channels), providing that they were productive, because the level of administration is apt to be higher on these than on rural projects. Such schemes are eminently visible and success or failure — which depends upon a degree of administration — is, despite the disgrace of the long-gestating Peligre hydroelectric project, clear to everyone.

Pierre-Charles proposes a somewhat different approach. His fundamental presupposition is that development has failed to take place in Haiti because of the opposition of the ruling classes. Fearing loss of control, and tolerating corruption because it suits their interests, they have consciously oppressed the masses. Only the

---

in peasant development, he asks, why not give power directly to the community council? This is the main local governmental institution, but it has always been controlled by the central government. If the central government is unwilling to give any power to the community council, does it make any sense to try to create rural cooperatives? Shouldn't the rural cooperative be one of the aims of a revitalized community council? (*L'Economie Haitienne* [Port-au-Prince, 1959], 177).
11 Moral, *Paysan*, 324, 327.
12 Rémy Bastien, *La Familia Rural Haitiana* (Mexico City, 1961); René Laroche, "Perspective d'Avenir," 51–71; William B. Gates, Jr., "Observations on Economic Development and Haiti," unpub. typescript (Williamstown, 1959), 31–32.

coming to power of a new progressive government supported by
poor and middle-level peasants, the workers, the national
bourgeoisie, the petite bourgeoisie, and the radical intellectuals
can, he believes, mobilize the peasantry through the organization
of cooperatives, new literacy campaigns, and public health
schemes, establish and operate publicly owned enterprises, nation-
alize foreign commerce in order to provide needed revenues, and
industrialize.[13] But the Pierre-Charles program makes sense only if
a government emerges in Haiti with a clear commitment to development and a willingness to lower the after-tax incomes of the
elite. It is doubtful that such a government could come to power
in the near future and, even if it could, such a regime is unlikely to
undertake all of the projects proposed by Pierre-Charles. State
control of foreign trade would possibly not provide substantial
new state revenues since the profits of private traders are not now
very large relative to the taxes already collected by the state.[14] Furthermore, even a new Haitian government would be hard-pressed
to eliminate corruption and administrative inefficiency. Pierre-
Charles is as over-optimistic as most other Haitian planners.

Most of the economists whose ideas have been discussed and rejected would probably contend that economic change in Haiti is
absolutely impossible without major political alterations. For
once, they may be overly pessimistic. We argue that some economic development is possible despite exceedingly dour political
prospects. Only by proposing a modest strategy which neither depends upon nor institutes radical social alterations can we maxi-
mize the present possibilities for economic progress. Given such an
assumption, the remainder of this chapter concerns itself with tactics in the major economic areas.

[13] Pierre-Charles, *Economie*, 219–252, esp. 224. For the interventionist policies
beloved of Latin American intellectuals, cf. Albert O. Hirschman, "Ideologies of
Economic Development in Latin America," in Hirschman (ed.), *Latin American
Issues* (New York, 1961), 3–42.
[14] For a discussion of the shares of the government, traders, and peasants in coffee
and cotton, see William B. Gates, Jr., "The Haitian Coffee Industry," unpub. typescript (Williamstown, 1959), 23–25; *idem.*, "The Haitian Cotton and Cotton Textile
Industries," *ibid.*, 10–12.

2. Policies for Education

The growth of formal education probably accounts for a substantial fraction of the increase in output per person in the United States, and for an equally substantial fraction of the differences in per capita incomes among countries.[15] Such conclusions rely upon the "education earnings" method of estimating the productivity of education: earnings are assumed to represent the productive contribution of the individual to society, and differentials in earnings associated with schooling (with age, sex, and race held constant) are attributed to education.[16]

The use of this approach for underdeveloped countries is subject to qualification, however. In most, a large fraction (sometimes more than half) of the graduates of secondary schools and universities is employed by the government, yet the theoretical justifica-

[15] Edward F. Denison, *The Sources of Economic Growth in the United States* (Washington, 1962), 67–79; Krueger, "Factor Endowments," 266.

[16] But educational attainment is also positively correlated with ability, motivation, and family connections — each of which raises earnings — so in order to allow for such indirect factors Denison attributed only 60 per cent of the earnings differentials to education itself. Attempts have been made to separate the influence of intelligence from that of education, but little progress has been made in removing the influence of motivation and family connections. (See Gary S. Becker, *Human Capital* [New York, 1964], 79–88.) Nevertheless, the usefulness of the education-earnings approach is clear at least for developed countries. It has also been used to provide the basis for recommendations about the size and composition of national expenditures on education in the developing world. For this purpose, estimates of the cost of education (direct costs plus earnings forgone) are combined with earnings differentials to obtain rates of return for different kinds of schooling. (For the problems, see Theodore W. Schultz, *The Economic Value of Education* [New York, 1963], 20–63.) In principle, however, the rate of return measures only the productive contribution made by an individual to the firm which employs him. These are the internal productive benefits, and do not include the benefits of education unrelated to production, i.e., the enhanced enjoyment of leisure activities. Also excluded from the rate of return are benefits external to the individual and his employer. For example, educated persons make civic contributions, encourage the education of their children and others, make original discoveries, etc. Education can also prove an instrument of cultural integration and greater tolerance of diversity. The spread of education additionally may increase dissatisfaction with the status quo and hence produce either a harmful instability or a predisposition to necessary change. "Rate of return," as used in this chapter, thus includes on the benefit side only the productive increments accruing directly to the individual or his employer. It is only a guide to the priority which should be put on education in a national budget, but if the rate of return is high the case for increasing allocations is particularly strong.

tion for using earnings as guides to productivity rests on the assumptions that earnings are determined in a competitive market, and that the employers are profit-maximizing firms (or that the workers are self-employed). Where the government, as in Haiti, is sufficiently dominant substantially to alter the salary scales of private employers, the earnings of the different classes of workers may have little to do with their productive contribution to society. Furthermore, in underdeveloped countries family connections are, as in Haiti, important in securing lucrative employment in the private sector. (Another objection, that very large changes may soon occur in the levels of industrial employment and school enrollment, making calculations out of date, does not apply to Haiti.) These objections are compelling, but they relate largely to secondary and higher education, and rate of return calculations may still be useful, so far as Haiti is concerned, with regard to basic literacy, primary education, and certain kinds of vocational training. This is particularly true if we remember that all data collected in other underdeveloped countries show a distinct earnings differential between literate and illiterate workers. That employers are prepared to pay more for literacy is evidence that these workers are more productive, especially since family connections play little role in this sphere and the correlation between ability and education is likely to be weaker in those countries where educational opportunity is limited than in countries where opportunity is widespread.[17]

In some other developing countries (Table 30) the rates of return for five or six years of primary education are high, even if the striking figures for Venezuela conceal considerable error.[18] These estimates are based upon the arbitrary assumption that 50 per cent

[17] Minimum wage laws and trade unions make labor markets less competitive than otherwise. These two imperfections, however, probably operate to narrow wage differentials and thereby produce an underestimation of the social rate of return to education.

[18] The estimate of the cost of primary education in Venezuela did not include earnings forgone which means that the estimated rate of return is too high. The same is true of the Indian study. It had previously been thought that the earnings forgone of primary students were negligible, but Carnoy found this not to be true of Mexico. See Martin Carnoy, "Rates of Return to Schooling in Latin America," *Journal of Human Resources*, II (1967), 359–374.

Table 30
Rates of Return to Primary Education, Various Countries[a]

Country	Year	Rate of Return
India	1960	16.8
Mexico	1963	12.5
Venezuela	1957	41
Chile	1958	12 (or 5.8)[b]
Colombia	n.a.	10

[a] Fifty per cent of the difference in earnings is attributed to education.
[b] Carnoy recalculates the Chilean estimate and reduces it by about half. See Carnoy, "Rates of Return," 369–370.

Sources: A. M. Nalla Gounden, "Investment in Education in India," *Journal of Human Resources*, II (1967), 352; Martin Carnoy, "Rates of Return to Schooling in Latin America," *ibid.*, 367–368.

of earnings differentials (after adjustment for age and sex) are attributable to education. In 1965, the rate of return for Northern Nigeria was also high since the benefit-cost ratio of primary education, calculated at a discount of 5 per cent, was given at 16.9 (or 8.5 if 50 per cent of the earnings differential is attributed to education).[19] Although similar education and earnings data are unavailable for Haiti, it seems likely that primary education is complementary with other factors of production, especially physical capital. The productivity of primary education (as measured by the earnings differential) increases when the percentage of the labor force with primary education remains constant while other factors are increased. In particular cases physical capital may substitute for primary education, but in industry as a whole the relationship is probably complementary. Overall, it is safe to say that different levels of education are complementary if they are far apart and substitutable if they are close together. Primary education is thus complementary with higher education and workers with five years of education are substitutes for illiterate workers in many industries, and for industry as a whole.

When the rate of growth of an economy increases, the rate of

[19] Samuel Bowles, "The Efficient Allocation of Resources in Education," *Quarterly Journal of Economics*, LXXXI (1967), 189–219.

return to education rises. This is not a necessary conclusion, however, for it depends to some extent upon the reason for the rise in the rate of growth. If, for example, the only source of growth came from increased education, then presumably the rate of return to education would fall. But if the source of growth is an increase in physical capital, or if the stock of physical capital grows more rapidly than the stock of educated manpower, then the rate of return to education should rise. If growth occurs because of a discovery of new natural resources, a rise in the world price of a critical export, or a shift away from unfavorable governmental policies, then the return to all factors may rise. The limited empirical evidence available for Latin American countries indicates a positive correlation between the rate of growth of GDP and the rate of return to education as a whole.[20] These generalizations are probably equally true with regard to primary schooling, and we would therefore expect this rate of return in Haiti to be comparatively low. Yet in no underdeveloped country has this rate been found to be low and, in any case, given present administrative capacities, the rate of return to investment in physical capital is also likely to be low in Haiti. Thus public expenditure on primary education is indicated, at least in the urban areas.

There is almost no relevant data with which to construct a table of rural rates of return, yet it is of interest to try to correlate differences in output and earnings in the peasant sector with literacy and illiteracy. There is evidence from many countries that migrants from rural to urban areas are better educated than those who remain behind. A plausible hypothesis is that the monetary returns to the skills of education are greater in urban than in rural areas, and this factor would account for a higher rate of migration for the educated. If the private monetary benefits in both rural and urban areas are roughly proportional to the social benefits in both sectors, the migration of the educated is hardly to be regretted on the grounds of efficiency. Unless the social cost of education is lower in rural than in urban surroundings, the rate of return from educating a rural child who becomes a farmer must be less than the return from educating an urbanite who becomes a worker. There are also *a priori* grounds for believing that in a traditional agricul-

[20] Carnoy, "Rates of Return," 370.

tural setting the benefits of primary education will be low. Those who favor primary education for farmers suggest that its return is high in a setting of transitional agriculture — where farmers are beginning to use new factors of production. In such a situation information about new techniques must be conveyed to cultivators, a process facilitated by primary education. But even fervid advocates admit that where the economic environment is so deficient that peasant agriculture remains traditional, schooling may have little economic value because there is hardly any information worth acquiring.[21]

There are other arguments for educating peasants. Exposure to values other than their own may make them more receptive to the ideas of an extension service.[22] Education may also foster cultural integration and broaden the base of political participation. The content of rural education conceivably could be made more enriching and effective if it were biased toward vocational instruction, but in Africa such shifts have brought no more success than the American efforts in Haiti during the 1920's. In Central America and Southeast Asia, education appears to be a force for social change only when that process is already underway.[23] In Jamaica, rural education has been emphasized since the nineteenth century, and by 1960 the literacy rate for the entire country was 82 per cent.[24] Jamaican peasants also enjoy other important advantages over Haitians: they are part of a more developed economy and have better roads, a competent extension service, and a nonpredatory government. Yet it may surprise enthusiastic supporters of rural literacy that Jamaican peasants in the middle 1950's had in-

---

[21] See Schultz, *Transforming Agriculture*, 204.

[22] Clifford R. Wharton, Jr., "Education and Agricultural Growth: The Role of Education in Early-Stage Agriculture," in C. Arnold Anderson and Mary Jean Bowman (eds.), *Education and Economic Growth* (Chicago, 1966), 207.

[23] Philip J. Foster, "The Vocational School Fallacy in Development Planning," in Anderson and Bowman, *Education and Economic Growth*, 142–166; Manning Nash, "The Role of Village Schools in the Process of Cultural and Economic Modernization," *Social and Economic Studies*, XIV (1965), 131–143.

[24] *UNESCO Yearbook, 1965*, 39. It is interesting that in Jamaica the illiteracy rate is lower for women (15.2 per cent) than for men (21.4 per cent). The data indicate that, among Caribbean countries with a predominantly Negro population, male literacy is higher than female at an early stage in the development of literacy, but, as literacy spreads, the female rates rise above the male rates. The data on literacy by age groups confirm this hypothesis. In several countries, at younger ages the females are more literate while at older ages the male literacy rates are higher.

comes only 40 to 80 per cent higher than those of Haitian peasants.[25]

Primary education of peasants is unlikely to prove beneficial so long as the economic environment of a country remains deficient and traditional. The education of urban workers will also prove only marginally beneficial if no growth occurs, but to raise the rate of return to primary education of this group it is necessary to begin industrial growth. It will increase the demand for workers and put a greater pressure on the wages of those who possess some education. Since the supply of labor lacking education will prove highly elastic, their wages will rise little compared with the wages of workers with schooling. The increase in earnings differentials will also raise the return to primary education of urban workers, an effect that will be strengthened if the new industries are more skill-intensive than the old.[26]

When industrial growth occurs, physical capital grows more rapidly than the supply of educated manpower, and the rate of return to primary education increases.[27] A rise in demand and production in the peasant agricultural sector, however, may bring about different results: Other factors may not increase relative to peasant labor as output expands. If the economic environment remains deficient, particularly with regard to the quality of the extension service, the availability of research results, and the insecurity of tenure, then peasant techniques are unlikely to change and there will be little or no growth in the return to primary education of farmers.[28]

[25] At the same time, Jamaican per capita income was around three times that of Haiti. Christopher K. Clague, "Jamaica and Haiti," unpub. typescript (April 1970); A. Ahiram, "Income Distribution in Jamaica, 1958," Social and Economic Studies, XIII (1964), 333–369.

[26] Nathaniel Leff, The Brazilian Capital Goods Industry, 1929–1964 (Cambridge, Mass., 1968), 69–72, describes how rapid industrial growth raised the skill differential in Brazil to a level substantially higher than that in industrial countries.

[27] The rate of return may also be affected by growth in the supply of workers with primary education compared with changes in the supply of complementary supervisory personnel, nearly all of whom would possess secondary or university education.

[28] This statement does not deny that a community development strategy should include primary education. If the government will send a teacher for a school built by the local community, it takes one step toward winning the confidence of the community. Community development in Haiti is frequently carried out by private groups, especially missionaries. Some are concerned primarily to save souls, but

If peasant farmers benefit only marginally from the provision of educational facilities, the benefit of educating one rural child to a given grade is less than educating the same child to the same grade in an urban setting.[29] Costs must also be considered, and, in primary education, they are the sum of the instructional costs plus earnings forgone. In Haiti, instructional costs seem less for village than for town schools (in 1963–1967, 59 gourdes in rural schools and 86 in urban secular public schools).[30] But rural students are concentrated in the lower grades more than they are in urban schools, 59 per cent of all rural students (41 per cent in the towns) being enrolled in kindergarten.[31] Moreover, many rural pupils probably leave schools without acquiring functional literacy and without deriving real benefit from their education. Quantification of the effects of such desertion on the cost of schooling is complicated, but the costs per unit of effective education in Haitian rural and urban schools are roughly equal (248 and 236 gourdes respectively).[32]

---

others devote much time, energy, and money to improvements in agriculture, health, and education. Such a program seems very appropriate for missionaries concerned with material improvement. For an example of a successful, if unique, community development project, see the series of articles on "The Transformation of Political, Legal, and Social Systems of Suppressed Peasant Societies: The Vicos Case," *American Behavioral Scientist*, VIII (1965), 3–33; especially Henry F. Dobyns, "The Strategic Importance of Enlightenment and Skill for Power," *ibid.*, 23–27.

29 The benefits of expenditure on urban primary education are measured by the rate of return plus ancillary factors, and benefits accruing to expenditure on rural education are indicated by the weighted average of both rural and urban benefits, the weights being assigned according to the proportion of rural residents with primary schooling who migrate to the towns.

30 *Tableaux de l'Ecole Haitienne* (Port-au-Prince, 1967), 7, 13.

31 This figure is affected by the fact that kindergarten lasts two years in the rural schools and usually only one in the urban schools. In spite of this fact, however, it is likely that the standards of achievement for a given grade are no higher in the rural than in the urban schools.

32 We assume that children who progress as far as the fourth grade acquire educational benefits proportional to the number of years they have been in schools; children who leave school after one of the three previous grades acquire benefits equal to half the number of years they have been in school; and children who never go beyond kindergarten acquire no benefits whatsoever. (The notion that the first couple of years of primary school are not so valuable as the last few years is documented in Carnoy, "Rates of Return," 368. He found the rate of return to years 3 through 5 to be substantially greater than to years 1 and 2.) It follows that the cost of a "unit of effective education" is the number of children in grades four through six added to half of the number of children in the first three grades, the total divided into instructional costs.

If costs of education are about the same in rural and urban areas, the benefit-cost ratio must be higher in the latter. This suggests that Haiti should continue to concentrate its educational dollars on the towns until such time as the proportion of urban children in school increases markedly. Consequently, if the benefits of primary education are reaped mainly in the higher grades, it might prove a better allocation of resources to direct attention and funds more toward reducing dropout rates than toward expanding enrollment.

It is difficult to make even such modest recommendations for Haitian secondary and higher education. There is a paucity of reliable national and comparative data; we know that Haiti has a small, highly cultured elite, who have for more than 150 years placed a high value on the education of their children. It is a qualification for upper-class status, promises (or formerly promised) financial security, and facilitated emigration in times of stress. Haitians have always emigrated, never more than during the era of Duvalier. Yet there is still no dearth of indigenous entrepreneurs given the availability of sufficient venture capital and conditions propitious to investment. The several caveats are probably insufficient to countermand any decisions in favor of moderate expansion of secondary and higher education. The economic return to public investment would probably prove sufficiently high, especially when the external benefits are considered. And if the pace of development should increase, so will the returns to secondary education rise.

3. Policies for Rural Development

We have already suggested that a strategy of economic development for Haiti should give low priority to the rural sector. Peasant uplift is popular in international aid circles, however, and Haitian governments can do so either by *dirigisme* or gradualism — by pumping large sums into a region and thereby changing the environment drastically or by introducing limited inexpensive changes in cultivation practices which can be implemented with a minimum of outside support. Missionary bodies are now the main practitioners of gradualism in Haiti, but the moderate rate of progress which it induces appeals only weakly to the government and its current advisers. The successful cooperative in Fermathe resulted from a gradualist approach. The Artibonite Valley irrigation scheme[33] was an example of *dirigisme*. It promised visible and politically useful results; but discontinuity of interest, corruption, and incompetence quickly vitiate projects which depend overwhelmingly on official direction. By contrast, gradualism is attractive because of its long-term potential for the diffusion of innovation. Yet, if large-scale directed schemes are prone to collapse, programs of gradualism equally often fail to take off, and, in Haiti, no examples of the spread of consciously introduced technological progress can be cited.

It is clear that Haitian governments have neither the patience and dedication for gradualism nor the administration and will required for *dirigisme*. The basic interests of the ruling elite are essentially directive, however, and, providing that international agencies are in a position to support and control such projects, the optimal strategy will continue to be highly *dirigiste* in character. The extent of innovational diffusion will continue to be negligible and Haitian governments will probably learn only slowly to administer such projects properly, but international organizations should cease believing that they can initiate economic growth in Haiti by showing the government what is possible. Aid-giving bodies will want to maintain a close supervision of their projects to prevent them from collapsing.

One kind of project which seems sensible is the reconstruction of irrigation channels, ditches, and dikes. Making the services of tractors available is another; by doing so it is possible to eliminate the problems connected with teaching peasants how to care for and use draft animals, and it sharply reduces the need for credit since peasants can simply purchase the services of a tractor (which are cheap compared with the purchase of a draft animal) when and if needed. Little emphasis should be put on general reafforestation

[33] For an intelligent discussion of irrigation projects in Haiti, see Mosher, *Technical Cooperation*, 94–99.

(with its diffused benefits) since the government of Haiti is unlikely to do so effectively and the international agencies have better uses for their limited funds. Much more reasonable are projects of reafforestation for very specific purposes, e.g., to prevent the
silting up of Lake Peligre or the inundation of Port-au-Prince. In
general, projects with clearly defined and measurable goals are to
be preferred, and such projects should be located in the regions of
the country which promise the greatest chance of success.

4. The Transport Sector

By 1929 American engineers had constructed about 1000 miles
of road, virtually all unpaved, and by the end of 1948 there were
about 2250 miles, only 50 of which had been paved. (For figures,
see Table 31.) The 50 paved miles were almost entirely located in
the cities; elsewhere gravel surface, which is more economical than
macadam or concrete where traffic volumes are low, predominated.
Throughout the period from about 1934 to 1950, however, maintenance was systematically neglected, and, as a result, the government of President Magloire decided to surface long stretches of the

Table 31
Roads in Haiti

	Paved Roads (kms.)	All Roads for Motor Vehicles[a] (kms.)
1929	n.a.	1600
1948	80	2700
1952	193	2980
1959	500	3065
1962	554	n.a.
1969	370[b]	3157

[a] Mostly earth and gravel roads, some passable during only part of the year.
[b] Two hundred three listed as being in good condition, 167 in bad condition.

Sources: 1929 and 1948: *Mission in Haiti*, 227–228; 1952: Robert S. Folsom, "Haitian
Economy" (1954), 166–167; 1959: Pierre-Charles, *L'Economie Haitienne*, 85 (primary
source not indicated); 1962: *Guide Economique de la République d'Haiti*, 86; 1969:
Planification et Développement, Bulletin du CONADEP, 2 (1969), 12.

arterial roads between cities. Faulty construction and poor maintenance soon led to the breaking up of this new asphalt covering, and to a state of deterioration probably worse than that before paving.[34] In 1956 the World Bank agreed to provide $2.6 million in foreign currency for the rehabilitation of the road network and the reorganization of the highway maintenance section of the Ministry of Public Works, but no improvements were ever discerned.

The total number of motor vehicles in Haiti remained about the same (see Table 32) until it increased markedly during the prosperous years of the Magloire administration. A decline in registrations followed to 1962, and perhaps through 1969, for the official figure is implausible in the light of current economic trends.[35] The decline in the number of trucks and buses from 1900 in 1956 to

Table 32
Motor Vehicles in Haiti

	Passenger Cars[a]	Trucks and Buses	Total
1929	n.a.	n.a.	c. 3000
1948	n.a.	n.a.	c. 3015
1950	3120	1137	4257
1956	7914	1883	9797
1958	7975	1508	9483
1962	7317	929	8246
1969	13,400[b]	800	14,200[b]

a Cars, station wagons, and jeeps.
b This figure is hard to accept in the light of the general economic trends.

Sources: See Table 31.

34 The utility of a road surface depends upon the quality of the base, the subbase, and the drainage facilities. It is possible to pave roads inexpensively if they are sited on poorly drained, inadequately prepared surfaces, but after a few years the paving crumbles. Roadworks undertaken by unscrupulous contractors can therefore prove an enormous waste of public funds. See Pan-American Union, *A Survey of Factors Which Affect Transportation Cost* (Washington, 1964), 46–47, 52.
35 It is hard to preserve comparability in a table of the total number of vehicles, for diplomatic, governmental, and military vehicles are not always included. The figures for 1950, 1956, and 1958 seem to have been complete, but those for 1929 and 1948 may have been somewhat understated. The peculiar rise in the number of passenger cars from 1962 to 1969 does not seem to be explicable in terms of differences in coverage.

about 800 in 1969 is striking, largely reflecting the dismal state of
the road network. Because of the inefficiency of the motor vehicle
routes, other forms of transportation remain important. In 1933
an estimated 400,000 horses, 650,000 donkeys, and 62,000 mules
were engaged in carrying goods and humans.[36] In 1952 there were
501 sailboats and 19 motor vessels engaged in coastal trade.[37] The
trains no longer carry passengers or private (non-sugar) traffic, and
space for airfreight is both in very short supply and expensive.

Public investments in the transport sector fortunately lend
themselves well — at least in principle — to quantitative cost-
benefit analysis. Many of the benefits are easily measurable and
the required data are usually inexpensive to collect. But modern
analysis of this kind is only beginning to be applied to investments
in transport in the developing countries, and data with which to
compare the Haitian case are scarce. When considering roads, we
want to know the costs of different kinds of construction and maintenance, vehicle operations, and loading and unloading, and existing and future volumes of traffic with alternative kinds of road-
ways. Yet the projection of future traffic densities is particularly
difficult in view of the multiplicity of products currently being carried and possibly to be transported in the future.[38]

The only available information on traffic flow in Haiti dates
from 1951, when the Institut Haitien de Statistique unsystemati-
cally observed traffic northward and southward from Port-au-
Prince for five days during the rainy season. The daily northward
traffic in tons was 1018, but only 65 tons moved southward. The
data on vehicle operating costs are also old (1954) and not particularly reliable (Table 33), but it is clear that rates were higher between outlying towns (when the road network was in better repair
than today) than in the vicinity of Port-au-Prince and that costs by
sailboat between comparable towns were about 25 per cent less

36 Holly, *Agriculture*, 127.
37 *Bulletin Trimestriel de Statistique*, 14 (December 1954), 36.
38 Precise cost assessments are frequently unnecessary since specific projects often
appear to have either high or low benefit-cost ratios. Thorough discussions of
benefit-cost analysis for transport projects in underdeveloped countries may be
found in Hans A. Adler, *Sector and Project Planning in Transportation* (Baltimore,
1967); A. A. Walters, *The Economics of Road User Charges* (Baltimore, 1968).

than vehicle costs. (The precise proportion of facility costs in operating costs is not known, but it will be assumed here that taxes
comprise a small portion of the rates.) In the Peruvian jungle the
mule train costs were about 50 cents per ton kilometer during the
mid-1950's, and the rate for human porterage in Africa in 1950 was
about 32 cents per ton kilometer.[39] Finally, transport cost rates
must be compared with the value of the merchandise being carried.[40] A journey of 50 kilometers at the ton-kilometer rate of 8
cents would add a mere $4; by donkey the added cost per ton-
kilometer would be $25.

Table 33
Rates per Ton-Kilometer
Various Routes, Haiti, 1954

Route to the South	U.S. Cents per ton-km.	Distance (km.)
Port-au-Prince to Léogane	6.24	32
Port-au-Prince to Miragoâne	8.88	90
Port-au-Prince to Jérémie	10.08	298
Route to the North		
Port-au-Prince to Arcahaie	6.32	48
Port-au-Prince to Gonaïves	7.56	185
Port-au-Prince to Môle St. Nicolas	10.70	336

Note: The rates by road were converted into rates per passenger-kilometer, and
then into rates per ton-kilometer, using the assumption of 10 passengers per ton.

Source: *Bulletin Trimestriel de Statistique*, 14 (December 1954), 17.

Comparable Nigerian Costs per ton-km., mid-1950's

Tarred roads	4.34 cents
Laterite roads	4.34 to 5.43 cents
Dry-season roads	6.52 to 7.24 cents

Source: E. K. Hawkins, *Road Transport in Nigeria* (London, 1958), 72.

[39] George Wilson, *et al.*, *The Impact of Highway Investment on Development*
(Washington, 1966), 151; Gilbert Walker, *Traffic and Transportation in Nigeria*
(London, 1959), viii.
[40] Producers' prices in 1955 (in dollars per ton) were coffee, $677.4; cacao, $580.4;
fresh fish, $240.0; corn, $96.0; sweet potatoes, $36.0; manioc, $5.40. See Tripartite
Mission, *Annex*, Tables 9 and 10.

In 1969 the government of Haiti began to construct a concrete highway from Port-au-Prince to Cayes, a distance of 196 kilometers (122 miles) at a cost of $15 million, or $76,400 per kilometer.[41] If amortized over forty years at 5 per cent interest, and assuming maintenance costs of $605 per kilometer per year, the facility cost comes to $5053 per kilometer per year, or $13.84 per day. In order to assess the utility of such expenditures we shall assume that, as a result of the new road, traffic triples and operating costs are reduced from 10 cents to 3 cents per ton kilometer.[42] Even given these optimistic assumptions, the average present traffic flow over the whole of the new road needs to amount to at least one hundred tons per day if the project is to obtain a favorable benefit-cost ratio.[43]

Since the traffic flow in 1951 south from Port-au-Prince was only 65 tons a day, it is doubtful that the present and potential traffic flows are sufficiently large to justify the expense of such a highway. We have also made our calculations on the basis that traffic will be trebled, but even this increase is excessive. The principal commodities now carried along the existing gravel road are coffee, cacao, essential oils, cattle, and fowl. It is now and will probably remain cheaper to walk cattle than to ship them by truck.[44] For coffee, cacao, and essential oils, reductions in transport costs would probably have very little effect on producer prices and hence on supply. Almost certainly there are road projects with high benefit-cost ratios, but the route to Cayes as presently planned is not one of them. The limited availability in Haiti of funds for road construction requires that projects should be selected after a careful study of actual and potential traffic flows. Roads and other agricultural

[41] *Planification et Développement*, Bulletin du CONADEP, 2 (1969), 14. This cost is probably unrealistically low by a factor of $5 million.

[42] Pan American, *Survey*, 13.

[43] The calculation is as follows. Letting x be the initial traffic flow, the daily benefits, on the assumption that the traffic increase is 2x, become $(7¢) (x) + ½ (7¢) (2x) = (7¢) (2x)$. Setting this sum equal to $13.84 yields $x = 98.9$. It is worth noting that shortfalls of the actual traffic below the minimum required results in *proportional* reductions in the benefit-cost ratio of the project. Thus if the present traffic is 50 tons on the average instead of 100, the benefit-cost ratio is 0.5 (still on the assumption of a tripling of traffic volume).

[44] Assuming 500 kilos per head of cattle, at 3 cents a ton kilometer, the cost of transport by truck would be $3 against $2 on foot. The cattle lose less weight, however, when transported by truck. Transporting slaughtered beasts would probably prove more expensive.

investments should also be coordinated with each other and located in the most promising regions of the country, such as the Artibonite Valley.

Maintenance performance is a critical component of road construction calculations, and for Haiti it is logical to assume some degree of faulty maintenance in order to justify the higher costs of surfaces which are relatively maintenance free. This lies behind Duvalier's determination to lay a thick concrete pavement to Cayes. Another important effect of the assumption of inadequate maintenance is the implied reduction in the benefit-cost ratio on all road projects. If the conditions are so deficient that very poor (or no) maintenance may be assumed, then the priority on new construction should be low. The setting of this condition would, however, involve the expansion of the economy of Port-au-Prince, even higher import propensities than now prevail, and highly inefficient and extremely inegalitarian development. It will make more sense to mobilize sufficient resources for maintenance.

5. Priorities

Before examining the development plans proposed by the Tripartite Mission in 1962, and the Haitian Conseil de Développement et de Planification (CONADEP) in 1968, several general observations should be made. First, it is advisable on grounds of efficiency to leave as much as possible to the private sector; the public sector should be confined to those activities in which the ratio of total to private benefits is large. It is often argued that the private sector in underdeveloped countries lacks dynamism — that entrepreneurs have a low tolerance for risk, are poor managers, and have low savings propensities — but so far as Haiti is concerned these charges are exaggerated. Even were this not so, public undertakings in Haiti are and have been less efficient than private enterprise.[45] But there is still need for a publicly financed development bank to provide credit for the private sector. (In the industrial and modern commercial sectors, unlike traditional agri-

45 Even Pierre-Charles, *Economie*, 194–195, agrees.

culture, the provision of credit without either technical assistance
or close supervision can prove productive.) Second, the proposed
development should be kept to a manageable (not overdispersed)
size. The government should not be asked (as do both plans) to
spread its efforts too thinly.[46] Third, over-ambition by itself is not
necessarily a critical defect if the specified priorities are apposite at
lower levels of expenditures (when percentage allocations will also
shift). Yet at fairly minimal expenditure levels the Haitian government should not undertake a variety of pilot projects which are
each expected to become national programs requiring the outlay of
large sums of money. Fourth, when funds are exceedingly tight we
feel that public health schemes should receive a low priority.
Their return in terms of economic development or the well-being
of the majority of the population is not high. (This is not to say
that the health of most Haitians is not deplorable and does not
inhibit their capacity to work.[47]) The most desirable kinds of
health expenditures on economic grounds are those for preventive
medicine affecting the productive capacity of adults. Thus the
yaws and malaria eradication schemes are justifiable, and in future
the distribution of a cheap protein-rich food (composed of soy-
beans, fishmeal, etc.) might be sponsored, but it is advisable to
permit better organized developing countries to prove the feasibil-
ity of such schemes before they are attempted in Haiti. Fifth, it is
unrealistic to assume that any government of Haiti could avoid
supporting at least a few uneconomic prestige projects. The installation of thermal power units in Port-au-Prince probably would
have been more economic than electricity generated at the Peligre
dam, but the popular appeal of large-scale hydroelectricity is obviously great. And public housing has equal appeal but it would
make more sense to increase the money incomes of the poor and to
let them build new houses inexpensively than to invest in costlier
government-sponsored facilities.

[46] The Tripartite Mission plan envisaged the expenditure of about $29 million a
year, about $14 million of which would have had to be contributed by Haiti. But
it was clearly well outside the bounds of historical experience for Haiti to spend
anything like that amount on development. And when U.S. aid was eliminated in
1963 the plan became utterly utopian.
[47] See Chapter VII above.

The allocations of the two existing development plans are displayed in Table 34. Since they show a broad similarity in their percentages by category they can be discussed together. We would alter their provisions by increasing expenditures on educa-

Table 34

Allocation in Development Plans

	Tripartite Mission Plan		Government Plan	
	$ Million	%	$ Million	%
1. Agriculture	17.8	24.5	1.74	13.7
2. Industry	10.0	13.7	1.24	9.7
3. Electricity	7.0	9.6	1.78	14.0
4. Transport and Communication	20.1	27.6	3.94	31.0
5. Education	4.5	6.2	.78	6.1
6. Public Health (includes water systems)	9.1	12.5	3.08	24.2
7. Community Development	0.3	0.3	.16	1.3
8. Public Housing	4.0	5.5	0.00	
9. Tourism	0.0		.40	
10. Bilateral Projects not Classifiable by Sector	0.0		.80	
11. Pre-investment and Research	0.0		.58	
Totals	72.8		14.50	
Totals, minus items 9–11	72.8	100.0	12.72	100.0

Sources: *Tripartite Mission Report*, 113; *Plan d'Action Economique et Sociale, 1968–69,* CONADEP, 1968, 58.

tion, transportation, and agriculture while reducing allocations to public health, and eliminating those for public housing. Although the Tripartite Mission wanted to redress the disparity between rural and urban education by concentrating resources in the former sector and by constructing new schools, it will probably prove wiser to expand the current educational budget — to hire additional teachers and give them more books, paper, and pencils with which to work. (The salaries of teachers need to be raised, but the supply elasticity of teachers is probably not low.)

A high priority on teacher training and on raising the teacher-student ratio (in order to combat high dropout rates) will be appropriate. Expansion of the numbers of children who attend school is not indicated.

Both of the existing plans list a number of important projects in the agricultural and transport sectors. But they are economically dispersive, and we suggest concentrating the development of agriculture and road construction together in the same limited regions in order to achieve a significant and visible impact. The irrigation and drainage canals in the Artibonite Valley could well be cleaned and extended, and their construction completed, while roads in the valley and from the valley to the capital are improved. Despite the prevailing rhetoric, neither the Tripartite Mission nor CONADEP urged the allocation of significant funds for erosion control, which is justified.

Although the Tripartite Mission expected the private sector to provide necessary investments in industry, CONADEP postulated a large role for Haiti's development bank, which had already begun initiating enterprises. It now operates a cotton factory in Gonaïves and a butter factory, slaughterhouse, and electricity generating plant in Cayes. The butter factory was inherited from the F.A.O. in 1961 and has always operated with large losses. The cotton establishment is about five years old and still unprofitable. The slaughterhouse, inaugurated in 1968, was poorly conceived and demand for meat prepared by modern methods is limited. As presently organized, it will probably always be unprofitable. (The plant is poorly designed for export.) Profitability in the short run is hardly the best criterion of social productivity, but it is in the long run unless external benefits are especially high. In none of these development bank projects are the external benefits as prepossessing as the financial losses. There is an "industrial city," however, which was allocated $400,000 in the CONADEP plan. It would include factories erected at government expense and rented to exporters of manufactured goods. Companies thereby benefit by the reduction in initial investment, the government eventually reaps the rewards of increasing internal employment, demand, and ancillary investment, and the climate for exports might improve markedly. This is a sensible proposal, and one of the limited kind worth recommending.

Although the development prospects in Haiti are bleak, they are not hopeless. In addition to tourism, most promising at present is probably the export of manufactured goods to the United States. But doing so depends upon U.S. policy, particularly with regard to Section 807 of the tariff law.

X

The Functioning of the
Predatory State and Its Future

"OUR GOVERNMENTS," once wrote Duvalier about Haiti's past, "never cared about the national inheritance and never attempted to stop social griefs. They talked a lot about liberty, only to fool the free world instead of using it fairly as a domestic policy. The country is split into two groups: the exploiters — [a] restless and foolhardy minority — monopolize the administrative power and paralyze the progress of the masses; the exploited — the great majority — [are] victims of a wrongful and cruel system. There are exploiters in all strata of society. Originated from the mass, they are sometimes more dangerous. All stunning blows to the collectivity's interests come directly from them. To enrich themselves with all possible speed, they will betray anyone for a mess of pottage. Do not trust them." [1] He wrote also, and with equal accuracy, of his own regime — of a government focused upon predation (the predatory state is defined as one in which brigandage is the predominant form of power, where effective power is exercised by praetorian specialists in violence who insure the safety of and respect for the formal center of power) and the development of an apparatus of total control (but not regimentation) obedient to the will (and whim) of a single, all-powerful individual.[2] It is

1 Quoted in Gingras, *Cyclone*, 105–106.
2 The predatory state is a species of what Harold D. Lasswell and Abraham Kaplan (*Power and Society: A Framework for Political Inquiry* [New Haven, 1950]) called virocracy — the form of rule in which the elite is "recruited in terms of well-being (vigor, vitality, prowess)" (211). Lasswell and Kaplan (222–223) would probably have found the notion of "total control" without "regimentation" and technology disconcerting, but the lack of regimentation is a function of incapacity rather than infirmity of will. And in Haiti it is possible to assert effective control without regimentation. For praetorianism, see Samuel P. Huntington, *Political Order in Changing Societies* (New Haven, 1968), 196–197. It should also be said that the

apt to recall that in an institutionalized civic polity the rise to the
top broadens a man's horizons but that "in a praetorian system it
narrows them." In the Haitian variant of these classical systems, it
is the individual who makes all of the vital (and many of the non-
vital) decisions affecting the state and its citizenry, operates as the
state, and personifies all of the functions usually exercised by an
ongoing government of a modern nation-state. He makes and en-
forces the rules — the laws and the tacit understandings which
accompany them — and provides machinery for the maintenance
of civil order, the adjudication of disputes, the punishment of
transgressors, and the secular operation of the bureaucracy without which even the most illusory state would cease to have meaning. He ordains social change and stagnation and provides direction for the process of political development and decay. In
combination, this personalization of the power of the state fits the
Latin American syndrome and is associated with the permanent
instability that typifies politics in so many small, underdeveloped,
marginal nations.[3]

Duvalier fancies himself the Leviathan: He is the King of the
Proud, and nothing on earth is "to be compared with him. He is
made so as not to be afraid. He seeth every high thing below him;
and is King of all the children of pride. But because he is mor-
tall, and subject to decay, as all other Earthy creatures are; and
because there is that in heaven . . . that he should stand in fear
of, and whose Lawes he ought to obey," there are diseases and
causes of mortality.[4] But when rule of the king is absolute, and
sanctioned by might rather than by any divine or natural pre-
scription, then the king will be anxious and insecure even when
his psyche is not prey to paranoia or allied with a national re-
flex of suspicion. If the ruler is alone on a lofty pinnacle of

---

predatory state is more than a mere kleptocracy, to use the neologism of Stanislav
Andreski, *Parasitism and Subversion: The Case of Latin America* (New York, 1967),
62–69, where graft and corruption are institutionalized.

3 For "permanent instability," see Martin C. Needler, *Political Development in
Latin America: Instability, Violence, and Evolutionary Change* (New York, 1968),
30, 48, 157–158. More generally, see Huntington, *Political Order*, 3. It should be
noted that Kenneth E. Johnson's "Causal Factors in Latin American Political Instability," *Western Political Quarterly*, XVII (1964), 435–441, do not fit the Haitian
case with any precision.

4 Thomas Hobbes, *Leviathan* (London, 1651), Cap. XXVIII, 167. Original emphasis
removed.

power, has made its ascending slopes slippery with the blood of opponents, and reigns without reference to viziers, astrologers, or the advice of strong persons in his court, then he is apt to devote himself unremittingly to the pursuit and maintenance of power rather than to the beneficial and transformational utilization of that power. The state, in the hands of such a sovereign, becomes no more than a juggernaut of oppression, its energies being concentrated upon the liquidation of internal rivalry and the defense of borders, not the sharing of its mandate.

Duvalier, like contemporary autocrats (Chiang Kai-shek, whose photograph is prominently displayed behind Duvalier's desk, and Trujillo come to mind) and the despots of old (Cesare Borgia and the Visconti, among others), sits like a solitary spider in the middle of a finely spun web, each filament transmitting authority outward and intelligence inward. Survival consequently depends upon maintaining the centrifugal tendencies of the radia, of minimizing any circumferential or horizontal linkages, and of tugging here and then there on the lines without weakening the strength and the control of the innermost ring. In contemporary Haiti there are no intermediary structures of relevance, no hierarchies of importance, and no competing foci of institutional loyalty. Where they existed, they have been eliminated: Duvalier, as Trujillo was in the Dominican Republic,[5] is the only boss.

No one shares Duvalier's power or helps him to exercise it in anything other than a menial way. There is no oligarchy; Duvalier operates on his own, not on behalf of a claque as had his predecessors. He alone (like Haile Selassie in Ethiopia, Kamuzu Banda in Malawi, and others) decides whether the capital will be provided with new storm sewers, whether generators will be transported to the Peligre dam via Port-au-Prince or St. Marc, whether foreigners will receive economic concessions, local businessmen special favors, and ordinary Haitians exile permits. He personally examines and decides whether or not to authorize minor research projects, grants university degrees, selects the kind of material to be used for a new highway, and determines the orthography to be employed for literacy training in Creole.

5 Crassweller, *Trujillo*, 123.

From the beginning of Duvalier's tenure in office, observers noted that this detailed personal intervention imparted no added efficiency to the government. The president, wrote an editor of a Haitian newspaper, "bogs down in the minutiae he insists upon handling, and the last man to get his ear frames the directive. This can result in any number of people being sent in any number of directions on the same errand. When you add to this a great knack for selecting the wrong man for the wrong job, it becomes evident why the great crusade has never, as Duvalier admits, got off the ground." [6] It goes without saying that he makes the major decisions: who is to be taxed, who is to be tried in a court of law, who is to be promoted in the army, who is to be permitted to extort and in what amounts, and who is to be killed and who spared. Even in the international sphere, Duvalier makes policy as if he were the state, and without reference to his nominally responsible minister of foreign affairs or his various ambassadors. For example, he alone decided to startle the world by recognizing Biafra: when he was a student at the University of Michigan he became friendly with a Nigerian physician from what was Biafra; in 1969, when the physician arrived in Haiti, Duvalier was only too willing to honor their hoary friendship by making Haiti the fifth country, and the first outside of Africa, to afford Biafra diplomatic recognition. Without giving it much thought, he told his foreign minister to prepare the necessary protocol and to make a suitable announcement. In terms of impact, the gesture was meaningless, but to Duvalier Haiti is but an extension of his own personality, and the action — no matter how frivolous — might, he believed, at least demonstrate his own independence. This idiosyncratic assertion of independence, and the flouting of normal protocol, was demonstrated again in 1969 when he kept a visiting delegation of Barbadians, including the country's deputy prime minister (together with his own very embarrassed and frightened minister of foreign affairs), waiting nearly three hours for an audience. [7]

6 Grossberg, "Explosive Buffer," 84.
7 Unless otherwise attributed, the examples and conclusions presented in this chapter are derived from material contained in preceding chapters, or collected in person (by observation, participation, and interview) in Haiti during 1968 and 1969.

Since Barbot's time, no Haitian has shared significantly, if at all, in Duvalier's decision-making process. Even his chief gunmen and advisers are no more than functionaries (to call them lackeys is probably too strong); he delegates specific responsibilities only, never general supervision of programs or proposals. Among his cabinet ministers, Duvalier has high regard primarily for Clovis Désinor, who is more alert and knowledgeable than any of the others. The son of a well-known journalist, Désinor was born in 1914 in St. Marc and attended the national university. He joined the Griots and was a prominent member of Fignolé's Mouvement. During the late 1940's he was a civil servant in the ministries of health (where he knew Duvalier) and the interior. Later (during the Magloire administration), he became secretary-general of the presidential office and the ministry of foreign affairs and director of the national economic planning bureau. Now a *macoute* as well as minister of finance, Désinor manages to elicit Duvalier's consent for projects of mutual interest more often and more easily than his compatriots, but the scope of his own autonomy is only marginally wider and can be exercised with only slightly less caution than is theirs.

Unofficial counselors of the president, such as Gérard de Catalogne, the Corsican publicist, have far less demonstrable power and, because they well know the penalties of overenthusiasm and indiscretion, use what little influence they possess warily. Zacherie Delva, a middle-aged homosexual who is the *macoute* satrap of Gonaïves and the watchdog of the north, provides a sole exception to the general precept that no one, even parochially, may by his posture or activities dim the luster of Duvalier. No other sectional leader of the *macoutes* — neither André Simon in the southeast nor Mme. Max Adolphe (female *macoutes* are not uncommon, although most are men) in Port-au-Prince — has real power of a kind which could be transformed into a base for centripetal departures. The ease with which Duvalier in 1969 purged Eloüs Maître and Luc Désir, the two leading *macoutes* attached to the presidential palace, testified to their relative impotence. Until early 1969 it was generally thought that Mme. Francesca Foucard St. Victor, the president's domineering personal secretary (and sister of Luc-Albert Foucard, the director of tourism, who married Nicole Duvalier), would play a lasting and decisive role in affairs of state, but she was ousted when Marie-Denise and Max Dominique, the president's daughter and son-in-law, were allowed to return from exile. Marie-Denise took Mme. St. Victor's position and her husband strolled the corridors of the palace. Together, they had access to the president's ear, and may have had designs on the succession after his demise, but by 1970 their influence had faded and both were once again in exile.[8]

It has already been asserted that the predominant motive for Duvalier's acquisition of and maintenance of power is power itself.[9] Here power is defined broadly as a "deference value" — "to have power is to be taken into account in others' acts (policies)."[10] Power, to be sure, generates sources of enrichment which provide the wherewithal to feed the repressive forces without which the continued maintenance of power within the Haitian context would prove impossible. The personal enrichment of the head of state is not the primary goal of Duvalierism; if it were, leverage would exist which could be manipulated by opponents and envious supporters to subvert the juggernaut from within. Duvalier's predecessors (and Trujillo) were as interested in riches as in power, especially since displayed wealth provided a cultural definition of power and was recognizable as such within the elite circles which dominated Haitian political life. But the psychological needs of the great mass of Haitians who can never hope to accumulate wealth are more readily satisfied, for the reasons given in Chapter I, by sheer power. Although Duvalier is not a representative of the masses, he epitomizes their hunger for power in ways which would have been understood by Weber.[11] He is the "polit-

[8] For earlier references to these individuals, see 255 above. In mid-1969, Dominique, Simone Duvalier, and Jean-Claude Duvalier went to Paris while Marie-Denise remained, for a short time, in the palace. In early 1970 Duvalier forced Foucard to divorce Nicole. She was said to be interested in marrying Franz Adam, a young army lieutenant. Foucard and his sister fled to the United States. At about the same time, Marie-Denis went to Paris and Jean-Claude came home. Luckner Cambrone, out of power for several years, replaced Maître and Désir in the palace.
[9] See above, 213, 257.
[10] Laswell and Kaplan, *Power and Society,* 77.
[11] See H. H. Gerth and C. Wright Mills (trans. and eds.), *From Max Weber: Essays in Sociology* (New York, 1958), 180.

ical man" who "demands the maximization of his power in relation
to all his values, who expects power to determine power," but who
does not — as the proposition states — identify "with others as a
means of enhancing power position and potential." [12] Hobbes
knew the inclination of all mankind to be "a perpetuall and rest-
lesse desire of Power after power, that ceaseth only in Death. And
the cause of this, is not alwayes that a man hopes for a more intensive delight, than he has already attained to; or that he cannot be
content with a moderate power; but because he cannot assure the
power and means to live well, which he hath present, without the
acquisition of more." [13] For Duvalier we must read "sustain his
power" for "live well." Even so, Duvalier's love of power seems
more than a mere aberration of the normal quest.

Psychic needs and drives may obviously determine the hunger
for power that many individuals possess and of which the case of
Duvalier appears an extreme example. An evaluation of what we
know of his personality is therefore necessary. Yet it is idle to
pretend that his personality can be easily assessed without the
data derived from a complete psychological evaluation (were such
an evaluation conceivable). Popularly, he has often been described in gross terms as a paranoid and a megalomaniac. Paranoia is technically characterized by well-systematized, stable,
slowly developing delusions of persecution and/or grandeur.
There is intense suspicion and good contact with reality except in
the areas of well systematized delusion. There is little or no intellectual deterioration, and the elaboration of the delusion is
logically constructed so that if the basic premise is granted all
consequent thinking is reasonable. Megalomania often accompanies paranoia and is a product of infantile feelings of omnipotence
which are retained and recalled in later life. That Duvalier feels
omnipotent and often expatiates upon the extent and range of his
omnipotence seems well established. His complaint is also self-
validating, for he now is, within the range of his endeavors, truly
omnipotent. Megalomania has a variegated and complicated etiology: it can be associated with tertiary syphilis, a malady with

[12] Lasswell and Kaplan, *Power and Society*, 78.
[13] *Leviathan*, Cap. XI, 47.

which it was once thought that Duvalier was afflicted. But this connection is unlikely since tertiary syphilis is easily eradicated by penicillin, or as a by-product of penicillin treatments, which Duvalier may well have received for other medical reasons. Furthermore, persons harboring tertiary syphilis are usually incapable of making plans and decisions of any kind, a failing which Duvalier has never exhibited. If the search for a causal explanation of his megalomania is to prove successful, material on Duvalier's early years, which is now inaccessible, must be made available. Megalomania may be related to a failure to progress normally from the oral phase of development, but Duvalier's first became publicly apparent after his accession to the presidency (and before his first heart attack and coma)[14] when he was aged fifty.[15] There is, as has also been mentioned, paranoia in the majority of Haitians. It is, at least to a certain level, the norm. Thus it is possible to speculate that the unusual degree to which Duvalier may suffer from megalomania and paranoia is merely an accentuation of normal Haitian personality traits and gives his own dealings as a political man that sense of extra urgency. The combination of megalomania and paranoia — not unknown in the history of tyrants — would also give to his ceaseless worship of naked power the appearance of rationality.

The persons who knew Duvalier in the 1950's and before, and whose comments have already been reported,[16] all remembered him as someone who was withdrawn, vocally muted to the point of inaudibility, unassertive in public (despite his writings), very secretive and markedly unambitious, and totally lacking in affect. For psychoanalysts these are possible indicators of a schizoid personality. The outstanding characteristics of such a character disorder are aloofness, an inability to enter into warm interpersonal relationships, and the avoidance of direct contact with life. Schizoids show a strong dependence upon daydreaming and seek compensation and satisfaction in fantasies of glory and omnipotence.

14 See above, 220.
15 But for earlier expressions of megalomania, see Abderrahman, *Souvenirs d'Autre Fois, 1926–1948* (Port-au-Prince, 1968), 58. Abderrahman, which means "The Victorious," was the pen name of Duvalier.
16 Above, 177–179. See also Diederich and Burt, *Papa Doc*, 35, 56.

The pattern of their unsociability is discerned early, and is often accompanied by fearfulness, avoidance of competition, and severe emotional detachment. They are exceedingly shy, retiring, and hypersensitive, and are inclined at times to withdraw into intro-version. Yet they are incapable of fully appreciating the reactions of others. They are tense, highly individualistic, overabstract, and — in some ways — autistic. Adult schizoids are known to attempt to make reality of their fantasy; they often write extensively, and tend to begin large-scale projects which are never completed. There are delusions, and, if the disorder is severe, psychosis is a conceivable result.

Whatever the psychological factors driving Duvalier, his hold on power is maintained exclusively by terror, force, and the pre-vention of supplantive violence. As has been stressed repeatedly, there is no ideology which binds (or blinds) the masses, and the ruler himself is no rabble-rouser.[17] His very lack of a prepossess-ing physique, his softspokenness, and his attire do, however, lend him an air of mystery and, to some, imply a preternatural and therefore unchallengeable hold on power.[18] Duvalier is the kind of man who can sit stolidly and unemotionally through four- and five-hour parades (the last was in 1964) without once seeking to arouse the emotions of his audience of thousands. He is not a fly-whisk waving orator of the African mold, nor a messianic per-suader capable of seeming or promising to enrich the lives of his listeners. He rarely strays from the confines of his wing of the presidential palace, preferring to see his people — if he must — from the permanent reviewing stand erected between the anti-aircraft batteries on the palace lawn. Very occasionally he drives through the town, usually without prior announcement. He has not been in the north, in Cap Haitien or Gonaïves, since 1959, and he has probably not traveled to the southwest since the election campaign of 1957. He startled Haitians of all backgrounds when he began 1969 by driving furtively (between 3 and 10 A.M.) to St. Marc and Peligre. All consultations are held in his relatively small, high-ceilinged office, where he sits cloistered behind a massive

17 See above, 208, 256–257.
18 See Bastien, "Voudon and Politics," 60.

mahogany desk on which repose an open Bible, French periodicals, a photograph of his wife and family, and a white antique telephone. His chair conceals — among the cushions — a .357 magnum revolver, and there are *macoutes* behind the nearest door. (When journalists interview the president the *macoutes* often lounge about the inner chambers with loaded rifles or submachine guns.)

Duvalier, it is clear, is not interested in the masses, in uplifting them, in educating them politically, or in mobilizing them for the greater glory and security of the state and his own person. The massive propaganda machine beloved of commentators is a myth,[19] and the Parti d'Unité Nationale is an evanescent phenomenon of no particular importance even in the capital. Duvalier, more systematically than his predecessors, and with a greater degree of obsessive singlemindedness, relies for the maintenance of his system upon loyalties secured from a comparatively small number of Haitians by patronage, and from the remainder by fear. Like Hitler (and others), he successfully manipulates men, each of whom hopes to supplant the others by monopolizing the leader's confidence.[20] Without willing gunmen, and masses accustomed to subservience, Duvalier's canny ability to juggle Haitian political variables would avail him little.

In order to sustain his regime, Duvalier has created as totalitarian a state as can be achieved with the underdeveloped technology at his disposal.[21] Strictly speaking, however, Duvalier's Haiti is not a totalitarian state: like Trujillo's Dominican Republic and a number of African states, it lacks an official ideology "focused and projected toward a perfect final state of mankind," a single mass party, or a centrally directed economy. It satisfies only three other conditions: a system of terroristic police control, a monopoly of all means of effective mass communication, and a monopoly of effective armed combat.[22] Because of the relative inefficiency of

19 But see Edward Luttwak, *Coup d'Etat: A Practical Handbook* (London, 1968), 171.
20 See also Bastien, "Voudon and Politics," 57.
21 Rayford W. Logan and Martin C. Needler, "Haiti," in Martin C. Needler (ed.), *Political Systems of Latin America* (Princeton, 1964), 159.
22 Carl J. Friedrich and Zbigniew K. Brzezinski, *Totalitarian Dictatorship and Autocracy* (Cambridge, 1965; rev. ed.), 22.

the regime and its concentration upon short- rather than long-term gains, there has been no attempt to institute a process of thought control or mental indoctrination. However, dissent of all kinds has been prohibited and stifled by force whenever and under whatever circumstances it arose.

The local press consists of two major and six less important daily newspapers in the capital; it also has five weeklies of interest. The largest of the dailies rarely runs to more than six or eight large-size pages of eight columns. Nor by the most generous estimate is its paid circulation more than about 3000 daily. The front page of each of the newspapers is devoted almost exclusively to pronouncements by the president and other officials, or to long accounts of the reaction of foreigners to a Haitian diplomatic or other initiative. Important news from France or the United States often finds its way to the front pages. Most other foreign news is crowded onto the last two pages, in a series of small items from the agencies. Otherwise, the bulk of most of the dailies is devoted to long reports of cultural events, gossip, home economics, verbatim texts of presidential speeches, and news of sports. One major daily gives two or more full front-page columns to chatty and obsequious notes about particular tourists and returning foreign residents — the hotel and nightclub scene. There is little news of crime and virtually no mention of anything remotely connected with politics unless it emanates from official sources. There are the expectedly sycophantic editorials, some of which are supplied by the government. Duvalier subsidizes several of the dailies and weeklies, and supplies them all with allocations of newsprint. None can publish without his personal approval. It should be obvious that the Haitian press has no independence whatsoever, and individual writers deviate from the norm only at the risk of being eliminated. Similarly, the television station in Port-au-Prince, which beams American movies and presidential messages to several thousand homes for about four hours nightly, and the twenty-five independently owned medium-wave radio stations, which for the most part broadcast popular music,[23] avoid

23 There are three other radio stations owned and operated by evangelical missionary groups. They broadcast church music, services, and programs of home improvement.

any acts which could be construed as hostile by the regime. All private "ham" wireless transmitters are forbidden (as are all privately owned airplanes). In addition, incoming foreign publications are censored, if sporadically, the president himself often marking up offending issues of the *New York Times, Time,* etc. Outgoing news dispatches by foreigners are delayed or prohibited when necessary. And private mail is still read. But the state has insufficient resources regularly to jam the hostile daily radio broadcasts in Creole from Cuba.[24]

The *macoutes* remain the eyes, ears, and arms of the regime. Ivan the Terrible had his Oprichnina, a forerunner of Stalin's N.K.V.D., Hitler had the Gestapo, and tyrants — large and small, mad and sane — throughout history have relied upon bullyboys to attain and preserve personal monopolies of power. The ways in which Duvalier has used and continues to use the *macoutes* as instruments for the spread of terror have already been detailed.[25] They continue to extort and blackmail, to inform — many taxi drivers are *macoutes* — to keep the army under surveillance, to torture prisoners, and to maim and kill dissidents on order, or arbitrarily. They number, according to the best estimates (careful records, if kept, are unavailable), about 7500, of whom approximately 1500 constitute the hard core — the trusted killers — and are based in the presidential palace. The latter have been and are recruited for the most part from among the ranks of the semiliterate underprivileged (no composite biography is possible for want of even the most rudimentary data) of the capital and provincial towns. On or off duty all wear civilian suits with hip or shoulder holsters, but they are far less omnipresent, and far more restrained in public and when unprovoked, than they were a few years ago. They are consciously being held in check by the president, but more because of his success than because of any newly developed morality or sense of timing. The other 6000 *macoutes* are also less openly offensive, especially in the cities where they have even be-

---

24 Haitian exiles in the United States broadcast every morning in Creole from New York until pressure (from Duvalier?) and threats of violence directed toward the firm owning the rented transmitting facilities, combined with increased expenses, terminated the programs in 1968.
25 See above, 215–216, 227–229.

gun to function as a kind of labor brigade. Not all of this group
— which can be equated with the *Volontaires de la Sécurité Nationale* — are black, and mulattoes are among their more prominent leaders, but the ranks of the *macoutes* are composed largely
of otherwise unemployed or semi-employed illiterates, and only
under princelings like Delva are they capable of disciplined combat as well as individual violence.

Macoutes are everywhere. The army has its quota, as does the
civil service. There are *macoutes* in the printing works and on
the docks watching and supplementing the police. *Chefs de section* are now very often *macoutes*. So are many *vodun* priests or
their assistants. Even an august personality like the *prefect* of Cap
Haitien carries a revolver beneath his nicely starched white suit.
So does a sub-minister of agriculture or a statistician in the bank.
And all of these men carry their guns only with the permission of
the president. Duvalier chooses all of his retainers and henchmen
and commands their individual and direct loyalty. There are
macoute commanders and assistant commanders, and the usual
complement of men who give orders to other men, but there is no
national or even regional chain of command. Although Delva is
the "boss" of the north, the leading *macoute* in Cap Haitien (either
the *prefect* or the postmaster, depending on the time of year or
whim of the president) is expected to report directly to the president about his local area and to defer to Delva only when he himself is proximate. There is a pecking order which is respected
within localities, but not otherwise, and even within districts it
can be circumvented — if necessary — by seeking a direct audience with Duvalier. The position, status, and worth of any man is
necessarily vague, for by maintaining uncertainty Duvalier mag-
nifies his own power and lessens the likelihood of challenges from
within. He understands and makes good use of the great power
which is derived from manipulation and thus is able to influence
"the behavior of others without making explicit the behavior
which he thereby wants them to perform." [26]

Duvalier has used the weapons of purge, infiltration, and re-

---

[26] Herbert Goldhamer and Edward A. Shils, "Types of Power and Status," *American
Journal of Sociology,* XLV (1939), 172.

organization to weaken the army,[27] but three of its branches —
faute de mieux — still play critically important roles in his overall
strategy of security while the remainder is, since the *macoutes* are
untrained in the arts of warfare and lack sophisticated weapons,
Haiti's only bulwark against invasion or large-scale internal subversion. The 5000 men under General Constant, who was
brought up in Port-au-Prince and attended one of the best Roman
Catholic secondary schools there, include 400 officers. Eight full
colonels constitute the general staff, and Constant's deputy is
Colonel Jacques Laroche, a light-skinned confirmed Duvalierist
who has been in the army since 1939 (when he was seventeen),
has taken a degree in law and a diploma in ethnology from the
national university, is fluent in English and Spanish, has extolled
the regime in numerous pamphlets and supported it as the chief
prosecutor or judge at all of the important trials before military
courts since 1960, and has been assistant chief of staff since 1963.
Laroche is too close to Duvalier not to have made innumerable
enemies within the army and the ranks of the *macoutes,* but he is
able and not so unsophisticated in the ways of the world as General Constant, his nominal superior, and several fellow colonels.
There are four other full colonels on the headquarters staff:
Henry Namphy, in charge of personnel; Lecestre Prosper, intelligence; Kessler Blain, operations and logistics; and Roger St.
Albin, head quartermaster.

Colonel Georges Danache commands the 200-man air force with
its three DC-3's (C-47's), two C-45's, three F-51's, and three single-
engined (AT-6 or T-28) trainers. Colonel Octave Cayard was the
admiral of Haiti's minuscule coast guard — a buoy tender, a small
tanker, and several small patrol boats — or navy (like the air force,
it has been a part of the army since the Marine reorganization of
1924) before he fomented a mutinous and abortive shelling of the
palace in April 1970. (He and most of the coast guard fled to Puerto
Rico.) Colonel Frédéric M. Arty has, since the early 1960's, been
the capital's chief of police. He commands about 300 soldiers
called policemen. If somewhat more roughly, they perform the
tasks of policemen the world over, but only within the confines of

27 See above, 202–203, 214.

the capital. Outside of its boundaries there are about 550 rural policemen attached to the various *chefs de section,* and within the other towns the army proper assumes police-like functions whenever necessary.

The strength of these different sections of the army pales beside that of the two "elite" battalions upon which Duvalier relies (in addition to the *macoutes*) for security in case of attack. Colonel Gracia Jacques leads the palace guard, whose 700 members actually use the basement of the palace as a barracks and have traditionally made and unmade Haitian presidents. Behind the palace, in the yellow-painted Caserne Dessalines, are the 500 men in Colonel Breton Claude's "tactical battalion." [28] Both Claude and Jacques report directly to the president without following the normal military chain of communication, are consciously rivals for his favor, and, if they were to work together, are well placed to frustrate attempts by the *macoutes* or other groups within the army to overthrow Duvalier or determine his successor. Claude's battalion has been given a monopoly of modern weapons, and his men are widely thought to be the best trained and militarily most able within Haiti. The army has outdated weapons — most of the rifles, for instance, are Belgian Mausers, forty-year-old American M-1903's, and M-1917 Enfields — and has a limited supply of twenty-five-year-old M-3 carbines, submachine guns, machine guns, and mortars. What newer weapons exist are at Claude's disposal, as is the bulk of the available ammunition not otherwise sequestered by the president and stored somewhere in the palace.

In a situation of limited warfare, the neighboring Dominicans would have unquestioned superiority, and it is not inconceivable that the Haitian army would, if faced with full-scale combat, break down in the manner of the Congolese army during the 1960's. Nevertheless, the Haitian army represents a force sufficient to repel invasions of the kind that have been mounted by exiles, quell anything less than a full-scale internal rising, and, if unity can be achieved, intervene to decide the direction of Haitian history.

Since Haiti has always lacked the informal attitudes and behavioral expectations which could have supported the legitimate pos-

[28] See above, 203, 253.

session of political authority or sanctioned its peaceful transfer and, like nearly all of the other Latin American nations, has regularly ignored the provisions of her carefully drafted constitutions because they reflected aspirations rather than fundamental political realities, the absence of intermediary structures capable of articulating and aggregating the interests of the majority of Haitians, and of resisting the rise and curbing the excesses of a tyrannical dictatorship, comes as no great surprise.[29] The executive in Haiti has always ruled supreme, as much during the American occupation as before or since. The legislature (and the cabinet) and the judiciary have always been comparatively meaningless, never acting for long as significant checks on the authority of the executive. Duvalier has effectively emasculated the remaining power of these institutions and eliminated informally important ones — such as the organization of merchants, the students' union, and the Masonic lodges — as well. Overt expression of opposition in any of these sectors or in the bureaucracy has, of course, also been suppressed totally. None of the structural components of government is, in short, strong enough to serve as a source of countervailing power or, in the event of any radical alterations in the distribution of authority, to provide the means of durable continuity during a period of difficult transition.

The fifty-eight members of the Chamber of Deputies in most cases have no bases of support except those resulting from their association with the president.[30] More than 50 per cent of them belong to Haiti's social as well as her new ruling elite, and only a few are of peasant stock. The language of parliamentary discourse is still French. About twenty-five, so far as can be ascertained, are

[29] For the model of interest articulation and aggregation in a normally functioning stable polity, see Gabriel A. Almond, "A Functional Approach to Comparative Politics," in Gabriel Almond and James S. Coleman (eds.), *The Politics of the Developing Areas* (Princeton, 1960), 33–45. See also Lucian W. Pye, "The Non-Western Political Process," *Journal of Politics*, XX (1958), 469–475, 485–486; Hélio Jaguaribe, *Desenvolvimento Econômico e Desenvolvimento Político* (Rio de Janeiro, 1962), 78; Needler, *Instability*, 25, 47.

[30] Although a detailed survey of the backgrounds and attitudes of the deputies, cabinet officials, judges, military leaders, and major *macoutes* was prepared and cooperation elicited from Haitian intellectuals and several of the potential respondents, it could be distributed only with the authorization of the president, who ignored various requests. Thus we lack more than randomly acquired information (from a number of interviews) and impressions of the composition of Haiti's political elite. This is not, however, the "political elite" of Eisenstadt, *Empires,* 116.

macoutes or allied to men influential in the *macoutes*. Most deputies reside in Port-au-Prince and, even if they possess homes in the areas which they represent, visit their constituencies only rarely. The most conscientious welcome their constituents in Port-au-Prince, visit parts of their districts monthly, and try to intercede on behalf of groups or individuals who are in difficulty with Duvalier or the *macoutes,* or who seek physical improvements usually provided by a central government — like schools, wells, or roads. In this way the more responsible or acquisitive deputies perform a recognizable political function in a clientage-type society; they use informal networks of influence (most deputies know the president and have become deputies only because he could thus pay off old political debts)[31] to redress grievances or ameliorate the conditions under which their constituents live. When the chamber meets, it does so only in order to ratify legislation put before it by the executive or, as has happened so often, to declare its impotence openly by delegating its powers to the president.

Latin American constitutions are "verbally honored, repeatedly cited, and promulgated anew to justify each revolution retroactively." [32] It is the same with their elaborate, codified bodies of law. Haiti, which makes use of the Napoleonic Code in a number of modern and locally adapted recensions, plus a version of the "punitive articles" of the U.S. Navy regulations for trials under martial law, is equally culpable. Despite decades of legal sophistication and a historically influential and active bar, the Haitian judiciary is now so accustomed to political direction as to make discussion of legal values meaningless and insulting. It is possible to explain the status and functions of the civil courts, from the smallest presided over by a *juge de paix* in a rural village or a corner of a town, through the thirteen *tribunaux civile* in the major cities, to the four appeals courts in Port-au-Prince, Cayes, Gonaïves, and Cap Haitien, to the supreme court. These courts deal with ordinary civil and commercial matters and with what in

---

31 One deputy owned a radio station and backed Duvalier wholeheartedly during the campaigns of 1957. He has a photograph of Duvalier which is inscribed "You are my Goebbels."
32 Needler, *Instability,* 25.

Anglo-American law would be termed misdemeanors and minor felonies. There is another hierarchy of courts in which criminal matters are heard, from the village and town level directly to the supreme court. According to the constitution, the executive cannot tamper with or direct the decisions of the various courts, but whenever states of emergency are declared (which is frequently) the normal rules of justice are suspended and the president convokes *ad hoc* military tribunals responsible to him. Furthermore, since judges are appointed by the executive for short terms, who would dare render a decision — even in the most trivial civil matter — which could possibly displease the president, or local officials with his ear? [33]

Presidents of Haiti before Duvalier limited the extension of their sway to the politically important urban areas, but since 1957 the direction of government has grown more centralized. Cities and towns, and in some areas villages, are nominally run by communally elected *magistrats* and *assesseurs*. Except in the smallest hamlets, the selection of such local officials is routinely made or sanctioned by Duvalier. In the rural areas the *chefs de section* have traditionally been despots, appointed by the local military commander; under Duvalier little has changed except the method of appointment and the kind of person selected. No longer need he be someone of pre-existing importance.[34] No longer, too, is there as sharp a separation between the chain of military command — from the lieutenant colonels commanding a military district through the commandants of subdistricts to the *chefs de section* — and that of civil authority — from the minister of the interior through his provincial *prefects* to the communal *magistrats*. The existence of the *macoutes* has also confused normal lines of authority — precisely the kind of situation which pleases an archmanipulator like Duvalier.

The cabinet, to complete this survey of the formal institutions

---

[33] The above is derived from a number of interviews with practicing lawyers and retired justices. A similar description can be found in Jean-Claude Garcia Zamor, *La Administracion Publica en Haiti* (Guatemala City, 1966), 71–72. See also Wingfield, "Haiti," 218.

[34] See also Richard P. Schaedel, "Preface," in Courlander and Bastien, *Religion and Politics,* xii; Comhaire, "The Haitian 'Chef de Section,'" 620–621.

of government, exists as a façade. Except for Désinor, it is composed of nonentities. Some of its present members, and Léonce Viaud, the minister of education from 1961 to 1968 and now the rector of the university, have been closely associated with the president since their days together as secondary school pupils in Port-au-Prince (at the Lycée Pétion), in the Groupes des Griots, or as followers of Estimé. None is young and innovative, none — including Désinor — has independent redoubts of power, and all must rise or fall with the president. None has served the president continuously since 1957, although Paul Blanchet, in 1969 minister of coordination and information, held that post from 1959 to 1962, from 1964 to 1965, and from late 1968. Désinor, who entered the government in 1958 as under secretary of commerce, became minister of commerce in early 1959, was ousted in late 1959, reinstated in 1960, omitted in 1963, reinstated in 1964 as a minister without portfolio, and then made minister of finance in 1965 — a position he retains. Aurèle A. Joseph, the minister of the interior and national defense, returned to office in 1967 after an absence of five years. Except for 1963, René Chalmers has been Haiti's foreign minister continuously since 1961. Simon Desvarieux, in 1969 a minister without portfolio, was minister of justice in 1961, 1962, and 1967, and ambassador to the Vatican from 1963 to 1967. Before Lebert Jean-Pierre became minister of commerce and industry in 1965, a position he maintained through 1969, he had been the administrator of the national bank. André Théard, in 1969 minister of agriculture and natural resources, entered office in 1958 as minister of commerce, industry, and finance, was dropped in 1959, was minister of agriculture from 1960 through 1963, and then became ambassador to the United States. Rameau Estimé, a president of the Chamber of Deputies, became minister of justice in 1963, a position he held until 1967, when he was imprisoned in Fort Dimanche for two months. In late 1968 he again became minister of justice. Raoul Lespinasse has served as minister of public works, transport, and communications only since 1967. Max Adolphe, husband of the leading female *macoute,* became minister of public health in 1968. In 1968 Frédéric Kebreau was appointed minister of education.

None of these men is in a position to make decisions or run his ministry independently of the president. This is not a peculiarly Haitian failing, but in Haiti cabinet ministers are more obviously ciphers and placemen than, for example, in Malawi, a comparably sized and impoverished country with an autocratic president. There, however, Dr. Banda permits the demonstrably competent to exercise a decision-making function within agreed and expanding limits. In Haiti it is wiser not to act than to act in error. It is a wonder that anything ever gets done, for ministers are used primarily as front men and foils. They are, however, permitted to discover and milk their own sources of additional remuneration. This is a surprising zone of *laissez-faire* which, however, fits into the Haitian and Duvalierist pattern.

It is perhaps obvious why Duvalier, having successfully routinized the use of enforcement terror,[35] suppressed all civil liberties, made nullities of potential personal and institutional rivals, and rebuffed five attempted invasions — in short, having fully justified his own pretensions to omnipotence — should now rule Haiti more securely and serenely than ever before. In 1970 Haiti had achieved a noticeable, if subdued, stability. Admittedly this was the stability of permanent instability, but, having reigned for so long and survived so many possible crises — such as his illness in mid-1969 — Duvalier had also achieved a measure of legitimacy. That is — and its enunciation seems like a contradiction in terms — he and his regime had begun, in a curious, convoluted fashion, to "satisfy" and be accepted by Haitians. It was better than no government at all, and more desirable in many eyes than the chaos of a revolution. It had also become less repressive — there were fewer Haitians in Fort Dimanche and the other prisons. And the Haitians who remained at home, for one reason or another refusing or being unable to emigrate, had learned to endure, to regard Duvalier as monstrous but ineluctably theirs and, after all the hard years, bearable.

This was the legitimacy of a Salazar, a Trujillo, a Somoza, or a Stroessner — of rulers who had so fully become father figures (a particularly apt analogy considering the nature of Haitian child

35 See above, 227.

rearing) that their removal or demise would evoke ambivalent
fears, feelings of great loss, and elemental insecurity, and occasion
a vacuum of legitimacy. This is not to say that the elite — almost
to a man — and most Haitians of some sophistication who are not
parts of the ruling machine, would not *also* welcome a change and
the overthrow of Duvalier, if only they could be assured of the
benevolence of his successor. There is a sense in which the elite,
disenchanted with Duvalier as they doubtless are, fear (and presume) that he will (and can only) be succeeded by someone
equally harsh, if possibly slightly less odious. Such is the Haitian
way.

These conclusions are necessarily based upon conversations and
interviews with a nonrepresentative but relatively large sample
of the elite. In the absence of the systematic attitude surveys that
— for the obvious reasons — were completely out of the question,
they may be regarded as suggestive rather than valid in any specifically predictive sense. Even so, with regard to elite opinion,
these conclusions have a certain credibility. More decisive for the
future of Duvalier and Haiti, however, are the views and visceral
feelings of the great mass of Creole-speaking peasants and ordinary men and women of the country. The president claims widespread support from this class of Haitians and, numerically if not
politically, they are the ultimate judges of legitimacy. In order to
evaluate their opinions, a short, twenty-eight-category questionnaire was administered covertly (that is, without the knowledge
or approval of the government) in Creole to fifty Haitians resident
in rural districts of both northern and southern Haiti (thirty-four
lived in the West Province). This is a tiny and, statistically, in-
valid sample of non-elite opinion. Because the interviewers posed
questions concerning legitimacy and, indeed, asked questions at
all, they necessarily were constrained to be extraordinarily cir-
cumspect. They were able to collect only fifty interviews, and the
interviewees were chosen both because, *a priori,* they seemed
representative and because they were available.[36] (That is, neither
army, *macoutes,* nor informers were within earshot; interviews
were conducted atop buses, in fields, along highways, etc.)

[36] As far as can be ascertained, this was the first political attitude survey ever attempted in rural Haiti.

Of the 50 respondents, 21 were peasant farmers, 3 were laborers, 12 worked in service industries, 7 were artisans, 5 worked for the government, and 2 were students. Only 13 could be classified as middle class or elite. Twenty, in age, were between 36 and 50, 13 were over 50, and 13 between 25 and 35. One respondent was under 25. Twenty-seven claimed to be able to read and write both French and Creole, although only 12 had spent more than 9 years in school. They were non-parochial, that is, they were acquainted with town life on the basis of more than two visits a year to Port-au-Prince or another large city (32) and the ownership of a radio (29). In other words, this sample was weighted more heavily than would probably be representative toward the "modern" end of any rural scale. The respondents were unusually literate and educated, particularly for middle-aged Haitian rural males (there were only three female respondents). Farmers were disproportionately few. As a group, they were surprisingly non-parochial.

Because of cultural differences, the decisive questions consciously were phrased simply, even naïvely. The respondents were asked whether they judged themselves better or worse off (materially and generally) than they had been five and ten years before. Only one, an elderly subsistence farmer with fewer than 9 years of schooling, asserted that he was neither better nor worse off. Only 16 of the others said that they were better off; in this group the students, artisans, and government employees predominated. Nineteen (all but 2) of the farmers and 9 of the 12 service employees felt that they were worse off. This category included 30 of the 36 persons who had been classified as "non-elite" and 16 of the 21 persons aged 36 to 50. The better-educated members of the sample said that they were better off. Of the persons who reported that they were worse off, 9 (the largest single aggregate) said, in answer to an open-ended question, that they would like the central government to assist them by improving the roads. Six asked for improved agricultural services, and four wanted employment. Of those who were better off, four asked for roads and four for improved schools.

"Sometimes," each interviewee was asked, "outsiders invade Haiti. If the invaders came near your village, would you join

them, oppose them, or do nothing?" [37] Two either failed to comprehend the question or refused to answer, no one said that he would
help the invaders, 27 said that they would oppose them, and 21 said
that they would do nothing — that they would wait to see what
happened. The government employees (including one *macoute*)
all said that they would oppose the invaders; the two students
opted for neutrality. The other occupational categories were almost equally divided, as were the respondents when broken down
by class (although 9 of the 13 "elite" respondents agreed to oppose
the invaders), by age, by education (the literate were 2–1 in opposition and the illiterate 2–1 neutral), parochialism (although
the less parochial were marginally opposed to the invaders), and
according to their province of residence or whether or not they
thought conditions in Haiti had improved or declined (two-thirds
of those who said that their conditions had improved were willing
to oppose the invaders).

Only 8 of the respondents said that they "knew" the president
in the sense that they had come into contact with him or perceived
him through tertiary acquaintance. Five lived in the West Province, 6 were of the elite, 4 worked for the government, all were
over thirty-six, all were literate, 5 reported that their conditions of
life were better, and 7 positively "liked" (approved of) Duvalier
(the other respondent refused to answer this question).

The answers to the questionnaire accorded well with previous
hypotheses. Worsening of conditions in the countryside was reported to be perceptible; very few "knew" their president (nearly
all "knew" their *chef de section, macoute* boss, and deputy); and,
although no one declared that he would join the invaders, a reasonably large number of the respondents predicted that they
would do nothing if the government were attacked. They would,
implicitly, avoid making decisions or taking sides. "Tell us who is
going to win," some asked. This impression of caution, passivity,
and true prudence is heightened when the open-ended responses
of the persons who said they would positively oppose the invaders

[37] The ambiguity contained in "outsiders," meaning Haitian exiles returning with
or without the help of others, is apparent, but the translation into Creole was
intended to eliminate purely patriotic responses.

are examined. Sixty per cent of this group said that they would either attack "or do nothing." It was expected of them by the government (and, by extension — they thought — perhaps by the interviewer) that they would defend the regime, but, if possible, they would be only too pleased to avoid this exaction and would happily sit on the sidelines. Few showed enthusiasm for their predicted role as protectors of the government, and, in some instances, although they should be given little weight, the interviewer noted that he doubted whether the respondent really intended his posture of opposition to be taken literally. In fact, the primary finding of the survey is that Duvalier and Duvalierism are neither strikingly legitimate nor illegitimate. They exist, and peasants and their compatriots are prepared, essentially, to co-exist. The dominant impression is that the central government affects the lives of the very parochial marginally, at least in ways which are not seen as being especially original, and that while there is no overwhelming enthusiasm for the present government, there also is no startling disenchantment. All Haitian governments are grasping and oppressive, and prudent rural folk simply try to keep out of harm's way.[38]

This attitude, if it may truly be attributed to the majority of Haitians — and whether it is termed an intelligent learned response (a laboratory rat avoids pressing the levers which produce shocks), a system-induced coping mechanism, submissiveness reminiscent of slavery, apathy produced by nutritional deficiencies, or sheer political atrophy — helps to explain why Duvalier has survived so long, why there have been no agrarian revolts, why he has not been assassinated, why invaders have failed to elicit support, why his tactics of terror have proved so efficacious and the *macoutes* have largely gone unchallenged, and why it is unlikely that he will be overthrown from within. Haitians clearly lack the subjective and political competence; they do not believe that they can — that it is possible to — influence the decisions of government, or that they can better their own environment by appealing

[38] See also Roland Wingfield and Vernon J. Parenton, "Class Structure and Class Conflict in Haitian Society," *Social Forces*, XLII (1965), 340, 345; Simpson, "Social Structure," 645.

to the government.[39] "The government is something for the people in the cities," said a Portuguese farmer recently, using a formulation of words that any Haitian, or southern Italian peasant, would understand.[40] Haitians know from childhood that authority is rarely responsive and that deviance is dangerous; only obedience is rewarded. They lack the self-assertiveness "to take the sustained action necessary to reorder their social situation." [41] *Au fond,* what at present is totally absent among Haitians is an awareness that their relative deprivation is capable of being assuaged. They are a rare contemporary example of the historically common phenomenon of a people who are accustomed to adjusting their expectations downward as their capabilities decline. They have never known lasting collective improvement and have become so inured to misery that even a prolonged decline across the subsistence threshold does not occasion the violence inherent in a society with stable or improving conditions.[42]

The intensity of discontent, and the ability and willingness to alleviate it "seems to be in inverse proportion to the distance from the object fervently desired." [43] Conditions, we can also suggest, must be improving before change is perceived to be possible, a postulate which studies of the French Revolution — to choose only the best known — bear out. If the goal is remote, and there is no sudden rise in aspiration level, spontaneous revolt is unlikely and will almost certainly fail to be sustained. If the possibility of effecting change is perceived to be remote, even the most charismatic figure will have difficulty (unlike Castro) recruiting substantial numbers of followers willing to risk their lives by fomenting rebellion. This is the Haitian condition.

Haiti and Haitians residing in Haiti fall so far below the threshold of revolution that it is reasonably safe to presume that Duva-

39 Gabriel A. Almond and Sidney Verba, *The Civic Culture: Political Attitudes and Democracy in Five Nations* (Princeton, 1963), 181–182, 214–221.
40 Richard Eder, "Apathy Evident on Salazar Issue," *New York Times,* September 23, 1968. For southern Italy, see Edward C. Banfield, *The Moral Basis of a Backward Society* (Chicago, 1958), 17, 33. But Haiti cannot be understood exclusively in terms of Banfield's formulation of "amoral familism."
41 Needler, *Instability,* 57.
42 I owe this formulation to Ted Robert Gurr, in a letter of December 2, 1969.
43 Eric Hoffer, *The True Believer* (New York, 1951), 28.

lier will not be toppled by a revolt of the masses, or — for other reasons connected with the effectiveness of his apparatus of terror — an attack (or assassination) by the elite. There are no free or potentially free labor unions or syndicates which could put pressure upon the regime. Nor are there underground political parties of significance. In theory, Haitian exiles in sufficient number could overthrow the present government from without. Given modern armaments, ample logistical support, administrative competence, and determination, they would not need the backing or assistance of the masses to topple Duvalier, disperse the *macoutes*, and neutralize the army. From the masses they would require what they can easily obtain — passivity. But at present it is unlikely that the existing organizations of exiles can on their own amass the matériel and provide the competence necessary for success. The Haitian Coalition, based in New York, has fewer than 3000 members in North America, but claims a network of cells within Haiti.[44] In 1969 it had a yearly budget of $60,000. Some of its leading members were involved in a training camp in 1968 in the Bahamas, but the organization itself asserts no responsibility for any of the recent invasions or attempted invasions of Haiti. (Cayard, however, was an active sympathizer.) The Coalition, which is Western- and democratically-oriented and was established in 1965, is the successor to several earlier anti-Duvalier alliances formed by the supporters of Déjoie, Magloire, and Jumelle. The leadership of the Coalition is now in the hands of younger Haitians who would not want to return any of the older politicians to power. President Magloire, who lives in New York, has glaucoma and is no longer seriously interested in or hoping for a return to prominence;[45] although President Fignolé lives in Brooklyn, he and the Coalition have little time for each other; and Déjoie is dead. The Coalition also professes to be patient. It realizes that poorly prepared invasions are counterproductive, and only bolster Duvalier's pretensions. Its leaders, who include Raymond Joseph, an evangelically trained graduate student of anthropology, ex-Lieutenant Roland Magloire, Joseph L. Déjean, a lawyer, and

44 Interview with Raymond Joseph, secretary of the Coalition, March 18, 1969.
45 Interview with President Magloire, April 21, 1969.

ex-Colonel Robert Bazille, of the staff of the O.A.S., believe that
their best hope of success is to educate exiles and cadres within
Haiti slowly and to husband the strength of their movement until
Duvalier dies or is somehow overthrown, or until there are the
kinds of cataclysmic occurrences which can be diverted to the advantage of the Coalition. Theirs is a policy of prudence.

Several other groups, not organizations, of Haitian exiles exist.
(The majority of Haitians are in exile for economic rather than
political reasons, and most — whether to protect relatives still in
Haiti or from personal fear or detachment — refrain from plotting.) [46] Their memberships constantly shift and are recruited
from the ranks of former military officers and recent, young, and
semiskilled Haitian emigrés. They are usually organized for a
specific purpose — the fomentation of supplantive violence —
and nearly always are intended to be vehicles for the return to
power and the dominance of particular individuals. The invasions of Haiti have nearly all been of this type, as was the recent
bombing attack directed by ex-Colonel René J. Léon. He had
earlier been implicated in connection with a secret training camp
for Haitians in the Florida Everglades, which was raided early in
1969 by the Monroe County police, and was said to be backed from
Montreal by the Movement of Democratic Patriots of Haiti.[47]

Whether or not Duvalier has in fact eradicated the underground Haitian Communist movement,[48] there are clusters of
Marxist-thinking Haitians in Montreal, Paris, Mexico City, Caracas, and Havana who would be pleased to help overthrow Duvalier.
Most stem from the ranks of the intelligentsia and operate as individuals. In Cuba the number of Haitians (most are cane cutters
who failed to return to their homeland and are now assimilated)
is sufficient to mount an invasion — if the Castro government were
not loath to embroil itself in such an adventure.[49] Cubans do,

[46] For the exile predicament, see Wingfield, "Haiti," 264.
[47] New York Times, March 13, 1969; Long Island Press, June 18, 1969. See also
above, 255. In 1970 he was sentenced to a prison term of three years "on charges
of violating United States neutrality laws" (New York Times, February 27, 1970).
[48] See above, 255. For the earlier role of Communism in Haiti, see Wingfield,
"Haiti," 258–262.
[49] The government of Cuba failed to respond to a series of requests for permission
to visit and talk with Haitians in Cuba.

however, beam three hours of propaganda daily to Haiti, and, given new developments there, it is not unlikely that Castro would facilitate the transfer of Cuban experience to Haiti. The leading Haitian in Cuba is René Dépestre, an embittered but very capable poet and demagogue who also is an exponent of black power. "I did not choose to be born in this false century," he writes, "to be part of the body of this ugly earth; I came after joy had died . . . but one day love will come with a kiss and lift me up from the mud." [50] But it is not known how influential or determined he is, or the extent of his backing. The involvement of large numbers of Soviet-directed Communists within or outside of Haiti remains unlikely, although in mid-1969 Tass announced the formation of the Parti Unifié des Communistes Haitiens from the Parti d'Entente Populaire and the Parti Populaire de Liberation Nationale.[51]

Duvalier's attitude toward Communism can be stated rather simply and baldly. Like Trujillo, he has opposed Communism only for the same reasons that he has opposed every political influence which was not his own — because its strength and appeal, and its discipline, are a threat to his own power. Those aspects of Communism which do not threaten him personally, however, and individual Communists who have assured him of their neutrality are tolerated.

What is certain is that the short-run prospects for violently induced change are negligible unless there is massive outside assistance, or elements within the army or the *macoutes* decide to strike preventively against other military personnel who are suspected of preparing a *putsch* or are believed to be serious rivals for power. In neither of the last two cases would the perpetuators be concerned with doing more than supplanting Duvalier. Of the anti-Duvalierists, only the Communists can claim to be acting in accord with a carefully thought-out program of social reform. The leaders of the Coalition, although they implicitly favor a reorientation of Haiti's political, social, and economic framework, have

---

[50] René Dépestre, *Gerbe de Sang* (Port-au-Prince, n.d.), 69.
[51] For the earlier labels of these parties, see Gérard R. Latortue, "Tyranny in Haiti," *Current History*, LI (1966), 351.

not as yet articulated it fully or in any kind of recognizably workable form. Furthermore, they, no less than the other opponents of Duvalier, realize that following any assumption of power in Haiti they would necessarily be compelled by circumstances and the structure of politics to rule arbitrarily for a period of several years.

Haiti is not ready for representative government. The necessary ingredients — support in informal attitudes, functional mechanisms for the articulation and aggregation of the interests of the diverse components of society, subjective and political competence, and what Erikson calls basic trust (the acceptance of the self as an integrated identity and the related ability to retain confidence in oneself when confronted by threats from without) are missing.[52] (At a less profound but equally significant level, Haitian leaders have failed to exhibit behavior which, put most simply and tritely, may be called "honorable." As a Nigerian politician of international prominence recently wrote of his own country: "Here . . . such a sense of honour as is exhibited by public men in Britain and in most civilized countries is unknown.") [53] For the long run the absence of these components, and of any drastic changes in the predominant patterns of child rearing, the level of mass politicization, and the art of mutual association, will make highly unlikely the development of modes of governance drastically different from the present.[54] When Duvalier goes, naturally or otherwise, a brief period of chaos and unsettlement will be followed by the installation of a dictatorship, if hopefully less bestial in its methods, comparable to that of the present, and similar to those of the past. The potential for real change is limited — whether or not someone from within like Désinor, Claude, Laroche, or Dominique, or someone now in exile, succeeds in replacing Duvalier — until such time as Haiti is transformed into a politically viable society.

52 Erikson, *Childhood and Society,* 248–249; above, 20–21.
53 Obafemi Awolowo, *The People's Republic* (London, 1968), 285.
54 The Haitian case makes nonsense of some recent generalizations about tyranny, notably those of Maurice Latey, *Tyranny: A Study in the Abuse of Power* (London, 1969). "Tyranny," he writes, "is, so to speak, a nervous break-down of the body politic. Society succumbs to stresses that are too great for it" (278). In Haiti tyranny is a natural outgrowth of the social and political matrix.

The possibilities for effecting such change from without are limited. They may be stated succinctly:

1) International organizations or the United States and other powers could decide to support Duvalier more vigorously than at present. Only the government of South Africa, however, and for perverse reasons, might find this course of action attractive.

2) The United Nations, the Organization of American States, the United States, the Soviet Union, and the other governments and associations, all of which can rightfully concern themselves with pockets of injustice, inhumanity, instability, poverty, and backwardness in the world, and which tend to spend their working days elaborating and discussing methods of improving the lot of the peoples of the globe, could nonetheless view the problems of Haiti as intractable and, because they have so many equally pressing and more readily resolved conundrums with which to deal, refuse to give the present and future of Haiti more than passing attention.

The adoption of this second and most seductive alternative would accord well with many notions of opportunity cost, the logic of international parsimony, and the prudence of common sense. It would also satisfy most articulate Haitians. They welcome foreign aid, but abhor such strings as may be attached, and urgently desire to retrieve their own misfortunes without outside interference or any action as humiliating as an intervention or an occupation. "The Haitian situation is not hopeless," wrote one exiled intellectual. "We do not need any international trusteeship or occupation. Haitians can solve their problems if they find a certain understanding from their friends all over the world." [55]

Even so, and conscious of such widely held sensitivities, it probably behooves the governments of America, collectively through the O.A.S., and the United States separately, as the international parties most sensitive to and affected by Haiti's present squalor, to consider what, if anything, can be done to alleviate and eradicate it. The purely commercial involvement of the United States is not particularly large. In 1968 Haiti supplied the United States with a mere .08 per cent of its imports, and took only .07 per cent

[55] Gérard R. Latortue, "Is Haiti Hopeless?" *San Juan Review*, II (March 1966), 28.

of its exports. Of the total United States foreign direct investment, Haiti accounted for only .08 per cent, and there were no individual large investors.[56] Nor is Haiti of particular diplomatic significance. She is isolated within the Latin American community, and, unlike Cuba and despite her own diplomatic overtures, the new nations of Africa have disassociated themselves from her because of the nature of the present regime and the absence of any real affinities. France now has no particular stake in or involvement with her onetime colony. Despite Duvalier's espousal of black power, the black community in the United States has not aligned itself with his cause. In short, there is no politically articulate or economically potent body of opinion supporting Duvalier.

Nevertheless, the United States cannot simply ignore the Haitian problem. Haiti is still of interest strategically to planners in the Pentagon even though the desire to protect the transit of shipping through the Windward Passage is no longer as overriding as it once was because of overwhelming United States air- and seapower.[57] The government of the United States worries most about the possibility of its international antagonists gaining a foothold 600 miles (and a few missile minutes) from Miami. The United States also wants to prevent the coming to power in Haiti of a Castro-type government which would export revolution to other parts of the hemisphere. Furthermore, the United States is anxious to safeguard its apparent gains in the Dominican Republic. If Haiti were to harbor elements hostile to the Dominican experiment, then the United States (and the O.A.S.) would necessarily become involved, and anxious, even though such a threat would probably serve an integrative function in the Dominican Republic. Otherwise, the United States and the members of the O.A.S. can only assert an overriding humanitarian responsibility for the great mass of Haitians, and for the future of their decaying country.

[56] U.S. Bureau of the Census, *U.S. General Imports,* FT 155, 1968; U.S. Bureau of the Census, *U.S. Exports,* FT 455, 1968; Manigat, *Haiti of the Sixties,* 17; U.S. Bureau of the Census, *Statistical Abstract of the United States,* 1968, 791.
[57] But see Major General Roland H. del Mar, "Strategic Characteristics of the Caribbean," in A. Curtis Wilgus (ed.), *The Caribbean: Its Hemispheric Role* (Gainesville, 1967), 155–160.

3) On the economic plane, the O.A.S., Canada, and the United States can markedly increase the supply of their aid (for some of the projects enumerated in the previous chapter, and following the strategy enunciated there) in the hope that some of it will prove productive, have a multiplier effect, and gradually seep down to the level of the people they are attempting to help.[58] It would be likely, however, that under present circumstances new funds and goods would, at best, be wasted, and, more probably, be diverted to the coffers of Duvalier's regime. The injection of larger amounts of aid could not at present or in the immediate future be supervised sufficiently strictly to ensure that it would not be wasted.

4) If the O.A.S. and the United States (and other powers) want to sponsor progress in Haiti they must first find a means of altering the motives and methods of Haitian government. In order to accomplish such a short-term redefinition of official priorities Duvalier himself, and his entire entourage, must be removed from power. Given the military superiority of the members of the O.A.S., and the unlikelihood of more than official and momentary resistance within the country, an internationally organized and equipped force could intervene and occupy Haiti within days. It could establish an administration capable of governing effectively and justly. But it would be forced to contemplate an occupation of lengthy duration. What is more, invasions and occupations of this kind would never be sanctioned by the O.A.S., and for any individual member state to contemplate such gross interference in the affairs of another is unthinkable. Certainly public opinion within the United States would find such action — no matter how beneficent the motivation — unwarranted.

5) Admittedly, neither the O.A.S. nor the United States would

---

58 John N. Plank, "Neighborly Relations in the Caribbean," in *ibid.*, 168, suggests "the conscious use of trade policy as an instrument of regional development." Basically, he advocates differential access to the North American market and, therefore, "a sharp departure from what is now regarded as desirable international trade practice." He recognizes the practical difficulties, and the extent to which such a policy would violate U.S. commitments to the General Agreement on Tariffs and Trade. But he literally sees "no other way out" for the lands of the Caribbean. Unfortunately, for Haiti anyway, even agricultural preferences on a grand scale would not be expected to result in dramatic economic advances, and the costs for United States trade would be as large as the benefits would be minimal. The reasons are set out in the previous chapter.

need to intervene openly. They could surreptitiously sponsor an armed incursion by exiled Haitians. If such a filibustering expedition were supported by large outlays of foreign capital, supplied with abundant modern arms, and carefully trained by one of the more efficient American armies or assault teams, the likelihood of success would be high. But no American government would want this kind of precedent to be established in the hemisphere; few are sufficiently secure to condone, much less participate in, such a venture. Furthermore, no matter how covert the international or national backing, the major role played by outsiders would — as nearly always happens with these kinds of ventures — be discovered. Among statesmen, only a determined crusader against tyranny or a rash international speculator would in this way risk the moral outrage of his own citizens. And he would do so only if a stable, friendly government could be assured — which it could not and cannot.

6) The concerted imposition of economic or diplomatic sanctions (if it were possible to develop a broad general policy of sanctions acceptable to the members of the O.A.S.) might harm Haiti, but it is unlikely, for the reasons advanced earlier, that it would bring about either the demise of Duvalier or radical improvements in his methods of rule. The results of the imposition of sanctions against Cuba and Rhodesia have hardly proved commensurate with the efforts and the propaganda involved. Even if Haiti were brought to an absolute halt economically, international airlines ceased bringing tourists, American and European brokers stopped handling sugar, coffee, sisal, and other exports, and the flow of imports were curtailed, Duvalier would endure and, by intensifying the application of the instruments of terror, make his people pay for foreign-induced dislocations. Furthermore, sanctions often prove counterproductive: in this case Duvalier would be expected to appeal successfully to the pride and patriotism of his people in the midst of what would be called an attack by racist imperialists. Then, too, as the nations of Eastern Europe and some of Asia have taken advantage of the sanctions against Rhodesia to purchase commodities inexpensively, so these same countries would probably try to trade with and ob-

tain diplomatic bases in Haiti. In this connection Duvalier, it need hardly be emphasized, would have few scruples.

7) Once it is accepted that neither the O.A.S. nor the United States is or is apt to be (or should be, for practical as well as moral reasons) willing to depose Duvalier, then those who are anxious about the future of Haiti must prepare for his peaceful departure. He may become sufficiently infirm to relinquish power to a hand-picked successor, someone like Dominique or Désinor, both of whom would try to maintain the inherited mechanisms of rule. Or Dominique could, if Duvalier's health again deteriorates,[59] gradually make his father-in-law's power his own. In either case the potential for intensive rivalry and renewed chaos (on the 1957 model, if more brutal) would be likely. Or Duvalier could suddenly die without naming or assuring the elevation of a successor. In these circumstances there would be a tendency for the succession to be settled by violence. The army and the *macoutes* would compete, and the army might engage in internecine conflict. If power were not consolidated quickly, Haiti might soon find itself in a state of internal war. It is for such contingencies that both the O.A.S. and the United States plan.

8) Conceivably the United States could groom a distinguished Haitian now in exile (a number of Haitians currently holding responsible positions in the United Nations come to mind) for the presidency, try to gain a general support among exiles and exile organizations (an impossible task), back him diplomatically and financially, and help him to mobilize support within the country when Duvalier dies or retires. None, however, has an existing base of power on which to build. Alternatively, the United States could choose to back a figure already in Haiti and embroiled in its politics. Désinor is the most able of the men around Duvalier, but he doubtless would seek to perpetuate the present pattern of dictatorial rule. However, he would probably need assistance to survive the strains occasioned by Duvalier's demise, and American policy-makers might (rationally) prefer continued strong rule if it facilitated the implementation of responsible programs of economic development. In other words, Americans might and per-

59 See above, 255.

haps should be willing to sacrifice dramatic improvements in the immediate political and social well-being of Haiti for short-term economic benefits, a de-escalation of terror, and the possibility of a long-term enhancement of the political order. This option (whichever man were chosen) would minimize bloodshed, help to ensure stability, and provide a degree of leverage over the incumbent; it might inaugurate an epoch of reorganization and reorientation sufficiently transformational to make possible a degree of societal modernization.

9) Only the imposition of new terms of reference from outside would ensure such a transformation. If the O.A.S. and the United States together (but certainly not separately or independently) were to agree that Haiti was the sick man of the Western Hemisphere, and that the demise of Duvalier called for unusual measures to prevent Haiti from being plunged, again, into the abyss of instability — thus endangering the security of her neighbors — then an occupation might have some merit. Haitians of all strata would deplore it, but they might enjoy the freedom from tyranny and the potential for development which such an internationally mounted occupation would encourage. To occupy in order to smooth the transition between Duvalier and his successors, and in order to prevent civil war, would be viewed as less reprehensible than an invasion or intervention to oust an incumbent. Yet to bring about the desired changes in this way, or at least their commencement, implies a period of tutelage (and, cynically, an interlude of violent upheaval) which, to be effective, might of necessity last five or ten years. Such a policy of renewed colonialism would muster few votes in the O.A.S. or the United Nations or support elsewhere.

10) The O.A.S. (acting without Haiti) could choose as the best of a set of morally suspect and generally impractical alternatives to combine features from the above three options: when Duvalier departs it could intervene, with the support of the navies of the Americas, in order to install a predetermined person, committee of public safety, or exile group. Agreement (which is unlikely) among the members of the O.A.S. for such a plan would have to be obtained well beforehand if it were to stand a chance of suc-

cess. Its rapid implementation would be essential. For policy-makers, however, the knottiest problem would still remain: From the collection of potential successors or successor teams, how is it possible to choose infallibly? Will not even the most promising candidate or candidates soon become mired in the slough of Haitian politics? Is any Haitian capable, without exceptional skills and massive external backing, of overcoming the structural difficulties of national life?

An appreciation of Haiti's tortured past and a feeling for her present predicament provide ample reason for pessimism and a strong predisposition to extreme caution in considering any and all policy alternatives. There are no easy and sure remedies for the Haitian malaise, no panaceas capable of wreaking miraculous cures in the short run, and only a pollyannish hope for the future. If nothing else, policy-makers must perceive and accept the extent to which Haiti's contemporary crisis is less a passing illness than a product of deep, long-festering wounds. Only patient and careful rehabilitation — assisted if necessary internationally — can provide the basis for lasting structural improvements.

Haiti, after all, has demonstrated a penchant for clinging to the depressing end of all of the usual scales that are designed to measure national progress. It embodies institutional and structural failings carried to an unusual extreme. But this is not to say, when viewed from the perspective of history and a knowledge of the possible consequences of stagnation in today's world of the developing nations, that Haiti is exceptional. It may provide a paradigm of horror for African and Asian planners precisely because others, in earlier times, have fallen into a similar slough — what Huntington has suggestively called political decay.[60] As he demonstrates at length, the emergence of nations from the quicksand of decay is difficult and, as in Haiti's case, frequently serves merely to trap the unfortunate polity more securely.

Rapid political and economic improvement in Haiti is unlikely, even if we assume the possibility of effecting change by one of the more practical of the ten alternatives already postulated. Haitians are too numerous, underfed, diseased, disturbed, and uneducated

[60] Huntington, *Political Order*, 86 and *passim*.

for a mere shift of government to overcome the consequences of decades of neglect and oppression. The limited potential for economic development was indicated in the previous chapter. Political modernization equally is limited by an absence of supportive informal mechanisms or traditional sanctions. Governments in Haiti have rarely governed, and most have by their actions denied all of the commonly accepted normative goals of government. Brigandage has become a standard procedure and governments have been maintained more by the unconscionable use of terror than by consensus, no matter how broadly defined. Haiti has perfected the modern version of the predatory state, a polity the character of which can only very approximately be encompassed and expressed by the usual indices of political stability and instability, social change and stagnation, and economic development and underdevelopment.

There is little reason to contemplate the short-run future of Haiti with any optimism. But to be pessimistic is not to imply that some of the material improvements in the quality of economic and physical life suggested in the previous three chapters could not be realized — given abundant outside financial and technical assistance and a responsible government — within a decade. Certainly, Haiti, unlike the new states of Africa at the times of their independence, is fortunate in having a large pool of trained manpower, which, if its members can be attracted home and rewarded for utilizing their acquired knowledge, could help to transform the republic's outward appearances and elevate the per capita standard of living. Haiti does not want for most kinds of entrepreneurial initiative. But it does dramatically lack the social, psychological, and historico-experiential behavioral expectations and modes of response without which good (just, representative, effective, and stable) government and national economic and social progress become a chimera.

Appendices

Appendix A

Notes on the Estimation of Saint-Domingue's Exports

THIS APPENDIX describes how the data in Table 1 (p. 28) were calculated. The data in constant prices were calculated first, using quantity figures from the official returns and multiplying them by 1787–89 prices. These prices were obtained from the official returns, as reported by Edwards, *St. Domingo*, III, 144. The current price data in the second part of Table 1 were obtained by multiplying the quantity series by price indexes.

Sugar. The official figures on production of clayed and muscovado sugar are given in Table A–1. The table also shows the "muscovado equivalent total," which was calculated on the basis that one pound of clayed equals 1.75 pounds of muscovado. (See below for calculation of this ratio.) Figures from d'Auberteuil, *Considérations*, 65–74, were disregarded because, not being based on official returns, they are not comparable with the figures for other years. For some reason, other scholars (e.g., Moral, *Paysan Haitien*, 282, and Placide-Justin, *Histoire Politique*, 500–501) have accepted d'Auberteuil's sugar statistics for 1774 and 1776, which are substantially higher than the official figures for those years. (He apparently makes an allowance for smuggling in the case of sugar. His coffee figures are unaccountably lower than the official figures.) Moral, *Paysan*, 282, thus comes up with the following figures for sugar exports:

	Clayed	Muscovado	Apparent source
1767	51.5	73	Raynal
1774	59	88	D'Auberteuil
1776	61	92	D'Auberteuil
1788	70	93	Official returns—variety of sources

These figures give the impression that there was virtually no increase in sugar production from 1776 to 1788, whereas Table A–1, based entirely on official returns, gives a different impression.

The calculation of the value of sugar exports is shown in Table A–2. The 1787 price of 26.7 livres tournois per quintal of muscovado is taken from the official returns, as reported by Edwards, *St. Domingo*, III, 144. The comparable price of British sugar in 1787–89 was around 30 shillings per hundredweight (equivalent to livres tournois per quintal). The price in London was 38.2 shillings, but about 8 shillings must be subtracted for transport costs. (See Edwards, *St. Domingo*, V, 23.) There are some prices for Nantes, which give a figure of 28 livres in 1787–89. In the West Indies, this would presumably be around 20 livres. This price is too far below the London price to be comparable with it; the Nantes figures must refer to a low-quality muscovado, while the London figure refers to a high quality one. (On this point see Deerr, *Sugar*, II, 529.)

While the London and Nantes prices are not comparable with each other because of the quality problem, each price series is presumably consistent. The two series are used here to construct an index of price changes over time in Saint-Domingue. (This assumes transport costs were fairly constant.) The construction of our index is shown in Table A–3.

As mentioned above, the sugar production index weighted a ton of clayed sugar 1.75 times as much as a ton of muscovado. This was derived from the prices contained in Edwards, *St. Domingo*, III, 144. Other sources give somewhat different figures. See Frank Pitman, *The Development of the British West Indies* (New Haven, 1917; reprinted 1967), 186; Samuel Ricard, *Traité General du Commerce* (Amsterdam, 1781), I, 150; and d'Auberteuil, *Considérations*, I, 72. These sources give price ratios respectively of 1.45, 1.60, and 2.0. (The first two sets of figures were adjusted for transport costs to obtain West Indian prices.) The ratio 1.75 has the virtue of lying somewhere near the middle of these divergent estimates.

Coffee, Cotton, and Indigo. In each of these crops, export quantities were taken from authors citing official returns. These figures and the sources are shown in Table A–4. Also listed there are the nonofficial figures, which have been frequently cited by researchers, of d'Auberteuil.

The 1787–89 prices for each crop were taken from official returns, as reported by Edwards, *St. Domingo*, III, 144. The coffee prices for other years were taken from a variety of sources, as indicated in Table

A–5. The calculation of the value of coffee exports in current and constant prices is given in Table A–6.

Table A–1
Sugar Exports (Official Figures), 1767–1789
(figures in millions of French pounds)

Date	Clayed	Musco-vado	Total	Muscovado equivalent total [a]	Source
1767	51.6	72.7	124.3	163.0	Coke, from Raynal
1774	39.6	60.7	100.3	130.0	Dubuisson
1775			123.0		Ducoerjoly
1776	51.8	84.1	135.9	174.8	Dubuisson
1777	42.5	71.9	114.4	146.3	"
1783	77.4	44.3	121.7	179.8	"
1784	65.1	77.3	142.4	191.2	Warehouse Committee Report
1785	66.6	83.6	150.2	200.2	" " "
1786	71.1	61.9	133.0	186.3	" " "
1787	56.2	72.9	129.1	171.3	" " "
1788	70.2	93.2	163.4	216.1	" " "
1789	47.5	91.9	139.4	175.0	" " "

[a] Calculated on the basis of 1 ton clayed = 1.75 tons muscovado.

Sources: Thomas Coke, *A History of the West Indies* (London, 1811), III, 364; Pierre Ulric Dubuisson, *Nouvelles Considérations sur Saint-Domingue* (Paris, 1780), 27–44; S. J. Ducoerjoly, *Manuel des Habitants* (Paris, 1802), I, 138–140; Report from the Committee of Warehouses of the United East India Company Relative to the Culture of Sugar, 1792; this is Appendix 1 in *East India Sugar, Papers Respecting the Culture and Manufacture of Sugar in British India* (London, 1822).

Table A–2
Value of Sugar Exports

	Production muscovado equivalent[a] (1)	1787–89 price of muscovado (2)	Value in 1787–89 prices (3) = (1) × (2)	Price ratio[b] t / 1787–89 (4)	Value in current prices (5) = (3) × (4)
1787–89	187.5	.4	75.0	1.0	75.0
1783–84	190.5		76.2	.92	70.1
1774–76	152.4		61.0	.96	58.6
1767	163.0		65.2	1.0	65.2

[a] Calculated on the basis of 1 ton clayed = 1.75 tons muscovado. See Table A–1.
[b] Ratio of price in period t to price in 1787–89. From A–3.

Table A-3
Sugar Prices in London and Nantes, Selected Years

	London	Index	Nantes	Index	Index employed in Table A-2
1787–89	38.2	1.00	28	1.00	1.00
1783–84	34.0	.89	26.5	.95	.92
1774–76	36.5	.96	27	.96	.96
1767	37.5	.98	29	1.04	1.00

Figures are in shillings per cwt., or livres tournois per quintal, which are equivalent.

Sources: Noel Deerr, *History of Sugar*, II, 530–531; Thomas Cook and William Newmarch, *History of Prices* (London, 1838–56), I, 344 (London prices); and Guy Josa, *Les Industries du sucre et du rhum à la Martinique* (Paris, 1931), 111.

Table A-4
Export Quantities of Coffee, Indigo, and Cotton
(figures in millions of French pounds)

	Coffee	Indigo	Cotton
1787–89	71.5	1.018	6.654
1783–84	48.8	1.712	4.814
1774–76	43.7	1.758	2.497
1767	12.2	1.769	2.966

Sources: 1783–84, 1787–89: Warehouse Committee Report; 1775: Raynal, *Historie Philosophique*, VII, 140–141; 1774, 1776: Dubuisson, *Nouvelles Considérations*, 27–44; 1767: Raynal, as reported by Coke, *History*, III, 364.

D'Auberteuil's figures (*Considérations*, 65, 72, 74)

	Coffee	Indigo	Cotton
1776	32.5	1.8	3.5
1774	29.7	1.85	3.5
1767	15.6	1.5	2.55

Table A–5
Coffee Prices
(figures in colonial livres per pound)

Price		Source
1787–89	1.0	Edwards, *St. Domingo*, III, 144
1783	.75	Moral, *Paysan*, 265, primary source not cited
1776	.6	D'Auberteuil, *Considérations*, 65–74
1774	.6	D'Auberteuil, *Considérations*, 65–74
1767	1.2	D'Auberteuil, *Considérations*, 65–74

Table A–6
Value of Coffee Exports

Coffee	Production[a] (1)	1787–89 price (2)	Value in 1787–89 prices (3) = (1) × (2)	Price ratio[b] $\frac{t}{1787-89}$ (4)	Value in current prices (5) = (3) × (4)
1787–89	71.5	1.0	71.5	1.0	71.5
1783–84	48.8		48.8	.75	36.6
1774–76	43.7		43.7	.6	26.2
1767	12.2		12.2	1.2	14.6

a From A–4.
b Ratio of price in period t to price in 1787–1789. From Table A–5.

Appendix B

The Haitian Economy in the Nineteenth Century

I. Exports

Tables B–1, B–2, and B–3 give the quantities, prices, and values of major Haitian export commodities from 1821 to 1914. By and large the quantity figures in different nineteenth-century sources are mutually consistent, indicating that they have derived from a common original — probably some unpublished Haitian records. (Since there were heavy taxes on these commodities, there was a need to keep official records; on the other hand, there must have been some smuggling, but no estimates of smuggling have been found.)

The price statistics are largely unit values of U.S. imports. Export values in Tables B–7, 8, & 9 were obtained by multiplying the quantities of Tables B–2, 3, & 4 by the prices of Tables B–1, 5, & 6. The U.S. wholesale price index employed was the Warren and Pearson index in *Historical Statistics of the United States, 1789–1945* (Washington, 1949), 231–232.

Table B–1
Prices of Logwood, Cacao, and Mahogany, 1835–64

	Logwood	Cacao	Mahogany
1835	4.07	7.52	4.70
1838–39	5.20	6.24	7.20
1863	5.51	7.09	n.a.
1864	4.32	6.45	n.a.

Units are as follows: Logwood, dollars per thousand French pounds; cacao, cents per U.S. pound; mahogany, dollars per thousand board feet.

Sources: St. John, *Hayti,* 373, 378.

Table B–2
Export Quantities, 1821–42

	Coffee (million pounds)	Logwood (million pounds)	Cotton (million pounds)	Cacao (million pounds)	Mahogany (millions of board feet)
1821	30.0	3.6	.8	.2	
22	24.2	7.4	.6	.4	
23	33.4	6.2	.4	.4	
24	44.2	3.8	1.0	.4	
25	36.8	3.6	1.0	.4	
26	33.2	5.0	.6	.6	
27	49.6	5.4	.8	.8	
28	44.4	8.2	1.4	.4	
29	39.8	7.6	1.0	.8	
30	42.4	16.0	1.4	.4	
31	40.4	21.0	1.2	.4	
32	49.0	17.4	1.0	.4	
33	31.6	23.8	1.8	.4	
34	46.4	16.4	1.2	.4	
35	48.0	11.0	1.6	.4	5.413
36	37.0	5.8	1.0	.4	
37	31.0	6.0	1.0	.2	
38	50.0	7.8	1.2	.4	4.881
39	37.8	26.8	1.6	.4	5.903
40	46.0	29.2	1.0	.4	
41	34.0	45.0	1.6	.6	
42	40.6	19.0	.8	.4	4.097

Sources: All figures for 1821–42 are from Benoit, *Cent Cinquante Ans,* 22, 32, 36, 55, except for the mahogany figures, which are from Candler, *Brief Notices,* 105, and St. John, *Hayti,* 372–373. Candler, writing in 1841, says that mahogany exports have been increasing (106). Tobacco exports have been excluded because they came primarily from the eastern, or Spanish, part of the island.

Table **B–3**
Export Quantities, 1845–90

	Coffee	*Logwood*	*Cotton*	*Cacao*	*Mahogany*
1845	41.0	n.a.	.56		7.90
59	41 [M]	88.2	.94	1.40	2.69
60	60.5	104.3	.67	1.58	2.26
61	45.7	105.8	1.14	1.31	1.66
62	54 [M]	167.0	1.47	1.74	2.44
63	71.6 [B]	116.7	2.22	2.34	2.02
64	45.2	152.2	3.24	1.40	2.37
73	64.8				
74	54.7				
75	72.6 [B]				
76	72.2 [B]				
77	53.0				
78	63.3				
79	47.9				
80	55.6	321.7	.96	2.73	
85	74.0	297.5	2.57	3.94	
86	58.1	282.6	2.04	3.16	
87	41.6 [B]	280.0 [P]	n.a.	n.a.	
88	84.0 [B]	240.2 [B]	2.0 [B]	4.0 [B]	
89	57.6 [B]	133.2 [B]	1.0 [B]	.8 [B]	
90	56.6 [B]	190.8 [B]	1.6 [B]	4.2 [B]	

Sources: All figures are from St. John, *Hayti*, 374–376, 364–365, except where indicated otherwise. The symbols are B = Benoit, *Cent Cinquante Ans*, 22, 32, 36, 55; M = L. J. Marcelin, *Haiti, Ses Guerres Civiles*, 32 (coffee); P = Paul Moral, *Paysan Haitien*, 120.

Table B–4
Export Quantities, 1891–1914

	Coffee	Logwood	Cotton	Cacao
1891	79.4	160.0	1.0	2.8
92	68.0	114.4	1.2	4.0
93	70.8	128.8	1.2	3.0
94	58.4	142.0	.8	2.4
95	75.4	138.0	.2	2.2
96	47.6	115.8	.4	2.2
97	73.0	66.6	.8	2.2
98	67.4	66.6	1.2	4.0
99	61.4	82.8	1.4	4.0
1900	72.0	106.0	1.0	4.2
1905	45.2	78.0	3.2	5.0
06	56.4	87.6	3.8	4.6
07	58.8	136.2	4.2	4.4
08	60.6	82.0	3.0	6.0
09	39.2	73.8	3.4	4.4
10	77.4	87.0	3.8	4.0
11	51.6	74.6	4.2	3.2
12	77.8	92.2	4.4	6.8
13	57.4	62.6	4.4	3.8
14	81.2	65.8	3.4	6.6

Source: All figures are from Benoit, *Cent Cinquante Ans,* 22, 32, 36, 55.

Table B–5
Prices of Coffee and Cotton, 1821–1914
(All figures in U.S. cents per U.S. pound)

	Coffee	Cotton		Coffee	Cotton		Coffee	Cotton
1821	20.2	15	1842	7.9	7	1890	16.0	10.1
22	21.1	14	45	5.7	6.0	91	n.a.	10.0
23	17.3	11	59	9.4	11.7	92	n.a.	8.7
24	12.7	16	60	10.8	10.9	93	14.0	8.5
25	9.7	n.a.	61	11.1	11.7	94	16.4	7.8
26	10.5	10	62	11.3	23.3	95	14.7	5.8
27	7.5	10	63	12.5	58.4	96	14.6	8.1
28	9.4	12	64	12.0	82.4	97	11.1	7.4
29	9.2	10	73	15.0	*	98	7.5	5.9
30	8.3	10	74	19.3	*	99	6.5	5.4
31	7.7	9	75	15.8	*	1900	6.7	7.7
32	6.9	10	76	16.7	*	1905	6.66	6.94
33	10.0	12	77	16.2	*	06	9.00	11.77
34	10.1	12	78	16.8	*	07	8.17	13.78
35	10.2	18	79	12.5	*	08	5.66	11.19
36	9.9	17	80	13.5	11.5	09	6.19	10.63
37	9.6	10	85	8.2	10.6	10	6.13	15.75
38	8.6	10	86	7.6	9.9	11	9.05	16.17
39	9.0	14	87	10.7	9.5	12	11.22	13.85
40	8.8	8	88	14.0	9.8	13	11.13	12.92
41	9.0	10	89	13.0	9.9	14	7.73	14.10

Note: Figures are unit values of total U.S. imports, except cotton, 1821–45.
* Not calculated because no export data are available.

Sources: *Foreign Commerce and Navigation of the United States.* For cotton, 1821–45: Arthur H. Cole, *Wholesale Commodity Prices in the United States 1700–61, Statistical Supplement* (Cambridge, 1938).

Table B–6
Prices of Logwood and Cacao, 1891–1914

	Logwood	Cacao
1891	11.52	6.93
92	10.97	8.04
93	10.75	8.72
94	11.80	9.92
95	12.27	7.55
96	11.21	5.93
97	8.82	9.65
98	7.75	13.50
99	6.77	16.13
1900	6.19	16.55
1905	5.92	11.45
06	6.53	9.63
07	5.36	11.63
08	4.63	14.83
09	3.46	8.41
10	5.27	8.34
11	n.a.	9.00
12	5.19	9.49
13	5.91	10.69
14	5.06	9.70

Logwood prices in dollars per thousand French pounds. Cacao prices in cents per U.S. pound. All figures are unit values of Haitian imports into the United States.

Source: *Foreign Commerce and Navigation of the United States.*

Appendices

Table B–7
Export Values, 1821–42
(Values in thousands of U.S. dollars)

	Coffee	Logwood	Cotton	Cacao	Mahogany	Total
1821	6560	18	130	14	(100)	6822
22	5530	37	90	28	(100)	5785
23	6530	31	50	28	(100)	6739
24	6080	18	180	28	(100)	6406
25	3870	16	180	28	(100)	4194
26	3780	25	70	42	(100)	4017
27	4030	27	90	56	(100)	4303
28	4520	41	180	28	(100)	4869
29	3970	37	110	56	(100)	4273
30	3810	80	150	28	(200)	4268
31	3370	105	120	28	(200)	3823
32	3660	87	110	28	(200)	4085
33	3420	119	230	28	(200)	3997
34	5080	82	160	28	(200)	5550
35	5300	45	310	28	254	5937
36	3970	29	190	28	(300)	4517
37	3220	30	110	14	(300)	3674
38	4660	56	130	25	351	5222
39	3680	139	240	25	425	4509
40	4380	146	90	28	(300)	4944
41	3310	225	180	42	(300)	4057
42	3470	95	60	28	193	3846

Figures in parentheses were estimated arbitrarily. Values were calculated by multiplying quantities in Tables B–2, B–3, and B–4 by prices in Tables B–1, B–5, and B–6. For coffee, cotton, and cacao, prices had to be multiplied by 1.083 to convert U.S. pounds into French pounds.

Table B–8
Export Values, 1845–90

	Coffee	Logwood	Cotton	Cacao	Mahogany	Total
1845	2,530		37		371	
59	4,170	441	108	106	126	4,951
60	7,080	522	79	120	106	7,907
61	5,490	529	144	100	78	6,341
62	6,610	835	371	130	115	8,061
63	9,690	584	1,404	180	95	11,953
64	5,870	761	2,892	98	111	9,732
73	10,530					
74	11,430					
75	12,420					
76	13,060					
77	9,300					
78	11,520					
79	6,490					
80	8,130	4,021	119	207	negligible	12,477
85	6,570	2,386	295	299		9,550
86	4,780	2,190	219	239		7,428
87	4,820	2,540				
88	12,740	3,003	212	303		16,258
89	8,110	1,665	108	61		9,944
90	9,810	2,385	285	318		12,798

Table B–9
Export Values, 1891–1914

	Coffee	Logwood	Cotton	Cacao	Total
1891	13,760 [1]	1843	108	210	15,921
92	11,780 [1]	1255	108	349	13,492
93	10,730	1385	108	284	12,507
94	10,370	1676	66	258	12,370
95	12,000	1693	14	180	13,887
96	7,530	1298	35	141	9,004
97	8,780	587	60	230	9,657
98	5,470	516	78	585	6,649
99	4,320	561	76	699	5,656
1900	5,220	656	83	753	6,712
1905	3,260	462	240	621	4,583
06	5,500	572	484	480	7,036
07	5,200	730	627	554	7,111
08	3,710	380	364	964	5,418
09	2,630	255	391	401	3,677
10	5,140	458	649	362	6,609
11	5,060	390	735	312	6,497
12	9,450	479	660	699	11,288
13	6,920	370	615	440	8,345
14	6,800	333	519	693	8,345

[1] 1890 price used.

II. Population

Population figures were estimated by interpolating between the estimate of 700,000 for the whole island in 1824 given by Placide-Justin, *Histoire Politique, 503,* and the revised 1950 census estimate of 3.38 million, calculated by Jacques St. Surin, *Indices Démographique et Perspectives de la Population d'Haiti de 1950 à 1980* (Port-au-Prince, 1962), 15. From the 700,000 estimate for the whole island, the population of the Spanish part must be subtracted. According to Spanish official documents, this was 152,640 in 1785 (from Placide-Justin): 122,640 whites and 30,000 slaves. Assuming that a good many whites departed as a result of the wars and the Haitian takeover of 1822, the population in the Spanish part of the island may have numbered about 100,000. This leaves 600,000 for Haiti proper in 1824.

In interpolating the population for the intervening years, a higher growth rate was assumed for the 1920–1950 period than for the pre-occupation period. If the population is put at 2.0 million in 1922, which Millspaugh, *American Control,* 13, regards as the "general estimate" for that year, the implied rates of population growth are 1.9 per cent for 1922–50 and 1.24 per cent for 1824–1922. These assumptions yield the following population estimates:

	Population (million)
1824	.600
1860	.935
1890	1.355
1914	1.823
1922	2.000
1950	3.380

III. Education

Table B–10 presents the structure of the educational system in 1877 and 1895. The pupils in the different categories of schools in 1895 were estimated by the crude procedure of making use of the number of pupils per school in 1877. When the number of schools in 1895 was multiplied by the pupils per school in 1877, a total of 41,001 students was obtained. The actual number of 1895 (excluding the private school students, who were not included in the calculation) was 38,039. Scaling down the 41,001 to 38,039 by equal percentage reductions in all groups gives the figures shown in Table B–10. There is some independent confirmation for the 9779 figure for national religious enrollment in 1895. Total Catholic school enrollment was 8000 in 1891 and 11,300 in 1905. (See Logan, "Education," 439.)

Table B–10
Structure of Educational System,
1877 and 1895

| | Publicly Supported Schools | | | | Private (Prim. & Sec.) | Total |
| | Secular Urban | | National Religious (Prim. & Sec.) | Rural (Prim.) | | |
	Primary	Above Primary				
1877						
Schools	165[a]	17[a]	(11)[b]	200[a]		
Pupils	11,784[a]	1527[a]	(2000)[b]	5939[a]	3914[c]	25,164
1895						
Schools	197[d]	20[d]	51[d]	505[d]	102[d]	
Pupils	(13,053)[e]	(1666)[e]	(9779)[e]	(13,541)[e]	6503[d]	44,452[d]

Figures in parentheses are author's estimates.

[a] From official sources, as reported in Bureau of American Republics, *Bulletin*, No. 62 (1892), 38.
[b] Estimated from information in Logan, "Education," 436–437, and William B. McCormick, "The Christian Brothers in Haiti," *America* (February 4, 1922).
[c] *Exposé*, 1875, 51–2.
[d] From official sources, as reported in Sténio Vincent and L.-C. Lherisson, *La Législation de l'Instruction Publique* (Paris, n.d. but 1896), 94–95.
[e] Estimated. See text.

Table B–11
Public Debt, 1825–1875

Date	New Obligations	Debts Outstanding	Principal Paid	Interest Paid	Total Payments	No. Yrs.	Annual Rate of Payment
I. Loan of 1825 (in millions of francs)							
1825	30						
1827		28.8	1.2	0	1.2	1	1.20
1839		33.16	5.6		5.6	12	.47
1843		27.26	5.9	3.6	9.5	4	2.38
1849		33.66	0	0	0		0
1859		14.9	17.76	6.9	24.66	10	2.47
1875		0	14.9	3.6	18.5	16	1.16
II. Indemnity (in millions of francs)							
1825						1	5.30
1838		60					0
1843		50.9	9.1			5	1.82
1849		50.9					0
1859		32.0	18.9			10	1.89
1875		8.0	24.0			16	1.50

III. Combined Annual Rates of Payment (in millions of dollars)

Debt Service	1825	1827	1828–38	1839–43	1843–48	1849–59	1859–75
Payments	1.023	.232	.091	.811	0	.841	.513
Government Receipts				1.4			2.6
Ratio, Debt Payments to Govt. Receipts				.58			.20

Sources: 1825–43: Lepelletier de Saint-Remy, *Saint Domingue*, II, 114–126; 1849–59: Alexandre Bonneau, *Haiti: Ses Progres, Son Avenir* (Paris, 1862), 69; 1875: Folsom, "Haitian Economy," unpub. typescript (1954), 392–393.

IV. The Public Debt

Tables B–11 and B–12 show the public debt outstanding at various dates. It was assumed that repayment of principal and interest took place at constant annual rates between the dates shown. Thus the average annual repayments calculated are not necessarily applicable in any particular year. The interest rates on the various loans were as follows: Indemnity: none; Loan of 1825; initially 5 per cent, reduced to 3 per cent in 1838; Loan of 1865: initially 6 per cent, reduced to 5 per cent in 1885; Loan of 1896: 6 per cent; Loan of 1911: 5 per cent. The calculated annual payments of principal and interest on the foreign debt, together with customs receipts, which account for the great bulk of government revenue (aside from the proceeds of inflationary finance), are shown in Table B–13.

Table B–12
Public Debt, 1876–1914
Debt Outstanding, Selected Years
(millions of francs)

	Loan of 1875	Loan of 1896	Loan of 1911
1876	35.0		
1885	35.0		
1890	24.5		
1896	22.0	50.0	
1902	19.25	46.64	
1911	19.25	41.59	65.0
1914	19.25	37.64	64.02

Sources: Banque Nationale de la République d'Haiti, *Reseignements Financières, Statistiques, et Economiques de la République d'Haiti,* various years; Bureau of American Republics, *Bulletin,* No. 62 (1892), 96–111.

Table B–13
Annual Rates of Payment, 1876–1914
(millions of francs except where indicated otherwise)

	Indemnity	1876 Loan	1896 Loan	1911 Loan	Combined Annual Payments Francs	Dollars
1876–79	.8	2.10			2.90	.556
1880–85	.8	2.10			2.90	.556
1886–90		1.23			1.23	.237
1891–95		1.68			1.68	.324
1896		1.68	2.65		4.33	.836
1897–1902		1.42	3.44		4.86	.938
1903–1910		1.00	3.15		4.15	.801
1911		1.00	3.15	2.42	6.57	1.268
1912		1.00	3.70	3.56	8.26	1.594
1913		1.00	3.70	3.56	8.26	1.594
1914		1.00	3.70	3.56	8.26	1.594

	Customs Receipts (dollars)	Ratio, Debt Payments to Customs Receipts
1876–79	$3.9	.14
1880–85	3.9	.14
1886–90	5.6	.04
1891–95	7.2	.05
1896	5.6	.15
1897–1902	4.7	.20
1902–1910	3.2	.25
1911	4.1	.31
1912	6.9	.23
1913	5.2	.31
1914	5.0	.32

Sources: Table B–12. Customs receipts: 1818–25, 1860–86: St. John, *Hayti;* 382–387; 1837–40: Candler, *Brief Notices,* 115–116; 1890–1914: *Report of the Financial Adviser-Receiver General,* 1927–28, 55.

Appendix C

U.S. Tariff Rates on Items of Interest to Haiti

			TARIFF RATES (PERCENT)	
SITC Group	*TSUS No.*	Description (1968 exports in parenthesis)	*Pre-KR[a]*	*Post KR[a]*
655	315.20	Binder twine (1428)	Free	Free
8944	734.56	Softballs (1298)	15	7.5
841	— [b]	Clothing (850)	27.4	24.5
851	700.55.45	Footwear, vinyl uppers, women and child (745)	12	6
831	— [b]	Travel goods (427)	20.4	15.6
656	389.60	Misc. textile articles (273)	30	15
897	740.38	Misc. jewelry, 20¢ to $5 per doz. (225)	55	27.5
632	206.95; 207.00	Misc. wood products (about 100)	16.7	8.5
698	657.20	Misc. iron and steel products (72)	19	9.5
722	685.90	Switchboard panels (117)	17.5	8.5
722	686.10.60	Resistors (45)	12.5	6.5
724	685.20.40	Misc. TV parts (36)	10	5

[a] Pre-Kennedy Round, Post Kennedy-Round. Kennedy Round cuts began on Jan. 1, 1968 and will be completed by Jan. 1, 1972.
[b] Exports in this category are too diversified to be listed here. Tariffs are averages for entire group weighted by total U.S. imports in 1966. They were obtained from worksheets of Bureau of International Commerce, Department of Commerce.

Source: U.S. Import and Tariff Statistics, Census Bureau and Tariff Commission.

Tariff Commission, *Tariff Schedules of the United States Annotated (1968)*; Bureau of the Census, *U.S. Imports for Consumption and General Imports*, FT246, 1968.

Bibliography

Bibliography

THE LITERATURE on Haiti is surprisingly large. Much is in French, but English, Spanish, German, and even Polish studies are also important. Haitians themselves have for two centuries supported a succession of periodical and other outlets for the discussion of current problems and past solutions. Even today, and throughout the reign of Duvalier, the main historical, ethnological, and literary reviews have continued to appear; new journals for sociology and psychiatry have also been printed and distributed. Haitians continue to be prolific writers and publishers of full-length works; neither for the era of Duvalier nor for earlier eras is there a shortage of commentary. Amid the welter of articles and full-length discourses, however, there are now (and have always been) too few studies of real worth. In this sense, despite the flood of material available to any diligent student of Haiti, the people of that republic have been poorly served. Much, whether in French or in English, or whether written by Haitians or by outsiders, is at best tendentious and at worst trivial. Objectivity is unusual. The literature is replete with self-serving narratives and court biographies. Propaganda has often been confused with scholarship. The following list of books and articles therefore represents a guide, albeit one severely selective, to the literature relevant to a study of the history, politics, and economy of Haiti. For economy of space, the entries are annotated with symbols:

* = particularly valuable
+ = popular and/or especially evocative

Abderrahman (pseud. François Duvalier), *Souvenirs d'Autrefois, 1926–1948*. Port-au-Prince, 1968.

Agullo, María Jesús C., "Duvalier, dos veces excomulgado por S.S. Juan XXIII; vodú, miseria y tiranía," *Bohemia Libre Puertorriqueña*. Caracas, LIV (23 June 1963), 34ff.

Alba, Victor, *Politics and the Labor Movement in Latin America.* Stanford, 1968, 110–111, 119, 286–287.

Alexander, Richard, "The Hell of Haiti," *The Nation,* CXCVI (2 February 1963), 98–99.

Allen, John H., "An Inside View of Revolutions in Haiti," *Current History,* XXXIII (May 1930), 325–329.

Alphonse, Emile J., *Jets de Lumière.* Port-au-Prince, 1961.

Antoine, Charles, *Quelques Considérations sur le Milieu Rural à Deseaux: Une Expérience de Développement Communautaire dans la Vallée de l'Artibonite.* Port-au-Prince, 1959.

Ardouin, Beaubrun, *Etudes sur l'Histoire d'Haiti, Suivies de la Vie du Général J.-M. Borgella.* Port-au-Prince, 1924–1926, 2v.

Ardouin, C. N. Celigni, *Essais sur l'Histoire d'Haiti.* Port-au-Prince, 1865.

Armbrister, Trevor, "Is There Any Hope for Haiti?" *The Saturday Evening Post,* CCXXXVI (15 June 1963), 78–81.

Arty, Daniel, "Haití: aspectos de la crisis," *Bohemia.* Havana, LV (6 December 1963), 92–95ff.

Astor, Brooke Russell, *Patchwork Child.* New York, 1962.

D'Auberteuil, Hilliard, *Considérations sur l'État Présent de la Colonie Française de Saint-Domingue: Ouvrage Politique et Legislatif.* Paris, 1776–1777, 2v.

Aubourg, Michel, "La Diffusion des Techniques dans la Formation de nos Ouvriers," *Revue du Travail.* Port-au-Prince, XII (1 May 1963), 9–12.

Auguste, G., "Die Tragödie Haitis," *Neue Zeit,* XLII (1965), 14–16.

Balch, Emily Greene (ed.), *Occupied Haiti.* New York, 1927.

Baptiste, Jean, "Nadie está libre de los 'Ton Ton Macoute'; la opresión haitiana al desnudo!" *Ahora.* Santo Domingo, II (2–15 February 1963), 12–14.

Barré de St. Venant, Jean, *Des Colonies Modernes sous la Zone Torride, et Particulièrement de celle de Saint-Domingue.* Paris, 1802.

*[Barskett, James], *History of the Island of St. Domingo from its First Discovery by Columbus to the Present Period.* London, 1818.

Bastien, Rémy, *La Familia Rural Haitiana.* Mexico City, 1961.

———, "Haitian Rural Family Organization," *Social and Economic Studies,* X (1961), 478–510.

———, "Haitian Rural Family Organization," in Sidney Mintz and William Davenport (eds.), *Working Papers in Caribbean Social Organization.* Mona, 1961, 380–535.

————, "The Role of the Intellectual in Haitian Plural Society," *Annals of the New York Academy of Sciences,* LXXXIII (1960), 843–849.

Beach, Edward Latimer, "Admiral Caperton in Haiti," unpub. typescript (1919), privately held.

————, "From Annapolis to Scapa Flow," unpub. typescript (1919), privately held.

————, "Haiti and its People," unpub. typescript (1919), privately held.

Beals, Carleton, " 'Papa Doc,' emperador de Haití," *Politica.* México, IV (1 March 1964), 34–35.

Beaulier, Philippe, "The Church and Haiti," *Center of Intercultural Formation Reports.* Cuernavaca, III, 12 (1964), 1–13.

Beghin, I., W. Fougere, and Kendall W. King, "Enquête Clinique sur l'État de Nutrition des Enfants Préscolaires de Fond-Parisien et de Gauthier (Haiti): Juin, 1964," *Annales des Sociétés Belges de Médecine Tropicale,* XLV (1965), 577–602.

———— *et al.,* "Le Centre de Recuperation," *ibid.,* 557–576.

Behar, M., and Nevin S. Scrimshaw, "Epidemiology of Protein Malnutrition," in I. Galdston (ed.), *Human Nutrition, Historic and Scientific.* New York, 1960, 257–273.

Bekker, L. J. de, "The Massacre at Aux Cayes," *The Nation,* CXXX (12 March 1930), 308, 310.

Bellegarde, Dantès, *Dessalines a Parlé.* Port-au-Prince, 1948.

————, *Ecrivains Haitiens: Notices Biographiques et Pages Choisies.* Paris, 1950; 2nd ed.

————, *Haiti and Her Problems.* Rio Piedras, 1936.

————, *Histoire du Peuple Haitien (1492–1952).* Port-au-Prince, 1953.

————, "Pétion et Bolivar," *Revue de la Société d'Histoire et de Géographie d'Haiti,* XII (October 1941), 1–13.

————, *Pour une Haiti Heureuse: II. Par l'Education et le Travail.* Port-au-Prince, 1929.

————, *La Résistance Haitienne.* Montreal, 1937.

Belshaw, Cyril S., "Monetized Peasant Marketing," in Cyril S. Belshaw, *Traditional Exchanges and Modern Markets.* Englewood Cliffs, 1965, 53–83.

Bengoa, J. M., "Nutritional Rehabilitation Programmes," *Journal of Tropical Pediatrics,* X (1964), 63–64.

Berle, Adolf A., "Is Haiti Next?" *The Reporter,* XXVIII (23 May 1963), 16.

Bernstein, Marvin D. (ed.), *Foreign Investment in Latin America: Cases and Attitudes.* New York, 1966.

*Bird, Mark B., *The Black Man: Or, Haytian Independence, Deduced from Historical Notes, and Dedicated to the Government and People of Hayti.* New York, 1869.

Blassingame, John W., "The Press and American Intervention in Haiti and the Dominican Republic, 1904–1920," *Caribbean Studies,* IX (1969), 27–43.

Boissonade, Prosper, *Saint-Domingue à la Veille de la Révolution.* Paris, 1906.

*Bonhomme, Colbert, *Révolution et Contre-Révolution en Haiti de 1946 à 1947.* Port-au-Prince, 1957.

Bonsal, Stephen, *The American Mediterranean.* New York, 1912.

Bosch, Juan, *The Unfinished Experiment: Democracy in the Dominican Republic.* New York, 1965.

Boulos, Carlos, "Une Enquête Alimentaire en Haiti," *Bulletin de l'Association Médicale Haitienne,* VL (1954), 185–188.

Bourguignon, Erika E., "Class Structure and Acculturation in Haiti," *The Ohio Journal of Science,* LII (1952), 317–320.

———, "Possession Trance in the Americas," *Dance Perspectives,* XXXV (Autumn 1968), 26–41.

———, "Visionary Trance," *ibid.,* 20–25.

Bowers, Margareta K., "Hypnotic Aspects of Haitian Voodoo," *International Journal of Clinical and Experimental Hypnosis,* IX (1961), 269–282.

*Brand, Willem, *Impressions of Haiti.* The Hague, 1965.

Breathett, George, "Catholic Missionary Activity and the Negro Slave in Haiti," *Phylon,* XXIII (1962), 278–285.

Breda, Jeremie, "Life in Haiti: Voodoo and the Church," *The Commonweal,* LXXVIII (24 May 1963), 241–244.

Bretones, G. J., "Expériences de Développement Communautaire en Haiti," *International Review of Community Development,* X (1962), 75–88.

Brierre, Jean F., *Dessalines Nous Parle. . . .* Port-au-Prince, 1953.

*Brown, Jonathan, *The History and Present Condition of St. Domingo.* Philadelphia, 1837, 2v.

Brown, Robert K., "The Plot Against Papa Doc," *National Review,* XIX (24 January 1967), 91–92.

Brun, Gérard, "Lengua y Literatura: Dos Aspectos de la Cultura del Pueblo Haitiano," *Thesaurus,* XI (1966), 194–198.

Brutus, Edner, *Instruction Publique en Haiti, 1492–1945.* Port-au-Prince, 1948.

Buell, Raymond Leslie, "The American Occupation of Haiti," *Foreign Policy Information Service,* V (27 November–12 December 1929), 327–391.

Calixte, Démosthènes Pétrus, *Haiti: The Calvary of a Soldier.* New York, 1939.

*Candler, John, *Brief Notices of Hayti: With Its Condition, Resources, and Prospects.* London, 1842.

Capo, José María, "Haití, o la Crisis Permanente," *Boricua.* San Juan, I (September 1961), 32–33ff.

Carey, Alida L., "Our Choice in Haiti: Duvalier or the People," *The Commonweal,* LXXV (2 March 1962), 587–590.

Casimir, Jean, "Aperçu sur la Structure Economique d'Haiti," *America Latina,* VII (1964), 37–54.

———, "Aperçu sur la Structure Economique d'Haiti," *ibid.,* VIII (1965), 40–61.

Catalogne, Gérard de, "El Escalvo que llegó a ser rey," *Bohemia.* Havana, LV (15 February 1963), 13–15.

———, *Haiti Devant son Destin.* Port-au-Prince, n.d. but 1940.

Célestin, Clément, *Compilations pour l'Histoire.* Port-au-Prince, 1958–1959, 3v.

Cesaire, Aimé, "La tragédie du Roi Christophe," *Presence Africaine,* XLVI (1963), 163–183.

———, *Toussaint L'Ouverture: la révolution française et le probleme coloniale.* Paris, 1962.

*Chapman, Charles E., "The Development of the Intervention in Haiti," *The Hispanic American Historical Review,* VII (1927), 299–319.

*Charlevoix, Pierre-François Xavier de, *Histoire de l'Isle Espagnole ou de S. Domingue.* Amsterdam, 1733, 4v.

Chatelain, Joseph, *La Banque Nationale.* Port-au-Prince, 1954.

Chevalier, George-Ary, "Un colon de Saint-Domingue pendant la Révolution. Pierre Collette, Planteur de Jean-Rabel," *Revue de la Société d'Histoire et de Géographie d'Haiti,* XII (January 1940), 29–45; (April 1940), 25–45; (July 1940), 1–38; (October 1940), 26–48; XIII (January 1941), 1–38.

———, "Etude sur la colonisation française en Haiti: Origines et développement des propriétés Collette," *ibid.,* IX (October 1938), 11–46.

————, "Etude sur la colonisation française en Haiti: Un fortune coloniale au XVIIIᵉ siècle," *ibid.,* X (April 1939), 17–41.

Chevillard, André, "Les desseins de S. E. de Richelieu pour l'Amérique," *Annales des Antilles,* XI (1963), 59–73.

Christiansen, S., *Rapport sur le Projet d'Eradication du Pian en Haiti.* Geneva, 1966.

Clausson, L. J., *Précis Historique de la Révolution de Saint-Domingue.* Paris, 1819.

Cole, Hubert, *Christophe: King of Haiti.* London, 1967.

Comhaire, Jean L., "The Haitian 'Chef de Section,'" *American Anthropologist,* LVII (1955), 620–623.

Comhaire-Sylvain, Suzanne, "Courtship, Marriage and Plasaj at Kenscoff, Haiti," *Social and Economic Studies,* VII (1958), 210–233.

————, "Les Fiancailles dans la région de Kenscoff, Haiti," *Bulletin du Bureau d'Ethnologie,* III, 23–25 (March–September 1960), 27–35.

————, "The Household in Kenscoff, Haiti," *Social and Economic Studies,* X (1961), 192–222.

————, and Jean Comhaire-Sylvain, "A Statistical Note on the Kenscoff Market System — Haiti," *ibid.,* XIII (1964), 397–404.

Cook, Francis J., "Haiti Today; Letter from the Caribbean," *National Review,* XVI (21 April 1964), 312.

Cook, Mercer (ed.), *An Introduction to Haiti.* Washington, 1951.

*Cooper, Donald B., "The Withdrawal of the United States from Haiti, 1928–1934," *Journal of Inter-American Studies,* V (1963), 83–101.

*Courlander, Harold, *The Drum and the Hoe: Life and Lore of the Haitian People.* Berkeley, 1960.

*Courlander, Harold, and Rémy Bastien, *Religion and Politics in Haiti.* Washington, 1966.

Crassweller, Robert D., *Trujillo: The Life and Times of a Caribbean Dictator.* New York, 1966.

Dale, Ernest "The Terror in Haiti," *New Statesman.* London, LXV (10 May 1963), 706, 708.

Dale, George A., *Education in the Republic of Haiti.* Washington, 1959.

Dalencour, François, *Biographie du General François Cappoix.* Port-au-Prince, 1956.

————, *La Fondation de la République d'Haiti par Alexandre Pétion.* Port-au-Prince, 1944.

————, *Précis Methodique d'Histoire d'Haiti: Cinq Siècles d'Histoire 1492–1930.* Port-au-Prince, 1935.

————, *Le Sauvetage National par le Retour à la Terre.* Port-au-Prince, 1923.

Dalmas, M., *Histoire de la Révolution de Saint-Domingue, Depuis le Commencement des Troubles, Jusqu'à la Prise de Jérémie et du Môle S. Nicolas par les Anglais; Suivie d'un Memoire sur le Rétablissement de cette Colonie.* Paris, 1814.

David, Placide, *L'Héritage Colonial en Haiti.* Madrid, 1959.

+Davis, H. P., *Black Democracy: The Story of Haiti.* New York, 1936.

————, "Haiti after 1936," *Outlook and Independent* (19 March 1930), 443–446.

Debien, Gabriel, *Le Commerce Nantais et la Perte de Saint-Domingue d'après une Correspondance de la Maison Lebourg (1784–1800).* Port-au-Prince, n.d.

————, *Etudes Antillaises (XVIIIᵉ Siècle).* Paris, 1956.

————, *Lettres de Colons.* Dakar, 1965.

————, "Le Marronage aux Antilles Françaises au XVIIIᵉ Siècle," *Caribbean Studies,* VI (October 1966), 3–43.

————, "Les Origines des Esclaves aux Antilles," *Bulletin de l'Institut Fondamental d'Afrique Noire,* XXIX (B) (1967), 536–558.

*————, *Plantations et Esclaves à Saint-Domingue.* Dakar, 1962.

Delmas, Gérard, "Quand l'espoir devient réalité; le développement des centres d'artisanat rural," *Revue du Travail.* Port-au-Prince, XII (1 May 1963), 69–75.

Demas, William G., *The Economics of Development in Small Countries, with Special Reference to the Caribbean.* Montreal, 1965.

*Denis, Lorimer, and François Duvalier, "La Civilisation Haitienne: Notre Mentalité est-elle africaine ou gallo-latine?" *Revue de la Société d'Histoire et de Géographie d'Haiti,* VII (May 1936), 1–31.

*————, *Le Problème des Classes à Travers l'Histoire d'Haiti.* Port-au-Prince, 1948 and 1958; also reprinted in Duvalier, *Oeuvres Essentielles,* I, 304–365.

Dépestre, René, *Gerbe de Sang.* Port-au-Prince, n.d.

Deren, Maya, *Divine Horsemen: The Living Gods of Haiti.* London, 1953.

Deschamps, Léon, *Les Colonies Pendant la Révolution: la Constituante et la Réforme Coloniale.* Paris, 1898.

Désinor, Yvan M., *Tragédies Américaines.* Port-au-Prince, 1962.

Despois, J., "Une étude sur la vie rurale en Haiti," *Annales de Géographie,* LXXI (1962), 426–427.

Dhormoys, Paul, *Une Visite chez Soulouque: Souvenir d'un Voyage dans l'Ile d'Haiti.* Paris, 1864.

+Diederich, Bernard, and Al Burt, *Papa Doc: The Truth About Haiti Today.* New York, 1969.

Dillard, J. L., "The Writings of Herskovits and the Study of the Language of the Negro in the New World," *Caribbean Studies,* IV (July 1964), 35–41.

*Douglas, Paul H., "The American Occupation of Haiti," *Political Science Quarterly,* XLII (1927), 228–258, 368–396.

*———, "The National Railway of Haiti: A Study in Tropical Finance," *The Nation,* CXXIV (19 January 1927), 59–61.

Douyon, Emerson, "Research Model on Trance and Possession States in the Haitian Voodoo," in Richard P. Schaedel (ed.), *Research and Resources of Haiti.* New York, 1969, 415–427.

———, "La transe vaudouesque: un syndrome de déviance psycho-culturelle," *Acta Criminologica,* II (January 1969), 11–70.

Douyon, Lamarque, "Phenoménologie de la crise de possession," *Revue de la Faculté d'Ethnologie.* Port-au-Prince, XII (1967), 28–40.

Dubucq, J. B., and Pierre Ulric Dubuisson, *Lettres Critiques et Politiques sur les Colonies et le Commerce des Villes Maritimes de France, Adressées à G. T. Raynal.* Geneva, 1785.

Durand, Rony, "Les conditions de la croissance économique d'Haiti," *Revue de la Faculté d'Ethnologie,* VII (1963), 41–56.

Duvalier, François, "Les Civilisations Négro-Africaines et le Problème Haitien," *Revue de la Société d'Histoire et de Géographie d'Haiti,* VII, (January–April 1936); reprinted in *Oeuvres Essentielles,* I, 229–247.

———, *Histoire Diplomatique: Politique Etrangère; Géographie Politique: Politique Fronterale.* Port-au-Prince, 1968.

———, *Message à la Nation.* Port-au-Prince, 1966.

*———, *Oeuvres Essentielles: I. Eléments d'une Doctrine.* Port-au-Prince, 1968, 2nd ed.

———, *Oeuvres Essentielles: II. La Marche à la Presidence.* Port-au-Prince, 1968; 3rd ed.

———, "La Tragédie des Protagonistes des Questions de Classes à Travers l'Histoire d'Haiti," *Les Griots* (23 January 1948); reprinted in *Oeuvres Essentielles,* I, 289–303.

——— (trans. John E. Pickering), *A Tribute to the Martyred Leader of Non-Violence, Reverend Dr. Martin Luther King, Jr.* Port-au-Prince, 1968.

————, Arthur Bonhomme, and Lorimer Denis, *Les Tendances d'une Génération.* Port-au-Prince, 1933.

————, and Lorimer Denis, "Les Civilisations de l'Afrique Noire et le Problème Haitien," *Revue de la Société d'Histoire et de Géographie d'Haiti,* VII (January–April 1936), 19–41.

Dwinelle, J. H. *et al.,* "Evaluation of Penicillin in the Treatment of Yaws," *American Journal of Tropical Medicine,* XXVII (1947), 633–641.

Eder, Richard, "Haití: un tirano llamado Duvalier," *Bohemia.* San Juan, LV (7 March 1965), 16–18ff.

Edwards, Bryan, *An Historical Survey of the French Colony in the Island of St. Domingo.* London, 1797.

*Efron, Edith, "The 'New Movement' in Haiti," *Caribbean Quarterly,* IV (January 1955), 14–31.

+Elie, Louis E., *Histoire d'Haiti.* Port-au-Prince, 1944–1945, 2v.

Erasmus, Charles John, "Agricultural Changes in Haiti: Patterns of Resistance and Acceptance," *Human Organization,* II (Winter 1952), 20–26.

Evanson, Philip, "The Third Dominican-Haitian War and the Return of General Pedro Santana; Part of a Long Story," *Caribbean Studies,* IV (1964), 13–23.

Fagg, John Edwin, *Cuba, Haiti, and the Dominican Republic.* Englewood Cliffs, 1967.

+Fermor, Patrick Leigh, *The Traveller's Tree: A Journey Through the Caribbean Islands.* London, 1950, 245–333.

Fièvre, Michel, "Nissage Saget, 1810–1880," *Revue de la Société d'Histoire et de Géographie d'Haiti,* IV (July 1933), 1–38.

Folsom, Robert S., "Haitian Economy," unpub. typescript (1954).

Forbes, Warren, "Report Covering Haiti Prepared in the Division of Latin American Affairs, January 1, 1930," unpub. typescript (1930).

Fouchard, L. M., "La recherche sociologique et les problèmes de la vie rurale en Haiti en relation avec la développement économique et l'amelioration du niveau de vie," document presented at the Seminario sobre la Investigacion Sociolgica y los Problemas de la Vida Rural en America Central, Mexico. Paris, 1962, mimeo.

Francisque, Edouard, *Perspectives du Développement Economique en Haiti.* Port-au-Prince, 1968.

Franco, Victor, "A Haiti, enquête du Vaudou," *Connaissance du Monde.* Paris (October 1965), 74–83.

*Franklin, James, *The Present State of Hayti (Saint Domingo), With*

Remarks on its Agriculture, Commerce, Laws, Religion, Finances, and Population, etc., etc. London, 1828.

Friedmann, John R. P., "Development Planning in Haiti: A Critique of the U.N. Report," *Economic Development and Cultural Change,* IV (November 1955), 39–54.

Froude, James Anthony, *The English in the West Indies, or the Bow of Ulysses.* New York, 1900; 1st ed., 1888.

Gaillard, Roger, "La destinée de Carl Brouard," *Conjonction.* Port-au-Prince, C (December 1965), 29–61.

Galich, Manuel, and Fernando G. Campoamor, "Haití: reportaje de un país," *Bohemia.* Havana, LVII (27 August 1965), 4–18.

Gall, Norman, "Duvalier's Latest 'Housecleaning' May Be a Sign of Disintegration," *The Philadelphia Bulletin* (10 September 1969).

García Zamor, Jean-Claude, *La Administracion Publica en Haiti.* Guatemala, 1966.

Garnier, Apollo, "Autour de la mort de Pétion," *Revue de la Société d'Histoire et de Géographie d'Haiti,* II (January 1932), 1–17.

Garran, Jean Philippe, *Rapport sur les Troubles de Saint-Domingue.* Paris, 1797–1799, 4v.

Gates, William B. Jr., "The Haitian Coffee Industry," unpub. typescript (1959).

———, "The Haitian Cotton and Cotton Textile Industries," unpub. typescript (1959).

———, "Observations on Economic Development and Haiti," unpub. typescript (1959).

Gation, Louis R. E., *Aspects de l'Economie et des Finances d'Haiti.* (Port-au-Prince, 1944).

Georges, André, "La composition d'histoire au baccalauréat Haitien," *Cahiers Pedagogiques.* Port-au-Prince, II (August 1966), 152–309.

Georges-Jacob, Kléber, *Contribution à l'étude de l'homme haïtien.* Port-au-Prince, 1946.

+Gingras, Jean-Pierre O., *Duvalier, Caribbean Cyclone: The History of Haiti and its Present Government.* New York, 1967.

Girod-Chantrans, Justin, *Voyage d'un Suisse dans Différentes Colonies d'Amérique.* Neuchatel, 1785.

Gisler, Antoine, *L'Esclavage aux Antilles Françaises (XVIIe au XIX Siècle).* Fribourg, 1965.

+Gold, Herbert, *The Age of Happy Problems.* New York, 1962.

———, "Caribbean Caudillo: Magloire of Haiti," *The Nation,* CLXXX (5 February 1955), 118–120.

————, "Haunted Haiti," *Holiday,* XXXVII (March 1965), 64–69.

Grant, F. W., and D. Groom, "A Dietary Study in Haiti," *Journal of the American Dietetic Association,* XXXIV (1958), 708–716.

Gray, E., "Haitian Bogeyman," *Western Folklore,* XXI (April 1964), 120–121.

+Greene, Graham, *The Comedians.* London, 1966.

————, "Nightmare Republic," *The New Republic,* CXLIX (16 November 1963), 18–20.

Grossberg, Lynn, "Haiti Drifts Toward Explosion," *Minority of One,* IV (February 1962), 10–11.

————, "Haiti: The Explosive Buffer," *The Nation,* CXCI (20 August 1960), 83–85.

Grove, Gene, "The CIA, FBI & CBS Bomb in Mission: Impossible," *Scanlan's Monthly,* I, 1 (March 1970), 2–5ff.

Gruening, Ernest,* "Haiti Marches Toward Freedom," *The Nation,* CXXXII (1 April 1931), 362, 364, 366.

————, "Haiti under American Occupation," *The Century Magazine,* CIII (April 1922), 836–845.

————, " 'Memoir' on the Political, Economic, and Financial Conditions Existing in the Republic of Haiti under the American Occupation by the Delegates to the United States of the Union Patriotique d'Haiti," *ibid.,* CXII (25 May 1921), 751–775.

————, "More Dispatches on Haiti," *ibid.,* CXIII (21 December 1921), 737–739.

————, " 'Pitiless Publicity' for Haiti," *ibid.,* CXI (6 October 1920), 366–368.

————, "The Rape of Haiti," *ibid.,* CXIII (9 November 1921), 546–555.

————, "The Senators Visit Haiti and Santo Domingo," *ibid.,* CXIV (4 January 1922), 7–10.

————, "Why Haiti Has No Budget," *ibid.,* CXI (11 September 1920), 307–310.

+Haiti, Service d'Information, *Les Etapes d'un Relèvement: Le Président Magloire au Service du Peuple.* Port-au-Prince, 1956.

Hanna, S. W., *Notes of a Visit to Some Parts of Haiti, January–February 1835.* London, 1836.

Hardouin, A. C., "Haiti: A Study in Regression," *Mexico Quarterly Review,* II (1963), 77–86.

+Harvey, William Woodis, *Sketches of Hayti; From the Expulsion of the French, to the Death of Christophe.* London, 1827.

* Not all of the articles attributed to him were signed, but they bear his stamp.

Hassal, Mary, *Secret History, or, the Horrors of St. Domingo*. Philadelphia, 1808.

Hauberg, Clifford A., *Latin American Revolutions (Mexico, Central America, Panama and the Islands of the Caribbean)*. Minneapolis, 1968.

Hazard, Samuel, *Santo Domingo Past and Present: With a Glance at Hayti*. New York, 1873.

Heinl, Robert Debs, Jr., "Are We Ready to Intervene in Haiti?" *The Reporter*, XXIV (2 June 1966), 26–28.

———, "Bailing out Duvalier," *The New Republic*, CLVI (14 January 1967), 15–16.

———, "Haiti: A Case Study in Freedom," *ibid.*, CL (16 May 1964), 15–21.

———, "Haiti — Next Mess in the Caribbean?" *The Atlantic Monthly*, CCXX (November 1967), 83–89.

———, *Soldiers of the Sea: The United States Marine Corps, 1775–1962*. Annapolis, 1962, 170–180, 234–247.

Herring, Hubert, "Dictatorship in Haiti," *Current History*, XV (January 1964), 34–37.

Herskovits, Melville J., *Life in a Haitian Valley*. New York, 1937.

Hicks, Albert C., *Blood in the Streets: The Life and Rule of Trujillo*. New York, 1946.

Hoetink, Harmannus, "Over de Sociaal-Raciale Struuctur van Haiti," *Tijdschrift van het Koninklijk Nederlandsch Aardrijkskundig Genootschap*, LXXVIII (1961), 145–156.

Holden, David, "Bogeymen of Port-au-Prince," *Manchester Guardian Weekly*, LXXXVI (26 April 1962), 5.

Holly, Marc A., *Agriculture in Haiti*. New York, 1955.

Hubert, Giles A., "Some Problems of a Colonial Economy: A Study of Economic Dualism in Haiti," *Inter-American Economic Affairs*, III (Spring 1950), 3–30.

Hudicourt, Max L. (trans. Anita Dlyn Weinstein), *Haiti Faces Tomorrow's Peace*. New York, 1945.

Hughes, H. B. L., "British Policy Towards Haiti, 1801–1805," *The Canadian Historical Review*, XXV (1944), 397–408.

[Hunt, Benjamin S.], *Remarks on Hayti as a Place of Settlement for Afric-Americans; and on the Mulatto as a Race for the Tropics*. Philadelphia, 1860.

Hurston, Zora Neale, *Tell My Horse*. New York, 1938.

Huxley, Francis, "Haiti Chérie," *The Geographical Magazine*,

XXXVI (June 1963), 69–83.

+———, *The Invisibles*. London, 1966.

Inman, Samuel Guy, *Through Santo Domingo and Haiti: A Cruise with the Marines*. New York, 1919.

Innocent, Luc, "La Petíon y Bolívar; aspectos de la influencia de Haití en la independencia de América," *Boletin Cultural y Bibliografico*. Bogotá, V (February 1962), 142–146.

*James, Cyril L. R., *The Black Jacobins: Toussaint l'Ouverture and the San Domingo Revolution*. New York, 1963; 2nd ed.

———, *A History of Negro Revolt*. London, 1938.

Jan, J. M., *Monographie Religieuse des Paroisses du Cap-Haitien*. Port-au-Prince, 1950.

Janvier, Louis-Joseph, *Les Antinationaux (Actes et Principes)*. Port-au-Prince, 1962.

———, *Les Constitutions d'Haiti (1801–1885)*. Paris, 1886.

Jean-Baptiste, Saint-Victor, *Haiti, Sa Lutte pour l'Emancipation: Deux Concepts de l'Indépendance à Saint Domingue*. Paris, 1957.

Jean-Jacques, Manuel, "Terror en Haití," *Revista Internacional*. Prague, VII, 4 (1964), 90–91.

Jeannot, Pierre L., "La mission du général Nicolas Geffrard," *Revue de la Société Haitienne d'Histoire, de Géographie, et de Géologie*, XXV (January 1954), 3–19.

*Jelliffe, Derrick B., and E. F. Patricia Jelliffe, "The Nutritional Status of Haitian Children," *Acta Tropica*, XVIII (1961), 1–45.

———, "Prevalence of Protein Calorie Malnutrition in Haitian Preschool Children," *American Journal of Public Health*, L (1960), 1355–1366.

Jocelyn, Marcelin, "La Guerre de l'Indépendence dans le Sud," *Revue de la Société d'Histoire et de Géographie d'Haiti*, VI (April 1935), 1–70.

Johnson, James Weldon, "Self-Determining Haiti": I. "The American Occupation," *The Nation*, CXI (28 August 1920), 236–238; II. "What the United States Has Accomplished," *ibid.* (4 September 1920), 265–276; III. "Government Of, By, and For the National City Bank," *ibid.* (11 September 1920), 295–297; IV. "The Haitian People," *ibid.* (25 September 1920), 345–347.

Johnston, Harry H., *The Negro in the New World*. New York, 1910.

Joseph, Raymond Alcide, "Haiti: Ripe for the Marines?" *The Nation*, CCVIII (31 March 1969), 392–397.

Joseph, Richard, *Haiti*. Garden City, 1964; rev. ed.

Justin, Joseph, *Etude sur les Institutions Haitiennes.* Paris, 1894–1895, 2v.

Kelsey, Carl, "The American Intervention in Haiti and the Dominican Republic," *The Annals of the American Academy of Political and Social Science,* C (March 1922), 109–202.

Kiev, Ari, "Obstacles to Medical Progress in Haiti," *Human Organization,* XXV (Spring 1966), 10–15.

————, "Research and Resources in Psychiatry in Haiti," in Richard P. Schaedel (ed.), *Research and Resources of Haiti.* New York, 1969, 428–440.

————, "Spirit Possession in Haiti," *The American Journal of Psychiatry,* CXVIII (1961), 133–138.

King, Kendall W., "Nutrition Research in Haiti," in Richard P. Schaedel (ed.), *Research and Resources of Haiti.* New York, 1969, 347–370.

———— et al., "Food Patterns from Dietary Surveys in Rural Haiti," *Journal of the Amerian Dietetic Association,* LIII (1968), 114–118.

————, "Height and Weight of Haitian Children," *American Journal of Clinical Nutrition,* XIII (1963), 106–109.

————, "Response of Pre-School Children to High Intakes of Haitian Cereal-Bean Mixtures," *Archivos Latinamericanos de Nutricion,* XVI (1966), 53–64.

Klippstein, F. A., I. M. Samloff, and E. A. Schenck, "Tropical Sprue in Haiti," *Annals of Internal Medicine,* LXIV (1966), 575–594.

Korngold, Ralph, *Citizen Toussaint: A Biography.* New York, 1944.

Kreiger, Herbert M., *The Aborigines of the Ancient Island of Hispaniola.* Washington, 1929.

Kuser, Dryden J., *Haiti: Its Dawn of Progress After Years in a Night of Revolution.* Boston, 1921.

Lacombe, Robert, *Histoire monetaire de Saint-Domingue et de la République d'Haiti jusqu'en 1874.* Paris, 1958.

Langley, Jabez Ayodele, "Garveyism and African Nationalism," *Race,* XI (1969), 157–172.

Laroche, Jacques, "Ethno-Sociologie," unpub. paper (1969).

————, *Leadership and Religion.* Port-au-Prince, 1968.

————, *Year X of the Duvalier Revolution, Year XXI of the Duvalier Era.* Port-au-Prince, 1967.

Laroche, René, "Situation de l'Agriculture Paysanne Haitienne: Perspective d'Avenir," *Revista de Ciencias Sociales,* IV (1960), 166–168.

Lataillade, Nerva, "Broussais Brice, dit Brice Aîné, 1868–1870,"

Revue de la Société d'Histoire et de Géographie d'Haiti, III (October 1932), 22–38.

Latortue, François, *Le Droit du Travail en Haiti.* Port-au-Prince, 1961.

Latortue, Gérard R., "Haiti: Chaotic and Corrupt," *The Nation,* CCIII (21 November 1966), 539–541.

———, "Is Haiti Hopeless?" *San Juan Review,* III (March 1966), 5.

———, "Political Crises in Haiti," *New World,* III, 3 (1967), 45–50.

———, "Tyranny in Haiti," *Current History,* LI (December 1966), 349–353.

Laurent, Garvey, "Etude socio-économique de la vallée de Camp-Perrin: Plaine des Cayes — Haiti," *Bulletin Agricole,* V (1956), 1–63.

Laurent, Gérard M., *Politique Commerciale: Un Cri d'Alarme.* Port-au-Prince, 1935.

———, *Pages d'histoire d'Haiti.* Port-au-Prince, c. 1950.

——— (ed.), *Toussaint Louverture: À Travers sa Correspondance (1794–1798).* Madrid, 1953.

Léautaud, Jean-Casimir, *La República de Haïti, ensayo de interpretacion sociológica.* Mexico, 1962.

Lebeau, Auguste, *De la Condition des Gens de Couleur Libres sous l'Ancien Régime.* Poitiers, 1903.

Lebon, Jean, "Pour una anténtica independencia de Haití; carta de Puerto Príncipe," *Revista Internacional.* Prague, VI (April 1963), 86–88.

Leconte, Vergniaud, *Henri Christophe dans l'Histoire d'Haiti.* Paris, 1931.

Léger, Jacques Nicolas, *Haiti: Her History and her Detractors.* New York, 1907.

Legerman, Caroline J., "Kin Groups in a Haitian Market," *Man,* LXII (October 1962), 145–149.

Lens, Sidney, "The Frightened Land," *The Progressive,* XXVIII (February 1964), 27–29.

Léon, Rulx, *Les Maladies en Haiti.* Port-au-Prince, 1954.

*Lepelletier de Saint-Remy, R., *Saint-Domingue: Étude et Solution Nouvelle de la Question Haïtienne.* Paris, 1846, 2v.

*Lepkowski, Tadeusz, *Haiti: Poczatki Państwa i Narodu* [*Haiti: The Beginning of the State and Nation*]. Warsaw, 1964.

*Leyburn, James G., *The Haitian People.* New Haven, 1941.

*———, "The Making of a Black Nation," in George Peter Murdock (ed.), *Studies in the Science of Society* (New Haven, 1937), 377–394.

Lherisson, Justin, *La Famille des Petite-Caille.* Port-au-Prince, 1963.

——, *Zoune chez sa Ninnaine.* Port-au-Prince, 1953.

Lherisson, Lelia J., *Manuel de la Littérature Haitienne.* Port-au-Prince, 1955.

Limonade, Julien Prévost Comte de, *Relation des Glorieux Evénements.* Cap-Henry, 1811.

Lizarazo, J. A. Osorio, *La Isla Iluminada.* Santo Domingo, 1953.

Lobb, John, "Caste and Class in Haiti," *American Journal of Sociology,* XLVI (1940), 23–34.

+Loederer, Richard, *Voodoo Fire in Haiti.* London, 1935.

Logan, Rayford W., *The Diplomatic Relations of the United States with Haiti, 1776–1891.* Chapel Hill, 1941.

——, "Education in Haiti," *The Journal of Negro History,* XV (1930), 401–460.

+——, *Haiti and the Dominican Republic.* London, 1968.

——, "Les relations diplomatiques des Etats-Unis avec Haiti 1776–1891," *Revue de la Société Haitienne d'Histoire et de Géographie,* XVIII (April 1947), 13–49.

——, "The United States Colonial Experiment in Haiti," *World Today,* XVII (1961), 435–446.

——, and Martin C. Needler, "Haiti," in Martin C. Needler (ed.), *Political Systems of Latin America.* Princeton, 1964, 149–162.

Lubin, Maurice A., "Bibliographie sur l'éducation en Haiti," *Conjonction,* CIV (1967), 65–66.

——, "Ou en Sommes-Nous avec l'Elite Intellectuelle d'Haiti?" *Journal of Inter-American Studies,* III (1961), 121–132.

——, "Les premiers rapports de la nation Haitienne avec l'étranger," *ibid.,* X (1968), 277–305.

——, "Quelques aspects de l'économie Haitienne," *ibid.,* I (1959), 425–447.

——, "Quelques aspects des communautes rurales d'Haiti," *America Latina,* V (1962), 3–22.

Luttwak, Edward, *Coup d'Etat: A Practical Handbook.* London, 1968.

MacCorkle, William A., *The Monroe Doctrine in its Relation to the Republic of Haiti.* New York, 1915.

Mackenzie, Charles, *Communications Received at the Foreign Office Relative to Hayti.* London, 1829.

*——, *Notes on Haiti Made During a Residence in that Republic.* London, 1830, 2v.

MacLeod, Murdo J., "The Haitian Novel of Social Protest," *Journal of Inter-American Studies,* IV (1962), 207–221.

Magloire, Jean, *Dumarsais Estimé: Esquisse de sa Vie Politique.* Port-au-Prince, 1950.

Malo, Charles, *Histoire d'Haiti . . . Depuis sa Découverte jusqu'en 1824, Epoque des Dernières Negociations entre la France et le Gouvernement Haitien.* Paris, 1825.

Malval, Marc E., *La Politique Financière Extérieure de la République d'Haiti depuis 1910: La Banque Nationale de la République ou nos Emprunts Extérieurs.* Paris, 1932.

Manigat, Leslie F., "La Crise Haitiano-Dominicaine de 1963–1964," *Revue Française de Science Politique,* XV (1965), 288–296.

———, *Un Fait Historique: l'Avènement à la Présidence d'Haiti du Général Salomon: Essai d'Application d'un Point de Théorie d'Histoire.* Port-au-Prince, 1957.

*———, *Haiti of the Sixties, Object of International Concern.* Washington, 1964.

———, *La Politique agraire du gouvernement d'Alexandre Pétion (1807–1818).* Port-au-Prince, 1962.

———, "La substitution de la prépondérance américaine à la prépondérance française en Haiti au début du XXme siècle: la conjoncture de 1910–1911," *Revue d'Histoire Moderne et Contemporaine,* XIV (1967), 321–355.

Mar, Roland H. del, "Strategic Characteristics of the Caribbean," in A. Curtis Wilgus (ed.), *The Caribbean: Its Hemispheric Role.* Gainesville, 1967, 155–160.

Marcelin, L. J., *Haiti: Ses Guerres Civiles — Leurs Causes, Leurs Conséquences Présentes, Leur Conséquence Future et Finale.* Paris, 1892.

———, *Introduction à un Ouvrage sur Haiti.* Paris, 1892.

Marcelin, Milo, *Mythologie Vodou (Rite Arada).* Port-au-Prince, 1949.

Mars, Louis, "La crise de possession et la personnalité humaine en Haiti," *Revue de Psychologie des Peuples.* Le Havre, XVII (January–March 1962), 6–22; also in *Revue de la Faculté d'Ethnologie,* VIII (1964), 37–63.

———, "La mentalité Haitienne et la psychiatrie," *Revue de la Société d'Histoire et de Géographie d'Haiti,* VIII (March 1937), 1–27.

Martin, Gaston, *Nantes au XVIIIᵉ Siècle: L'Ere des Négriers (1714–1744).* Paris, 1931.

Mason, J., and P. Cavalie, "Malaria Epidemic in Haiti Following a Hurricane," *American Journal of Tropical Medicine and Hygiene,* XIV (1965), 533–545.

Mathon, François, "Dessalines, Législateur: Deux aspects du statut familial Haitien sous le premier empire (1805)," *Revue de la Société d'Histoire et de Géographie d'Haiti,* XI (October 1939), 1–14.

Maximilien, Louis, *Le Vodou Haitien, Rite Radas-Canzo.* Port-au-Prince, 1945.

McCloy, Shelby T., *The Negro in the French West Indies.* Lexington, 1966.

McCrocklin, James H. (ed.), *Garde d'Haiti, 1915–1934: Twenty Years of Organization and Training by the United States Marine Corps.* Annapolis, 1956.

Metcalf, Clyde H., *A History of the United States Marine Corps.* New York, 1939.

*Métral, Antoine, *Histoire de l'Insurrection des Esclaves dans le Nord de Saint-Domingue.* Paris, 1818.

+Métraux, Alfred (trans. Peter Lengyel), *Haiti: Black Peasants and Voodoo.* New York, 1960.

———, "Orígenes e historia de los cultos Vodú," *Casa de las Americas.* Havana, VI (May–August 1966), 42–62.

+———, *Voodoo in Haiti.* New York, 1959.

Michel, Antoine, *Avènement du Général Fabre Nicolas Geffrard à la Présidence d'Haiti.* Port-au-Prince, 1932.

Michel, Henri Adam, "Toussaint-Louverture et la liberté générale des esclaves," *Revue de la Société d'Histoire et de Géographie d'Haiti,* V (April 1934), 29–33.

Michelmore, Peter, *Dr. Mellon of Haiti.* London, 1965.

Millspaugh, Arthur C., *Haiti under American Control, 1915–1930.* Boston, 1931.

Mintz, Sidney W., "The Caribbean as a Socio-Cultural Area," *Journal of World History,* IX (1966), 912–937.

———, "The Employment of Capital by Market Women in Haiti," in Raymond Firth and B. S. Yamey (eds.), *Capital, Saving and Credit in Peasant Societies.* Chicago, 1964, 256–286.

———, "The House and the Yard Among Three Caribbean Peasantries," *Actes du VIe Congrès International des Sciences Anthropologiques et Ethnologiques,* II. Paris, 1960, 591–596.

———, "Internal Market Systems as Mechanisms of Social Articulation," *Proceedings of the Annual Spring Meeting of the American Ethnological Society* (1960), 20–30.

——, "Living Fences in the Fond-des-Nègres Region, Haiti," *Economic Botany,* XVI (1962), 101–105.

——, "Peasant Markets," *Scientific American,* CCIII (August 1960), 112–122.

——, "Pratik: Haitian Personal Economic Relationships," *Proceedings of the Annual Spring Meeting of the American Ethnological Society* (1961), 54–63.

——, "Standards of Value and Units of Measure in the Fond-des-Nègres Market Place, Haiti," *Journal of the Royal Anthropological Institute,* XCI (1961), 23–38.

——, "Le Système du Marché Rural dans l'Economie Haitienne," *Bulletin du Bureau d'Ethnologie,* III, 23–25 (March–September 1960), 3–14.

——, "A Tentative Typology of Eight Haitian Marketplaces," *Revista de Ciencias Sociales,* IV (1960), 15–57.

Mirabeau, Roch L., "Can Haiti be Helped; Background to Chaos," *The Nation,* CXCVI (18 May 1963), 416–418.

Mirville, Solon, *L'Ecole Primaire.* Port-au-Prince, 1959.

Mondestin Jean, N., "Essai de clinique historique: Jean-Jacques Dessalines," *Revue de la Société d'Histoire et de Géographie d'Haiti,* XVII (April 1946), 1–20.

*Montague, Ludwell Lee, *Haiti and the United States, 1714–1938.* Durham, 1940.

Monteforte Toledo, Mario, "Haití, dictadura rampante," *Entre Columnas.* México, XI (November 1962), 14–16.

Moore, O. Ernest, "Is Haiti Next?" *The Yale Review,* LI (1961), 254–263.

——, "Monetary-Fiscal Policy and Economic Development in Haiti," *Public Finance,* IX (1954), 230–253.

Moral, Paul, "La Culture du Café en Haiti: Des Plantations Coloniales aux 'Jardins' Actuels," *Cahiers d'Outre-Mer,* VIII (1955), 233–256.

——, *L'Economie Haitienne.* Port-au-Prince, 1959.

*——, *Le Paysan haïtien; étude sur la vie rurale en Haiti.* Paris, 1961.

Moran, Charles, *Black Triumvirate: A Study of L'Ouverture, Dessalines, Christophe — The Men Who Made Haiti.* New York, 1957.

*Moreau de Saint-Méry, Médéric-Louis-Élie, *Description Topogra-*

phique, Physique, Civile, Politique et Historique de la Partie Française de l'Isle de Saint-Domingue. Philadelphia, 1797, and Paris, 1958, 3v.

Mossell, C. W., *Toussaint L'Ouverture, The Hero of Saint Domingo, Soldier, Statesman, Martyr: Or Hayti's Struggle, Triumph, Independence, and Achievements.* Lockport, 1896.

Munro, Dana G., *Intervention and Dollar Diplomacy in the Caribbean, 1900–1921.* Princeton, 1964, 326–387.

Neal, Marian, "United Nations' Technical Assistance Programs in Haiti," *International Conciliation,* 468 (1951), 81–118.

Needler, Martin C., *Latin American Politics in Perspective.* Princeton, 1963.

———, *Political Development in Latin America: Instability, Violence, and Evolutionary Change.* New York, 1968.

——— (ed.), *Political Systems of Latin America.* Princeton, 1964.

Nemours, Alfred, *Les Présidents Lescot et Trujillo.* Port-au-Prince, 1942.

———, "La tentation et la mort du Christ noir: Toussaint Louverture," *Revue de la Société d'Histoire et de Géographie d'Haiti,* XV (July 1944), 20–35.

Nemours, Auguste, *Histoire Militaire de la Guerre d'Indépendance de Saint-Domingue.* Paris, 1925, 2v.

Nicolas, Hogar, *L'Occupation Américaine d'Haiti: La Revanche de l'Histoire.* Madrid, n.d. but 1956.

Noel, Ulrick, *Haiti: sa politique de defense sociale.* Port-au-Prince, 1963.

Opper, Conrad G., "Ataque Frontal Contra la Miseria: Como se Lleva a Cabo una Campaña de Educacion Fundamental," *El Correo,* III (1951), 5.

Padgett, James A., "Diplomats to Haiti and Their Diplomacy," *The Journal of Negro History,* XXV (1940), 265–330.

Paret-Limardo de Vela, L., "Quelques aspects des problèmes de la main-d'oeuvre haitïenne," *Journal of Inter-American Studies,* IV (1962), 121–144.

Pattee, Ricardo, *Haiti: Pueblo Afroantillano.* Madrid, 1956.

Paul, Edouard C., *L'Aphabétisation en Haiti.* Port-au-Prince, 1965.

Paul, Emmanuel, *Panorama du folklore haïtien.* Port-au-Prince, 1962.

Paul, J. H., and A. Bellerive, "A Malaria Reconnaissance of the Republic of Haiti," *Journal of the National Malaria Society,* VI (1947), 41–67.

Paulèus-Sannon, Horace, *Essai Historique sur la Révolution de 1843.*
Les Cayes, 1905.

———, *Histoire de Toussaint-Louverture.* Port-au-Prince, 1920–
1933, 3v.

Peterson, Arthur W., "Man-Land Relations in the Caribbean Region," in A. Curtis Wilgus (ed.), *The Caribbean: Its Health Problems.* Gainesville, 1965, 42–73.

Pettigrew, Robert L., *The Story of Fort Liberty and the Dauphin
Plantation.* Richmond, 1958.

*Pierre-Charles, Gérard, *La Economía Haitiana y su Vía de Desar-
rollo.* México, 1965.

———, *L'Economie Haitienne et sa Voie de Développement.* Paris,
1967.

Pierre-Louis, Ulysse (ed.), *Sortileges Afro-Haitiens (Contes et Lé-
gendes).* Port-au-Prince, 1961.

*Placide-Justin, *Histoire Politique et Statistique de l'Ile d'Hayti,
Saint-Domingue.* Paris, 1826.

Plank, John N., "Neighborly Relations in the Caribbean," in A.
Curtis Wilgus (ed.), *The Caribbean: Its Hemispheric Role.*
Gainesville, 1967, 161–170.

Polk, D. S., "Child Care in Haiti," *Clinical Pediatrics,* IV (1965),
293–304.

Posner, Walter H., "American Marines in Haiti, 1915–1922," *The
Americas.* Washington, XX (1964), 231–266.

Pressoir, Catts, "Historique de l'Enseignement en Haiti," *Revue de
la Société d'Histoire et de Géographie d'Haiti,* VI (January 1935),
33–57.

Price-Mars, Jean, *Ainsi Parla l'Oncle: Essais d'Ethnographie.* Com-
piegne, 1928.

———, "L'archéologie, l'ethnologie et la linguistique: état actuel de
ces sciences appliquées à l'aire géographique du Golfe du Mexique et du bassin des Caraibes, études comparatives et possibilités
de coordination scientifique," *Revue de la Société d'Histoire et de
Géographie d'Haiti,* XII (April 1941), 1–36.

———, *De Saint-Domingue à Haiti: Essai sur la Culture, les Arts et
la Littérature.* Paris, 1959.

———, "Jean-Jacques Dessalines, les origines, le milieu physique et
le milieu humain," *Revue de la Société d'Histoire et de Géographie d'Haiti,* IX (January 1938), 1–11.

———, *Jean-Pierre Boyer Bazelais et le Drame de Miragoane.* Port-
au-Prince, 1948.

————, "Lemba-Pétro: Un culte secret; son histoire, sa localisation géographique, son symbolisme," *Revue de la Société d'Histoire et de Géographie d'Haiti,* IX (January 1938), 12–31.

————, "La position d'Haiti et de la culture française en Amérique," *Journal of Inter-American Studies,* VIII (1966), 44–53.

————, *La République d'Haiti et la République Dominicaine: Les Aspects divers d'un problème d'histoire, de géographie, et d'ethnologie.* Port-au-Prince, 1953, 2v.

————, "Le Sentiment de la valeur personnelle chez Henry Christophe en fonction de son rôle de Chef. Psychologie d'un Homme d'Etat," *Revue de la Société d'Histoire et de Géographie d'Haiti,* V (January 1934), 19–39.

————, *Silhouettes de Negres et de Negrophiles.* Paris, n.d.

————, "L'Unité Politique de l'Ile d'Haiti," *Revue de la Société d'Histoire et de Géographie d'Haiti,* VIII (October 1937), 1–27.

————, *Vilbrun Guillaume Sam, ce méconnu.* Port-au-Prince, 1961.

+Prichard, H. Hesketh, *Where Black Rules White: A Journey Across and About Hayti.* London, 1900 and 1910.

Priestley, Herbert Ingram, *France Overseas Through the Old Régime: A Study of European Expansion.* New York, 1939.

Quintana, Jorge, "La independencia de Haití," *Bohemia Libre Puertorriqueña.* Caracas, II (30 December 1962), 70–72ff.

Ragatz, Lowell Joseph, *The Fall of the Planter Class in the British Caribbean, 1763–1833: A Study in Social and Economic History.* New York, 1928.

*Rainsford, Marcus, *An Historical Account of the Black Empire of Hayti: Comprehending a View of the Principal Transactions in the Revolution of Santo Domingo: With its Ancient and Modern State.* London, 1805.

Ravenscroft, Kent, Jr., "Spirit Possession in Haiti: A Tentative Theoretical Analysis," unpub. scholar of the house B.A. (hons.) thesis. Yale, 1962.

————, "Voodoo Possession: A Natural Experiment in Hypnosis," *The International Journal of Clinical and Experimental Hypnosis,* XIII (1965), 157–182.

Raynal, Guillaume T., *Histoire Philosophique et Politique des Etablissements et du Commerce des Européens dans les Deux Indes.* Geneva, 1784, VII.

Renaud, Raymond, *Le Régime Foncier en Haiti.* Paris, 1934.

Rice, Berkeley, "Haiti: Last Act of a Tragicomedy," *Harper's Magazine,* CCXXVI (May 1963), 65–75.

Rigaud, Candelon, "Histoire d'Haiti et Histoire de Port-au-Prince," *Revue de la Société d'Histoire et de Géographie d'Haiti,* V (October 1934), 20–38.

———, "Influence des Colonies Françaises sur le Commerce de la Métropole," *Revue de la Société d'Histoire et de Géographie d'Haiti,* II (December 1926), 1–35.

Rigaud, Milo, *La Tradition Voudoo et le Voudoo Haitien (Son Temple, ses Mystères, sa Magie).* Paris, 1953.

Ritter, Karl, *Naturhistorische Reise nach der Westindischen Insel Hayti.* Stuttgart, 1836.

+Rodman, Selden, *Haiti: The Black Republic.* New York, 1954.

Ronceray, Hubert de, "Images Mentales de l'Education en Haiti," *Les Cahiers du CHISS,* II, 3 (1968), 3–15.

———, "Une micro-collectivité rurale haitienne: Furcy," *Revue de la Faculté d'Ethnologie,* VII (1963), 3–25.

——— "Quelques reflexions sur le problème de la stratification sociale en Haiti," *Les Cahiers du CHISS,* II, 2 (1968), 1–13.

Rosenhouse, Harvey, "Come to Haiti and Meet Papa Doc's Police," *The New Republic,* CLVI (11 March 1967), 10–11.

Roucek, Joseph, "Haiti in Geopolitics," *Contemporary Review,* CCIV (1963), 21–29.

Roussier, Paul (ed.), *Lettres du Général LeClerc, Commandant en Chef de l'Armée de Saint Domingue en 1802.* Paris, 1937.

Saint-Rémy (Joseph), *Pétion et Haiti: étude monographique et historique.* Port-au-Prince, 1956.

+St. John, Spenser, *Hayti, or The Black Republic.* New York, 1889.

St-Juste, Laurore, "Les Archives Nationales d'Haiti hier, aujourd'hui et demain" *Caribbean Studies,* I (July 1961), 12–15.

Saintoyant, Jules François, *La Colonisation Française Pendant La Révolution (1789–1799). II: Les Evénements Coloniaux.* Paris, 1930.

St. Surin, Jacques, *Indices Démographiques et Perspectives de la Population d'Haiti de 1950 à 1980.* Port-au-Prince, 1962.

St. Whitelock, Otto V. (ed.), *Social and Cultural Pluralism in the Caribbean.* New York, 1960.

Salgado, Jean-Marie, "Survivances des cultes africains et syncrétisme en Haiti," *Revue de l'Université d'Ottawa,* XXXII (1962), 431–467.

Salmon, C. S., *The Caribbean Confederation, with a Map. A Plan for the Union of the Fifteen British West Indian Colonies*. London, 1888.

Samame, G. E., "Treponematosis Eradication with Especial Relation to Yaws Eradication in Haiti," *Bulletin of W.H.O.*, XV (1956), 897–903.

*Schaedel, Richard P., "The Human Resources of Haiti," unpub. typescript (1962).

———— (ed.), *Research and Resources of Haiti*. New York, 1969.

Scharon, Faine, *Toussaint L'Ouverture et la Révolution de St-Domingue*. Port-au-Prince, 1957–59, 2v.

*Schmidt, Hans R., Jr., "The United States Occupation of Haiti 1915–1934," unpub. Ph.D. thesis. Rutgers, 1968.

Schmidt-Schütt, Margarete, *Ärtzin auf Haiti*. Berlin, 1942.

Schoelcher, Victor, *Colonies Etrangères et Haiti: Résultats de l'Emancipation Anglaise*. Paris, 1843, 2v.

*————, *Vie de Toussaint-Louverture*. Paris, 1889; 2nd ed.

Schreadley, Richard L., "The American Intervention in Haiti," unpub. M.A.D.L. thesis. Fletcher School, Tufts University, 1969.

Scobie, Edward, "Haiti's Black Jacobins," *Flamingo*. London, III (August 1964), 20–21.

+Seabrook, W. B., *The Magic Island*. New York, 1929.

*Sebrell, W. H., Jr., *et al.* "Appraisal of Nutrition in Haiti," *The American Journal of Clinical Nutrition*, VII (1959), 1–48.

Sherman, George, "Nonintervention: A Shield for 'Papa Doc,'" *The Reporter*, XXVIII (20 June 1963), 27–29.

Simpson, George Eaton, "The Belief System of the Haitian Vodou," *American Anthropologist*, XLVII (1945), 35–59.

————, "Haitian Peasant Economy," *The Journal of Negro History*, XXV (1940), 498–519.

*————, "Haitian Politics," *Social Forces*, XX (1942), 487–491.

————, "Haiti's Social Structure," *American Sociological Review*, VI (1941), 640–649.

————, "Peasant Songs and Dances of Northern Haiti," *The Journal of Negro History*, XXV (1940), 203–215.

Slocum, Kenneth G., "Papa Doc Holds On," *The Wall Street Journal* (20 April 1968).

Spector, Robert M., "W. Cameron Forbes in Haiti [1930]: Additional Light on the Genesis of the Good Neighbor Policy," *Caribbean Studies*, VI (July 1966), 28–45.

+Steedman, Mabel, *Unknown to the World, Haiti*. London, 1939.

Steele, Martha L., "Constitutions of Haiti, 1804–1951," *Revue de la Société Haitienne d'Histoire, de Géographie, et de Géologie,* XXIII (January 1952), 17–48.

+Stoddard, T. Lothrop, *The French Revolution in San Domingo.* Boston, 1914.

Street, John M., "Historical and Economic Geography of the Southwest Peninsula of Haiti." Berkeley, 1960, mimeo.

*Streit, Clarence K., "Haiti: Intervention in Operation," *Foreign Affairs,* VI (1928), 615–632.

Stycos, J. M., "Attitudes Towards Family Size in Haiti," *Human Organization,* IX (1960), 21–27.

———, "Haitian Attitudes Toward Family Size," *ibid.,* XIII (1964), 42–47.

Sylvain, Georges, *Dix Années de Lutte pour la Liberté, 1915–1925.* Port-au-Prince, 1925, 2v.

+Taft, Edna, *A Puritan in Voodoo-Land.* Philadelphia, 1938.

Tannenbaum, Frank, *Slave and Citizen: The Negro in the Americas.* New York, 1947.

Thoby, Percival, "Nos crises économiques et financières," *Revue de la Société Haitienne d'Histoire, de Géographie, et de Géologie,* XXIII (January 1952), 49–68; XXIII (April 1952), 27–49; XXIII (July 1952), 58–68; XXIII (October 1952), 39–49; XXIV (April 1953), 48–56; XXIV (July 1953), 57–68; XXIV (October 1953), 12–42; XXV (January 1954), 68–84.

———, *Nos Crises Économiques et Financières: Nos Contrats de Banque, nos Émissions de Monnaies, nos Emprunts et la Réforme Monétaire, 1800 à 1888.* Port-au-Prince, 1955.

+Thomas, Lowell, *Old Gimlet Eye: The Adventures of Smedley D. Butler as Told to Lowell Thomas.* New York, 1933.

Tibbenhauer, Louis Gentil, *Die Insel Haiti.* Leipzig, 1893.

Tomasek, Robert D., "The Haitian-Dominican Republic Controversy of 1963 and the Organization of American States," *Orbis,* XII (1968), 294–313.

Trembley, William A., "The Status of the Church in Saint-Domingue During the Last Years of the French Monarchy, 1781–1793," *Caribbean Studies,* I (April 1961), 11–18.

Trouillot, Ernst, *Prospections d'Histoire; Choses de Saint-Domingue et Haiti.* Port-au-Prince, 1961.

Trouillot, Henock, "Le code rural de Boyer et la paysannerie haitienne," *Conjonction,* XCVI–XCVII (1964), 62–77.

———, "Economie et Finances de Saint-Domingue," *Revue de la*

Société Haitienne d'Histoire, de Géographie, et de Géologie, XXXIII (January–April 1965), 1–139.

Turnier, Alain, *Les États-Unis et le Marché Haitien.* Washington, 1955.

Underwood, Frances W., "The Marketing System in Peasant Haiti," in Sidney Wilfred Mintz (ed.), *Papers in Caribbean Anthropology.* New Haven, 1960, 36 pp.

———, and Irma Honigmann, "A Comparison of Socialization and Personality in Two Simple Societies," *American Anthropologist,* XLIX (1947), 557–577.

U.N.E.S.C.O., *The Haiti Pilot Project.* Paris, 1951.

U. S. State Department, Division of Latin American Affairs, "Report Covering Haiti" (1 January 1930), mimeo.

*Vaissière, Pierre de, *Les Origines de la Colonisation et la Formation de la Société Française à Saint-Domingue.* Paris, 1906.

———, *Saint-Domingue: La Société et la Vie Créoles sous l'Ancien Régime (1629–1789).* Paris, 1909.

Vallès, Marie-Thérèse, *Les Idéologies Coopérativistes et leur Applicabilité en Haiti.* Paris, 1967.

Vandercook, John W., *Black Majesty: The Life of Christophe, King of Haiti.* New York, 1928.

Vandergrift, A. A. (ed. Robert B. Asprey), *Once a Marine.* New York, 1964.

Vaval, Duraciné, "Alexandre Pétion. l'homme et sa vie," *Revue de la Société d'Histoire et de Géographie d'Haiti,* III (July 1932), 1–34.

———, "Le génie politique de Toussaint Louverture," *Revue de la Société Haitienne d'Histoire et de Géographie,* XIX (July 1948), 73–82.

———, "Le Gouvernement de Dessalines," *Revue de la Société Haitienne d'Histoire, de Géographie, et de Géologie,* XXVIII (October 1955), 63–74.

———, "Le Roi d'Haiti Henri Christophe: L'Homme et son Oeuvre de Gouvernement," *Revue de la Société d'Histoire et de Géographie d'Haiti,* II (June 1931), 1–37.

Velie, Lester, "The Case of our Vanishing Dollars in Haiti," *The Reader's Digest,* LXXX (March 1962), 122–126.

Venault de Charmilly, *Lettre à Bryan Edwards.* London, 1797.

Verschueren, J., (pseud. Henri Op-Hey) *La République d'Haiti.* Paris, 1948, 3v.

Viaud, Léonce, "La Personnalité de Joseph-Anténor Firmin," *Revue* de la Société Haitienne d'Histoire et de Géographie, XIX (January 1948), 1–22.

Victor, René, *Recensement et Démographie*. Port-au-Prince, 1944.

Viélot, Klébert, "L'enseignement primaire en Haiti," in Richard P. Schaedel (ed.), *Research and Resources of Haiti*. New York, 1969, 281–346.

Vieux, Serge A., "Les Problèmes de la Fonction publique haitienne et les perpectives de recherche dans ce domaine," in *ibid.*, 524–591.

Vilgrain, Jacques, "Stratification socio-économique de la République de Haiti," *Bulletin Trimestriel de Statistique*, 41–44 (1961), 1–11.

Vincent, Sténio, *Efforts et Résultats*. Port-au-Prince, n.d. but 1939.

———, *En Posant les Jalons*. Port-au-Prince, 1939, 5v.

———, *Outline of the Financial History of the Republic of Haiti*. Port-au-Prince, 1939.

Wagley, Charles, *The Latin American Tradition: Essays on the Unity and the Diversity of Latin American Culture*. New York, 1968.

Weatherly, Ulysses G., "Haiti: An Experiment in Pragmatism," *The American Journal of Sociology*, XXXII (1926), 353–366.

Wilgus, A. Curtis (ed.), *The Caribbean: Its Health Problem*. Gainesville, 1965.

——— (ed.), *The Caribbean: Its Hemispheric Role*. Gainesville, 1967.

——— (ed.), *The Caribbean: Natural Resources*. Gainesville, 1961.

Wilson, Edmund, *Red, Black, Blond and Olive. Studies in Four Civilizations: Zuni, Haiti, Soviet Russia, Israel*. New York, 1956, 69–146.

+Wilson, Ruth Danenhower, *Here is Haiti*. New York, 1957.

*Wimpffen, François Alexandre Stanislaus Baron de (trans. J. Wright), *A Voyage to Saint Domingo, in the Years 1788, 1789, and 1790*. London, 1817.

Wingfield, Roland, "Haiti, A Case Study of an Underdeveloped Area," unpub. Ph.D. thesis. Louisiana State, 1967.

———, and Vernon J. Parenton, "Class Structure and Class Conflict in Haitian Society," *Social Forces*, XLII (1965), 338–347.

Winkler, Max, *Investments of United States Capital in Latin America*. Boston, 1928.

+Wirkus, Faustin E., and Dudley, Taney, *The White King of La Gonave*. Garden City, 1931.

Wise, F. M., *A Marine Tells It to You*. New York, 1929.

Wood, Harold A., *Northern Haiti: Land, Land Use, and Settlement: A Geographical Investigation of the Departement du Nord.* Toronto, 1963.

————, "Physical Influences on Peasant Agriculture in Northern Haiti," *Canadian Geographer,* V (1961), 10–18.

Young, Maurice de, "Class Parameters in Haitian Society," *Journal of Inter-American Studies,* I (1959), 449–458.

————, *Man and Land in the Haitian Economy.* Gainesville, 1958.

Index

Index

(Prepared by Bernice S. Colt)

Robert I. Rotberg was born in 1935 in New Jersey. He took an A.B. from Oberlin College in 1955 and the M.P.A. from Princeton University in 1957. As a Rhodes Scholar, he earned a D.Phil. from the University of Oxford in 1960. He has held numerous grants for extended research in African affairs and other fields, among them a grant from the Rockefeller Foundation, the British Social Science Research Council, the American Philosophical Society, the Ford Foundation, and a Guggenheim Fellowship for 1970–71. He edits the *Journal of Interdisciplinary History* and is the author of several books: *The Rise of Nationalism in Central Africa; A Political History of Tropical Africa; Christian Missionaries and the Creation of Northern Rhodesia;* and *Joseph Thomson and the Exploration of Africa.* He is also the editor of *Protest & Power in Black Africa* and *Africa and its Explorers.* He was for a time a reporter with the *New York Times* and the Hartford *Courant.* He taught at Harvard University, where he still is a research associate of the Center for International Affairs, before becoming Associate Professor of Political Science and History at M.I.T.

Christopher K. Clague is Associate Professor of Economics at the University of Maryland. After taking a B.A. from Swarthmore College and a Ph.D. at Harvard University, he was a member of the staff of the Council of Economic Advisers.

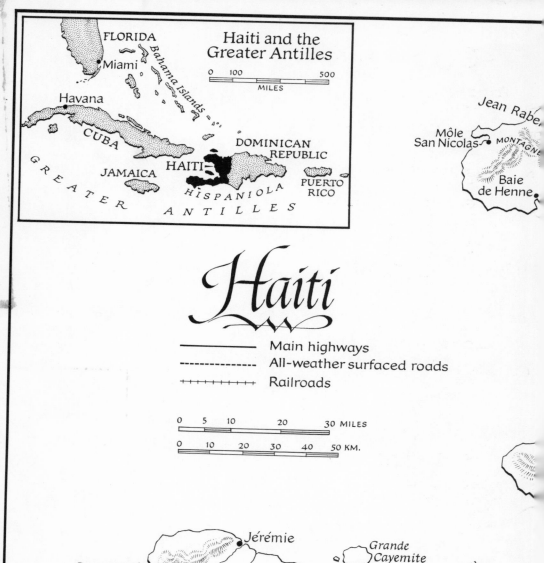

Haiti and the Greater Antilles

0   100   500
MILES

FLORIDA
Miami

Havana

CUBA

JAMAICA

Bahama Islands

HAITI

DOMINICAN
REPUBLIC

PUERTO
RICO

HISPANIOLA

G R E A T E R   A N T I L L E S

Jean Raber

Môle
San Nicolas

MONTAGNE

Baie
de Henne

Haiti

——————— Main highways
- - - - - - - - All-weather surfaced roads
+++++++++++ Railroads

0   5   10   20   30 MILES

0   10   20   30   40   50 KM.

Jérémie

Grande
Cayemite

Dame Marie

Anse d'Hainault

R. Bras à Droit

Corail

Pestel

Petit Trou
de Nippes

Anse-à-
Veau

Baradères

SUD

DÉPARTEMENT   DU

DE LA

HOTTE

Gde R. de Nippes

M A S S I F

R. de Pins

Cap Carcasse

Tiburon

Camp Perrin

Aquin

Les Anglais

Port-à-Piment

Las Cayes

Île-à-Vache

Sam! H. Bryant

Pte.-a-Gravois